THE WAR ON DRUGS II

The Continuing Epic of Heroin, Cocaine, Crack, Crime, AIDS, and Public Policy

THE WAR ON DRUGS II

The Continuing Epic of Heroin, Cocaine,
Crack, Crime, AIDS, and Public Policy

James A. Inciardi

University of Delaware

Mayfield Publishing Company
Mountain View, California
London • Toronto

Library of Congress Cataloging-in-Publication Data

Inciardi, James A.
    The war on drugs II : the continuing epic of heroin, cocaine, crack, crime, AIDS, and public policy / James A. Inciardi.
        p.   cm.
    Includes indexes.
    ISBN 1-55934-016-9
    1. Drug abuse—United States.   2. Narcotics, Control of—United States.   3. Heroin habit—United States.   4. Cocaine habit—United States.   5. Drug abuse and crime—United States.   I. Title.
HV5825.I543   1991
363.4'5'0973—dc20   91-24736
                                                                         CIP

Manufactured in the United States of America

10 9 8 7 6 5 4 3 2 1

Mayfield Publishing Company
1240 Villa Street
Mountain View, California 94041

Sponsoring editor, Franklin C. Graham; production editor, Lynn Rabin Bauer; copy editor, Colleen O'Brien; text designer, Jean Mailander; cover designer, Jill Turney. The text was set in 10/12 Palatino by Execustaff, and printed on 50# White Opaque by Malloy.

Credits: Cover photograph, chapter opening photographs, and photograph p. 78 courtesy of the Drug Enforcement Administration; p. 11, Bettmann Archive; p. 20, Historical Pictures Service, Chicago; p. 37, Courtesy of the Valley Forge Music Fair; p. 91, Copyright © 1991 by The New York Times Company. Reprinted by permission; p. 237, © American Professional Captain's Association; p. 274, © 1990 by Herblock in The Washington Post; p. 280, © Maricopa County Demand Reduction Program.

To the memory of my parents

CONTENTS

CHAPTER FIVE

LEGENDS OF THE LIVING DEAD   135
Unraveling the Drugs/Crime Connection

CHAPTER SIX

MAINLINING IN THE SHADOW OF DEATH   173
Probing the AIDS/Drugs Connection

PREFACE

The worlds of heroin, cocaine, crack, and crime are curious and often brutal worlds, populated by czars and kings, diplomats and merchants, peasants and slaves, and agents both legitimate and corrupt. There are numerous other participants: an odd assembly of drug users, dealers, and traffickers; prostitutes, pimps, and other players in the sex industry; mercenaries, assassins, insurgents, and arms traders; and small and scattered battalions of runners, lookouts, mules, moles, and other bizarre creatures of the streets. The worlds of drug-taking and drug-seeking are tragic and dangerous as well, where pain, suffering, violence, and death are commonplace. They are alien and exotic worlds, ranging from the poppy fields of Southeast and Southwest Asia, the jungles of Amazonia, and the highlands of the Andes, to the crack houses, shooting galleries, and streets of rural and urban America.

The War on Drugs II is a series of reflections on these worlds. Much of what is described is based on street research and outreach programs in Miami, the Florida Keys, across the Florida Straits, and New York and other locales. The information presented comes from a myriad of interviews and discussions with the drug users, drug dealers, and drug traffickers who inhabit the streets, and with the law enforcement agents and government officials charged with controlling drugs and crime in the streets. As such, the information is both systematic and anecdotal. The descriptions and characterizations are also based on numerous observations and conversations in South America—in the drug-trafficking capitals of Colombia, Bolivia, Ecuador, Peru, and Venezuela; in the coca fields and high cities of the Andes Mountains; in the jungle labs and drug-selling bazaars of Amazonia; and in the hills and along the tiled streets of Rio de Janeiro. In these distant places, the informants included peasant laborers, military officials and other foreign government representatives; drug users and sellers;

bandits and dealers in contraband; North and South American drug enforcement agents; members of the United States diplomatic corps; and drug abuse clinicians and their patients.

As a series of perspectives and reflections, this book is not intended to provide a definitive statement on any of the topics it covers, although at times the opinionated nature of the commentary may suggest this. But the events, viewpoints, and impressions are intended to provide an examination of American drug policy against the background of social and cultural change—where policy has been, where it appears to be now, and where it likely ought to be going. Moreover, rather than a revision of its predecessor, this volume represents an expansion and sequel. Hence the name, *The War on Drugs II.*

In this behalf, Chapter 1, "From Dover's Powder to Mexican Ditch Weed," traces the early history of drug taking in the United States from colonial times through the end of the Great Depression.

Chapter 2, "Along the Road from H to Ice," examines the drug problem in post–World War II America. Taken together, Chapters 1 and 2 focus on the many social and cultural events that shaped the nature and course of drug use and drug control policy.

Chapter 3, "Shit, Smack, and Superfly," provides an overview of heroin and cocaine trafficking and use—where the drugs come from, how they are refined and distributed, how they are prepared and used, and what effects they engender. This chapter is also somewhat of an adventure in exotic geography.

Chapter 4, "Hurricane Crack," examines the most talked about street drug of the late 1980s. In addition to descriptions of the history, pharmacology, and abuse patterns of crack, the reader is taken on a journey through a number of crack houses to witness the sex-for-crack exchanges, violence, and human suffering that is so associated with this form of drug use.

Chapter 5, "Legends of the Living Dead," offers a social history of the criminalization of drug use, combined with an examination of the complexities of the drugs/crime connection.

Chapter 6, "Mainlining in the Shadow of Death," probes the AIDS/drugs connection. Topics include the history and myths of AIDS, the characteristics of the HIV virus, the global epidemiology of the disease, and the AIDS risk factors associated with drug use and sexual behaviors.

Chapter 7, "From Miami to Mandalay and Tingo Maria to Katmandu," describes the social, economic, and political implications of the international drug trade, including a focused view of the more violent aspects of cocaine trafficking.

Chapter 8, "The Great Drug War and the Great Drug Debate," targets the drug legalization argument—the issues on both sides of the controversy, followed by a detailed judgment as to why legalizing heroin, cocaine, crack, and other drugs of abuse would be an extremely naive and high-risk alternative in the war on drugs.

Chapter 9, ''Where Do We Go From Here?'' evaluates contemporary American drug control policies and suggests how they might be strengthened.

The reflections and comments of many people who populate the worlds of heroin, cocaine, crack, and crime are included throughout this book. Reported verbatim, they are uncensored and often tend to be rather graphic.

Finally, the total number of debts one incurs in writing a book is surprisingly large. The vast majority must remain anonymous, but they know who they are, and their help is gratefully acknowledged.

CHAPTER ONE

FROM DOVER'S POWDER TO MEXICAN DITCH WEED

The Early History of Drug Taking in the United States

The beginnings of most social phenomena are relatively easy to trace. American jazz, for example, emerged a little more than a century ago in the city of New Orleans. It was a fusion of the existing musical art forms of black America—work songs, spirituals, and blues—combined with elements of white folk music, rhythms of Hispanic America and the Caribbean, melodies of French dances, and instrumentation of the marching band. The environmental movement of the late 1960s and early 1970s was an outgrowth of the writings of biologist Rachel Carson, combined with a better understanding of the effects of pollution on ecosystems. And similarly, the roots of today's attempt to rid American streets and highways of drunk drivers are also easily targeted. They began on a spring afternoon in 1980 when a 13-year-old California teenager was struck down and killed by a hit-and-run driver. Stunned that the operator of the automobile was not only drunk at the time but out on bail for his third drunk-driving offense and unlikely to be punished for the killing, the child's mother launched the organization of Mothers Against Drunk Drivers (MADD) and initiated a campaign of public outcry.

But the origins of other social trends can be more difficult to uncover. The roots of drug abuse are particularly obscure. The use of opium dates back at least to the ancient Greeks, and references to marijuana appear in early Persian, Hindu, Greek, Arab, and Chinese writings. Similarly, when the Spanish conquistador Francisco Pizarro stumbled upon the Inca empire in 1531, the chewing of coca had already been in Inca mythology for centuries. Even in the United States, a nation with a relatively short history, the onset of drug taking as a social phenomenon remains somewhat of a mystery.

THOMAS DOVER, OPIUM, AND THE GREAT AMERICAN MEDICINE SHOW

Perhaps it all began during the eighteenth century with Thomas Dover, a student of British physician Thomas Sydenham. Known as the "English Hippocrates" and the father of clinical medicine, Sydenham had been a strong advocate of the use of opium for the treatment of disease. In fact, he was so committed to the clinical value of opium that sometime before his death in 1689 he stated that "among the remedies which it has pleased the Almighty God to give to man to relieve his sufferings, none is so universal and so efficacious as opium."[1]

Following the path of his mentor, Dover developed a form of medicinal opium. Known as Dover's Powder, it contained one ounce each of opium, ipecac (the dried roots of a tropical creeping plant), and licorice, combined with saltpeter, tartar, and wine.[2] It was introduced in 1709, the same year that Dover, also an adventurer and privateer, rescued castaway Alexander Selkirk from one of the desolate Juan Fernandez Islands off the coast of Chile, thus inspiring Daniel Defoe's *Robinson Crusoe*. Dover's Powder made its way to America and remained one of the most widely used opium preparations for almost two centuries.

The attraction of Dover's Powder was in the euphoric and anesthetic properties of opium. For thousands of years, opium had been a popular narcotic. A derivative of the Oriental poppy (*Papaver somniferum L.*)—known to most Americans as the flower that interrupted Dorothy and Toto in their journey along the yellow brick road to the wonderful land of Oz—it was called the "plant of joy" some 4,000 years ago in the Fertile Crescent of Mesopotamia. In Homer's *Odyssey*, the potion that Helen of Troy mixed to "quiet all pain and strife, and bring forgetfulness of every ill," is believed to have contained opium. There is even speculation that the "vinegar mixed with gall," mentioned in Matt. 27:34, as an offering to Christ on the cross contained opium.[3]

The introduction of Dover's Powder apparently started a trend. By the latter part of the eighteenth century, patent medicines containing opium were readily available throughout urban and rural America. They were sold in pharmacies, grocery and general stores, at traveling medicine shows, and through the mail. They were marketed under such labels as Ayer's Cherry Pectoral, Mrs. Winslow's Soothing Syrup, McMunn's Elixir, Godfrey's Cordial, Scott's Emulsion, and Dover's Powder. Many of these remedies were seductively advertised as "painkillers," "cough mixtures," "soothing syrups," "consumption cures," and "women's friends." Others were promoted for the treatment of such varied ailments as diarrhea, dysentery, colds, fever, teething, cholera, rheumatism, pelvic disorders, athlete's foot, and even baldness and cancer. The drugs were produced from imported opium as well as from the white opium poppies that were being legally grown in the New England states, Florida and Louisiana, the West and Southwest, and the Confederate States of America during the Civil War.

The medical profession also fostered the use of opium. Dr. William Buchan's *Domestic Medicine*, first published in Philadelphia in 1784 as a practical handbook on simple medicines for home use, suggested for the treatment of coughs:

> A cup of an infusion of wild poppy leaves and marsh-mellow roots, or the flowers of coltsfoot, may be taken frequently; or a teaspoonful of the paregoric elixir (flowers of benzoin plus opium) may be put into the patient's drink twice a day. Spanish infusion (liquor combined with the syrup of poppy leaves) is also a very popular medicine in this case, and may be taken in the quantity of a teacupful three or four times a day.[4]

Buchan's treatise on home remedies, which was republished in several editions, also recommended tincture of opium for the treatment of numerous common ailments:

> Take of crude opium, two ounces; spirituous aromatic water, and mountain wine, of each ten ounces. Dissolve the opium, sliced, in the wine, with a gentle heat, frequently stirring it; afterward add the spirit, and strain off the tincture.[5]

Yet the mere appearance of Dover's Powder and other patent medicines in America was only minimally related to the evolution of drug taking; other more potent social forces had been of considerably greater significance. Along with Dover's opium concoction, similar remedies were initially shipped to the colonies from London, as were most of the medications of the period. They were available from physicians or over the counter from apothecaries, grocers, postmasters, and printers, but only in modest quantities. When trade with England was disrupted during the Revolutionary War, a patent medicine industry emerged in the United States, spirited also by the state of eighteenth-century and early nineteenth-century regular medicine. The prevailing vogue in American medical therapy had stressed extreme bleeding and purging. It was medicine's ''heroic'' age, but suspicion of heroic therapy led many to seek out home remedies or ''cures'' available through their local general store. These suspicions were further intensified with the rise of Jacksonian democracy and its antagonism toward intellectuals.

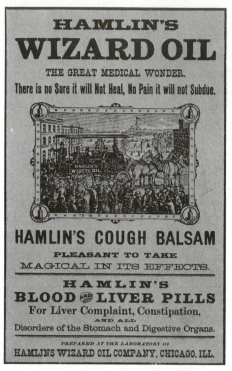

Hamlin's Wizard Oil, a nineteenth-century opium-based patent medicine.

Expansions in the patent medicine industry were also related to the growth of the American press. The manufacturers of the "medicines" were the first business entrepreneurs to seek national markets through widespread advertising. They were the first hucksters to use psychological lures to entice customers to buy their merchandise. They were the first manufacturers to help the local merchants who retailed their wares by going directly to consumers with a message about their products. In total national advertising, this segment of the drug industry ranked highest in expenditures. During the post–Civil War decades, some individual proprietors spent in excess of $500,000 each year for advertising. In the 1890s, for example, more than $1 million was spent annually for the promotion of Scott's Emulsion.[6] As to the number of different varieties of patent medicines available, an 1804 New York catalog listed some 90 brands of elixirs; an 1857 Boston periodical included almost 600; in 1858 one newspaper account totaled more than 1,500 patent medicines; and by 1905 the list had stretched to more than 28,000.[7]

Curiously, the widespread presence of opium in patent medicines was not altogether understood by the majority of the public, for the so-called "patent medicines" were actually unpatented. The patenting of a drug required revealing its ingredients so that all might know its composition, but unpatented patent medicines kept their contents secret. In fact, in 1881 the Proprietary Medicine Manufacturers and Dealers Association was organized as an effective lobby for all interests in the trade. For almost three decades it fought against disclosure laws while Dover's Powder and the other popular opium-containing drugs sold in massive quantities.

Even though opium had been the only known product of the Oriental poppy for the longest time, in 1803 a young German pharmacist, Frederick Serturner, isolated the chief alkaloid of opium.[8] Serturner had hit upon morphine, which he so named after Morpheus, the Greek god of dreams. The discovery was to have profound effects on both medicine and society, for morphine was, and still is, the greatest single pain reliever the world has ever known. Then the hypodermic syringe was invented, and the use of morphine by injection in military medicine during the Civil War and the Franco-Prussian War granted the procedure legitimacy and familiarity to both physicians and the public.[9] Furthermore, hypodermic medication had its pragmatic aspects—it brought quick local relief, its dosage could be regulated, and it was effective when oral medication was impractical. The regimen, however, was used promiscuously, for many physicians were eager to illustrate their ability to quell the pain suffered by their patients, who, in turn, expected instant relief from discomfort. Or as one commentator put it:

> There is no proceeding in medicine that has become so rapidly popular; no method of allaying pain so prompt in its action and permanent in its effect; no plan of medication that has been so carelessly used and thoroughly abused; and no therapeutic discovery that has been so great a blessing and so great a curse to mankind than the hypodermic injection of morphia.[10]

The use of morphine by needle had become so pervasive by the 1890s that technology soon responded with the production of inexpensive equipment for mass use. In the 1897 edition of the Sears Roebuck catalog, for example, hypodermic kits, which included a syringe, two needles, two vials, and a carrying case, were advertised for as little as $1.50, with extra needles available at 25 cents each or $2.75 per dozen.[11]

In addition to the uncontrolled use of opium in patent medicines and morphine by injection, the practice of opium smoking also was prevalent. The Chinese laborers who were imported to build the railroads and work the mines in the trans-Mississippi West had introduced it to America. It was estimated that by 1875 opium smoking had become widespread, particularly among prostitutes, gamblers, and other denizens of the underworld, but also among more respectable men and women of the middle and upper classes.[12]

As to the full volume of opium and morphine actually consumed during the nineteenth century, the picture is not altogether clear. The domestic production of opium was limited as a result of cultivation techniques that tended to yield a product considerably deficient in morphine, so one indicator of consumption could be drawn from import figures. According to data that the United States Public Health Service compiled in 1924, more than 7,000 tons of crude opium and almost 800 tons of smoking opium were imported during the four-decade period ending in 1899.[13] Estimates of the number of individuals actually addicted to opium during the latter part of the nineteenth century tended to be compiled rather loosely, ranging as high as 3 million.[14] Yet other, more rigorously collected data for the period did indicate that the use of narcotic drugs was indeed pervasive. In 1888, for example, one examination of 10,000 prescriptions from Boston-area pharmacies found that some 15% contained opiates,[15] and that was only in Boston. In 1900 it was estimated that in the small state of Vermont, 3.3 million doses of opium were sold each month.[16]

THE DIVINE GIFT OF THE INCAS

Beyond opium and morphine, the patent medicine industry branched even further. Although chewing coca leaves for their mild stimulant effects had been a part of Andean culture for perhaps a thousand years, for some obscure reason the practice had never become popular in either Europe or the United States. During the latter part of the nineteenth century, however, Angelo Mariani of Corsica brought the unobtrusive Peruvian shrub to the notice of the rest of the world. After importing tons of coca leaves to his native land, he produced an extract that he mixed with wine and called Vin Coca Mariani.[17] The wine was an immediate success, publicized as a magical beverage that would free the body from fatigue, lift the spirits, and create a lasting sense of well-being. Vin Coca brought Mariani immediate wealth and fame as well as a medal of appreciation from Pope Leo XIII who used the drink as a source of comfort in his many years of ascetic retirement.

Across the ocean during the same years, John Styth Pemberton of Atlanta, Georgia, had been marketing Triplex Liver Pills, Globe of Flower Cough Syrup, and a number of equally curious patent medicines. Noting Mariani's great success, in 1885 Pemberton developed a new product that he registered as French Wine Coca—Ideal Nerve and Tonic Stimulant. It was originally a medicinal preparation, but the following year he added an additional ingredient, changed it into a soft drink, and renamed it Coca-Cola.[18]

Although the extracts of coca may have indeed made Pemberton's cola "the real thing," the popularity of Coca-Cola in the years hence was hardly a reason for considering it a national health concern, for the stimulant effects of the drink were at best mild.[a] The full potency of the coca leaf remained unknown until 1859 when cocaine was first isolated in its pure form.[b] Yet little use was made of the new alkaloid until 1883 when Dr. Theodor Aschenbrandt secured a supply of the drug and issued it to Bavarian soldiers during maneuvers. Aschenbrandt, a German military physician, noted the beneficial effects of cocaine, particularly its ability to suppress fatigue.

Among those who read Aschenbrandt's account with fascination was a struggling young Viennese neurologist, Sigmund Freud. Suffering from chronic fatigue, depression, and various neurotic symptoms, Freud obtained a measure of cocaine and tried it himself. He also offered it to a colleague who was suffering from both a disease of the nervous system and morphine addiction, and to a patient with a chronic and painful gastric disorder. Finding the initial results to be quite favorable in all three cases, Freud decided that cocaine was a "magical drug." In a letter to his fiancee, Martha Bernays, in 1884, Freud commented on his experiences with cocaine:

> If all goes well I will write an essay on it and I expect it will win its place in therapeutics by the side of morphium and superior to it. I have other hopes and intentions about it. I take very small doses of it regularly against depression and against indigestion, and with the most brilliant success. . . . In short it is only now that I feel that I am a doctor, since I have helped one patient and hope to help more.[19]

---

[a] Today's Coca-Cola incorporates "decocainized" extracts of the coca leaf in one of its flavoring compounds. However, these extracts come not from the species of coca native to the eastern Andes Mountains of South America (*Erythroxylum coca Lam.*) from which street cocaine is derived, but from "Trujillo coca" (*Erythroxylum novogranatense var, truxillense*). Trujillo coca is a variety well adapted to the desert conditions found in coastal Peru and has been found in numerous archeological sites dating back as far as 1750 B.C. See Timothy Plowman, "The Identity of Amazonian and Trujillo Coca," *Botanical Museum Leaflets, Harvard University,* 27 (1979), pp. 45–51; M. N. Cohen, "Archeological Plant Remains From the Central Coast of Peru," *Nawpa Pacha,* 16 (1978), pp. 36–37; T. C. Patterson, "Central Peru: Its Population and Economy," *Archaeology,* 24 (1971), pp. 316–321.

[b] There appear to be numerous contradictions in the literature as to who first isolated cocaine and when. Although recent sources hold that it was the German chemist Friedrich Gaedecke in 1855, a more persistent search suggests that Gaedecke only isolated alkaloidal cocaine. It was not until 1859 that Dr. Albert Niemann of the University of Gottingen isolated the chief alkaloid of coca and actually named it "cocaine." See Carl Koller, "On the Beginnings of Local Anesthesia," paper presented at the annual meeting of the Brooklyn Ophthalmological Society, Brooklyn, New York, April 18, 1940; David F. Allen, *The Cocaine Crisis* (New York: Plenum Press, 1987).

COCA-COLA
SYRUP ✣ AND ✣ EXTRACT.

For Soda Water and other Carbonated Beverages.

This "INTELLECTUAL BEVERAGE" and TEMPERANCE
DRINK contains the valuable TONIC and NERVE STIM-
ULANT properties of the Coca plant and Cola (or Kola)
nuts, and makes not only a delicious, exhilarating,
refreshing and invigorating Beverage, (dispensed from
the soda water fountain or in other carbonated bever-
ages), but a valuable Brain Tonic, and a cure for all
nervous affections — SICK HEAD-ACHE, NEURALGIA,
HYSTERIA, MELANCHOLY, &c.

The peculiar flavor of COCA-COLA delights every
palate; it is dispensed from the soda fountain in same
manner as any of the fruit syrups.

J. S. Pemberton,
⤳ Chemist, ↝
Sole Proprietor, Atlanta, Ga.

Early Coca-Cola advertisements noted the drink's
coca content and stimulant properties.

In July 1884, less than three months after Freud's initial experiences with cocaine, his essay was published in a German medical journal and then reprinted in English in the *Saint Louis Medical and Surgical Journal* shortly thereafter.[20] Freud pressed the drug onto his friends and colleagues, urging that they use it both for themselves and their patients; he gave it to his sisters and his fiancee and continued to use it himself. By the close of the 1880s, however, Freud and the others who had praised cocaine as an all-purpose wonder drug began to withdraw their support for it in light of an increasing number of reports of compulsive use and undesirable side effects. Yet by 1890 the patent-medicine industry in the United States had also discovered the benefits of the unregulated use of cocaine. The industry quickly added the drug to its repertoire of home remedies, touting it as helpful not only for everything from alcoholism to venereal disease but also as a cure for addiction to other patent medicines. Since the new tonics contained substantial amounts of cocaine, they did indeed make users feel better, at least initially, thus spiriting the patent-medicine industry into its golden age of popularity.

THE PECULIAR LEGACY OF BAYER LABORATORIES

Research into the mysteries of opium during the nineteenth century led not only to Serturner's discovery of morphine in 1806 but to that of more than two dozen other alkaloids, including codeine, in 1831. Yet more importantly, in an 1874 issue of the *Journal of the Chemical Society*, British chemist C. R. A. Wright described a series of experiments he had carried out at London's St. Mary's Hospital to determine the effect of combining various acids with morphine. Wright produced a series of new morphine-like compounds, including what became known in the scientific literature as diacetylmorphine.[21]

The discovery of both codeine and diacetylmorphine had been the outgrowth of an enduring search for more effective substitutes for morphine. This interest stemmed not only from the painkilling qualities of opiate drugs but also from their sedative effects on the respiratory system. Wright's work, however, went for the most part unnoticed. Some 24 years later, though, in 1898, pharmacologist Heinrich Dreser reported on a series of experiments he had conducted with diacetylmorphine for Friedrich Bayer and Company of Elberfeld, Germany, noting that the drug was highly effective in the treatment of coughs, chest pains, and the discomforts associated with pneumonia and tuberculosis. Dreser's commentary received immediate notice, for it had come at a time when antibiotics were still unknown, and pneumonia and tuberculosis were among the leading causes of death. He claimed that diacetylmorphine had a stronger sedative effect on respiration than either morphine or codeine, that therapeutic relief came quickly, and that the potential for a fatal overdose was almost nil. In response to such favorable reports, Bayer and Company began marketing diacetylmorphine, under the trade name of Heroin—so named from the German *heroisch*, meaning heroic and powerful.[22]

Although Bayer's Heroin was promoted as a sedative for coughs and as a chest and lung medicine, it was advocated by some as a treatment for morphine addiction. This situation seems to have arisen from three somewhat related phenomena. The first was the belief that heroin was nonaddicting. As one physician wrote in the *New York Medical Journal* in 1900:

> Habituation [with Heroin] has been noted in a small percentage of the cases. All observers are agreed, however, that none of the patients suffer in any way from this habituation, and that none of the symptoms which are so characteristic of chronic morphinism have ever been observed. On the other hand, a large number of the reports refer to the fact that the same dose may be used for a long time without any habituation.[23]

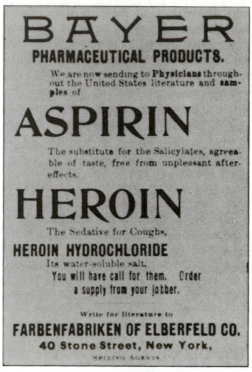

At the turn of the twentieth century, heroin was sold over the counter as a cough suppressant.

Second, since the drug had a greater potency than that of morphine, only small dosages were required for the desired medical effects, thus reducing the potential for the rapid onset of addiction. And third, at the turn of the twentieth century, the medical community did not fully understand the dynamics of cross dependence. Cross dependence refers to the phenomenon that among certain pharmacologically related drugs, physical dependence on one will carry over to all the others. As such, for the patient suffering from the unpleasant effects of morphine withdrawal, the administration of heroin would have the consequence of one or more doses of morphine. The dependence was maintained and withdrawal disappeared, the two combining to give the appearance of a "cure."

Given the endorsement of the medical community, with little mention of its potential dangers, heroin quickly found its way into routine medical therapeutics and over-the-counter patent medicines.

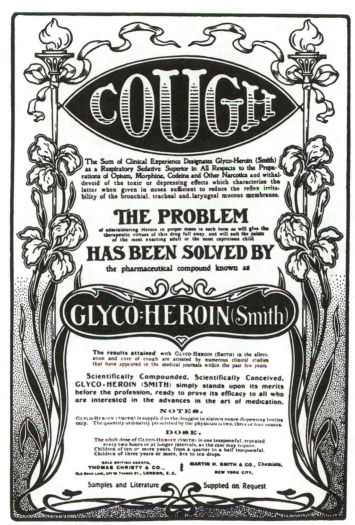

Like Bayer's *Heroin*, Smith's *Glyco-Heroin* was a potent narcotic widely advertised as an over-the-counter cough medicine.

ROCK OIL, DURHAM'S PURE BEEF LARD, AND THE QUEST OF FRANCIS BURTON HARRISON

By the early years of the twentieth century, the steady progress of medical science had provided physicians with a better understanding of the long-term effects of the drugs they had been advocating. Sigmund Freud had already recognized his poor judgment in the claims he had made about

cocaine, the addiction potential and abuse liability of morphine had been
well established, and the dependence-producing properties of Bayer's
Heroin were being noticed. Yet these drugs—cocaine, morphine, and
heroin—often combined with alcohol, were still readily available from a
totally unregulated patent medicine industry. Not only were these drugs
unregulated, many were highly potent as well. Birney's Catarrah Cure,
for example, was 4% cocaine. Colonel Hoestetter's Bitters had such a
generous amount of C_2H_5OH (alcohol) in its formula "to preserve the
medicine" that the fumes from just one tablespoonful fed through a gas
burner could maintain a bright flame for almost five minutes.

To these and others could be added even more quack medications,
which, even though not necessarily dangerous to the patient's health,
were pushed on the unsuspecting and gullible public by enterprising
and imaginative hucksters. Perhaps the most curious of these was
Samuel M. Kier's Rock Oil. During the better part of the nineteenth
century, salt was typically produced from brine drawn from deep
wells. Occasionally, the utility of such wells was ruined when a black
oily substance known as petroleum found its way into the underground reservoirs. One Kentucky businessman secured a number of
these abandoned and ruined salt wells, formed the American Medical
Oil Company, and sold hundreds of thousands of bottles of the greasy
brine as American Oil, advertising it as an effective remedy for almost
any ailment. But Kier, the profiteering son of a Pennsylvania salt
manufacturer, was even more enterprising. When oil began to flow
in quantity from his underground salt deposits, he initiated an active
campaign by giving testimony to the wonderful medicinal virtues of
"Petroleum, or Rock Oil; A Natural Remedy; Procured from a Well
in Allegheny County, Pennsylvania; Four Hundred Feet Below the
Earth's Surface." Kier's salespeople, equipped with ornamented
wagons and ready supplies of the wonder oil, brought the legendary
medicine show to rural and urban America, selling millions of half-
pint bottles along the way.[24]

For decades, however, the task of bringing about change in the
medicine industry seemed to have few results. As early as the 1870s,
while some physicians were actively cashing in on the gullibility of
the patient population, others expressed their reservations in print.
The medical writings, however, went unnoticed for the most part, for
few Americans other than doctors or pharmacists read the medical
journals. Newspapers, on the other hand, were a haven for the patent
medicine industry, and most producers of the dubious drugs made
sure that they would remain so. They invented a "red clause" that
would appear in advertising contracts. "It is mutually agreed," the
red type would indicate, "that this Contract is void, if any law is
enacted by your state restricting or prohibiting the manufacture or sale
of proprietary medicines."[25] Thus, the newspaper reader saw one

column after another of patent-medicine advertising with almost no questioning of the drugs' medical efficacy.

With the new century came a more progressive climate of opinion and a greater willingness to speak out for reform. The American Medical Association purged its journal of questionable advertising; the AMA Council on Pharmacy and Chemistry investigated the patent medicine industry; state chemists undertook analyses of the remedies; and all pooled their findings and turned them over to lay reporters. Then the muckraking journalists took over. William Allen White's *Emporia* (Kansas) *Gazette* ignored the infamous red clause and hosted a series of articles that pointed out the hazards of self-medication with patent medicines. At the same time, the *Ladies Home Journal* extended the attack to the remedies high in alcoholic content. Yet the most provocative effort was "The Great American Fraud," a long series of articles written by Samuel Hopkins Adams that began in 1905 in the pages of *Collier's* magazine. Wrote Adams in his opening essay:

> Gullible America will spend this year $75 million in the purchase of patent medicines. In consideration of this sum it will swallow huge quantities of alcohol, an appalling amount of opiates and narcotics, a wide assortment of varied drugs ranging from powerful and dangerous heart depressants to insidious liver stimulants; and, far in excess of other ingredients, undiluted fraud. For fraud, exploited by the skillfulest of advertising bunco men, is the basis of the trade.[26]

In subsequent articles Adams exposed the institution of the red clause and passionately described the powders and soothing syrups containing heroin, opium, morphine, and cocaine as part of a shameful trade "that stupefies helpless babies and makes criminals of our young men and harlots of our young women."

Adams's commentaries in *Collier's* did not go unnoticed, but the final indictment leading to the downfall of the patent-medicine industry was totally unrelated to the problems described in "The Great American Fraud." On $500 supplied by a socialist periodical, a young novelist lived for seven weeks in the stockyards' meat-packing district of Chicago, gathering data among the welter of new immigrant nationalities who were struggling there to adjust to the New World. His name was Upton Sinclair, and his goal was to point out the evils of capitalist exploitation and to bring laborers under the wing of the Socialist party.

With the 1906 publication of Sinclair's account, *The Jungle,* public attention concentrated not on the scandalous miseries of the proletariat in capitalist America but on the lurid and nauseating details of Chicago's handling of the meat that the entire nation had been eating.

Collier's
THE NATIONAL WEEKLY

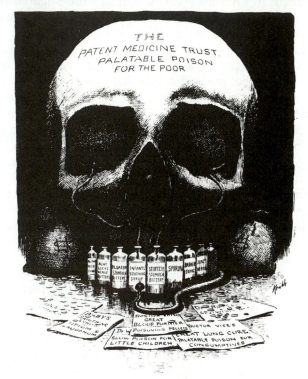

THE
PATENT MEDICINE TRUST.
PALATABLE POISON
FOR THE POOR

DEATH'S LABORATORY

Patent medicines are poisoning people throughout America to-day. Babies who cry are fed laudanum under the name of syrup. Women are led to injure themselves for life by reading in the papers about the meaning of backache. Young men and boys are robbed and contaminated by vicious criminals who lure them to their dens through seductive advertisement

DRAWN BY E. W. KEMBLE

From October 7, 1905 through February 17, 1906, a series in *Collier's* featured questionable practices in the patent medicine industry.

It seems that deviled ham was actually minced tripe (stomach lining) dyed red, and much of the packers' lamb and mutton was goat. They kept down infestations of rats in the packing plants by baiting the rodents with poisoned bread. Then, dead rats (poisoned bread and all) typically went into the hoppers of oddments used for human consumption in sausages and other processed meats. And, what no reader could manage to forget—now and then an employee slipped on a wet floor, fell into a vat of boiling meat scraps, and ''was overlooked for days, till all but his bones . . . had gone out to the world as Durham's Pure Beef Lard.''

The Jungle shocked both Congress and America and represented the needed impetus for legislative reform. By mid-1906 the Pure Food and Drug Act was passed, prohibiting the interstate transportation of adulterated or misbranded food and drugs. The act brought about the decline of the patent medicine industry because henceforth the proportions of alcohol, opium, morphine, heroin, cocaine, and a number of other substances in each preparation had to be indicated. Thus because of the mass media's having pointed out the negative effects of these ingredients, a number of the remedies lost their appeal. Moreover, it suddenly became difficult to market as a cure for morphine addiction a preparation that contained one or more other addicting drugs.

The new legislation merely imposed standards for quality, packaging, and labeling; it did not actually outlaw the use of cocaine and opiate drugs. Public Law No. 47, 63rd Congress [H.R. 1967], more popularly known as the Harrison Act, sponsored by New York Representative Francis Burton Harrison and passed in 1914, ultimately served in that behalf. At the same time, the new legislation went a long way to alter public and criminal justice responses to drug use in the United States for generations to come.

The Harrison Act required all people who imported, manufactured, produced, compounded, sold, dispensed, or otherwise distributed cocaine and opiate drugs to register with the Treasury Department, pay special taxes, and keep records of all transactions.[27] As such, it was a revenue code designed to exercise some measure of public control over drugs rather than to penalize the estimated 200,000 users of narcotics in the United States. In effect, however, penalization is specifically what occurred.

Certain provisions of the Harrison Act permitted physicians to prescribe, dispense, or administer narcotics to their patients for "legitimate medical purposes" and "in the course of professional practice." But how these two phrases were interpreted ultimately defined narcotics use as a crime.

On the one hand, the medical establishment held that addiction was a disease and that addicts were patients to whom drugs could be prescribed to alleviate the distress of withdrawal. On the other hand, the Treasury Department interpreted the Harrison Act to mean that a doctor's prescription for an addict was unlawful. The United States Supreme Court quickly laid the controversy to rest. In *Webb v. U.S.*,[28] decided in 1919, the high court held that it was not legal for a physician to prescribe narcotic drugs to an addict patient for the purpose

[c] Although cocaine is not a narcotic, the Harrison Act and subsequent court decisions defined it as such. Even in segments of contemporary drug legislation, at both state and federal levels, cocaine is still listed as a narcotic. A discussion of what constitutes a narcotic appears in Chapter 3 of this book.

of maintaining his or her use and comfort. In *U.S. v. Behrman*,[29] decided three years later, this ruling went one step further by declaring that a narcotic prescription for an addict was unlawful, even if the drugs were prescribed as part of a cure program.[c] The impact of these decisions combined to make it almost impossible for addicts to obtain drugs legally. In 1925 the Supreme Court emphatically reversed itself in *Lindner v. U.S.*,[30] disavowing the Behrman opinion and holding that addicts were entitled to medical care like other patients, but the ruling had almost no effect. By that time, physicians were unwilling to treat addicts under any circumstances, and a well-developed illegal drug marketplace had emerged to cater to the needs of the addict population.

SNOW PARTIES, GERMAN WAR PROPAGANDA, AND THE RISE OF THE CRIMINAL ADDICT

Many commentators on the history of drug use in the United States have argued that the Harrison Act snatched addicts from legitimate society and forced them into the underworld. As attorney Rufus King, a well-known chronicler of American narcotics legislation, once described it, "Exit the addict–patient, enter the addict–criminal."[31] But this cause-and-effect interpretation tends to be a rather extreme misrepresentation of historical fact.

Without question, at the beginning of the twentieth century, most users of narcotics were members of legitimate society. In fact the majority had first encountered the effects of narcotics through their family physician or local pharmacist or grocer. In other words, their addiction had been medically induced during the course of treatment for some other perceived ailment. Yet long before the Harrison Act had been passed, there were indications that this population of users had begun to shrink.[32] Agitation had existed in both the medical and religious communities against the haphazard use of narcotics, defining much of it as a moral disease. For many, the sheer force of social stigma and pressure served to alter their use of drugs. Similarly the decline of the patent-medicine industry after the passage of the Pure Food and Drug Act was believed to have substantially reduced the number of narcotics and cocaine users. Moreover, by 1912 most state governments had enacted legislative controls over the dispensing and sale of narcotics. Thus, it is plausible to assert that the size of the drug-using population had started to decline years before the Harrison Act had become the subject of Supreme Court interpretation. Then too, the combined effects of stigma, social pressure, the Pure Food and Drug Act, and state controls had also served to create an underworld of drug users and black-market drugs. By 1914 a number of commentators had noted this change. Some, however melodramatically, targeted the subterranean economy of narcotics use:

> Several individuals have come to the conclusion that selling "dope" is a very profitable business. These individuals have sent their agents among the gangs frequenting our city corners, instructing them to make friends with the members and induce them to take the drug. Janitors, bartenders, and cabmen have also been employed to help sell the habit. The plan has worked so well that there is scarcely a poolroom in New York that may not be called a meeting place for dope fiends. The drug has been made up in candy and sold to school children. The conspiring individuals, being familiar with the habit-forming action of the drugs, believe that the increased number of "fiends" will create a larger demand for the drug, and in this way build up profitable business.[33]

By the latter part of the decade, other observers were noting that although the medically induced addict was still prominent, a new population had recently emerged.[34] It was an underworld population composed principally of heroin and cocaine users who had initiated drug use as the result of associations with other criminals. Thus it would appear that the emergence of the criminal addict was not simply the result of a cause-and-effect criminalization process—the Harrison Act's definition of narcotics use as criminal. Rather it was likely the result of the effects of legislation combined with the emergence of a new category of users who were already within the underworld.

Although accurate data on the incidence and prevalence of drug use have been available only recently, by the early 1920s readers of the popular media were confronted, almost on a daily basis, with how drug use, and particularly heroin use, had become a national epidemic. Estimates were placed as high as 5 million, with any number of explanations for the increased number of users. Some blamed it on the greed of drug traffickers, others on the inadequate personalities of the users. A few argued that it was a natural consequence of the Prohibition amendment.[35] Most observers generally agreed, however, that more legislation was the answer to the problem. As an editorial in *Literary Digest* for June 10, 1922, stated:

> "Snow parties," which are said to have become so prevalent as to menace American civilization, will be made impossible by the Jones-Miller bill governing the manufacture, importation and exportation of habit-forming drugs, which has been passed by Congress and signed by President Harding. By

striking at the source of supply, the bill goes to the root of the
evil, and, in time, will eliminate it altogether.[36]

Snow, as the editorial suggested, referred to heroin and cocaine, and
the Jones-Miller Act was a piece of federal legislation that set fines of
up to $5,000 and imprisonment of up to 10 years for anyone involved
in the unlawful importation of narcotics.

Even though the Jones-Miller Act had little impact, other than to
further inflate the prices of heroin and morphine in the illicit drug
marketplace, some people argued that the drug "epidemic" was a
myth. One observer suggested that the exaggerated estimates were
no more than German war propaganda. Referencing a rumor that those
in charge of the draft during World War I would find no less than
500,000 addicts among the inductees, it was pointed out that of some
3.5 million men examined, only 3,284 were found to be addicts. By
applying that ratio to 1920 census figures, it was concluded that 100,000
was likely a more accurate estimate, and that drug addiction had
actually declined during the previous two decades.[37] Other data tended
to support this conclusion. In 1924 Dr. Lawrence Kolb and Dr. A. G.
Du Mez of the United States Public Health Service, after a careful
examination of all the available survey data on drug use, estimated
that there were probably only 110,000 addicts in the United States at
the end of 1922, reflecting a considerable decline since the turn of the
century.[38] Yet whatever the correct figures, everyone seemed to agree
that narcotics use was indeed a problem that needed to be addressed.

THE EVIL WEED OF THE FIELDS
AND RIVER BEDS AND ROADSIDES

The national concern over the use of narcotics during the 1930s was
not focused solely on heroin, for another substance was considered
by some to represent an even greater evil. One might expect that it
was cocaine, since the drug's stimulant effects had been promoted in
the United States well before the introduction of Bayer's Heroin. But
this was not the case. After the passage of the Pure Food and Drug
Act in 1906, cocaine use moved underground to the netherworlds of
the jazz scene and the bohemia of the avant-garde. There it remained
for decades, so much so that the Treasury Department's Bureau of
Narcotics, a federal agency that was often accused of grossly exaggerating the extent of drug use in the United States, concluded in 1939 that,
"The use of cocaine in the illicit traffic continues to be so small as
to be without significance."[39] No, not cocaine, but rather the more

insidious marijuana, alternatively called the "devil drug," "assassin of youth," and "weed of madness."

Marijuana, typically referred to a century ago as "cannabis" or "hashish," was introduced to the American public in essentially the same manner as were opium, morphine, cocaine, and heroin. A derivative of the Indian hemp plant *Cannabis sativa L.*, the drug appeared among the patent medicines hawked from the tailgates of medicine show wagons and was sold as a cure for depression, convulsions, hysteria, insanity, mental retardation, and impotence.[d] Moreover, during the late 1800s such well-known pharmaceutical companies as Parke-Davis and Squibb produced tincture of cannabis for the family pharmacist to dispense. As a medicinal agent, however, the drug quickly fell into disfavor. Because of its insolubility, it could not be

---

[d] *Cannabis sativa L.* is an annual plant that flourishes in most warm or temperate climate and varies in height from 3 to 10 feet or more. The leaves are long, narrow and serrated, and form a fan-shaped pattern; each fan has anywhere from 3 to 15 leaves but typically only 5 or 7 leaves. These leaves are shiny and sticky, and their upper surfaces are covered with short hairs. The psychoactive preparations derivative of cannabis are:

1. Marijuana, the crushed and dried twigs, leaves, and flowers.
2. Hashish, the resinous extract obtained by boiling those parts of the plant in a solvent that are covered with the resin, or by scraping the resin from the plant.
3. Hashoil, a dark, viscous liquid produced by a process of repeated extraction of cannabis material.

The active ingredient in cannabis is *delta-9-tetrahydrocannabinol*, or simply THC. Whereas the THC content of most marijuana ranges from 1% to 5%, in hashish this figure can be as high as 15% to 20%, and twice that for hashoil.

Cannabis products vary in both name and form in different parts of the world. In Asia, for example, there is "ganga," "charas," and "bhang." Ganja consists of the young leaves and flowering tops of the cultivated female plant and its resin, pressed or rolled into a sticky mass and then formed into flat or round cakes. Its color is dark green or greenish-brown, and it has a pleasant smell and characteristic taste. Charas is the prepared resin separated from the tops of the female plant. It is pounded and rubbed until it is a gray-white powder and then made into cakes or think almost transparent sheets, or it is left in dark brown lumps. Bhang consists of the older or more mature leaves of the plant and is often used by boiling in water and adding butter to make a syrup. Bhang is less potent than ganja, which in turn is considerably weaker than charas.

In the Middle East the word "hashish" is usually applied to both the leaves and the resin or a mixture of the two. In North Africa the resin and tops, usually reduced to a coarse powder, is known as "kif" in Morocco and "takrouri" in Algeria and Tunisia; in central and southern Africa "dagga" refers to the leaves and tops.

Despite these many differences in nomenclature, the subjective effects of marijuana are essentially the same, although varying in intensity depending on the THC content. At social-recreational use levels, these effects include: alteration of time and space perception; a sense of euphoria, relaxation, well-being, and disinhibition; dulling of attention; fragmentation of thought and impaired immediate memory; an altered sense of identity; and exaggerated laughter and increased suggestability. At doses higher than the typical recreational levels, more pronounced distortions of thought may occur, including a disrupted sense of one's own body, a sense of personal unreality, visual distortions, and sometimes hallucinations, paranoid thinking, and acute psychotic-like symptoms.

In the 1930s, Harry Anslinger's theories about marijuana were brought to mass audiences through numerous Hollywood productions.

injected, and taken orally it was slow and generally ineffective. Moreover, its potency was variable, making dosage standardization difficult. Yet as a recreational drug, marijuana had its devotees. By the middle of the 1880s every major American city had its clandestine hashish clubs catering to a rather well-to-do clientele.[40]

At the beginning of the twentieth century, what was referred to in Mexico as "marijuana" (also marihuana and mariguana) began to appear in New Orleans and a number of the Texas border towns. Having been used in South America and Central America for quite some time, "Mexican ditch weed," as some people called it, was a substance less potent than the hashish (often spelled hasheesh in the mass media) that was first smoked in the underground clubs decades earlier. Whereas hashish is the resinous extract of the hemp plant, marijuana is composed of the hemp plant's dried leaves, stems, and flowering tops.[e]

By 1920 the use of marijuana had become visible among members of minority groups—blacks in the South and illegal alien Mexicans in the Southwest. Given the social and political climate of the period, it is not at all surprising that the use of the drug became a matter of immediate concern. The agitation for reform that had resulted in the passage of the Harrison Act and the Pure Food and Drug Act was still active, and the movement for national prohibition of alcohol was at its peak. Moreover, not only was marijuana an "intoxicant of blacks and wetbacks" that might have a corrupting influence on white society, it was considered particularly dangerous because of its alien (spelled "Mexican") and un-American origins.

Through the early 1930s state after state enacted antimarijuana laws, usually instigated by lurid newspaper articles depicting the madness and horror attributed to the drug's use. Even the prestigious *New York Times*, with its claim of "All the News That's Fit to Print," helped to reinforce the growing body of beliefs surrounding marijuana use. In an article headlined "Mexican Family Go Insane," and datelined Mexico City, July 6, 1927, the Times reported:

> A widow and her four children have been driven insane by eating the Marihuana plant, according to doctors, who say that there is no hope of saving the children's lives and that the mother will be insane for the rest of her life.
>
> The tragedy occurred while the body of the father, who had been killed, was still in a hospital.
>
> The mother was without money to buy other food for the children, whose ages range from 3 to 15, so they gathered some herbs and vegetables growing in the yard for their dinner. Two hours after the mother and children had eaten the plants, they

---

[e] The etymological roots of the word *marijuana* have been debated at length and still remain unresolved. Some maintain that the word comes from what the Aztec Indians referred to as *mallihuan*, a term that imparted the idea of a substance that took possession of the user. A second position holds that marijuana is a corruption of the Portuguese *maranguango*, meaning intoxicating.

were stricken. Neighbors, hearing outbursts of crazed laughter, rushed to the house to find the entire family insane. Examination revealed that the narcotic marihuana was growing among the garden vegetables.[41]

Popular books of the era, as well, were as colorful as the press in describing marijuana and the consequences of its use. A 1928 publication, aptly titled *Dope*, offered the following:

> And the man under the influence of hasheesh catches up his knife and runs through the streets hacking and killing everyone he meets. No, he has no special grievance against mankind. When he is himself, he is probably a good-humored, harmless, well-meaning creature; but hasheesh is the murder drug, and it is the hasheesh which makes him pick up his knife and start to kill.
>
> Marihuana is American hasheesh. It is made from a little weed that grows in Texas, Arizona, and Southern California. You can grow enough marihuana in a window-box to drive the whole population of the United States stark, staring, raving mad.
>
> . . . but when you have once chosen marihuana, you have selected murder and torture and hideous cruelty to your bosom friends.[42]

In other reports, the link between the antimarijuana sentiment and prejudice was apparent. On January 27, 1929, the *Montana Standard* reported on the progress of a bill that amended the state's general narcotic law to include marijuana:

> There was fun in the House Health Committee during the week when the Marihuana bill came up for consideration. Marihuana is Mexican opium, a plant used by Mexicans and cultivated for sale by Indians. "When some beet field peon takes a few rares of this stuff," explained Dr. Fred Fulsher of Mineral County, "he thinks he has just been elected president of Mexico so he starts to execute all of his political enemies. . . ." Everybody laughed and the bill was recommended for passage.[43]

Although marijuana is neither Mexican opium nor a narcotic of any kind, it was perceived as such by a small group of legislators, newspaper editors, and concerned citizens who were pressuring Washington for federal legislation against the drug. Their demands were almost immediately heard by Harry J. Anslinger, the then recently installed Commissioner of the Treasury Department's Bureau of Narcotics of 1930. Although it would appear that Anslinger was a

Neanderthal ultraright-wing conservative who truly believed marijuana to be a threat to the future of American civilization, his biographer maintained that he was an astute government bureaucrat who viewed the marijuana issue as a mechanism for elevating himself and the Bureau of Narcotics to national prominence.[44] In retrospect, however, given what is now known about marijuana, Anslinger's crusade has been interpreted by many to have been no more than the ravings of a madman.

Using the mass media as his forum, Anslinger described marijuana as a Frankenstein drug that was stalking American youth. In an issue of *American Magazine* he wrote:

> The sprawled body of a young girl lay crushed on the sidewalk the other day after a plunge from the fifth story of a Chicago apartment house. Everyone called it suicide, but actually it was murder. The killer was a narcotic known to America as marijuana, and to history as hashish. It is a narcotic used in the form of cigarettes, comparatively new to the United States and as dangerous as a coiled rattlesnake. . . .[45]

Then there was Anslinger's "gore file," a collection of the most heinous cases, most with only the flimsiest of substantiation, that graphically depicted the insane violence that marijuana use engendered. For example, again from *American Magazine:*

> An entire family was murdered by a youthful addict in Florida. When officers arrived at the home, they found the youth staggering about in a human slaughterhouse. With an ax he had killed his father, mother, two brothers, and a sister. He seemed to be in a daze. . . . He had no recollection of having committed the multiple crime. The officers knew him ordinarily as a sane, rather quiet young man; now he was pitifully crazed. They sought the reason. The boy said that he had been in the habit of smoking something which youthful friends called "muggles," a childish name for marihuana.[46]

Much of the "gore file" also touched on the interracial fears of white society. For example:

> Colored students at the Univ. of Minn. partying with female students (white), smoking [marijuana] and getting their sympathy with stories of racial persecution. Result pregnancy.

> Two Negroes took a girl fourteen years old and kept her for two days under the influence of marihuana. Upon recovery she was found to be suffering from syphilis.[47]

As the result of Anslinger's crusade, on August 2, 1937, the Marijuana Tax Act was signed into law, classifying the scraggly tramp of the vegetable world as a narcotic and placing it under essentially the same controls as the Harrison Act had done with opium and coca products.[f]

POSTSCRIPT

As was the case with morphine and heroin, observers of the marijuana "problem" debated about the number of the drug's devotees. What everyone seemed to concur on, however, was that narcotics use was indeed a problem in the United States. Where little agreement existed was in the proper methods for handling it. Throughout the balance of the 1930s three points of view dominated. The medical establishment argued that addiction was a physical disease and should be treated as such; the law enforcement establishment saw addiction as a criminal tendency and favored harsh punishment for the sake of societal protection and deterrence; and then there was the political establishment. It believed that addiction could be simply legislated out of existence if enough comprehensive laws were passed. Each establishment worked in pursuit of its own position. A few treatment facilities were opened, addicts were arrested and imprisoned, and new legislation was passed. By the early 1940s narcotic addiction had all but disappeared in the United States. But it was not the result of medical, enforcement, or legislative efforts. World War II intervened to cut off the supplies of opium from Asia and interrupted the trafficking routes from Europe. As an editorial in *Time* put it in 1942, "The war is probably the best thing that ever happened to U.S. drug addicts."[48]

Notes

1. Charles E. Terry and Mildred Pellens, *The Opium Problem* (New York: Bureau of Social Hygiene, 1968), p. 56.
2. E. F. Cook and E. W. Martin, *Remington's Practice of Pharmacy* (Easton, PA: Mack Publishing Co., 1951).

---

[f] For decades after the passage of the Marijuana Tax Act, Anslinger continued to write about the evils of marijuana, the "Mexican ditch weed," almost as if he had to justify the wisdom of the law. See, for example, Harry J. Anslinger and William F. Tompkins, *The Traffic in Narcotics* (New York: Funk & Wagnalls, 1953); Harry J. Anslinger and Will Ousler, *The Murderers: The Shocking Story of the Narcotics Gangs* (New York: Farrar, Straus, and Cudahy, 1961).

3. Peter P. White, "The Poppy," *National Geographic*, Feb. 1985, p. 144. See also, Mark David Merlin, *On the Trail of the Ancient Opium Poppy* (Rutherford, NJ: Fairleigh Dickinson University Press, 1984).

4. William Buchan, M.D., *Domestic Medicine: or, A Treatise on the Prevention and Cure of Diseases by Regimen and Simple Medicines* (Philadelphia: Crukshank, Bell, and Muir, 1784), pp. 225–226.

5. Buchan, p. 520.

6. *Scientific American*, 5 Oct. 1985, p. 214.

7. James Harvey Young, *The Toadstool Millionaires: A Social History of Patent Medicines in America Before Federal Regulation* (Princeton, NJ: Princeton University Press, 1961), pp. 19–23.

8. Jerome H. Jaffe and William R. Martin, "Narcotic Analgesics and Antagonists," *The Pharmacological Basis of Therapeutics*, ed. Louis S. Goodman and Alfred Gilman (New York: Macmillan, 1970), p. 245.

9. See Roberts Bartholow, *A Manual of Hypodermatic Medication* (Philadelphia: Lippincott, 1891).

10. H. H. Kane, *The Hypodermic Injection of Morphia* (New York: C. L. Bermingham, 1880), p. 5.

11. *1897 Sears Roebuck Catalogue* (1897; rpt. New York: Chelsea House, 1968), p. 32 of insert on drugs.

12. Terry and Pellens, p. 73.

13. See Lawrence Kolb and A. G. Du Mez, "The Prevalence and Trend of Drug Addiction in the United States and the Factors Influencing It," *Public Health Reports*, 23 May 1924.

14. Terry and Pellens, pp. 1–20. See also H. Wayne Morgan, *Yesterday's Addicts: American Society and Drug Abuse, 1865–1920* (Norman: University of Oklahoma Press, 1974).

15. Virgil G. Eaton, "How the Opium Habit Is Acquired," *Popular Science Monthly*, 33 (1888), pp. 665–666.

16. A. P. Grinnell, "A Review of Drug Consumption and Alcohol as Found in Proprietary Medicine," *Medical Legal Journal*, 1905, cited in Terry and Pellens, pp. 21–22.

17. Hector P. Blejer, "Coca Leaf and Cocaine Addiction—Some Historical Notes," *Canadian Medical Association Journal*, 25 Sept. 1965, p. 702.

18. E. J. Kahn, *The Big Drink: The Story of Coca-Cola* (New York: Random House, 1960).

19. Ernest Jones, *The Life and Work of Sigmund Freud*, Vol. I (New York: Basic Books, 1953), p. 81.

20. Freud's paper "Uber Coca" (On Coca) has been reprinted in *Cocaine Papers by Sigmund Freud*, ed. Robert Byck (New York: New American Library, 1975), pp. 49–73.

21. C. R. A. Wright, "On the Action of Organic Acids and Their Anhydrides on the Natural Alkaloids," *Journal of the Chemical Society*, 12 July 1874, p. 1031.

22. Virginia Berridge and Griffith Edwards, *Opium and the People: Opiate Use in Nineteenth-Century England* (New Haven: Yale University Press, 1987), pp. xix–xx.

23. M. Manges, "A Second Report on the Therapeutics of Heroin," *New York Medical Journal*, 20 Jan. 1900, pp. 82–83.

24. James A. Inciardi, "Over-the-Counter Drugs: Epidemiology, Adverse Reactions, Overdose Deaths, and Mass Media Promotion," *Addictive Diseases: An International Journal*, 3 (1977), pp. 253–272.

25. James Harvey Young, *The Medical Messiahs: A Social History of Health Quackery in Twentieth-Century America* (Princeton, NJ: Princeton University Press, 1967), p. 29.

26. Cited in Young, p. 31.

27. The complete text of the Harrison Act, as well as those of other federal drug laws passed from 1909 through 1980, have been reprinted in Gerard P. Walsh (ed.), *Opium and Narcotic Laws* (Washington, DC: United States Government Printing Office, 1981).

28. *Webb v. U.S.*, 249 U.S. 96 (1919).

29. *U.S. v. Behrman*, 258 U.S. 280 (1922).

30. *Lindner v. U.S.*, 268 U.S. 5 (1925).

31. Rufus King, "The American System: Legal Sanctions to Repress Drug Abuse," in *Drugs and the Criminal Justice System*, eds. James A. Inciardi and Carl D. Chambers (Beverly Hills: Sage, 1974), p. 22.

32. See Morgan.

33. Perry M. Lichtenstein, "Narcotic Addiction," *New York Medical Journal*, 14 Nov. 1914, p. 962. It should be pointed out here that although Lichtenstein's comments were published almost a year after the passage of the Harrison Act, they were based on his treatment efforts with criminal addicts during prior years while he served as a physician at New York's Manhattan City Prison (more popularly known as "The Tombs"). The complete text of Dr. Lichtenstein's remarks have been reprinted in John A. O'Donnell and John C. Ball (eds.), *Narcotic Addiction* (New York: Harper & Row, 1966), pp. 23–34.

34. G. E. McPherson and J. Cohen, "Survey of 100 Cases of Drug Addiction Entering Camp Upton, New York," *Boston Medical and Surgical Journal*, 5 June 1919; Special Committee of Investigation, *Traffic in Narcotic Drugs* (Washington, DC: Department of Treasury, 1919); *Literary Digest*, 26 Apr. 1919, p. 32; *The Outlook*, 25 June 1919, p. 315; *The Survey*, 15 Mar. 1919, pp. 67–868; *American Review of Reviews*, July–Dec. 1919, pp. 331–332.

35. *Literary Digest*, 6 Mar. 1920, pp. 27–28; 16 Apr. 1921, pp. 19–20; 24 Feb. 1923, pp. 34–35; 25 Aug. 1923, pp. 22–23.

36. *Literary Digest*, 10 June 1922, p. 34.

37. *World's Work*, Nov. 1924, p. 17.

38. Lawrence Kolb and A. G. Du Mez, "The Prevalence and Trend of Drug Addiction in the United States and Factors Influencing It," *Public Health Reports*, 23 May 1924, pp. 1179–1204.

39. U.S. Treasury Department, Bureau of Narcotics, *Traffic in Opium and Other Dangerous Drugs* (Washington, DC: United States Government Printing Office, 1939), p. 14.

40. Larry Sloman, *Reefer Madness: A History of Marijuana in America* (Indianapolis: Bobbs-Merrill, 1979), p. 26. For a description of a late nineteenth-century hashish club, see H. H. Kane, "A Hashish-House in New York," *Harper's Monthly*, Nov. 1883, pp. 944–949, reprinted in Morgan, pp. 159–170.

41. *New York Times*. 6 July 1927, p. 10.

42. Winifred Black, *Dope: The Story of the Living Dead* (New York: Star & Co., 1928), p. 28.
43. Sloman, pp. 30–31
44. See John C. McWilliams, ,*The Protectors: Harry J. Anslinger and the Federal Bureau of Narcotics, 1930–1962* (Newark: University of Delaware Press, 1990).
45. Sloman, p. 34.
46. Sloman, p. 63.
47. Sloman, pp. 58–59.
48. *Time* 24 Aug. 1942, p. 52.

CHAPTER TWO

ALONG THE ROAD FROM H TO ICE
Drug Taking in Post–World War II America

The crusade against marijuana during the 1930s had attributed to drug taking a level of wickedness that could only have been matched by the Victorian imagery of masturbation and its consequences. The 1940s all but ignored the drug problem, principally because if it were indeed a "problem," it was an invisible one—hardly a topic that should divert attention away from the events of a world at war. Then came the 1950s, a time when everything seemed right but in many instances was quite wrong.

IN SEARCH OF THE ROAD TO H

Within three years after the close of World War II, the opium-heroin trafficking networks from Southeast Asia and Europe had been reestablished, and illicit narcotics once again began to reach American ports. During the opening years of the 1950s the prevailing image of drug use was one of heroin addiction on the streets of the urban ghetto. As summarized by the distinguished author and journalist Max Lerner in his celebrated work *America as a Civilization:*

> As a case in point we may take the known fact of the prevalence of reefer-and-dope addiction in Negro areas. This is essentially explained in terms of poverty, slum living, and broken families, yet it would be easy to show the lack of drug addiction among other ethnic groups where the same conditions apply.[1]

Lerner went on to explain that addiction among blacks was due to the adjustment problems associated with their rapid movement from a depressed status to the improved standards and freedoms of the era.

Yet Lerner's interpretation was hardly a correct one, and not only about
"reefer addiction" but also about the prevalence of drug abuse in other
populations—rich and poor, white and black, young and old.

In the popular media of the time a somewhat more detailed portrait of the problem was offered. *Time, Life, Newsweek,* and other major
periodicals spoke of how teenagers, jaded on marijuana, had found
greater thrills in heroin. For most, the pattern of initiation had been
the same. They began with marijuana, the use of which had become
a fad in the ghetto. Then, enticed in school yards by brazen Mafia
pushers dressed in dark suits, white ties, and wide-brimmed hats,
the youngsters were given their first dose of heroin free. By then,
however, it was too late; their fate had been sealed; they were already
addicted.[2] Or as a saying of the 1950s went, "It's so good, don't
even try it once!"

Hollywood offered a somewhat different image of the situation in
the 1955 United Artists' release of *The Man with the Golden Arm.* The
film was somewhat controversial in its day, for the Otto Preminger
production had touched upon a topic that most Americans felt should
remain in the ghetto where it belonged. In its actual content, like most
films of the comfortable, conservative, prosperous, classless, sexless,
and consensual paradise of the 1950s, it reflected majority attitudes
and served to confirm established visions of reality. Cast in the role
of a would-be professional musician, singer-actor Frank Sinatra was
the hero of the story. Plagued by the evils of heroin addiction, he was
unable to get his life together. Finally, however, through the help and
understanding of his girlfriend Molly (portrayed by Kim Novak), he
was saved from a life of pathetic degradation. As in the case of other
media images of the drug scene, *The Man with the Golden Arm* offered
only a contorted view, failing to probe even the most basic issues.

Within the scientific community, much of the literature and
research was almost as bizarre. As might be expected, most explanations of drug addiction focused on heroin in the ghetto. Young addicts
were believed to be either psychotic or neurotic casualties for whom
drugs provided relief from anxiety and a means for withdrawing from
the stress of daily struggle in the slum. Among the more celebrated
studies of the period was psychologist Isidor Chein's *The Road to H.*
Concerning youthful addiction in New York City, Chein concluded:

> The evidence indicated that all addicts suffer from deep-rooted
> personality disorders. Although psychiatric diagnoses are apt
> to vary, a particular set of symptoms seems to be common to
> most juvenile addicts. They are not able to enter into prolonged,
> close, friendly relations with either peers or adults; they have
> difficulties in assuming a masculine role; they are frequently
> overcome by a sense of futility, expectations of failure, and

general depression; they are easily frustrated and made
anxious, and they find frustrations and anxiety intolerable.[3]

By focusing on such maladies as "weak ego functioning," "defec-
tive superego," and "inadequate masculine identification," what Chein
was suggesting was the notion of a psychological predisposition to drug
use—in other words, an addiction-prone personality. The text went
on to imply that the series of predispositions could be traced to the
addict's family experiences. If the youth received too much love or not
enough, or if the parents were overwhelming in terms of their affec-
tion or indulgence, then the child would develop inadequately. As a
result, the youth would likely be unable to withstand pain and discomfort, to cope with the complexities of life in the neighborhood and
community, to assess reality correctly, and to feel competent around
others of more varied social experiences. Although this has certainly
been the case over the years with a number of addicts, it does not
explain all addiction. Chein concluded, however, that this type of youth
would be more prone to trying drugs than others of more conventional
family backgrounds.

The prevailing portrait of addiction in the scientific community,
then, was one of passive adaptation to stress. Drugs allowed the user
to experience fulfillment and the satiation of physical and emotional
needs. This general view was also supported by sociological attempts
to explain the broader concepts of deviance and delinquency. Given
this predisposition, consider what became known in the literature as
the "double-failure" hypothesis.[4] According to sociologists Richard A.
Cloward and Lloyd E. Ohlin, double failures were ghetto youths who
were unable to succeed in either the gang subculture or the wider
legitimate culture. They embraced drugs, in turn, as a way of finding
a place for themselves in society.

For those who lived in the ghetto, worked in the ghetto, took drugs
in the ghetto, policed the ghetto, or in some other fashion actively
observed or participated in ghetto life, the "addiction-prone personality," "double-failure," and other escapist theories of addiction were
found humorous. On the contrary, the conduct of most addicts
appeared to be anything but an escape from life. Much of their time
was spent in drug-seeking behaviors, in meaningful activities and relationships on the street centers surrounding the economic institutions
of heroin distribution. As the late urban anthropologist Edward Preble
once put it, they were "taking care of business":

> The brief moments of euphoria after each administration of a
> small amount of heroin constitute a small fraction of their daily
> lives. The rest of the time they are aggressively pursuing a
> career that is exciting, challenging, adventurous, and rewarding.

They are always on the move and must be alert, flexible, and resourceful. The surest way to identify heroin users in a slum neighborhood is to observe the way people walk. The heroin user walks with a fast, purposeful stride, as if he is late for an important appointment—indeed, he is. He is hustling [robbing or stealing], trying to sell stolen goods, avoiding the police, looking for a heroin dealer with a good bag [the street retail unit of heroin], coming back from copping [buying heroin], looking for a safe place to take the drug, or looking for someone who beat [cheated] him—among other things.[5]

"TIMOTHY LEARY'S DEAD . . ."

In many ways the 1950s had been a decade of waste. Caught up in a belief that the good life had arrived, Americans rushed to the suburbs to escape urban congestion. Throughout the country tract developments sprouted as landscapes were bulldozed flat. This mass migration to the suburbs left the cities to deteriorate. An overwhelming reliance on the automobile, brought about by a sudden romance with the family car and the construction of a 40,000-mile interstate highway system, resulted in a breakdown in mass transportation and, in turn, pollution and congestion. These problems were most deeply felt in the central cities where the poor had been left behind.

Another problem was the racism that persisted from earlier years. In the growing prosperity of the 1950s, blacks continued to face the legacy of Jim Crow. In the South, particularly, they were repeatedly the victims of mob murders, lynchings, and all forms of social disenfranchisement.

To compound these problems, American youth faced an enforcement of conformity, a transparency of sexual morals, and a set of cultural prescriptions and proscriptions that stressed achievement, prejudice, waste, compliance, and consensus yet failed to explain or recognize the confusion and absurdity of it all. As a result of such contradictions, a teenage ethic emerged that made serious negative value judgments about the nature and meaning of life. As social critic Kenneth Rexroth warned in an early issue of *Evergreen Review*:

> Listen You—do you really think your kids are like bobby soxers in those wholesome Coca-Cola ads? Don't you know that across the table from you at dinner sits somebody who looks on you as an enemy who is planning to kill him in the immediate future? Don't you know that if you were to say to your English class, "It is raining," they would take it for granted that you

were a liar? Don't you know they never tell you nothing? That they can't? that . . . they simply can't get through, can't, and won't even try anymore to communicate? Don't you know this, really? If you don't, you're in for a terrible awakening.[6]

The enforced conformity, youth rebellion, racism, cultural values that canonized consumption and waste, and the numerous other problems in American society that had been festering during the 1940s and 1950s seemed to merge during the following decade, resulting in one of the most revolutionary periods in recent history. The 1960s was a time characterized by civil rights movements, political assassinations, campus and antiwar protests, and ghetto riots.

Among the more startling events was the drug revolution of the 1960s. The use of drugs seemed to have leapt from the more marginal zones of society to the very mainstream of community life. No longer were drugs limited to the inner cities and half-worlds of the jazz scene and the underground bohemian protocultures. Rather, they had become suddenly and dramatically apparent among members of the adolescent middle-class and young-adult populations of rural and urban America. By the close of the decade, commentators on the era were maintaining that ours was "the addicted society," that through drugs millions had become "seekers" of "instant enlightenment," and that drug taking and drug seeking would persist as continuing facts of American social life.[7]

In retrospect, what were then considered the logical causes of the new drug phenomenon now seem less clear. A variety of changes in the fabric of American life occurred during those years, which undoubtedly had profound implications for social consciousness and behavior. Notably, the revolution in the technology and handling of drugs that began during the 1950s was of sufficient magnitude to justify the designation of the 1960s as "a new chemical age." Recently compounded psychotropic agents were enthusiastically introduced and effectively promoted, with the consequence of exposing the national consciousness to an impressive catalog of chemical temptations— sedatives, tranquilizers, stimulants, antidepressants, analgesics, and hallucinogens—which could offer fresh inspiration as well as simple and immediate relief from fear, anxiety, tension, frustration, and boredom.[8]

Concomitant with this emergence of a new chemical age, a new youth ethos had become manifest, one characterized by widely celebrated generational disaffection, a prejudicial dependence on the self and the peer group for value orientation, a critical view of how the world was being run, and mistrust for an "establishment" drug policy whose "facts" and "warnings" ran counter to reported peer experiences. On this latter point, it is no wonder that such mistrust developed. Many teenagers and young adults across the nation had become recreational users of marijuana. For most, the psychological reactions they experienced included euphoria, fragmentation of thought, laughter, spatial and temporal distortions, heightened sensuality, and increased sociability. A few experienced fear, anxiety, and panic. Yet what most of the brokers of drug education were saying to users and their peers was something totally different—something reminiscent of Anslinger's pontifications during the 1930s' era of reefer madness. In fact, in the early 1960s Anslinger was still saying essentially the same things about marijuana:

> Those who are accustomed to habitual use of the drug are said eventually to develop a delirious rage after its administration during which they are temporarily, at least, irresponsible and prone to commit violent crimes. The prolonged use of this narcotic is said to produce mental deterioration. . . . Much of the most irrational juvenile violence and killing that has written a new chapter of shame and tragedy is traceable directly to this hemp intoxication.[9]

With statements such as these coming from the Commissioner of Narcotics, drug educators, and parents—statements that for the most part were contrary to experience and untrue—it is no wonder that the youth of the day turned deaf ears to the antidrug messages.

Whatever the ultimate causes, America's younger generations, or at least noticeable segments of them, had embraced drugs. The drug scene became the arena of "happening" America; "turning on" to drugs for relaxation and to share friendship and love seemed to have become commonplace. And the prophet—the "high priest" as he called himself—of the new chemical age was a psychology instructor at Harvard University's Center for Research in Human Personality, Dr. Timothy Leary.

The saga of Timothy Leary had its roots not at Harvard in the 1960s but in Basel, Switzerland, just before the beginning of World War II. It was there, in 1938, that Dr. Albert Hoffman of Sandoz Research Laboratories first isolated a new chemical compound which he called D-lysergic acid diethylamide. More popularly known as LSD, it was cast aside in his laboratory where, for five years, it remained unappreciated, its properties awaiting discovery. On April 16, 1943, after absorbing some LSD through the skin of his fingers, Hoffman began to hallucinate. In his diary he explained the effect:

> With closed eyes, multihued, metamorphizing, fantastic images overwhelmed me. . . . Sounds were transposed into visual sensations so that from each tone or noise a comparable colored picture was evoked, changing in form and color kaleidoscopically.[10]

Hoffman had experienced the first consciously induced LSD "trip."[a]

Dr. Humphrey Osmond of the New Jersey Neuropsychiatric Institute neologized a new name for LSD. "Psychedelic," he called it, meaning mind-expanding. But outside the scientific community, LSD was generally unknown—even at the start of the 1960s. This was quickly changed by Leary and his colleague at Harvard, Dr. Richard Alpert. They began experimenting with the drug—on themselves, and with colleagues, students, artists, writers, clergymen, and volunteer prisoners. Although by 1963 their adventures with LSD earned them dismissals from Harvard, their message had been heard, and LSD achieved its reputation. Their messages were numerous and shocking to the political establishment and to hundreds of thousands of mothers and fathers across the nation.

In *The Realist*, a radical periodical of the 1960s, Leary commented:

> I predict that psychedelic drugs will be used in all schools in the near future as educational devices—not only marijuana and LSD, to teach kids how to use their sense organs and other cellular equipment effectively—but new and more powerful psychochemicals. . . .[11]

Elsewhere he wrote of the greatest fear that might be generated by psychedelic drug use, what he called "ontological addiction":

> . . . the terror of finding a realm of experience, a new dimension of reality so pleasant that one will not want to return. This fear is based on the unconscious hunch . . . that normal consciousness is a form of sleepwalking and that somewhere there exists a form of awakeness, of reality from which one would not want to return.[12]

And then, perhaps most frightening of all to the older generation, were Leary's comments to some 15,000 cheering San Francisco youths on

---

[a] Dr. Hoffman also experienced the first "bad trip." Regarding an April 19, 1943, experience with LSD, he later recalled in his *LSD: My Problem Child* (Los Angeles: J. P. Tarcher, 1983):

> The dizziness and sensation of fainting became so strong at times that I could no longer hold myself erect, and had to lie down on a sofa. My surroundings had now transformed themselves in more terrifying ways. Everything in the room spun around, and the familiar objects and pieces of furniture assumed grotesque, threatening forms. They were in continuous motion, animated, as if driven by an inner restlessness. The lady next door, whom I scarcely recognized, brought me milk—in the course of the evening I drank more than two liters. She was no longer Mrs. R., but rather a malevolent, insidious witch with a colored mask.

the afternoon of March 26, 1967. As a modern-day Pied Piper, Leary told his audience:

> Turn on to the scene, tune in to what's happening; and drop out—of high school, college, grade school . . . follow me, the hard way.[13]

Leary's downfall came shortly thereafter, the result of conviction and imprisonment on drug-trafficking charges followed by a period of time as a fugitive in Algeria and Afghanistan after a prison escape. But his demise was eulogized. At the opening of "House of Four Doors" on the album *In Search of a Lost Chord*, the Moody Blues sang: "Timothy Leary's dead . . . he's on the outside, looking in."

Actually, Leary was not quite dead. By 1976 he had straightened out his legal problems and become a free man. Since that time he has been "a cheerleader for scientific optimism," as he once put it. With the onset of the 1980s Leary joined the ranks of the most highly paid speakers on the college lecture circuit, often debating G. Gordon Liddy of Watergate fame. Quite curiously, Liddy was once his nemesis, having organized a raid in 1966 that led to one of Leary's early drug arrests. During the mid- and late 1980s Leary became successful in the computer support industry, creating a variety of educational and personal management software;[14] and in early 1989, regarding the amount and variety of drugs that were reportedly used during the LSD era, he was quoted as saying: "If you remember the '60s, you weren't there."[15] Most recently, Dr. Leary was heard arguing for a legalization of drugs and suggesting that pharmaceutical firms should be encouraged to develop non-addicting mood altering drugs.[16]

The hysteria over Leary, LSD, and the other psychedelic substances was threefold. First, the drug scene was especially frightening to mainstream society because it reflected a willful rejection of rationality, order, and predictability. Second, there was the stigmatized association of drug use with antiwar protests and antiestablishment, long-haired, unwashed, radical "hippie" LSD users. And third, there were the drugs' psychic effects, the reported "bad trips" that seemed to border on mental illness. Particularly in the case of LSD, the rumors of how it could "blow one's mind" became legion. One story told of a youth, high on the drug, taking a swan dive in front of a truck moving at 70 mph. Another spoke of two "tripping" teenagers who stared directly into the sun until they were permanently blinded. A third described how LSD's effects on the chromosomes resulted in fetal abnormalities. The stories were never documented and were probably untrue. What were true, however, were the reports of LSD "flashbacks." Occurring with only a small percentage of the users, individuals would reexperience the LSD-induced state days, weeks,

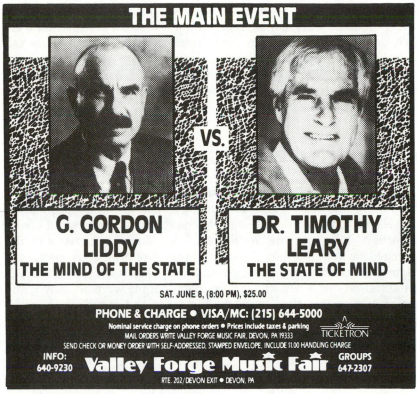

In the 1980s, the Liddy-Leary debates were popular on college campuses and at other public forums.

and sometimes months after the original ''trip'' without having taken the drug again.[b]

---

[b] Physiologically, the effects of LSD and other hallucinogens include increased pulse rate and blood pressure, dilated pupils, tremor, cold and sweaty palms, and at times, flushing, shivering, chills, pallor, salivation, and nausea.

Drug-induced activity lasts 8 to 12 hours, with the most intense changes in mood, sensation, and perception occurring during the first half of the experience. Mood alteration is the first obvious behavioral change observed. Along with this is a significant increase in sensory input, a kind of floating, with perceptual distortions and hallucinations. ''Synesthesia'' often occurs, involving sensory crossovers: subjects ''hear'' colors, ''taste'' sounds, and visualize music in colors. There is also ''tunnel vision,'' the focusing in on minute details not observed before.

The literature on LSD reports three different experiences when the user is under the influence of the drug: (1) *the good trip*, a predominantly pleasing experience; (2) *the bad trip*, a dysphoric experience characterized by anxiety, panic, feelings of persecution and fear, loss of control of time and space perception, and impaired performance; and (3) *the ambivalent state*, where the subject may simultaneously experience contrasting feelings of happiness and sadness, relaxation and tension.

The typical LSD dose is about 100 to 200 micrograms (1,000 micrograms = 1 milligram),

Despite the lurid reports, as it turned out, LSD was not in fact widely used on a regular basis beyond a few social groups that were fully dedicated to drug experiences. In fact psychedelic substances had quickly earned reputations as being dangerous and unpredictable, and most people avoided them.[c] By the close of the 1960s, all hallucinogenic drugs had been placed under strict legal control, and the number of users was minimal.[17]

FROM BLACK BEAUTY TO KING KONG

Throughout the 1960s heroin remained the most feared drug, and by the close of the decade estimates of the size of the addict population exceeded 500,000. Yet despite the hysteria about the rising tide of heroin addiction, LSD and the youth rebellion, Timothy Leary and the psychedelic age, and the growing awareness of drug abuse along the Main Streets of white America and the "Mean Streets" of black America, no one really knew how many people were actually using drugs. In fact, the estimates of the incidence and prevalence of marijuana, heroin, psychedelic, and other drug use were, at the very best, only vague and impressionistic. Although the reliability of political polling had long since demonstrated that the social sciences indeed had

---

may take doses as large as 2,000 micrograms. Physical dependence on LSD has not been observed.

[c] Other popular hallucinogenic drugs of the era were peyote, mescaline, psilocybin, MDA, and DMT.

Peyote is a spineless cactus native to central and northern Mexico whose top crown, or button, is a hallucinogenic drug. The button is dried, then ingested by holding it in the mouth until it is soft, and then swallowed whole. It takes about 3–4 buttons to experience a "trip." Tolerance is not known, and physical dependence has not been reported.

Mescaline is the principle alkaloid in the peyote cactus and perhaps the first hallucinogen to be chemically isolated (1897). Less potent than LSD, it is ingested orally, smoked, or injected. Tolerance is not known, physical dependence has not been reported, and interestingly, most confiscated samples of mescaline have been found to be PCP.

Psilocybin is the active ingredient in the Psilycybe Mexicana mushroom. Isolated in 1958 by Albert Hoffman, it is a white crystalline material. Potency is somewhere between mescline and LSD. It is the most rapid acting of the hallucinogens, with onset about 15 minutes after intake. The maximum intensity of the drug experience occurs after 90 minutes and effects last some 5 to 6 hours. No tolerance of physical dependence has been reported.

MDA is a semisynthetic drug produced by modifying the major psychoactive components of nutmeg and mace. First synthesized in 1910, MDA combines effects like those of mescaline and the amphetamines. MDA can be both toxic and lethal, but no tolerance or physical dependence has been reported.

DMT (dimethyltryptamine), commonly made synthetically, is also found in the seeds of certain South American and West Indian plants. It may appear as a crystalline powder or as a solution, or it may be mixed with such substances as tobacco or parsley. Its effects are similar to those of LSD, but the drug is much weaker and its effects shorter lived.

the tools to measure the dimensions of the "drug problem," no one at any time throughout the 1960s had gone so far as to count drug users in a systematic way. Yet several indicators existed. Studies were suggesting that the annual production of barbiturate drugs exceeded 1 million pounds, the equivalent of 24 one-and-one-half-grain doses for every man, woman, and child in the nation—enough to kill each person twice.[18] And for amphetamines and amphetamine-like compounds, the manufacturing figures came to some 50 doses per U.S. resident each year, with half the production reaching the illicit marketplace.[19]

The amphetamines were not new drugs, but their appearance on the street had been relatively recent. Having been synthesized in Germany during the 1880s, their first use among Americans had not come until World War II. Thousands of servicemen in all of the military branches were issued Benzedrine, Dexedrine, and a variety of other types as a matter of course to relieve their fatigue and anxiety. After the war, amphetamine drugs became more readily available, and they were put to a wider assortment of uses—students cramming for exams, truck drivers and others who needed to be alert for extended periods of time, in weight-control programs, and as nasal decongestants. Yet as strong stimulants with pharmacological effects similar to those of cocaine, in time they became popular drugs of abuse.

As the 1970s began, the first item on the government's agenda for drug reform was amphetamines, with Indiana Senator Birch Bayh conducting hearings. There was a parade of witnesses, and the worst fears about the the drugs were confirmed—or so it seemed.[20] Bayh and his committee heard the horror stories of the "speed freaks" who injected amphetamine and methamphetamine, who stalked the city streets suffering from paranoid delusions and exhibiting episodes of violent behavior at the onset of their psychotic states. They heard, too, of the hundreds, thousands, and perhaps hundreds of thousands of children and teenagers stoned on "ups," "bennies," "pinks," "purple hearts," "black beauties," and "King Kong pills." By that time, systematic surveys of the general population had finally begun, with the first, conducted in New York, empirically documenting that amphetamine use and abuse were indeed widespread.[21]

Almost immediately, new legislation was proposed by the Bayh committee and pushed through by the Senate. Tighter controls were placed on the prescribing and distribution of amphetamines, and legitimate production was ultimately cut by 90%. In so doing, it was thought that the drug problem, at least in terms of the dangerous amphetamines, would be measurably solved.

But suddenly something seemed to go terribly wrong. The Senate, oftentimes a sacred repository of culture lag, in its infinite wisdom had totally ignored, or at least misunderstood, the very nature of the youth drug scene of the day. True, many youths were getting "stoned" on amphetamines. And true, there were "speed freaks" out on the streets of America committing random acts of violence. But the actual numbers of amphetamine and methamphetamine "freaks" were comparatively few, and the frequency of their violent acts was even less. Moreover, the number of youths who had actually become dysfunctional as a result of amphetamine abuse was hardly what any sophisticated researcher or clinician would have called an epidemic. Most importantly, what the Senate missed was that the amphetamine-using youth of America were "drug-use habituated." That is, it was not amphetamines that were important to them but drugs, any drugs. So, when the amphetamines dried up on the streets, the youthful users simply went to another widely available drug. They chose methaqualone— "sopors," "ludes," and "Captain Quaalude." Thus one drug problem was simply replaced by another. But this time, rather than arriving in high school classrooms stoned, users began showing up in hospital emergency rooms and county morgues.

Meanwhile, the heroin epidemic continued, and cocaine began its reappearance, emerging from the netherworlds of crime and the avant-garde where it had been casually sequestered since the early years of the century.

THE MANY LIVES OF CAPTAIN QUAALUDE

The United States Senate was not the real instigator of the methaqualone problem, for the crisis that followed was one in which everyone seemed to be at fault—the pharmaceutical industry, the medical profession, the Food and Drug Administration, the federal narcotics establishment, and the media. In 1972, the *Washington Post* focused the blame somewhat differently:

> The methaqualone boom should make an interesting case study in future medical textbooks: How skillful public relations and advertising created a best-seller—and helped cause a medical crisis in the process.[22]

Methaqualone was initially synthesized in India during the early 1950s as a possible antimalarial agent. When its hypnotic (sleep-producing) properties were discovered later in the decade, many hoped that as a non-barbiturate methaqualone might be a safer alternative to the barbiturates.[23]

Barbiturate drugs had been available for the better part of the century. As potent central nervous system depressants, they were the drugs of choice for inducing sleep. Depending on the dosage level, they were also in common use for anesthesia, sedation, and the treatment of tension, anxiety, and convulsions. However, the barbiturates had their problems. They were widely abused for the "high" they could engender. Moreover, they produced addiction after chronic use, were life-threatening upon withdrawal, and could cause fatal overdoses—particularly when mixed with alcohol.

As an alternative to barbiturates, methaqualone was introduced in England in 1959, and in Germany and Japan in 1960. Despite extensive medical reports of abuse in these three countries, the drug was introduced in the United States under the trade names of Quaalude, Sopor, Parest, Somnafac, and later, Mequin. Although methaqualone was a prescription drug, the federal drug establishment ignored evidence of an abuse potential, decided it need not be monitored, and the number of times a prescription could be refilled need not be restricted. This, combined with an advertising campaign that emphasized the drug as a "safe alternative to barbiturates," led to the assumption by the medical profession, the lay population, and the media that methaqualone was nonaddicting. Even the prestigious *AMA Drug Evaluations*, as late as 1973, stated no more than "long-term use of larger than therapeutic doses may result in psychic and physical dependence."[24]

The most effective advertising campaign was launched by William H. Rorer pharmaceuticals. Given the success of the catchy double-a in their antacid Maalox, they named their methaqualone product Quaalude. Their advertising emphasized that it was a non-barbiturate. Free samples of Quaalude were shipped throughout the country, and physicians began overprescribing the drug.

Looking for a new and safe high, users sought out methaqualone, and the drug quickly made its way to the street. Rather than a safe alternative to whatever they had been taking previously, street users actually had a drug with the same addiction liability and lethal potential as the barbiturates. What they experienced was a pleasant sense of well-being, an increased pain threshold, and a loss of muscle coordination. The high was reputed to enhance sexual performance. Although no actual evidence confirmed that effect, it is likely that the depressant effects of the drug in men were serving to desensitize the nerve endings in the penis, thus permitting intercourse for longer periods without climaxing. Moreover, like alcohol, the drug was acting on the central cortex of the brain to slacken normal inhibitions. Also common was "luding out"—attaining an intoxicated state rapidly by mixing the drug with wine.

In early 1973, after reports of widespread abuse, acute reactions, and fatal overdoses, Birch Bayh convened more Senate hearings, the problems with methaqualone were fully aired, and rigid controls over the drug were put into force.[25] Shortly thereafter, the abuse of metha-qualone began to decline.[d] In the meantime the heroin problem persisted, and around 1970 cocaine base devotees on the West Coast began experimenting with a new variety of smokable cocaine "rock."

"EVERYBODY SMOKES DOPE"

While legislators, clinicians, and drug educators struggled with the methaqualone problem, marijuana use grew apace. From 1960 through the end of the decade, the number of Americans who used marijuana at least once increased from a few hundred thousand to an estimated 8 million. Given such widespread use, in 1969 the government launched an elaborate and determined effort to cut down the flow of marijuana into the United States. Known as "Operation Intercept" and based on the belief that Mexico was and would remain the primary source of marijuana for Americans, the effort was designed principally to tighten inspections of vehicles coming across the border from Mexico and to intercept smuggled drugs.[26]

Set for September 21, 1969, Operation Intercept was timed for the fall marijuana harvest. Along the 2,500-mile-long border, on land as well as in the sea and air, the surveillance network was intense, particularly so at the border crossings where vehicles and passengers could be individually searched. Within an hour after it all started, automobile traffic began to pile up as each vehicle waited to go through inspection. In no time, the backups were three miles long, and in some places they extended to six miles. Members of Congress and other officials immediately began to receive complaints—from Mexico because the effort was hurting tourism, from merchants on both sides of the border because it was affecting business, and from the American travelers who had spent many extra hours waiting to return home.

Twenty days later Operation Intercept was abandoned. Although the government deemed it a success, there had been no major seizures of marijuana. In fact, during the three weeks of the operation the actual seizures averaged 150 pounds per day, a rate no different from that

---

[d] For those who missed the first wave of methaqualone abuse, another began in 1978 and persisted into the early 1980s. In 1980 some 4 tons of the drug were produced legally in the United States, and it is estimated that another 100 million tons were smuggled in, principally from Colombia. In 1982 when tight restrictions were placed on the importation of methaqualone powder from West Germany to Colombia, trafficking in the drug declined substantially. In 1984 all legal manufacturing of methaqualone was halted in the United States, and since that time the abuse of the drug has been, at best, modest.

which had existed earlier in 1969. Operation Intercept did have other effects, however. The temporary shortage that it created pushed up the street price of the drug; it led to increased imports of a more potent marijuana from Vietnam; and it stimulated the cultivation of domestic marijuana.[e]

By the early 1970s marijuana use had increased geometrically throughout all strata of society. Expounding on this situation, a Miami attorney offered an interesting explanation of the prevalence of marijuana use in America:

> *Everybody smokes dope!*
> This profound statement should not be taken to mean that every person in the country smokes marijuana. It merely means: Policemen smoke dope. Probation officers smoke dope. Narcotic agents smoke dope (and sell it). Judges smoke dope. Prosecutors smoke dope. Plumbers, schoolteachers, principals, deans, carpenters, disabled war veterans, Republicans, doctors, perverts, and librarians smoke dope. Legislators smoke dope. Even writers of articles on drug abuse smoke dope. *Everybody smokes dope!*[27]

Given such pervasive use of marijuana and arrests that were affecting the careers and lives of so many otherwise law-abiding citizens, legislation was introduced that reduced the penalties for the simple possession of the drug—first at the federal level and later by the states. In Alabama, judges were no longer required to impose the mandatory minimum sentence of five years for the possession of even one marijuana cigarette; Missouri statutes no longer included life sentences for second possession offenses; and in Georgia, second sale offenses to minors were no longer punishable by death.

Then there was the issue of decriminalization—the removal of criminal penalties for the possession of small amounts of marijuana for personal use. The movement toward decriminalization began in 1973 with Oregon, followed by Colorado, Alaska, Ohio, and California in 1975; Mississippi, North Carolina, and New York in 1977; and Nebraska in 1978. Given that there were an estimated 50 million users of marijuana in the United States by the close of the 1970s, many hoped that decriminalization, and perhaps even the legalization of marijuana use, would become a national affair, but the movement suddenly

---

[e] A State Department official indicated to the author in 1971 that given the vast outflow of U.S. dollars into Mexico for wholesale purchases of marijuana, the real purpose of Operation Intercept was to stimulate the production of domestic marijuana and thus keep the American dollar on this side of the border. This reasoning, however, has never been confirmed.

stalled for a variety of reasons.[28] Principally, Congress failed to pass legislation that would have decriminalized marijuana under federal statutes. The issue had not been salient enough throughout the nation as a whole to result in concerted action in favor of decriminalization. The lobbying on behalf of marijuana law reform never demonstrated the power and influence necessary for repeal. Perhaps most important of all, marijuana had always been viewed as a drug favored by youth.[f]

By the close of the 1970s and the onset of the 1980s, evidence indicated that marijuana use in the United States had actually declined. In 1975 surveys showed that some 30 million people were users.[29] By the early 1980s this figure had dropped to 20 million, with the most significant declines among people ages 25 and under.[30] Perhaps the younger generation had begun to realize that although marijuana was not the "devil drug," "assassin of youth," or "weed of madness" that Harry Anslinger and his counterparts had maintained, it was not

---

[f] A rather curious but interesting indicator of the popularity of marijuana over the years is the number of different street terms that have been used to designate the substance. Over the last 100 years, no other drug has generated as many slang labels, including: A-bomb, Acapulco Gold, ace, African black, ashes, aunt mary, baby, bale, Bambalacha, bammy, banji, bats, bhang, birdwood, black gungeon, black gunion, black gunny, black meat, black mo, black moat, bo, Bob Marley, bo-bo, bo-bo bush, bomb, bomber, boo, brick, broccoli, bud, budda, bush, butter flower, buzz, C-weed, California red, Canadian black, carpet weed, charas, charge, cheddar, cheese, cheese stick, chiba, Chicago green, chocolate, churrus, coli, Colombian, Colombian gold, Colombian red, columbia red, creeper, dagga, daha, dew, dick, dick weed, ditch weed, dogie, donjem, doobie, dope, dry high, elbow, erb, faggot, fatty, fingers, flowers, foo, fu, funny stuff, fuck, fuckjoint, fuck-stuff, fuckweed, gage, Gainesville green, geek, greenie, ganga, gangster, ganja, gauge, gigglesmoke, giggleweed, gold, gold Colombian, golden leaf, gonga, goof, goof-ball, goofbutt, grass, grass weed, greafa, greapha, greefa, greefp, green, grefa, greta, grifa, grillo, grunt, gunny, gyve, hash, Hawaiian, hay, heathen, he-ho weed, hemp, herb, homegrown, hooch, hop, humble, humble weed, Illinois green, Indian hay, Indian hemp, J, jane, jay smoke, Jersey green, jimmy-john, jive, Johnson, Johnson grass, johnnie, joint, joystick, joyweed, juane, juanita, juiana weed, keef, kick, kick stick, kidstuff, kif, killer, killer weed, kilter, kind, kind bud, kona bud, lambsbreath, limbo, Lipton's, lobato weed, loco, loco weed, loveboat, loveweed, lumbo, M, mach, maggie, margie, mari, mariquita, maria juana, mariguano, mary, mary and johnnie, maryann, maryjane, mary-jane superweed, mary warner, mary weaver, Maui, Maui-wowie, megg, merry, messerole, Mexican brown, Mexican ditch weed, Mexican green, Mexican guano, Mexican locoweed, Mexican red, Mexican shit, mezz, M.J., mohasky, mooca, moocah, moota, mootah, mooters, mootie, moshky, mota, mother, mu, muggles, musta, muta, mutah, mutha, nickel, number, Panama gold, Panama red, panatella, pin, pitillo, pod, poke, pot, potiguava, punk, ragweed, rainy day woman, rama, reaper, red, red dirt, reefer, reefer weed, refrigerator weed, reggae, righteous bush, roach, roof weed, root, rope, rough stuff, rug, salt & pepper, sassafras, sativa, scissors, seaweed, sex weed, shishi, shit, shitweed, sinsemilla, skinny, skunk, skunk weed, smoke, snop, spinach, splay, spleef, spliff, splim, square grouper, stick, stinkweed, straw, stuff, stum, superpot, sweet lunch, sweet lucy, sweet lunch, sweet maryjane, T, Tai, Tai weed, tea, Texas tea, Thai sticks, thirteen, thumb, tin, tree, tripweed, turf, twigs, twist, Vermont green, viper's weed, vonce, wackytabbacky, wackyweed, weed, weed tea, wheat, yerba, yesca, and Zacatecas purple.

a totally innocuous substance either. Perhaps the change occurred because of the greater concern with health and physical fitness that became so much a part of American culture during the 1980s, or as an outgrowth of the antismoking messages that appeared daily in the media. Whatever the reason, it was clear that youthful attitudes had changed. Over the period from 1979 through the close of the 1980s, the proportion of seniors in American high schools who saw "great risk" in using marijuana even once or twice rose from 9.4% to 23.6%, while the proportion who had ever experimented with marijuana declined from 60.4% to 43.7%—representing a 15-year low.[31]

Despite the declining use (and interest) in marijuana within the youth culture, the drug remained in the news. A new organization calling itself The National Anti-Drug Coalition began a crusade against marijuana that was reminiscent of the reefer madness era of the 1930s.[32] "Prescription pot" became a reality in 1985 when the Food and Drug Administration gave approval to Unimed, Inc., a New Jersey research firm, to produce Marinol, a THC derivative effective for treating the nausea associated with cancer chemotherapy.[33] And finally, while arguments for the legalization of marijuana resurfaced,[g] the possession of small amounts of marijuana for personal use was recriminalized in Oregon through a statewide referendum in 1986, with a similar action occurring in Alaska in 1990.[34]

Meanwhile, the heroin problem endured, cocaine emerged as the new drug of choice, and Caribbean islanders emigrating to Miami and New York brought a variety of smokable cocaine with them—a drug that would become known worldwide as crack.

TIC, ROCKET FUEL, AND
THE SPECTER OF THE LIVING DEAD

The propaganda campaigns that have periodically emerged to target specific drugs as the root causes of outbreaks of violent crime were not restricted to the Anslinger era of "reefer madness." More recently, PCP emerged as the new "killer drug," which changes the user into a diabolical monster and a member of the "living dead."

PCP, or more formally phencyclidine, a central nervous system excitant agent having anesthetic, analgesic, and hallucinogenic properties, is not a particularly new drug. It was developed during the 1950s, and following studies on laboratory animals, it was recommended

---

[g] The debate over the legalization of marijuana and other drugs is examined at length in Chapter 8.

for clinical trials on humans in 1957.[35] Parke, Davis & Company marketed the drug under the trade name of Sernyl. Originally, phencyclidine was used as an anesthetic agent in surgical procedures. Although it was found to be generally effective, the drug often produced a number of unpleasant side effects—extreme excitement, visual disturbances, and delirium. As a result, in 1967 the use of phencyclidine was restricted to "veterinary use only." Under the trade name of Sernylan, it quickly became the most widely used animal tranquilizer.[h]

The initial street use of PCP (also known as rocket fuel, horse tranquilizer, animal trank, aurora borealis, DOA, elephant, elephant juice, dust, goon, green snow, mist, sheets, angel dust, fairy dust, dummy dust, monkey dust, devil's dust, devil stick, hog, THC, Tic, tic tac, supergrass, flakes, and buzz) appeared in the Haight-Ashbury underground community of San Francisco and other West Coast and East Coast cities during 1967. It was first marketed as the PeaCe Pill; hence, the name PCP quickly became popular.

Characteristic of the hallucinogenic drug marketplace has been the mislabeling and promotion of one substance as some other more desirable psychedelic, and for a time PCP occupied a conspicuous position in this behalf. Samples of mescaline (the hallucinogenic alkaloid found in the peyote cactus) sold in Milwaukee, for example, were invariably PCP.[36] During the late 1960s and early 1970s, tetrahydrocannabinol (THC), the active ingredient in marijuana, was frequently sought after in its pure form as a prestige "fad" drug. Yet THC has never been sold on the street, for in its isolated form it is so unstable a compound that it quickly loses its potency and effect. During 1970 analyses of "street drugs" from the greater Philadelphia area revealed that PCP was a common THC substitute.[37] In an experiment undertaken in 1971, samples of alleged LSD, THC, mescaline, and PCP were secured from street suppliers in New York City's Greenwich Village. Laboratory analyses identified the THC and mescaline samples to be PCP, and the PCP sample to be LSD, with only the LSD sample having accurate labeling. In a second experiment carried out during early 1972 in Miami's Coconut Grove area, 25 individual samples of alleged THC were purchased from an equal number of street drug dealers. Under laboratory analysis, 22 of the "THC" samples were found to be PCP. One was Darvon (a prescription painkiller), another was an oral contraceptive, and the last a chocolate-covered peanut.[38] It was quickly learned that these apparent deceptions had been aimed at "plastic," or weekend, hippies and "heads"—those children of two cultures whose social schizophrenia placed them partially in the straight world

---

[h] Dog and cat owners who request medication from a vet to sedate a pet during a plane or long automobile trip are generally given PCP.

and partially in the new underground, never fully being a part of either. In both the New York and Miami drug subcultures, however, and probably in most others, THC was simply accepted as another name for PCP, perhaps explaining why the latter drug was called "Tic" for more than a decade in many cities.

The stories describing PCP as a "killer drug" date to its first introduction to the street community. In 1969, for example, a New York City chief of detectives commented:

> Let me tell you, this stuff is bad, real bad. One dose of it and we're talking about some serious instant addiction. I keep telling these kids that if they keep playing around with that shit they are going to blow their fucking minds.[i]

Similarly, a number of news stories at approximately the same time described PCP as a synthetic drug so powerful that a person could become high simply by touching it—instantly absorbing it through the pores.[39] These early reports ran counter to both medical and street experiences,[40] and the drug quickly became relegated to the lengthening catalog of street substances that after their initial appearance received little public attention. Most of those using PCP during those early years were not found among the populations addicted to narcotic drugs. Rather, they were multiple-drug users manifesting patterns of long-term involvement with marijuana and/or hashish, combined with the experimental, social-recreational, or spree use of hallucinogens, sedatives, tranquilizers, and stimulants.

During 1978 the hysteria over PCP emerged once again, but this time in earnest. In one episode of the popular "60 Minutes" television program, CBS News commentator Mike Wallace described PCP as the nation's "number one" drug problem, reporting on bizarre incidents of brutal violence—reminiscent of Harry J. Anslinger's "gore file"—allegedly caused by the new killer drug. Shortly thereafter, a *People* magazine article touted PCP as America's most dangerous new drug—the "devil's dust."[41] In these and other reports, violence was always associated with PCP use, as well as its propensity to destroy the user's mind and hence to create new recruits to the growing army of the living dead. During special hearings on August 8, 1978, a senator described PCP as "one of the most insidious drugs known to mankind," and a congressman declared that the drug was "a threat to the national security and that children were playing with death on the installment plan."[42] Then the syndicated columnist Ann

---

[i] All undocumented quotations in this and subsequent chapters are comments made directly to the author during the course of fieldwork.

Landers—the seemingly self-proclaimed expert on almost everything
from aardvark to zymotechnics—offered the following comment
about "angel dust" (PCP) as part of her 10-year campaign against
marijuana use:

> Unless a teenager is a chemist, there is no way he can be sure
> of what he is ingesting. The possibility of getting angel dust
> sprinkled in with pot should be enough to scare even the
> dumbest cluck off the stuff for life. Angel dust can blow your
> mind to smitherines.[43]

Research during 1978 and 1979 quickly demonstrated that comments such as these may have been overstated. In 1978 when PCP was
labeled by "60 Minutes" as the number-one drug problem and responsible for more emergency room admissions than any other drug,
estimates from the Drug Abuse Warning Network found PCP to
account for only 3% of all reported drug emergencies.[j] Furthermore,
ethnographic studies of PCP users in Seattle, Miami, Philadelphia,
and Chicago demonstrated that the characterizations of users' experiences were slanted and misleading.[44] The studies found something
quite different from the monster drug that the media presented as some
live enemy making users lose complete control of rationality and being
so overpowered by PCP that they helplessly and inescapably moved
directly to either a psychotic episode, suicide, homicide, or a state of
suspended confusion, which only an indefinite confinement in a mental
hospital would hopefully reverse. Users were typically aware that PCP
was a potent drug, and except for the few who sought a heavily
anesthetized state, most used it cautiously. They aimed to control its
effects. Although some had adverse reactions to the drug, violence was
rarely a factor. In fact, among the more than 300 PCP users contacted
during the studies, almost all were baffled by the connection of the
drug with violent behavior. The only known episodes of violence
occurred during "bad trips" when someone tried to restrain a user,
and these were extremely unusual. Furthermore, the few who exhibited
aggressive behavior typically had already developed a reputation for
violence that was independent of PCP use.

None of this should suggest, however, that PCP is a harmless
drug. On the contrary, hallucinations, altered mood states, feelings

---

[j] The Drug Abuse Warning Network, more commonly known as DAWN, is a large-
scale, data-collection effort designed to monitor changing patterns of drug abuse in the
United States. Hundreds of hospital emergency rooms and county medical examiners
in 26 metropolitan areas report regularly to the DAWN system. However, since a number
of limitations are built into the DAWN data, they are far from representative of the
actual character of drug abuse in the United States as a whole.

of depersonalization, paranoia, suicidal impulses, and aggressive behavior have been reported, only not to the extent that some commentators have suggested. In terms of acute drug reactions reported to the DAWN system involving PCP that resulted in a visit to a hospital emergency room, the numbers were significant during the 1980s, peaking in 1987 with almost 8,000 incidents and dropping to under 5,000 by the close of the decade.[45] However, many of these involved PCP in combination with some other drug, and curiously, the data reflected a striking regional variation. Of the cases nationwide, half were typically from Washington, D.C.,[k] and one out of every six was reported from the city of Los Angeles—a phenomenon that has been characteristic of PCP use almost every year since the mid-1970s.

In the 1980s it appeared that PCP use in the general population was relatively low. Among national samples of high school seniors surveyed annually, the proportions having used PCP at least once dropped from 13% in 1979 to less than 3% by 1990.[46] Moreover, the proportions who had used PCP during the 30-day period prior to the survey contact had declined from 2.4% to only 1% over the same 10-year period.[47] Nevertheless, press reports continued to describe the bizarre behavior that PCP users were exhibiting. Yet despite the media attention, all systematic attempts to study the alleged relationship between PCP use and violent behavior continued to conclude that only a very small minority of users committed bizarre acts while in a PCP-induced state.[48]

POSTSCRIPT

As America moved through the 1980s and into the 1990s, both heroin and cocaine use persisted,[l] and crack-cocaine smoking reached epidemic proportions in many inner city neighborhoods.[m] At the same time, a curious variety of fad drugs came to pass—some new, and others quite old.

"Ecstasy" (MDMA)

Perhaps first of the fresh arrivals to the American drug scene of the 1980s was MDMA (3, *4-methylenedioxymethamphetamine*). Better known

---

[k] During much of the 1980s, PCP put so many of its users into Washington's St. Elizabeth's Hospital that with a grim irony the drug became known in the nation's capital as the "key to Saint E's."

[l] Heroin and cocain are addressed at length in Chapter 3.

[m] The crack epidemic is examined in Chapter 4.

as "Ecstasy" and sometimes referred to as "XTC" and "Adam," it is a synthetic compound related to both mescaline and the amphetamines, commonly labeled as a hallucinogen.[n]

Interestingly, Ecstasy was not an altogether new drug when it first received widespread notice. Having been developed by Merck & Co. as an appetite suppressant during the early years of the century (but never marketed), it made its initial appearance on the street in the early 1970s and became the successor to MDA—the "love drug" of the late 1960s hippie counterculture.[49] Information about Ecstasy was first disseminated largely by word of mouth and in anonymously written "flight guides" which provided instructions on its proper use. For a time it was used by psychiatrists and other therapists for facilitating client communication, acceptance, and fear reduction.[50] It was argued by a number of therapists, for example, that patients "opened up" while under the influence of the drug, becoming less defensive and less fearful and recalling events of the past they had been repressing for years.[51]

As the therapeutic and recreational use of the drug became more widespread during the early 1980s, it drew the attention of both the media and the Drug Enforcement Administration (DEA).[52] In spite of the arguments of several psychiatrists and researchers who strongly believed in Ecstasy's therapeutic potential, a DEA chemist concluded that the drug had a high potential for abuse and should be strictly controlled. By the close of 1986 Ecstasy had become a Schedule I drug, which meant that its manufacture, distribution, and sale was a violation of federal law.[53]

In the aftermath of federal control, the mild euphoric effects of Ecstasy were sought by small segments of undergraduate student populations;[54] "Ecstasy parties" became popular in a few New York nightclubs;[55] the drug became a focus of attention in Europe because of its widespread use at disco "acid house parties";[56] deaths related to the use of MDMA (and its analog MDEA, also referred to as MDE and known on the street as "Eve") were reportedly few in number, but nevertheless apparent, particularly in individuals with cardiac disorders;[57] reports of serious and prolonged psychotic reactions to MDMA began to accumulate;[58] and preliminary studies at the Addiction Research Center in Baltimore suggested that Ecstasy destroyed nerve cells in the brain that produced the neurotransmitter serotonin—the chemical messenger that modulates feeling, sexual behavior, and responses to pain and stress.[59]

---

[n] Technically, MDMA is one of a group of drugs designated as methylated amphetamines.

"Crank" (Methamphetamine)

As Ecstasy disappeared from the headlines, it was replaced in 1988 and 1989 by crank, better known as methamphetamine.° A central nervous system stimulant chemically related to the amphetamines, methamphetamine was developed in Japan in 1919 and first used widely during World War II by German soldiers to counter the fatigue of prolonged troop movements. Like the amphetamines, methamphetamine is a potent stimulant with an action on the body similar to the effects of adrenalin. It has been used in the clinical management of psychiatric depression, obesity and weight control, chronic fatigue and narcolepsy, hyperkinetic activity disorders in children, as an analeptic in sedative overdose, and as a vasoconstrictor for inflamed mucosal membranes.[60]

Since the early 1970s the therapeutic applications of methamphetamine have been notably curtailed. Its use in weight control is highly problematic since its appetite-suppressing effects endure for only a short time and its potential for psychic dependence is considerable. Moreover, other drugs have been found to be more effective in the management of psychiatric depression, and for fatigue it is prescribed only in extraordinary circumstances. Significant, as well, in the restricted clinical use of methamphetamine has been its notable abuse potential. It is typically abused for its energizing and euphoric properties. Although it can be taken orally for such purposes, the effects tend to be far more profound when taken intravenously. Chronic intravenous use typically leads to psychotic reactions and paranoid delusions.[P]

Although methamphetamine abuse had been a noticable part of the American drug scene since the 1960s, it seemed to become more prominent during the latter part of the 1980s, particularly in large urban areas west of the Mississippi. Referred to in the media as "white man's crack" and the "national drug crisis for the 1990s," crank was being produced in illegal laboratories in California, trafficked by Hell's Angels and other biker gangs, and sold primarily to members of the white working class.[61] Although slated to be the drug of the '90s, its popularity remained generally low.

° Although methamphetamine is most commonly referred to as "crank," it's other street names include crystal, meth, speed, go-fast, go, crystal meth, eight ball, glass, zip, zoom, chris, and christy.

P Two curiosities associated with these effects are meth monsters (grotesque, monstrous apparitions) and meth midgets (extremely small human shapes), which are commonly hallucinated by chronic methamphetamine users.

"ICE" (Methamphetamine)

If crank was to be the drug of the 1990s, ice was the expected "menace," "craze," and "epidemic" of the new decade.[62] Although crank was a relatively familiar drug, ice was something new. Both drugs are chemically the same in that they are methamphetamine. However, they are structurally quite different. Crank is usually obtained in powder form and in varying levels of purity; it can be ingested orally, smoked, snorted, and injected; and the effects last 2 to 4 hours. By contrast, ice is a crystalline form of methamphetamine having the appearance of rock salt. Its purity ranges from 90 to 100%; it is typically smoked; and its effects last 7 to 24 hours. The drug is produced in Hong Kong, Korea, Thailand, and the Phillipines, and reports indicated that its rapid onset caused intensive euphoria and often psychoses and violent behavior.[63]

Despite the media hype, however, by the beginning of the 1990s the anticipated ice epidemic turned out to be a plague that never was. Although ice appeared to be a problem in Hawaii, its use elsewhere appeared to be generally unknown.[64]

Finally, although the beginning of the last decade of the twentieth century experienced no significant new drugs of abuse, a war on drugs had been declared, the legalization of drugs was debated, the use of heroin and cocaine persisted, and the crack epidemic continued in the inner city. Moreover, dealing with problems of drugs became further complicated by the spread of AIDS within populations of drug users and their sex partners.

Notes

1. Max Lerner, *America as a Civilization: Life and Thought in the United States Today* (New York: Simon & Schuster, 1957), p. 666.
2. See *Newsweek*, 20 Nov. 1950, pp. 57–58; 29 Jan. 1951, pp. 23–24; 11 June 1951, pp. 26–27; 25 June 1951, pp. 19–29; 13 Aug. 1951, p. 50; 17 Sept. 1951, p. 60; *Life*, 11 June 1951, pp. 116, 119–122; *The Survey*, July 1951, pp. 328–329; *Time*, 26 Feb. 1951, p. 24; 7 May 1951, pp. 82, 85; *Reader's Digest*, Oct. 1951, pp. 137–140.
3. Isidor Chein, Donald L. Gerard, Robert S. Lee, and Eva Rosenfeld, *The Road to H: Narcotics, Juvenile Delinquency, and Social Policy* (New York: Basic Books, 1964), p. 14.
4. Richard A. Cloward and Lloyd E. Ohlin, *Delinquency and Opportunity* (New York: Free Press, 1960), pp. 178–186.
5. Edward Preble and John J. Casey, "Taking Care of Business: The Heroin User's Life on the Street," *International Journal of the Addictions*, 4 (1969), p. 2.
6. Kenneth Rexroth, "San Francisco Letter," *Evergreen Review*, Spring 1957, p. 11.

7. See Richard H. Blum and Associates, *Students and Drugs* (San Francisco: Jossey-Bass, 1970); Leslie Farber, "Ours Is the Addicted Society," *New York Times Magazine*, 11 Dec. 1966, p. 43; Joel Fort, *The Pleasure Seekers: The Drug Crisis, Youth, and Society* (New York: Grove Press, 1969); A. Geller and M. Boas, *The Drug Beat* (New York: McGraw-Hill, 1969); Helen H. Nowlis, *Drugs on the College Campus* (New York; Doubleday-Anchor, 1969); J. L. Simmons and B. Winograd, *It's Happening: A Portrait of the Youth Scene Today* (Santa Barbara, CA: Marc-Laired, 1966).

8. James A. Inciardi, "Drugs, Drug-Taking and Drug-Seeking: Notations on the Dynamics of Myth, Change, and Reality," in *Drugs and the Criminal Justice System*, James A. Inciardi and Carl D. Chambers, eds., (Beverly Hills: Sage, 1974), pp. 203–222; George Johnson, *The Pill Conspiracy* (Los Angeles: Sherbourne, 1967).

9. Harry J. Anslinger and William F. Tompkins, *The Traffic in Narcotics* (New York: Funk & Wagnalls, 1953), pp. 37–38.

10. Cited in William Manchester, *The Glory and the Dream: A Narrative History of America, 1932–1972* (Boston: Little, Brown, 1974), p. 1362.

11. *The Realist*, Sept. 1966.

12. Timothy Leary, "Introduction," in *LSD: The Consciousness-Expanding Drug*, ed. David Solomon (New York: G. P. Putnam's, 1964), p. 17.

13. Cited in *Manchester*, p. 1366.

14. *Newsweek*, 22 Dec. 1986, p. 48; Steve Ditles, "Artificial Intelligence," *Omni*, 9 (April 1987), p. 23; "Timothy Leary," Interview by David Sheff in *Rolling Stone*, 10 Dec. 1987, pp. 226–228.

15. *Newsweek*, 13 Feb. 1989, p. 13.

16. Timothy Leary,"On the Drug War," *New Perspectives Quarterly*, 6 (Fall 1989), p. 62.

17. National Commission on Marihuana and Drug Abuse, *Drug Abuse in America: Problem in Perspective* (Washington, DC: United States Government Printing Office, 1973), p. 81.

18. Carl D. Chambers, Leon Brill, and James A. Inciardi, "Toward Understanding and Managing Nonnarcotic Drug Abusers," *Federal Probation*, Mar. 1972, pp. 50–55.

19. John C. Pollard, "Some Comments on Nonnarcotic Drug Abuse," paper presented at the Nonnarcotic Drug Institute, Southern Illinois University, Edwardsville, June 1967; John Griffith, "A Study of Illicit Amphetamine Drug Traffic in Oklahoma City," *American Journal of Psychiatry*, 123 (1966), pp. 560–569.

20. U.S. Cong., Senate, Subcommittee to Investigate Juvenile Delinquency of the Committee on the Judiciary, *Legislative Hearings on S. 674, "To Amend the Controlled Substances Act to Move Amphetamines and Certain Other Stimulant Substances from Schedule III of Such Act to Schedule II, and for Other Purposes," July 15 and 16, 1971* (Washington, DC: United States Government Printing Office, 1972).

21. Carl D. Chambers, *An Assessment of Drug Use in the General Population* (Albany: New York State Narcotic Addiction Control Commission, 1970); James A. Inciardi and Carl D. Chambers, "The Epidemiology of Amphetamine Use in the General Population," *Canadian Journal of Criminology and Corrections*, Apr. 1972, pp. 166–172.

22. *Washington Post,* 12 Nov. 1972, p. B3.
23. For an overview of the history and clinical experiences related to metha-qualone, see James A. Inciardi, David M. Petersen, and Carl D. Chambers, "Methaqualone Abuse Patterns, Diversion Paths, and Adverse Reactions," *Journal of the Florida Medical Association,* Apr. 1974.
24. AMA Department of Drugs, *AMA Drug Evaluations* (Acton, MA: Publishing Sciences Group, 1973), p. 313.
25. U.S. Cong., Senate, Subcommittee to Investigate Juvenile Delinquency of the Committee on the Judiciary, *Legislative Hearings on the Methaqualone Control Act of 1973, S. 1252* (Washington, DC: United States Government Printing Office, 1973).
26. For a thorough analysis of Operation Intercept, see Lawrence A. Gooberman, *Operation Intercept: The Multiple Consequences of Public Policy* (New York: Pergamon Press, 1974).
27. Steven M. Greenberg, "Compounding a Felony: Drug Abuse and the American Legal System," in Inciardi and Chambers, *Drugs and the Criminal Justice System,* p. 186.
28. See Eric Josephson, "Marijuana Decriminalization: Assessment of Current Legislative Status," paper presented at the Technical Review on Methodology in Drug Policy Research, Decriminalization of Marijuana, National Institute on Drug Abuse, Rockville, MD, 20–21 Mar. 1980; James A. Inciardi, "Marijuana Decriminalization Research: A Perspective and Commentary," *Criminology,* May 1981, pp. 145–159.
29. The Domestic Council Drug Abuse Task Force, *White Paper on Drug Abuse* (Washington, DC: U.S. Government Printing Office, 1975), p. 25.
30. The White House, Drug Abuse Policy Office, Office of Policy Development, *National Strategy for Prevention of Drug Abuse and Drug Trafficking* (Washington, DC: United States Government Printing Office, 1984), p. 19.
31. *NIDA Notes,* Spring 1990, pp. 11, 20, 27; Office of National Drug Control Policy, *Leading Drug Indicators* (Washington, DC: The White House, 1990); National Institute on Drug Abuse, *National Household Survey on Drug Abuse: Population Estimates 1990* (Rockville, MD: NIDA, 1990).
32. See *War on Drugs,* June 1980. (*War on Drugs* is a publication of the National Anti-Drug Coalition and should not be confused with any book with the same title.) It should be added here that Harry J. Anslinger and the National Anti-Drug Coalition were not the only ones to overstate the problems with marijuana. Consistently conspicuous in this behalf has been Dr. Gabriel G. Nahas, a professor of anesthesiology at Columbia University's College of Physicians and Surgeons. In his *Keep Off the Grass: A Documented Report on the Hazards of Marijuana* (Middlebury, VT: Paul S. Eriksson, 1985), Nahas argues that marijuana is a highly addictive drug and that its use actually eroded a number of ancient civilizations.
33. *Business Week,* 24 June 1985, p. 104. See, also, Roger A. Roffman, *Marijuana as Medicine* (Seattle: Madrona Publishers, 1982).
34. *Time,* 19 Nov. 1990, p. 47; *Drug Enforcement Report,* 23 Nov. 1990, p. 8.
35. Phencyclidine (PCP), *NCDAI Publication 18* (Rockville, MD: National Clearinghouse for Drug Abuse Information, 1973).
36. A. Reed and A. W. Kane, "Phencyclidine (PCP)," *STASH Capsules,* Dec. 1970, pp. 1–2.

37. Sidney H. Schnoll and W. H. Vogel, "Analysis of 'Street Drugs,' " *New England Journal of Medicine*, 8 Apr. 1971, p. 791.
38. Both of these experiments were conducted by the author.
39. *Long Island Press*, 28 Nov. 1970.
40. E. F. Domino, "Neurobiology of Phencyclidine (Sernyl), A Drug with an Unusual Spectrum of Pharmacological Activity." *Internal Review of Neurobiology*, 6 (1964), pp. 303–347.
41. *People*, 4 Sept. 1978, pp. 46–48; See also Ronald L. Linder, *PCP: The Devil's Dust* (Belmont, CA: Wadsworth, 1981).
42. Select Committee on Narcotics Abuse Control, Executive Summary, *Hearings on Phencyclidine*, August 8 (Washington, DC: United States Government Printing Office, 1978).
43. *Cincinnati Post*, 2 June 1979, p. 23.
44. Harvey W. Feldman, "PCP Use in Four Cities: An Overview," in *Angel Dust*, ed. Harvey W. Feldman, Michael H. Agar, and George M. Beschner (Lexington, MA: Lexington Books, 1979), pp. 29–51.
45. National Institute on Drug Abuse, Division of Epidemiology and Statistical Analysis, *Annual Data, 1983, Data from the Drug Abuse Warning Network* (Rockville, MD: National Institute on Drug Abuse, 1984), pp. 200–201; National Institute on Drug Abuse, *Semiannual Report, Trend Data Through June 1988, Data from the Drug Abuse Warning Network* (Rockville, MD: National Institute on Drug Abuse, 1989); National Institute on Drug Abuse, *Annual Report, Data from the Drug Abuse Warning Network* (Rockville, MD: National Institute on Drug Abuse, 1990).
46. University of Michigan News and Information Services, 24 Jan. 1991.
47. *NIDA Notes*, Spring 1990, p. 27.
48. R. K. Siegel, "PCP and Violent Crime: The People vs. Peace," *Journal of Psychedelic Drugs*, 12 (1980), pp. 317–330; Eric D. Wish, "PCP and Crime: Just Another Illicit Drug?" *Phencyclidine: An Update*, ed. Doris H. Clouet (Rockville, MD: National Institute on Drug Abuse, 1986), pp. 174–189.
49. See Marsha Rosenbaum, "Why MDMA Should Not Have Been Made Illegal," *The Drug Legalization Debate*, ed. James A. Inciardi (Newbury Park, CA: Sage, 1991), pp. 135–146.
50. Jerome Beck, "The Popularization and Resultant Implications of a Recently Controlled Psychoactive Substance," *Contemporary Drug Problems*, 13 (1986), pp. 23–63.
51. Joe Klein, "The New Drug They Call 'Ecstasy,' " *New York*, 20 May 1985, pp. 38–43.
52. *Time*, 10 June 1985, p. 64; *New York Times*, 1 June 1985, p. 6; *USA Today*, 30 May 1985, p. D1; C. Dye, "XTC: The Chemical Pursuit of Pleasure," *Drug Journal News*, 10 (1982), pp. 8–9; *Newsweek*, 15 Apr. 1985, p. 96; *Discover*, Aug. 1986, p. 34.
53. For a thorough history and analysis of the MDMA controversy, see Jerome Beck and Marsha Rosembaum, "The Scheduling of MDMA ('Ecstasy'), in *Handbook of Drug Control in the United States*, ed. James A. Inciardi (Westport, CT: Greenwood Press, 1990), pp. 303–316.
54. S. J. Peroutka, "Incidence of Recreational Use of 3, 4-methylenedioxy-methamphetamine (MDMA, Ecstasy) on an Undergraduate Campus,"

New England Journal of Medicine, 317 (1987), p. 1542; D. M. Barnes, "New Data Intensify the Agony Over Ecstasy," *Science,* 239 (1988), pp. 864–866.
55. *New York Times,* 11 Dec. 1988, p. 58.
56. Charles Kaplan, "Ecstasy in Europe: Acid House Parties," *Street Pharmacologist,* Spring 1989, pp. 6–7; Bonn *Die Welt,* 5 Feb. 1990, p. 3.
57. *Street Pharmacologist,* Apr. 1987, p. 4.
58. Marjory Roberts, "MDMA: 'Madness, not Ecstasy,'" *Psychology Today,* June 1986, pp. 14–15.
59. G. Ricaurte, G. Bryan, L. Strauss, L. Seiden, and C. Schuster, "Hallucinogenic Amphetamine Selectively Destroys Brain Serotonin Nerve Terminals," *Science,* 229 (1985), pp. 986–988; C. J. Schmidt, "Neurotoxicity of the Psychedelic Amphetamine, Methylenedioxymethamphetamine," *Journal of Pharmacology and Experimental Therapeutics,* 240 (1987), pp. 1–7; Errol B. De Souza and George Battaglia, "Effects of MDMA and MDA on Brain Serotonin Neurons: Evidence from Neurochemical and Autoradiographic Studies;" Khursheed Asghar and Errol De Souza (eds.), *Pharmacology and Toxicology of Amphetamine and Related Designer Drugs* (Rockville, MD: National Institute on Drug Abuse, 1989), pp. 196–222; *NIDA Notes,* Fall 1987, p. 7.
60. See Oriana Josseau Kalant, *The Amphetamines: Toxicity and Addiction* (Toronto: University of Toronto Press, 1966); Erminio Costa and Silvio Garattini (eds.), *International Symposium on Amphetamines and Related Compounds* (New York: Raven Press, 1970).
61. *Street Pharmacologist,* Summer 1988, pp. 1–7; *Substance Abuse Report,* 1 Oct. 1988, pp. 1–3; *NIDA Notes,* Winter 1988/1989, p. 15; *Newsweek,* 3 Apr. 1989, pp. 20–21; Sacramento *News & Review,* 31 Aug. 1989, pp. 15–18.
62. *Drug Enforcement Report,* 24 Oct. 1989, p. 8; Time, 18 Sept. 1989, p. 28; *Alcoholism and Drug Abuse Week,* 25 Oct. 1989, pp. 7–8; *Substance Abuse Report,* 15 Nov. 1989, pp. 3–4; *Newsweek,* 27 Nov. 1989, pp. 37–40; *Miami Herald,* 25 Oct. 1989, pp. 1A, 11A.
63. *Street Pharmacologist,* 13 (1989), pp. 3, 10.
64. *Drug Enforcement Report,* 3 Jan. 1990, p. 7; *Substance Abuse Report,* 15 July 1990, pp. 1–2; *Drug Enforcement Report,* 8 Jan. 1991, p. 5.

CHAPTER THREE

SHIT, SMACK, AND SUPERFLY
Considerations on the Nature and Use of Heroin and Cocaine

English language usage is replete with any number of rather curious oddities. One of these is the euphemism, a delightfully ridiculous and roundabout word or phrase used to replace some other term or expression considered to be coarse, offensive, or otherwise painful. Among the most famous of these linguistic fig leaves are *affair* to communicate the idea of marital infidelity; *gay* for homosexual; *irregularity,* first posed by a 1930s adman as a genial substitute for that abnormal condition of the bowels known as constipation; and *making love* and *sleeping with* to cover all manner of copulation and fornication. More recent examples, also products of the advertising industry, include *pre-owned vehicle* for used car, *periodic pain* for menstrual cramps, *feminine hygiene* for the vaginal douche and sanitary napkin, and from the Red Lobster chain of seafood restaurants there is *call-ahead seating* to replace making a reservation. From the political-military complex there is *neutralization* or executive action (the murdering of some enemy agent), death by *friendly fire* or *misadventure* (the accidental killing of American service personnel by their own comrades), and *delivering ordnance* (dropping bombs).[a] Not to be forgotten as well are the sweeping changes that have occurred in jailhouse nomenclature, where prisons and penitentiaries have become *correctional facilities,* wardens have become *superintendents,* guards have become *correction officers,* and prisoners and convicts have become *inmates.*[b]

---

[a] In proper military terminology there are also hard and soft targets. Hard targets are those made of brick, concrete, and steel, whereas soft targets are flesh and bone. And especially suitable for attacking soft targets is selective ordnance (napalm).

[b] No doubt one of these days someone will invent a substitute term for hemorrhoid, a truly ugly word well in need of a euphemism. It would not be surprising if the new expression came from Parke-Davis, the makers of a hemorrhoid relief preparation that they have cleverly named *Anusol,* and which they even more cleverly pronounce *An-u-sol.*

A second peculiarity of language is the redefinition of words, either through simple ignorance or deliberate intent. This variety of linguistic manipulation has been a particular problem in the drug field for quite some time. Few words in the English language, for example, have been as misdefined, misused, and misunderstood as *narcotic* and *addiction.* The consequences of these linguistic abuses have become apparent in the areas of drug-abuse legislation, prevention, education, and treatment.

The wide and inconsistent usage of the word narcotic appears not only in the popular media but in legal and scientific circles as well. Sometimes narcotic is used to characterize any drug-induced stupor, insensibility, or sleep, thus embracing a breadth of substances ranging from alcohol to heroin. It is used to classify compounds that are addiction producing, a situation that creates even further confusion since addiction is defined so haphazardly. In legal matters, narcotic often designates any drug that is allegedly "dangerous," is widely abused, or has a high potential for abuse. As a result, such substances as marijuana, cocaine, PCP, and amphetamines have been considered along with heroin and morphine in narcotics regulations, despite having little in common with true narcotics. Cocaine, for example, has effects that are almost totally opposite those of heroin. In medicine, a field in which greater specificity would be expected, the terms *narcotics, opiates, dependence-producing drugs,* and *morphine-like drugs* are used interchangeably. Elsewhere, narcotics are simply "habit-forming" drugs.

In pharmacology, a science that focuses on the chemical nature, structure, and action of drugs, the designation of narcotic is quite specific.[1] It includes the natural derivatives of *Papaver somniferum L.*— the opium poppy—having both analgesic and sedative properties and any synthetic derivatives of similar pharmacological structure and action. Thus the range of substances that can be properly called narcotics is quite limited and encompasses four specific groups:

Natural narcotics
- opium, derived directly from *Papaver somniferum L.*
- morphine and codeine,[c] derived from opium

Semisynthetic narcotics
- heroin

---

[c] Like morphine, codeine is a narcotic analgesic and is present in both the opium poppy and opium. Most codeine is processed from morphine and is available as a white crystalline powder, in elixirs, and in pill and injectable forms. The drug's analgesic effects are similar to those of morphine, but its potency is considerably less. As a result, abuse and addiction are relatively uncommon since large quantities must be taken to produce such effects.

- hydromorphone (Dilaudid)[d]
- oxycodone (Percodan)[e]
- etorphine
- "designer drugs"

Synthetic narcotics with high potency

- methadone (Dolophine)[f]
- meperidine (Demerol)[g]

Synthetic narcotics with low potency

- propoxyphene (Darvon)[h]
- pentazocine (Talwin)[i]

---

[d] Hydromorphone, better known under the name of Dilaudid, is a semi-synthetic narcotic analgesic marketed in both tablet and injectable form. Although shorter acting than morphine, its potency is from two to eight times greater, and hence, a highly abusable drug. In some communities, Dilaudid is the substitute drug of choice among narcotics addicts when heroin supplies are low.

[e] Oxycodone (Percodan) is similar to codeine but more potent and with a higher addiction liability. It is effective orally and is marketed in combination with other drugs for pain relief. Abusers take Percodan orally or dissolve the tablets in water, filter out the insoluble material, and inject the active drug.

[f] Methadone was synthesized during World War II by German chemists when supply lines for morphine were interrupted. Although chemically unlike morphine or heroin, it produces many of the same effects. Methadone was introduced in the United States in 1947 and quickly become the drug of choice in the detoxification of heroin addicts.

Since the 1960s methadone has been in common use for the treatment of heroin addiction. Known as methadone maintenance, the program takes advantage of methadone's unique properties as a narcotic. Like all narcotics, methadone is cross-dependent with heroin. As such, it is a substitute narcotic that prevents withdrawal. More importantly, however, methadone is orally effective, making intravenous use unnecessary. In addition, it is a longer acting drug than heroin, with one oral dose lasting up to 24 hours. These properties have made methadone useful in the management of chronic narcotic addiction. Yet on the other hand, methadone is also a primary drug of abuse among some narcotic addicts, resulting in a small street market for the drug. Most illegal methadone is diverted from legitimate maintenance programs by methadone patients. Hence illegal supplies of the drug are typically available only where such programs exist.

[g] Meperidine (Demerol) is chemically dissimilar to morphine but resembles it in its analgesic potency. It is among the most widely used drugs for the treatment of moderate to severe pain, and is administered both orally and by injection. Meperidine is uncommon as a primary drug of addiction. More commonly it is used recreationally by members of the health professions and others who have ready access to it.

[h] Propoxyphine, sold under the trade names of Darvon and Dolene, was first marketed in 1957 for the treatment of mild to moderate pain. Less dependence producing than other narcotics, it is also less effective as an analgesic. Once the most widely prescribed analgesic drug in the United States, propoxyphine's limited effectiveness and significant abuse potential led to its placement into Schedule IV of the Controlled Substances Act in 1977.

[i] Pentazocine, sold under the trade name of Talwin, is a potent analgesic that is equivalent in effect to codeine. A recurrent problem with pentazocine has been the periodic appearance of T's and Blues. T's and Blues involve a combination of pentazocine

Many other drugs are in the latter three categories, but the examples indicated are the best known and most widely abused.[j]

A characteristic effect of narcotic drugs is addiction, a phenomenon that has had many meanings over the years. The addiction label has been used interchangeably with "dependence producing," "habit forming," and "habituation." There are also the metaphors of "physical dependence" and "psychological dependence." If addiction truly meant all these things, almost anything could be addicting— from Coca-Cola to sex, watching MTV and listening to rock music, even eating, sleeping, playing chess, and breathing. Marijuana, PCP, Ecstasy, and numerous other drugs have been called addicting, which they are not.

Addiction is a physiological phenomenon with a very specific meaning. Addiction is a craving for a particular drug, accompanied by physical dependence, which motivates continuing usage, resulting in tolerance to the drug's effects and a complex of identifiable symptoms appearing when it is suddenly withdrawn. Heroin is an addicting drug. Morphine is an addicting drug. The barbiturates are addicting drugs.[k]

Thus, although drugs and their actions should be designated in terms of their chemical structure and their effects on cellular biochemistry or physiological systems, there has been the tendency to classify most drugs according to the prevailing attitudes of the dominant cultural group and its most vocal representatives. Yet to be precise in the definitions of narcotic and addiction is not an attempt to engage in any semantic game (as has been the case with recent attempts to differentiate between illicit drug use, misuse, and abuse).[2] Narcotics and addiction are based on objective pharmacological criteria as opposed to the nominalist view that a narcotic is anything that someone may wish to call a narcotic. In the final analysis, however, with so

---

(Talwin/T's) and the antihistamine tripelennamine (Blues). Typically, two pentazocine tablets and one tripelennamine are crushed, dissolved in water, and injected intravenously. The IV use of this mixture reportedly produces a rush roughly equivalent in intensity to that of heroin, but lasting only 5 to 10 minutes. If several successive injections are made, the euphoric effects are reported to last 1 to 2 hours. In several parts of the United States T's and Blues are the drug of choice among narcotics addicts when heroin supplies are limited or of poor quality.

[j] It should be noted here that most drugs have a variety of different names, such as chemical, proprietary, and generic names. For an explanation of these alternative designations, see Appendix I: General Concepts. Additional topics covered in Appendix I are basic drug groups, dependency terms, drug reactions, routes of administration, and relevant pharmaceutical terms.

[k] It has been argued that in addition to the narcotics and barbiturates, cocaine and related coca products (such as crack) are also addicting drugs. This point is addressed later in this chapter.

many different applications and usages of addiction and narcotics, the terms have become relatively useless concepts. And in fact many researchers in the drug field have abandoned them for this very reason, preferring such designations as heroin users, cocaine users, and drug dependence.

HEROIN: "THE MOST DANGEROUS SUBSTANCE ON EARTH"

Known to its users as shit, smack, horse, harry, henry, H, jones, boy, brown, black tar, or simply dope or junk, by many in the law enforcement community and the general public, heroin has been called "the most dangerous substance on earth."[3] Indeed, heroin is a powerful narcotic. Several times more potent than morphine, it suppresses both respiratory and cardiovascular activity, has strong analgesic effects and a high addiction potential. At overdose levels heroin can produce coma, shock, and ultimately respiratory arrest and death. For the better part of the twentieth century, heroin has been the most widely discussed drug of abuse and the most feared. Yet for those involved in the production, distribution, sale, and use of this crystalline powder, heroin is something entirely different. It represents the cornerstone of several unique worlds with their own peculiar goals, values, rules, needs, and achievements.

Adventures on the Opium Express

The opium express is a network of production and trafficking that stretches around the globe from Asia to the United States. It is an enterprise that involves millions of peasant farmers and tens of thousands of corrupt government officials, disciplined criminal entrepreneurs, and street-level dealers.

A focal point in the trafficking complex of opium and heroin is the Golden Triangle, a vast area of Southeast Asia comprising the rugged Shan hills of Burma, the serpentine ridges of northern Thailand, and the upper highlands of Laos. This geographic area emerged during the late 1960s and early 1970s as the world's largest producer of illicit opium,[4] providing yields of some 700 metric tons annually.[1] For a time, the Golden Triangle also dominated the heroin-refining markets of Western Europe, and there is considerable agreement that the

---

[1] Both coca- and opium-production figures are typically expressed in metric tons—one metric ton equal to 1,000 kilogrms or 2.2046 pounds. In this example, 700 metric tons would be the equivalent of some 1.54 million pounds.

growing of opium in the region was introduced by Chinese political refugees. Using the Netherlands as their principle importation and distribution area, Chinese traffickers virtually controlled the heroin market—arranging for the purchase of raw opium, overseeing its conversion into heroin, and managing the international smuggling network. By 1978 to 1979, however, rivalries among the various Chinese drug syndicates, law-enforcement efforts against Asian traffickers, and declining production due to poor crop yields served to reduce the importance of the region as a center of opium trade.[5] A second focal point in the opium-heroin trafficking complex is what has become known as the Golden Crescent, an arc of land stretching across Southwest Asia through sections of Pakistan, Iran, and Afghanistan. Emerging as the leading opium producer in the world during the late 1970s, the Golden Crescent successfully challenged its Southeast Asian counterpart by generating a raw material for heroin that was less expensive and generally more potent. By the mid-1980s over half the heroin entering the United States originated as opium in the Golden Crescent. Iran was the key opium producer, and Pakistan and Afghanistan were the primary heroin refiners and shippers, having numerous illicit laboratories on both sides of the Khyber Pass. By the close of the decade, however, with estimates suggesting that the combined yield of Southeast and Southwest Asian opium production exceeded 3,000 metric tons, the Golden Triangle had reemerged as the world leader in opium production.[6] Moreover, with illicit opium-poppy farming apparent in Guatemala, Lebanon, Mexico, and perhaps other nations, the annual world production available for refining into heroin is likely in the vicinity of 4,000 to 5,000 metric tons (see Table 3.1).

The actual process culminating in the use of heroin on the streets of rural and urban America begins in the remote sections of the Golden Triangle and Golden Crescent. There, hill-tribe farmers use the most basic agricultural techniques to cultivate the opium poppy.[7] The annual crop cycle begins in late summer as farmers scatter poppy seeds across the surface of their freshly hoed fields. Three months later the plant is mature—a greenish stem topped by a brightly colored flower. Gradually the petals fall to the ground, exposing a seedpod about the size and shape of a small egg. Inside the pod is a milky white sap that is harvested by cutting a series of shallow parallel incisions across the surface of the pod. As the sap seeps from the incisions and congeals on the surface of the pod, it changes to a brownish-black color. This is raw opium, which the farmers collect by scraping the pod with a flat, dull knife.

The farmers then carry the raw opium on horseback to a local refinery where it is immediately converted into morphine—a practice that traffickers prefer, since compact morphine bricks are easier and safer to smuggle than are bundles of sticky, pungent opium. The

Table 3.1 Opium Production Estimates, 1986–1990

Country	1990 (Metric Tons)	1989 (Metric Tons)	1988 (Metric Tons)	1987 (Metric Tons)	1986 (Metric Tons)
Afghanistan	500–800	585	700–800	400–800	400–500
Iran	200–400	300	200–400	200–400	160–160
Pakistan	118–128	130	190–220	190–220	160–160
Total SW Asia	818–1,328	1,015	1,090–1,420	790–1,420	760–1,060
Burma	2,780	2,625	1,065–1,500	925–1,230	770–1,100
Laos	300–450	375	210–300	150–300	100–290
Thailand	40	50	23–33	20–45	20–25
Total SE Asia	3,120–3,270	3,050	1,298–1,833	1,095–1,575	890–1,415
Guatemala	6	14			
Lebanon	45	45			
Mexico	85	85	45–55	45–55	35–50
Total	136	144			
Total Opium	4,074–4,734	4,209	2,433–3,308	1,930–3,050	1,595–2,525

SOURCE: Bureau of International Narcotics Matters, Department of State, *International Narcotics Control Strategy Report* (Washington, DC: Department of State, March 1990), p. 18.

conversion of raw opium into pure morphine is an exercise in rudimentary chemistry. The opium is first dissolved in drums of hot water. Lime fertilizer is added to the steaming solution, precipitating out organic wastes and leaving the morphine suspended near the surface. Any residual waste matter is removed, and the morphine is transferred to another drum, where it is heated, stirred, and mixed with concentrated ammonia. The morphine solidifies and drops to the bottom of the container and is filtered out in the form of chunky white kernels. Once dried and packaged, the morphine weighs about 10% of the original raw opium from which it was extracted.

The process of transforming morphine into heroin is a bit more complex, and there was a time, from the end of World War II through the 1960s, when Hong Kong and Marseilles were the heroin-refining capitals of the world. More recently, this industry has become increasingly dispersed, with precision laboratories also in the opium-growing regions of Southeast and Southwest Asia, and in Turkey, Malaysia, and South America. The refining process occurs in five stages to chemically bind acetic acid to the morphine molecule, thereby generating a substance that can be transformed into the powder known as heroin. Ten kilograms of morphine can produce an equivalent amount of heroin that ranges from 80% to 99% pure.

The trafficking of the refined heroin from the clandestine laboratories to United States ports involves an elaborate organizational web

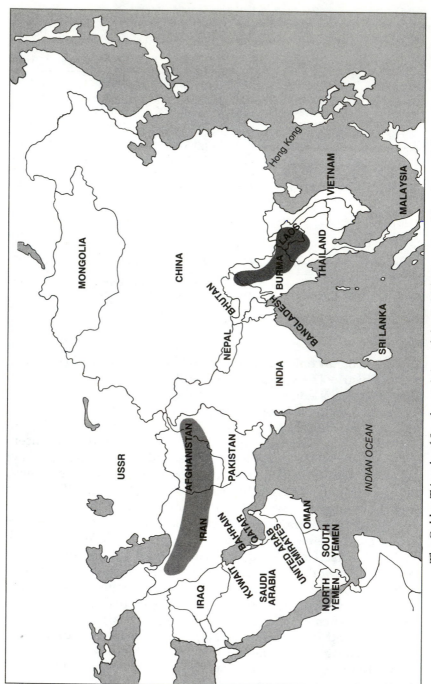

The Golden Triangle of Southeast Asia and the Golden Crescent of Southwest Asia

of transportation routes, couriers, and payoffs. Depending upon the particular trafficking organization, the drug may be transshipped by way of established routes through Indonesia, the Philippines, Syria, Egypt, Kenya, Nigeria, Italy, France, England, West Germany, the Netherlands, Canada, or a combination thereof. If the circumstances demand it, an organization can quickly and ingeniously design alternate routes. In early 1983, for example, a Miami heroin trafficker indicated that as the result of an arrest in Turkey, an assassination in Kuwait, and a plane crash in Corsica, one shipment of drugs had to be diverted through at least eight countries before it finally reached its final destination:

> As the story got to me, which I'm sure is true knowing where it came from, the stuff [heroin] started out in a small lab near Ou Neua. That's a place in north Laos, I think somewhere up near the Chinese border. It made its way to Bangkok okay where it was supposed to be flown to Athens, Amsterdam, New York, and then to Miami by car. But then things really got fucked up. The guy who's supposed to make the transfer in Athens gets picked up for somethin' or other, so they fly it to Singapore instead. They had someone there who could take it most of the way . . . but he decides to get himself killed in Kuwait before he even gets there. So get this: It goes back to Bangkok, to somewhere in India, then somewhere else in the Middle East, and then up the fucking Nile to Egypt. Then there's this mule [cocaine courier] in Corsica that's gonna take it, but he freaks out when his girlfriend finds out she don't know how to fly her plane too well and ends up cashing it in. . . . Somehow it finds its way to South Africa . . . it goes by ship to Uruguay, and then up through South America—Ecuador, Colombia, Peru and all that—to Panama, Mexico City, Chicago, Detroit, New York, and then Miami. . . . It's one for the Guinness book of fucking records.[m]

The couriers who actually carry heroin across the world and into the United States are as diverse as the personalities who use the drug—members of the trafficking organizations traveling alone or with their families as tourists, diplomats, pilots and other airline personnel, professional athletes, students, ship captains and seamen, teachers, physicians, judges, and numerous others—even Playboy playmates. Recently, a number of heroin-smuggling operations have focused on

---

[m] As already noted in Chapter 2, all undocumented quotations throughout this volume are personal communications to the author.

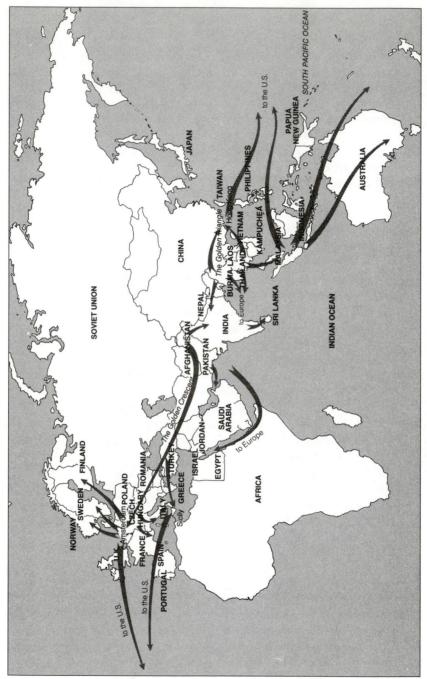

Heroin-Trafficking Routes

attractive women. Lebanese traffickers, for example, are known to recruit svelte Scandinavian women who bypass the traditional heroin depots in New York's Harlem, flying directly to Arab communities in East Coast cities.[8]

Once in the United States, heroin may be *stepped on* (diluted) as many as 7 to 10 times. What started out in some remote Asian laboratory as 99% pure heroin is cut with lactose (milk sugar, a by-product of milk processing), quinine, cornstarch, or almost any other powdery substance that will dissolve when heated. Heroin is also mixed with cleansing powder and dirt, and even arsenic or strychnine if the user is singled out for a *hot shot* (fatal dose). Ultimately, the heroin sold on the street is less than 10% pure and sometimes as little as 1% to 4% pure.

Concomitant with the trafficking and dealer dilution of heroin is the geometric increase in its price. In one trafficking operation, a kilogram of morphine base sold in Italy for $12,500; converted into heroin, that kilogram yielded an estimated $1.7 million in street sales.[9] Even more dramatically, although villagers in India's Siah Valley could earn the equivalent of $300 for 10 kilograms of raw opium during the 1980s, converted into heroin in New Delhi the price was $10,000,[10] with an escalation to $1.5 million on the streets of New York City—an overall increase of some 5,000%.

H Is for Heaven. H Is for Hell. H Is for Heroin. . . .

Why people use heroin, or any illicit drug for that matter, is not altogether understood. Theories are legion, so much so that one publication of the National Institute on Drug Abuse devoted its entire 488 pages to outlining the major views.[11] A number of investigators have described heroin users as maladjusted, hostile, immature, dependent, manipulative, and narcissistic individuals, suggesting that drug use is just one more symptom of their disordered personalities.[12] Others suggest that since drug use is an integral part of the general culture that surrounds the user, it is learned behavior.[13]

Sociologist Alfred R. Lindesmith's view, among the more often quoted, most simplistic, and perhaps least helpful theories of heroin use, explains addiction on the basis of the user's association of the drug with the distress accompanying the sudden cessation of its use.[14] Using heroin, he contends, is one thing, for people have various motivations for trying the drug. Becoming addicted, Lindesmith argues, is another. Users who fail to realize the connection between the withdrawal distress and the drug manage to escape addiction. Those who link the distress to the drug use, and thereafter use it to alleviate the distress symptoms, invariably become addicted.

There are other explanations: the bad-habit theory, disruptive-environment theory, cognitive-control theory, social-deviance theory, biological-rhythm theory, subcultural theory, social-neurobiological theory, and many more.[15] Among the more novel is Sandra Coleman's "incomplete mourning theory," an explanation holding that addictive behavior is a function of an unusual number of traumatic or premature deaths, separations, and losses that the drug user has not effectively resolved or mourned.[16]

Then there is the theory of the "addiction-prone personality," elucidated by Dr. Kenneth Chapman of the United States Public Health Service more than three decades ago:

> . . . the typical addict is emotionally unstable and immature, often seeking pleasure and excitement outside of the conventional realms. Unable to adapt comfortably to the pressures and tensions in today's speedy world, he may become either an extremely dependent individual or turn into a hostile "lone wolf" incapable of attaching deep feelings toward anyone. In his discomfort, he may suffer pain—real or imaginary. The ordinary human being has normal defense machinery with which to meet life's disappointments, frustrations, and conflicts. But the potential addict lacks enough of this inner strength to conquer his emotional problems and the anxiety they create. In a moment of stress, he may be introduced to narcotics as a "sure-fire" answer to his needs. Experiencing relief from his pain, or an unreal flight from his problems, or a puffed-up sense of power and control regarding them, he is well on the road toward making narcotics his way of life.[17]

Stated differently, when "stable" people are introduced to drugs, they will discard them spontaneously before becoming dependent. Those who have "addiction-prone personalities," because of psychoses, psychopathic or psychoneurotic disorders, or predispositions toward mental dysfunctioning "become transformed into the typical addict."[18]

To the great misfortune of the heroin-using population, the concept of the addiction-prone personality dominated much of the thinking in the drug-abuse treatment industry for almost six decades. Although the theory evolved from studies of addicts in psychiatric facilities during the early years of addiction treatment, it was applied universally and continues to be accepted by many.[19] Yet as researchers who have gone beyond the confines of their laboratories, hospitals, and university campuses to study addicts in their natural environments understand, and likely always did, users who come to the attention of psychiatric facilities are often quite different from those who remain active on the street for extended periods of time. Given this fact, it is no wonder that segments of the field of addiction treatment have had limited success over the years.

The difficulty with the concept of the addiction-prone personality, and all other theoretical explanations of heroin addiction, has been the assumption that one single theory will account for the entire spectrum of drug-using behaviors—a problem that has plagued discussions of deviant behavior in general. Unfortunately, this kind of thinking is not altogether that remote, at least in its logical structure, from the arguments of Dr. Benjamin Rush two centuries ago that there was a theory of disease rather than distinct theories of separate diseases. In all likelihood, there are as many reasons for using drugs as there are individuals who use drugs. For some it may be a function of family disorganization, or cultural learning, or maladjusted personality, or an "addiction-prone" personality, or even "incomplete mourning." For others heroin use may be no more than a normal response to the world in which they live. And in all likelihood there is a population of heroin users for whom Lindesmith's withdrawal-avoidance approach fits.

As the motivations for heroin use vary, so too do the patterns of initiation. Some careers in drug use are therapeutic in origin—through the chronic use of morphine, Demerol, Talwin, or another narcotic analgesic that was prescribed for the treatment of pain or some other ailment. For most, however, heroin is a later stage in a life-style of drug taking that began during early adolescence with the use of alcohol, codeine cough syrup, organic solvents, marijuana, and/or amphetamines. Whatever the pattern of initiation, addiction to heroin, if it occurs at all, is a lengthy process. Despite the "one shot and you're hooked" myth, to become addicted to heroin, one must work at it— particularly since much of the heroin available in the street community is frequently of low potency. Moreover, most people do not begin their heroin use by mainlining (intravenous injection). The recollections of David K., a New York City heroin user interviewed during the 1980s, illustrate a pattern of onset that is not altogether uncommon:

> One day my cousin comes over and he's using heroin, and he throws this 10-dollar bag of junk on the kitchen table and says, "Try some." I say, "Listen Alfie, I ain't about to put any of your shit into my veins." He says, "No man, just snort some of it, it's great."
>
> So I decide to snort some of Alfie's shit. I close off one nostril and sniff the shit out of the shit. . . . It blew my fucking head off, really fucked me up. I got such a bad pain in my head that I thought I was fucking brain damaged. I puked my guts out. I was really sick. . . .

A few weeks later I see Alfie again and ask him for some stuff, you know, just to try it again. You'd think that after that first time I might have learned something. But no. It's like when you try your first cigarette. You get dizzy and upset in your gut, but you do it again anyway because you want to be cool and since everybody else is doin' it there must be something to it.

So I snort again and ho-ly fucking shit! I felt like I died and went to heaven. My whole body was like one giant fucking incredible orgasm.

What David K. had experienced was his first *rush*. Or as described somewhat more vividly by former New York City heroin addict Manual J. Torres:

. . . it's really something else. I mean, it's like the shit really hit the fan . . . you can't describe it. All the colors of Times Square tumble right over your forehead and explode in your eyeballs like a million, jillion shooting stars. And then, each one of them goddamn stars novas in a cascade of brilliant Technicolor. And the world levels out. You know what I mean? There's no right, no wrong. Everything's beautiful, and it's like nothing's happening baby but clear, crisp light. The mambo beat is like hot fuck notes bouncing off lukewarm street scenes. The drummer downstairs in the park is onto life's whole fucking secret, and the primitive urge of his swinging soul becomes a mellow sharpness in your ears. And you want to gather all of creation inside you; maybe for a minute you do. What a perfect Manny Torres you become for a moment![20]

After snorting on and off for several months, and still not addicted, David K. moved into the next stage of heroin use:

I ran into this lady that I used to fuck and hang out with a couple of years ago and she asks me if I want to come along with her while she makes her connection [buys heroin] and fixes [injects the drug]. After a while she asks me if I want to try the needle and I say no, but then I decide to go halfway and skin-pop [injecting into the muscle just beneath the skin]. Well, man, it was wonderful. Popping was just like snorting, only stronger, finer, better, and faster.

For David, skin-popping lasted for three months, although not on a daily basis. "I don't think I was addicted then," he said, "because sometimes I'd go for almost a whole week without popping and I didn't get sick." Then he began to mainline:

Travelin' along the mainline was like a grand slam home run fuck, like getting a blow job from Miss America. The rush hits you instantly, and all of a sudden you're up there on Mount Olympus talking to Zeus.

Two months later David decided that he was *hooked* (addicted). He was using heroin regularly, spending more than $200 daily on his habit, and getting sick when more than six to eight hours would pass without fixing. And then, although he had no intentions of quitting his heroin use, he did admit that addiction had its drawbacks:

Any damn junkie that says that he doesn't like his shit is a fucking liar. They all love their dope. But your whole damn life revolves around your shit.

Or as Manny Torres described it:

See, once you're hooked you're not your own boss any more. You belong to your habit. Plain and simple. You plan, and scheme, and con, and lie, and hustle for your habit. Anybody and everybody becomes fair game. Look, you leave mother, brother, sister, father, friend for heroin. When you're hooked you gotta score. It ain't maybe I'll score, maybe I won't. It's, man, I'm gonna score and all hell ain't gonna stop me! And scoring can take time; it can be downright frustrating and uncomfortable. I've waited for over three hours on a street corner for a cat with a bag to surface. And you don't leave, 'cause he's the only one holding and if you miss him someone else will get the stuff and you'll be left holding air.[21]

As mentioned earlier, Alfred R. Lindesmith and others have claimed that, once addicted, the rush, kick, and euphoria that heroin produces become of only minor importance in explaining continued usage; and that it is the fear of the withdrawal symptoms—the yawning, sneezing, crying, running nose, gooseflesh, rapid pulse, hot and cold flashes, nausea and vomiting, diarrhea, stomach cramps, and muscular spasms—that motivates further use.[22] Yet by contrast, Dr. David P. Ausubel once argued:

The popular misconception that addicted individuals deprived of the drug suffer the tortures of the damned, and that once caught in the grip of physiological dependence the average person is powerless to help himself, are beliefs that have been touted on a credulous public by misinformed journalists and by addicts themselves.[23]

On this point, David K. commented:

> Listen, white brother, that's a crock of pure mule shit! Sure, you hurt, you hurt bad all over. But what you're really doin' is chasin' the rush and that wonderful feeling that you and the whole fucking world around you is cool. That's what you're really after, the high, the wonderful high. True, when you get busted and have to kick cold [without medication] in some dirty fucking stinking jail you raise hell and put on a show so maybe you'll get some medicine, but it's never as bad as you make it. . . . When it comes time to die, I want it to be an OD [overdose] on smack. That would be the greatest way to take the ride over the edge of the fucking world.

And, too, an ex-addict counselor in a Florida drug-treatment program added:

> When we are sure that the new resident has no concurrent addiction to some other drug, we just put him on the couch in the living room, give him a blanket, and ignore him. He'll start putting on his act, trying to get some sympathy. He'll look around the room and see some guy waxing the floor, somebody else at an ironing board, or somebody just reading a book. They're people who were shooting with him once out in the street and now they're all ignoring him. Pretty soon he settles down. He hurts, but it wears off in 24 to 48 hours.

The myth that heroin withdrawal is similar to the tortures of hell has a long history. As early as 1917 in a paper read before the California State Medical Association, Dr. A. S. Tuchler of San Francisco stated:

> When one is placed in confinement and deprived of the drug, the suffering, both physical and mental, endured by the addict, is beyond comprehension and belief.[24]

More recently, the myth has been a product of the media, vividly presented in such films as *The Man with The Golden Arm* (1955), *Monkey on My Back* (1957), *French Connection II* (1975), and numerous episodes of ''Hill Street Blues,'' ''Police Story,'' ''Miami Vice,'' and other television series. But researchers and clinicians in the drug field, and many heroin users as well, tend to agree that withdrawal is no different, and no more severe, than the chills, cramps, and muscle pains that are associated with a good dose of the flu—something that almost everyone has experienced.[n]

Gambling with Death

Unlike the situation with many other drugs, chronic heroin use seems to produce little direct or permanent physiological damage. Street heroin users tend to neglect themselves, however, and commonly reported disorders include heart and lung abnormalities, *tracks* (scarred veins), malnutrition, weight loss, endocarditis (a disease of the heart valves), stroke, gynecological and obstetrical problems in women, and particularly hepatitis, local skin infections, and abscesses.[25] Many heroin users live on the street, in alleys or abandoned buildings, and in general ignore the standard practices that encourage good health. In this regard a Philadelphia heroin user stated:

> When you spend most of your time hustling on the streets, scoring, fixing, scoring, fixing, hustling again, and living in some damp cellar that has dripping fungus on the walls you don't have time for such frills as fresh laundry, perfume baths, and gourmet food. . . .

And as David K. remarked:

> . . . once in a while I go home and I find that my sister has left me some clean clothes, but most of the time I wear the same fucking things from week to week. . . . I don't know how long it's been since I had a good shower, and for food it's either a taco, a Big Mac, or french fries and sour balls washed down with Coca-Cola and cheap wine.

For some women heroin users, there can be a number of additional problems. A heroin-using, part-time prostitute in Miami recently commented:

> When you find yourself fucking for money, fucking for drugs, and sometimes fucking or sucking a hairy prick for something to eat or a place to sleep, you're not too careful about avoiding the cruds. What's more, since you're stoned most of the

---

[n] It must be emphasized here that this is not necessarily the case with all addicting drugs. The unsupervised non-medical withdrawal from barbiturates and other sedative drugs can bring on shock, coma, and death.

time you don't feel much in the way of pain, or either that
your whole body hurts and you can't tell where the trouble
is. . . . When some kind of mess starts leakin' from my crotch
like toothpaste from a tube I know it's time to get my ass off
to the clinic.

Even though the infections and malnutrition are the result of poor
eating habits and lack of personal hygiene, hepatitis is the result of
needle sharing. And associated with this in recent years is acquired
immunodeficiency syndrome (AIDS), a topic that is addressed in detail
in Chapter 6.

Next, there is the problem of heroin overdose, a phenomenon that
is still not fully understood. Some users OD as the result of too much
heroin or a too-potent heroin. In these instances, if death occurs, it
is the result of respiratory depression, that is, suffocation. In other
instances death is so rapid that the needle is often still in the user's
arm when he or she is found. Such deaths are the result of asphyxia-
tion caused by acute pulmonary edema (an accumulation of fluid in
the lungs). Overdose deaths are more often the result of heroin intake
combined with the concurrent use of alcohol and another sedative.
There is also the difficulty posed by the adulterants used to cut heroin.
Quinine is popular. An irritant, it can cause vascular damage, acute
and potentially lethal disturbances in heartbeat, depressed respiration,
coma, and respiratory arrest. Moreover, heroin plus quinine can have
an unpredictable compounding effect.[26]

Overdose can also be a natural consequence of the very nature of
the drug-taking and drug-seeking behaviors of heroin users. In their
endless pursuit of the high, users continually seek out *good stuff* (strong,
potent heroin) and they have several alternatives. They can make their
purchases from their regular dealer, one with whom they have been
successful in the past. They can use the street grapevine—an informal,
and often erroneous, communication network that lets them know
where they can connect for "dynamite stuff." And finally, associated
with the street grapevine are "brand names"—a phenomenon apparent
in New York, Philadelphia, Miami, Chicago, St. Louis, Los Angeles,
and other urban areas across the United States when heroin is
generally available.

The labeling of drugs with brand names, studied most extensively
by ethnographer Paul J. Goldstein in New York City, has become a
popular merchandising technique in the drug black market. The process
occurs chiefly with heroin and involves distinctive packaging prior to
sale. The bag containing the heroin is labeled with a name, symbol,
or number, usually in a specific color. Brand names touted as good
stuff in New York City have carried such epithets as Black Magic, Chako
Fan, Death Row, 888, Fuck Me Please, Good Pussy, 90%, Kojak,

The Beast, 32, and The Witch.[27] In Miami, some highly sought-after names during the mid- and late 1980s included Chain Saw, Savage Cunt, Mexican Satan, Hand Job, Golden Girl, Rambo, Slime, Jail Bait, Sweet Lucy's Tit, Tubbs, and Miami's Vice. And during the early 1990s, the best known heroin labels in Miami were Chill, Afghan Delight, Overtown Max, and Saddam's Ass ("shoot up Saddam's ass" as one Miami heroin dealer advertised during the war with Iraq in 1991). With respect to the functions of heroin labeling, Goldstein explained:

> Most [users] have limited capital to expend on heroin. There are a multitude of street dealers to choose from. Getting beat on a heroin purchase or buying inferior quality heroin is an omnipresent risk. The quality of heroin that is commonly available is poor. Heroin users have either experienced or heard reminiscences of the superior dope of yesteryear and may have occasionally encountered highly potent heroin themselves in more recent years. Heroin users always look to obtain the highest quality heroin in a confusing and uncontrolled market-place. Most seem to feel that labeling bags of heroin assists them in their quest.[28]

Yet whether it is through brand names or grapevine rumor, the pursuit of the best heroin can have lethal consequences. During February 1975, for example, word quickly spread throughout the Miami drug community that a dealer in North Miami Beach had a supply of heroin so potent that he was hesitant to sell it. As one user put it: "It's supposed to be a gift from God, a god by the name of Bentley." The dealer ultimately sold his supply but a sample was obtained for analysis. As it turned out, the drug was etorphine, one of several compounds discovered by K. W. Bentley of Edinburgh during the early 1960s through a manipulation of the morphine molecule.[29] Bentley's compound had a potency several thousand times that of morphine. Before it finally disappeared from the streets, more than a score of heroin users in South Florida had tried it and fatally overdosed.[o]

Miami's etorphine incident was not an isolated case, for the drug has periodically reappeared on the streets of South Florida in the years hence. Then there was China White, a pure but rare and perhaps mythical strain of heroin from Southeast Asia that was a fantasy among

---

[o] Under the Controlled Substances Act of 1971, etorphine is classified as a Schedule I drug, which means that, like heroin and LSD, it has no accepted medical use in the United States and its mere possession is a violation of federal law. Etorphine hydrochloride, a less potent variety, is used occasionally by veterinarians to immobilize wild animals. In fact, even this milder form is so strong that a 2-cc dose is capable of immobilizing a 4-ton elephant.

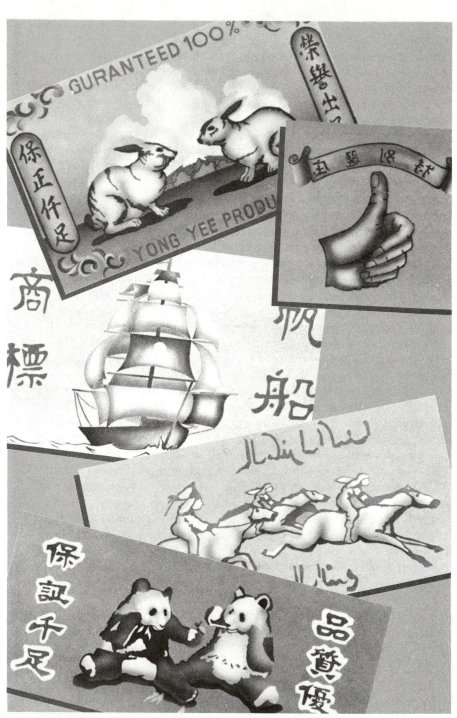

Heroin labeling is by no means new. Throughout this century, packages of heroin trafficked into the United States have been trademarked with exotic and colorful labels. Those illustrated here are among the many accumulated in recent years by the Drug Administration.

many West Coast users for more than a decade. *"Getting down* [shooting up] on it is a never-ending dream," said one user from Sacramento. In late 1980, the dream finally came true, or so it seemed. Word spread through southern California that China White had finally arrived on American shores. But the drug was not China White at all, and users began dying from it. It was *3-methylfentanyl,* or TMF, a chemical similar in structure to fentanyl, a synthetic narcotic analgesic 80 to 100 times more potent than morphine.[30] Moreover, TMF was the first in a continuing series of what have become known as designer drugs. So-named because they are new substances designed by slightly altering the chemical makeup of other illegal or tightly controlled drugs, they are typically more potent and often contaminated versions of either fentanyl, Demerol, or some other synthetic narcotic. One variety has been found to destroy brain cells; another produces the symptoms of Parkinson's disease and accelerated aging; a third paralyzes its users; and a fourth has a potency 6,000 times that of heroin—producing instantaneous death.[31] And the California episode was not an isolated one. During the early weeks of 1991 in the New York City area, no less than 18 heroin users died, with an additional 233 hospitalized, from a designer drug batch sold in the South Bronx under the label Tango & Cash. Again, the drug was either fentanyl or a fentanyl analog.[32] As such, designer drugs have posed such a threat to heroin users seeking a fix that one recently testified: "I don't know if the next dose will kill me."[P]

The precise number of overdoses from heroin (and other illicit narcotics) use is probably impossible to estimate. Users, unless their conditions appear especially life threatening, are rarely brought to hospital emergency rooms for treatment. In the case of lethal overdoses, it is not always possible to classify the exact cause of death. On the basis of data from the Drug Abuse Warning Network, more than 20,000 heroin overdoses in major cities result in emergency room treatment each year, with at least an additional 3,000 resulting in a stop at the county morgue.[33]

The Heroin Epidemics

Although opiate use in its various forms has been common throughout United States history, its current and most typical manifestation—the intravenous use of heroin—apparently developed during the 1930s and became widespread after 1945.[34] Between 1950 and the early 1960s,

---

[P] Curiously, while China White was the purest of the fantasy-heroin, more recently the designation of China White has also been applied to high quality heroin arriving from Southeast Asia. Moreover, whereas black tar is the street name associated with Mexican heroin (so designated because of its color), China White has become synonymous with pure Asian heroin. See *Drug Enforcement Report,* 25 April 1988, p. 8.

most major cities experienced a low-level spread of heroin use, particularly among black and other minority populations. Thereafter, use began to grow rapidly, rising to peaks in the late 1960s and then falling sharply. The pattern was so ubiquitous that it came to be regarded as epidemic heroin use.[35] More recent epidemics occurred in 1973–1974, 1977–1978, and 1982–1983, defined as such on the basis of the numbers of new admissions to heroin-treatment facilities. Yet interestingly, no one really knew how widespread heroin use was during those years, and even today the estimates are often no more than scientific guesses.

Throughout the 1960s, the Treasury Department's Bureau of Narcotics would periodically announce the number of active narcotics addicts in the United States. As of December 31, 1967, for example, it set the number at 62,045.[36] This figure—not 60,000 or 65,000, but 62,045—suggested considerable precision. New York City's many drug-abuse researchers, clinicians, and members of law-enforcement groups found the estimate suspect, however, since from their experiences the heroin problem was much greater. In fact, a heroin user from New York's Harlem area jokingly stated that "... there are more junkies than that just on my street."

The suspicions were justified, of course, for the bureau's figure was based almost exclusively on reports from local police departments. New York had its own such file at the time, one that reported almost twice the national bureau's number of new cases for the same year.[37] In an attempt to foist some scientific rationality into the estimates of heroin prevalence, in 1969 John C. Ball of Temple University and Carl D. Chambers of the New York State Narcotic Addiction Control Commission combined data from the New York and National Bureau of Narcotics files with figures provided by the federal drug-treatment facilities in Lexington, Kentucky, and Fort Worth, Texas. Through a complex series of ratios and correction factors, they came up with a figure of 108,424 heroin addicts for the year 1967.[38] Even Ball and Chambers, however, were not altogether confident of their estimate, for they were acutely aware of the potentially vast number of unreported cases.

In 1970, using scientific survey methodology, cross-sectional studies of the general population finally reached the drug field.[39] As indicators of heroin use, however, the data were disappointing. It was known at the outset that general population surveys could access only the more stable at-home populations, thus excluding residents of jails and penitentiaries, mental institutions, migrant workers, the homeless, the residents of welfare hotels and skid row shelters and lodging houses, others living on the street, and the members of drug subcultures who either had no stable living quarters or were typically away from them.[40]

As the drug field moved through the 1970s, the National Institute on Drug Abuse developed what it called "heroin trend indicators," relative estimates generated from a composite of reported heroin-related deaths, hospital emergency room visits, heroin-treatment admissions, and high school and household surveys. On the basis of these data, the estimated number of heroin users in the United States for 1977 ranged from 396,000 to 510,000.[41]

Throughout the 1980s government reports were maintaining that the number of heroin users in the United States was somewhere in the vicinity of 500,000, having been at that level for about a decade and a half.[42] At the beginning of the 1990s, however, there were indications that the number of heroin users might be on the increase, a situation brought about, at least in part, by the use of heroin to mediate the stimulant effects of *crack-cocaine* (see Chapter 4).

COCAINE: "THE MOST DANGEROUS SUBSTANCE ON EARTH"

Cocaine is known to its users as shit, coke, bernice, big C, corrine, lady snow, toot, nose candy, and in some circles as Super Fly (from the 1972 Warner Brothers movie of the same name). When barely a week apart during June 1986, two well-known athletes died of cocaine overdoses—University of Maryland basketball forward Len Bias and Cleveland Browns defensive back Don Rogers—numerous observers referred to the drug as "the most dangerous substance on earth." But wait, there seems to be a contradiction here. Earlier, heroin was reportedly the "most dangerous" of all. But then, at different times and in various media such drugs as marijuana, LSD, PCP, the amphetamines, Quaalude, Ecstasy, and most recently crank, crack, and ice, have each been designated as the world's most dangerous substance.

Regardless of the epithets, the aura surrounding today's coke is quite different from that of Angelo Mariani's Vin Coca, John Pemberton's French Wine Coca, or even Sigmund Freud's cocaine. Cocaine use in contemporary America is considered a major health problem, with estimates of the number of regular users in recent years ranging as high as 10 to 20 million.[43]

Adventures Along the Cocaine Highway

At the end of the 1880s when Sigmund Freud and his colleagues discovered that cocaine was not the all-purpose wonder drug that they had hoped for, they quickly withdrew their support for its applications in medical therapy. Aside from the drug's use by the patent-medicine industry until the passage of the Pure Food and Drug Act in 1906, cocaine moved underground, and remained there for the better part of a century. Its major devotees included prostitutes, jazz musicians, fortune-tellers, criminals, and blacks. Its relegation to the netherworlds of crime and the bizarre should not suggest, however, that people in this country were unconcerned with the use of cocaine by alien sub-cultures. Quite the contrary. During the early decades of the twentieth century, commentaries about cocaine took on racial overtones, pre-cipitated by white fears of blacks' sexual and criminal impulses. In 1910, for example, testimony before a committee of the House of Represen-tatives referenced these fears and also included almost every white stereotype of blacks:

> The colored people seem to have a weakness for it [cocaine]. It is a very seductive drug, and it produces extreme exhilara-tion. Persons under the influences of it believe they are millionaires. They have an exaggerated ego. They imagine they can lift this building, if they want to, or can do anything they want to. They have no regard for right or wrong. It produces a kind of temporary insanity. They would just as leave rape a woman as anything else and a great many of the southern rape cases have been traced to cocaine.[44]

In later decades cocaine use was associated with such exotic groups as the beatniks of New York's Greenwich Village and San Francisco's North Beach, the movie colony of Hollywood, and to such an extent with the urban smart set that coke became known as the rich man's drug.

During the late 1960s and early 1970s, cocaine use began to move from the underground to mainstream society, to a great extent the result of a series of decisions made at the time in Washington, D.C. First, the United States Senate and the federal drug-enforcement bureaucracy sponsored legislation that served to reduce the legal pro-duction of amphetamine-type drugs in the United States and to place strict controls on Quaaludes and other abused sedatives. Second, and most importantly, the World Bank allocated funds for the construc-tion of the Pan American Highway through the Huallaga River valley in the high jungles of Peru. These two factors combined to usher in the cocaine era.

The growing of coca leaves had always been popular on the slopes of the Peruvian Andes, but cultivation was for the most part limited for local consumption in tea or for chewing. Only relatively small amounts of the leaves were available for processing into cocaine. Travel throughout the rugged Andes terrain was difficult, and the coca leaves had to be carried out by mule pack. The World Bank's construction of a paved thoroughfare through the Huallaga valley opened up transportation routes for the shipping of coca, and the reduced availability of amphetamines and sedatives in the United States helped

Table 3.2 Worldwide Coca Production Estimates, 1986–1990

Country	1990 (Metric Tons)	1989 (Metric Tons)	1988 (Metric Tons)	1987 (Metric Tons)	1986 (Metric Tons)
Bolivia	64,000	65,998	57,445–78,355	46,000–67,000	44,000–52,920
Columbia	33,360	33,487	19,000–24,200	18,000–23,000	12,000–13,600
Peru	108,544	123,828	97,000–124,000	98,000–121,000	95,000–120,000
Ecuador	170	270	300–500	400	1,000
Total Coca	206,074	223,583	173,745–227,055	162,400–211,400	152,000–187,520

SOURCE: Bureau of International Narcotics Matters, Department of State, *International Narcotics Control Strategy Report* (Washington, DC: Department of State, March 1990), p. 18.

to provide a ready market for the new intoxicant. With the North Americans' increasing usage of cocaine, South American growers and entrepreneurs responded by opening vast new areas for the cultivation of coca.

The cocaine highway begins in the Andes Mountains of South America where the coca leaves are grown. There are the Chapare, Beni, and Yungas regions of northern and central Bolivia—areas characterized by spectacular mountain peaks with lofty snowcapped passes and thundering waterfalls that roller coaster down into subtropical valleys and moist tumbling lowlands. In Peru there are remote high jungles surrounding the Upper Huallaga River, a tributary of the mighty Amazon. In Ecuador there are highlands on both sides of the equator and areas adjacent to Guayaquil, that nation's largest city. In southeastern Colombia there is the vast and virtually uninhabited Amazonas territory; and there are plantations in East Asia, Bali, and the Caribbean. In these regions, on some 250,000 hectares (1 hectare=2.47 acres) of scattered fields, peasant farmers cultivate coca. As indicated in Table 3.2, more than 200,000 metric tons of leaf are produced annually, the majority of production occurring in Bolivia and Peru.[45]

The production of cocaine begins with the coca leaf. In the natural greenhouses of the Chapare, the Upper Huallaga, and similar forsaken tropical slopes and lowlands, rows of *Erythroxylum coca Lam.* are neatly planted. At harvest time the leaves are carefully picked, dried, and bundled for pack carriers who transport them to the clandestine processing laboratories. In Peru's Upper Huallaga the labs are usually nearby, but in the Bolivian Chapare, often the carriers must bear their loads across hundreds of miles of footpaths to the Beni, a jungle and savanna province the size of Kansas with no paved highways and few roads of any kind.

At the jungle refineries the leaves are sold for just a few dollars a kilo. The leaves are then pulverized, soaked in alcohol mixed with benzol (a petroleum derivative used in the manufacture of motor fuels, detergents, and insecticides), and shaken. The alcohol-benzol mixture is then drained, sulfuric acid is added, and the solution is shaken again. Next, a precipitate is formed when sodium carbonate is added to the solution. When this is washed with kerosene and chilled, crystals of crude cocaine are left behind. These crystals are known as coca paste. The cocaine content of leaves is relatively low—0.5% to 1% by weight as opposed to the paste, which has a cocaine concentration ranging up to 90%.

From the coca fields and refineries, the cocaine highway leads to Amazonia—a land of superlatives and the largest single geographical feature of the South American continent. Amazonia, known to the world as the Amazon, is a river, a valley, and a tropical rain forest. The river begins high in the Peruvian Andes and runs more than 4,000 miles along the equator to the Atlantic Ocean. Drawing its initial strength from hundreds of small mountain streams, it tumbles through steep gorges and eventually opens out into a mile-wide flow in northern Peru. The Amazon is also fed by 200 major tributaries, 17 of which are more than 1,000 miles long. At points along its course in Brazil, the river is several hundred feet deep and often more than seven miles across. When it finally reaches the Atlantic Ocean, the river discharges 3.4 million gallons of water each minute, staining the sea brown with silt for 150 miles. The river valley and tropical rain forest cover 2.5 million square miles of Brazil, Peru, Colombia, Ecuador, Bolivia, Venezuela, Suriname, and Guyana. If it were a country, Amazonia would be the ninth largest in the world, more than half the size of the United States.[46] Impossible to patrol, yet near cities closely linked to the outside world, Amazonia offers almost limitless potential as a drug base.

At the edge of Amazonia in eastern Bolivia is Santa Cruz. Two decades ago the city looked much like a small town on the Texas panhandle. Horses roamed its dusty streets, few people could be seen, and about the only sound that could be heard was the howling wind. Then came the discovery of oil and natural gas and finally the trafficking in cocaine. The once pathetic outpost suddenly became a boom town. Still hot and dusty, Santa Cruz is now Bolivia's second largest city. It has a university, an international airport, golf and tennis clubs, and several hotels and restaurants. As a key point along the cocaine highway, the city is a gathering place for Colombian and American buyers of coca paste.q

---

q The influence of drug trafficking has made Santa Cruz a rather unpleasant place. There seems to be no escape, for example, from plainclothes police fining foreigners (particularly North Americans) for one misdeamenor or another, such as having an invalid visa, or failing to pay the airport tax upon departure, or perhaps even carrying too many U.S. dollars. Failure to pay the appropriate fines can result in a trip to the police station, or even to jail.

In the paradise of lush, subtropical vegetation of western Amazonia is Tingo Maria, Peru. It is a jungle town of 20,000, situated in the cloud forest region of the Andes and surrounded by heavy tropical vegetation and often misty hillsides. It is also one of the few places in the world where jet aircraft land on a grass runway. Tingo Maria itself is an architectural nightmare. Most of the buildings appear hastily built of cinder blocks with little paint or other finishing work. In a few places the streets are paved but only haphazardly. Tingo Maria has a hotel, built during World War II for U.S. military officers and mining engineers. Described as already run-down in the 1950s,[47] it is now the State Tourist Hotel—still run-down but in a more-or-less state of arrested decay. The primary business enterprise of Tingo Maria is coca leaves and coca paste, which are sometimes openly bartered on its dusty streets.[48] While traders deal in their coca products, a small garrison of the Peruvian military is often present, its efforts directed exclusively against members of the Sendero Luminoso (Shining Path) antigovernment insurgent group.[r]

Some 400 miles north of Tingo Maria is Iquitos, deep in Peruvian Amazonia. It is a relatively modern city of 350,000 and is located directly on the west bank of the great river. As a port 2,300 miles upriver from the Atlantic that can be reached by oceangoing freighters, it is a pivotal point in the cocaine commerce. To understand this, one need only visit a few of the many waterfront and backstreet bars in Iquitos. Picturesque adventurers and other characters seemingly from grade B movies can be readily overhead making deals in coca paste.

A few hundred miles downriver on the Amazon is Leticia, Colombia, a town of perhaps 15,000. Overpowered outboards as well as Magnums, Cigarettes, Excaliburs, Scarab Sports, and other high-performance racing boats of a vintage that might be seen on TV's "Miami Vice" fill the small marinas that dot the riverbank. Fairly common, too, are rows of small seaplanes docked incongruously among the muddy decay that is characteristic of almost every jungle river town. Parts of Leticia are quite fascinating, particularly the local bustling street markets—typified by stalls selling giant fillets of piracucu fish the size of garbage can lids, buzzards sitting on lamp posts after a hard rain spreading their broad wings to dry, and of course, the many coca and coca paste merchants. In fact, it would appear that Leticia exists for no reason

---

[r] Perhaps most fascinating in the Tingo Maria area is the Cueva de las Lechuzas (Owl's Cave), just 6 km. from town. Reminiscent of the cave on Skull Mountain in the original 1933 RKO production of *King Kong*, on its towering walls and ceilings are perched any manner of bats, owls, nocturnal parrots, and parakeets. With the help of a torch, one can also see the cave's many other inhabitants, including roach-like bugs the size of mice. A common attracton for hikers, Cueva de las Lechuzas has become dangerous recently. It would appear that during late 1990, two British ornithologists were shot to death in the cave, apparently mistaken by Sendero Luminoso insurgents as agents of the U.S. Drug Enforcement Administration (Madrid *EFE*, 1838 GMT, 28 Oct. 1990).

but smuggling. The thousands of surrounding small tributaries and inlets make it impossible to control boat and seaplane traffic. Moreover, located just west of Brazil and east of the Peruvian frontier, Leticia is an ideal haven for anyone attempting to move goods from one country to another. The traffic, by the way, is not only in coca products but in stolen art and jewelry, guns, counterfeit money from many nations, rare animals (alive and skinned), and even the notorious Jivaro *tsanta*.[s]

Less than three miles southeast of Leticia is the port of Tabatinga, Brazil, a place that writers of South America guidebooks seem to leave out. The name used by the aborigines, which means "red mud," aptly portrays this garrison town of some 30,000 inhabitants at the edge of the Solimeos River.[t] Crisscrossed by dirt roads, Tabatinga is constantly under a cloud of dust from the many taxis, trucks, and vans which handle its precarious collective transportation. The enigma of Tabatinga is that although there is no industry, and agriculture is subsistence, the economy is nevertheless bustling. Not surprising, however, is that much of this activity is associated with the drug trafficking that originates in Leticia. A great number of Tabatinga's river boats, both passenger and fishing, transport coca paste and cocaine to other parts of Brazil.

From Santa Cruz, Tingo Maria, Iquitos, Leticia, Tabatinga, and other remote outposts, the coca paste works its way through Peru, Ecuador, and Brazil to Colombia. The principal destinations in Colombia

---

[s] The Jivaro live in the Amazonian rain forest of Ecuador and Peru in an area known as the *ceja de la selva* (eyebrow of the jungle), located on the eastern slopes of the Andes. A widely known characteristic of Jivaroan society is their persistent intra-tribal warfare, and tales of the Jivaro have both fascinated and terrified travelers into this part of South America for several centuries. The Jivaro are best known for their now-abandoned customs of "headhunting," and shrinking and preserving human heads to make *tsantas* or trophy heads.

A *tsanta* consisted of the entire skin removed from an enemy's head and gradually shrunk until it was about one-third its original size. Although the Jivaro practiced this craft for hundreds of years, during the early decades of the current century it was worked by numerous entrepreneurs using the heads of unclaimed dead in Panama, which they then passed off to tourists as authentic Jivaro *tsantas*. Although headhunting has been outlawed by the Peruvian and Ecuadorian governments for almost four decades, the process of shrinking heads is not a lost craft. *Tsantas* appear on the market now and then, but most are made from the heads of monkeys and tree sloths. In Leticia, however, it is claimed that authentic Jivaro *tsantas* can still be had. For a discussion of the Jivaro, and the history and significance of *tsantas*, see Michael J. Harner, *The Jivaro: People of the Sacred Waterfalls* (New York: Doubleday/Natural History Press, 1972); Elman R. Service, *Profiles in Ethnography* (New York: Harper & Row, 1978); Judith Davidson, *Jivaro: Expressions of Cultural Survival* (San Diego: San Diego Museum of Man, 1985).

[t] At this point in Brazil, the Amazon River does not actually go by the name *Amazon*. Brazilians refer to it as *do Rio Solimoes*. It is not until the Solimoes is joined by the Rio Negro, just west of Manaus, Brazil, that South Americans refer to it as Amazonas.

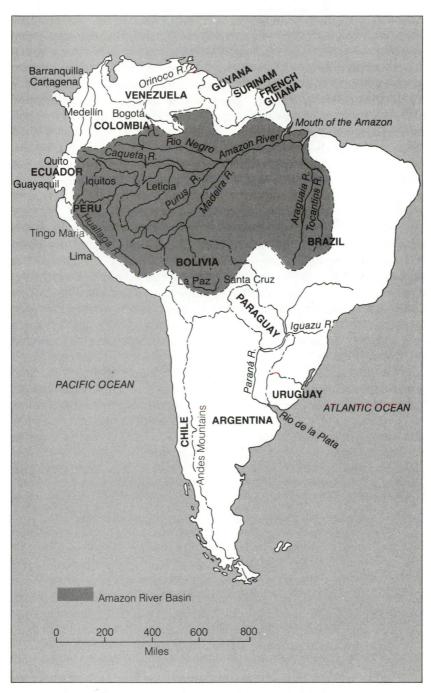

Barranquilla
Cartagena
Orinoco R.
VENEZUELA
GUYANA
SURINAM
FRENCH
GUIANA
Medellín
Bogotá
COLOMBIA
Mouth of the Amazon
Rio Negro
Amazon River
Caqueta R.
Quito
ECUADOR
Guayaquil
Iquitos
Leticia
Purus R.
Madeira R.
Araguaia R.
Tocantins R.
PERU
Tingo Maria
Huallaga R.
BRAZIL
Lima
BOLIVIA
La Paz
Santa Cruz
PARAGUAY
Iguazu R.
PACIFIC OCEAN
Paraná R.
URUGUAY
ATLANTIC OCEAN
CHILE
Andes Mountains
ARGENTINA
Rio de la Plata

Amazon River Basin

0   200   400   600   800
Miles

Amazonia

where the paste is refined into cocaine include the areas surrounding the cities of Bogota, Medellin, Cali, Barranquilla, and Cartagena. There the paste is treated with kerosene, washed in alcohol, filtered and dried, dissolved in sulfuric acid, and then processed with potassium permanganate with ammonium hydroxide, and filtered and dried once more. What is left is a relatively pure cocaine alkaloid known as cocaine base. Although the base can be smoked, it cannot be inhaled through the mucous membranes in the nose. Thus, to create a cocaine good for snorting, the base is then treated with ether, acetone, and hydrochloric acid, resulting in a cocaine that is typically 85% to 97% pure, with no toxic adulterants. From beginning to end: 100 kilos of coca leaves yield 1 kilo of paste; 2.5 kilos of paste yield 1 kilo of base; and 1 kilo of base yields just under 1 kilo of powder-cocaine.[49]

The distribution and transport of cocaine is in the hands of the notorious Medellin (pronounced Med-ah-een) Cartel, and the lesser known Cali, Bogota, Cartagena, and North Atlantic Coast cartels. The two largest cartels—Medellin and Cali—are named after, respectively, Colombia's second and third largest cities, in which they are based, with the Bogota Cartel named after that nation's largest urban complex. Collectively, the five cartels control approximately 70% of the cocaine processed in Colombia and supply 80% of the cocaine distributed in the United States.[50]

The final segment of the cocaine highway extends by air through a series of refueling and transshipping stops in the Caribbean and Bahama Islands, Central America, Cuba, and Mexico to Miami, Tampa, New Orleans, Dallas, New York, Atlanta, Boston, or one of many small Atlantic or Gulf Coast ports. The penetration of U.S. borders occurs at major airports, deserted airstrips, and through a variety of obscure air-sea routes chosen because of their impossibility to control. In this regard, a small-time Miami trafficker explained:

> With the combination of good coordination, good connections, good navigation equipment, good navigation skills, plus a few payoffs here and there, coke can be safely brought in at any time. . . . In one operation we had, we had a guy fly out of Cartagena with refueling stops in Jamaica and Nassau. After a little money changed hands there with the right officials, then he headed towards Miami and dropped the 10-kilo watertight package out the window into the water, to a prearranged spot just a few miles offshore just the other side of the reefs. Then he landed at Miami International and went through customs like everyone else and came out perfectly clean. That was on a Saturday night. The next afternoon, when the water was full of Sunday boaters, another guy went out with a good set of

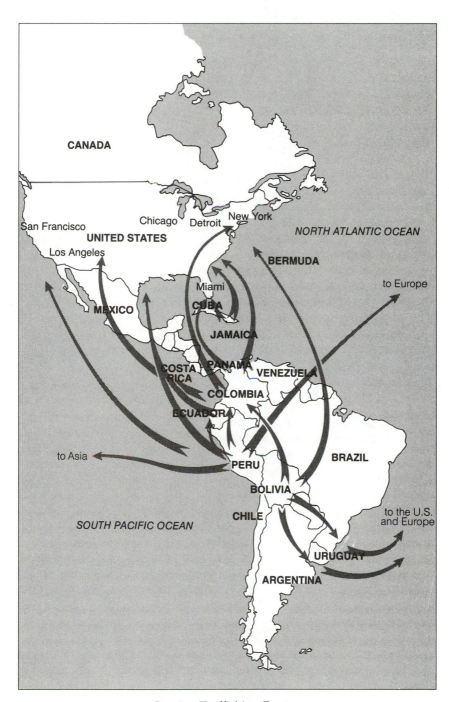

Cocaine-Trafficking Routes

Loran numbers.[u] He located the exact spot, went over the side with fins, mask, and snorkel and found the thing in 40 feet of water. Then he did some fishing and came back late in the afternoon with all the other boaters. He had his girlfriend and her kid with him, so everything looked ordinary and nobody looked suspicious. It's a clean arrangement.

By the time cocaine has been cut several times—with lactose, baking soda, caffeine, quinine, lidocaine, powdered laxatives, or even borax—to an average of 12% purity, it ranges in street price from $40 to $120 a gram. What started out as 500 kilograms of coca leaves worth $1,000 to $2,000 to the grower ultimately yields 8 kilos of street cocaine valued at perhaps $200,000.[v]

Fire in the Brain

Lured by the Lorelei of orgasmic pleasure, millions of Americans use cocaine each year—a snort in each nostril and the user is up and away for 20 minutes or so. Alert, witty, and with-it, the user has no hangover, no physical addiction, no lung cancer, and no holes in the arms or burned-out cells in the brain. The cocaine high is an immediate, intensely vivid, and sensation-enhancing experience. Moreover, it has the reputation of being a spectacular aphrodisiac: it is believed to create sexual desire, to heighten it, to increase sexual endurance, and to cure frigidity and impotence.

Given all these positives, no wonder cocaine became the all-American drug of the 1980s. And its use continues to permeate all levels of society, from Park Avenue to the inner city: lawyers and executives use cocaine; baby boomers and yuppies use cocaine; police officers, prosecutors, and prisoners use cocaine; politicians use cocaine; housewives and pensioners use cocaine; Democrats, Republicans, and Socialists use cocaine; students and stockbrokers and children and athletes use cocaine; even priests and members of Congress use cocaine.[51]

---

[u] Loran (from **LO**ng **RA**nge **N**avigation) is a navigational device that provides boaters with lines of positions derived from signals emitted from coastal-transmitting stations. Any given location offshore, described in terms of its Loran coordinates, can be found with almost pinpoint accuracy.

[v] Given changing demand, production levels, and interdiction efforts, the prices of coca and cocaine have fluctuated dramatically during the past decade. During the early 1980s, for example, the cocaleros (coca leaf growers) fetched $8 to $12 per kilo for their product. At the close of the decade this figure was down to $3.50, and at the beginning of the 1990s coca prices had collapsed to less than $1 per kilo. Similarly, a kilo of high-quality cocaine has fluctuated from a high of $65,000 in 1981 to a low of $14,000 in 1989 but back up to $30,000 to $35,000 in mid-1990. See *South Florida*, Nov. 1987, p. 74; *U.S. News & World Report*, 27 June 1988, p. 15; *New York Times*, 14 June 1990, pp. A1, B8; *Miami Herald*, 14 Aug. 1990, pp. 1A, 18A.

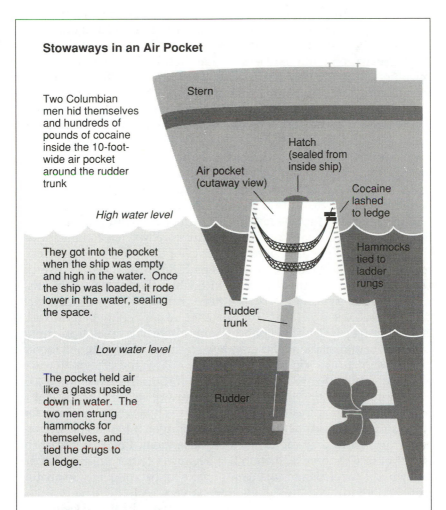

Stowaways in an Air Pocket

Two Columbian men hid themselves and hundreds of pounds of cocaine inside the 10-foot-wide air pocket around the rudder trunk

High water level

They got into the pocket when the ship was empty and high in the water. Once the ship was loaded, it rode lower in the water, sealing the space.

Low water level

The pocket held air like a glass upside down in water. The two men strung hammocks for themselves, and tied the drugs to a ledge.

Stern

Hatch (sealed from inside ship)

Air pocket (cutaway view)

Cocaine lashed to ledge

Hammocks tied to ladder rungs

Rudder trunk

Rudder

Two Men and Cocaine

On January 24, 1991, police scuba divers in New York Harbor were inspecting the hull of an oil tanker and came upon an unusual discovery: 366 pounds of cocaine, and two Colombian nationals tucked under the ship's rudder compartment. The stowaways had rafted to the compartment a few days earlier, when the ship was docked in Cartagena, and boarded the tanker while it was still above water, before it was loaded with its cargo of oil. While their smuggling routine was unique, they became prisoners by their own hands. They survived five stormy days at sea, eating only fruit and cheese, in the small compartment next to the roar of the ship's propeller. The two were arrested and charged with importation of a controlled substance.

The pleasure and feelings of power that cocaine engenders make its use a problematic recreational pursuit. In very small and occasional doses it is no more harmful than equally moderate doses of alcohol or marijuana, and infinitely less so than heroin, but there is a side to cocaine that can be very destructive. That euphoric lift, with its feelings of confidence and being on top of things that comes from but a few brief snorts, is short-lived and invariably followed by a letdown. Since the body does not develop any significant tolerance to cocaine, and since physical dependence similar to that on heroin never develops, the drug has been said to be nonaddicting. Yet there are many who would argue this position, pointing to the many chronic users who compulsively indulge in cocaine. Sidney Cohen of the Neuropsychiatric Institute at the Los Angeles School of Medicine, for example, suggests that the notion that cocaine does not produce addiction comes from the early professional literature, written at a time when the quantities of the drug used were smaller than those taken by contemporary users.[52] He adds that the high doses of cocaine currently used, combined with the frequency with which they are taken, produce a withdrawal syndrome characterized primarily by psychological depression. Others feel that what seems to be happening in these cases is only strong psychic dependence. Compulsive users seek the extreme mood elevation, elation, and grandiose feelings of heightened mental and physical prowess induced by the drug. When these begin to wane, a corresponding deep depression is felt, which is in such marked contrast to the users' previous states that they are strongly motivated to repeat the dose and restore their euphoria. Thus when chronic users try to stop using cocaine, they are often plunged into a severe depression from which only the drug can arouse them. But as noted at the outset of this chapter, addiction has become a rather imprecise term, and whether addiction to cocaine is physical or psychogenic (emanating from the mind), cocaine dependence is very real.[w]

In addition to the dependence potential, chronic cocaine use typically causes hyperstimulation, digestive disorders, nausea, loss of appetite, weight loss, tooth erosion, brain abscess, stroke, cardiac irregularities, occasional convulsions, and sometimes paranoid psychoses and delusions of persecution.[53] Moreover, repeated inhalation can result in erosions of the mucous membranes, including perforations of the nasal septum. A chronic runny nose is often a mark of the regular

---

[w] At the annual meeting of the Society for Neuroscience in 1985, researchers reported that the craving typically associated with cocaine cessation can be eased by drugs that stimulte dopamine production in the brain. Whether this finding will ultimately shed some light on the cocaine addiction debate is difficult to tell. See *New York Times*, 22 Oct. 1985, p. C5; Mary C. Ritz, R. J. Lamb, Steven R. Goldberg, and Michael J. Kuhar, ''Cocaine Receptors on Dopamine Transporters Are Related to Self-Administration of Cocaine,'' *Science*, 237 (Sept. 1987) pp. 1219–1223.

cocaine user. The reasons for these effects on the nose are well understood. Cocaine totally numbs the nasal membranes, which then shrink as their blood supply diminishes. When the drug wears off, the mucous membranes demand the blood supply that was withheld, and the nose becomes congested, with the symptoms of a head cold likely to follow. Any cocaine that remains undissolved in the nose can cause burns and sores, which can eventually lead to degeneration of the nasal mucous membranes or eat through the cartilage itself.[54]

Then there are the effects of cocaine use during pregnancy. Use of the drug reduces blood flow through the placenta, and such losses limit nutrients to the fetus, which retards growth. Cocaine-using women experience a significant increase in the rate of spontaneous abortion as compared with non–cocaine-using mothers. Maternal cocaine use contributes to the premature separation of the placenta from the uterus, resulting in both still births and premature infants. Babies who survive cocaine in utero suffer withdrawal symptoms and are at greater risk of stroke and respiratory ailments. Research findings also show an increased risk of Sudden Infant Death Syndrome (SIDS) in which the incidence among cocaine-exposed infants is 17% as compared with 1.6% in the general population.[55] As they grow, many cocaine-exposed infants experience emotional disorders, learning disabilities, and sensory-motor difficulties.[56]

These are the effects of snorting cocaine, the most common method of ingestion, but there are other ways of taking the drug, each of which can bring on an added spectrum of complications. One of these methods is freebasing, a phenomenon that has been known in the drug community for some two decades but moved into the mainstream of cocaine use only during the 1980s. Cocaine hydrochloride has a high melting point and thus cannot be efficiently smoked. As a result, some users produce a change in the cocaine salt form to a base form. More specifically, freebase cocaine is actually a different chemical product from cocaine itself. In the process of preparing freebase, street cocaine, which is usually in the form of a hydrochloride salt, is treated with a liquid base (such as buffered ammonia) to remove the hydrochloric acid. The free cocaine (cocaine in the base state, free of the hydrochloride acid, and hence the name freebase) is then dissolved in a solvent such as ether, from which the purified cocaine is crystallized. These crystals, having a lower melting point, are then crushed and used in a special heated glass pipe. Smoking freebase cocaine provides a quicker and more potent rush and a far more powerful high than regular cocaine and, as such, its use is that much more seductive. The freebasing process involves the use of ether, a highly volatile petroleum product that has exploded in the face of many a user.

Cocaine has also been used as a sex aid, a practice that has brought both pleasurable and disastrous results. A sprinkle of cocaine on the clitoris or just below the head of the penis will anesthetize the tissues and retard a sexual climax. But with persistent stimulation, the drug will ultimately promote an explosive orgasm. However, the urethra (the tube inside the penis or the vulva through which urine is eliminated) is very sensitive to cocaine. At a minimum, the drug will dry out the urethral membranes, which must remain moist to function properly. At a maximum, since the absorption rate of cocaine through the walls of the urethra is quite rapid, overdoses have been known to happen.[x]

As an aphrodisiac, cocaine is highly questionable. Research has found considerable differences in sexual responses to the same dosage level of cocaine, depending primarily on the setting of the usage and the background experiences of the user. Interestingly, the male sexual response to cocaine is different from that of women. For men, cocaine not only helps to prevent premature ejaculation, but at the same time permits prolonged intercourse before orgasm. Among women, achieving a climax under the influence of cocaine is often quite difficult. And finally, research also demonstrates that chronic, heavy users of cocaine typically experience sexual dysfunction.[57]

Among chronic users of cocaine, the intravenous use of the drug has become more noticeable in recent years. This route of administration produces an extremely rapid onset of the drug's effects, usually within 15 to 20 seconds, along with a rather powerful high. It also produces the more debilitating effects of psychoses and paranoid delusions similar to those of the amphetamine speed freak. These occur more rapidly than when cocaine is chronically snorted.[y] A related phenomenon is the intravenous use of cocaine in combination with another drug. Known as speedballing, the practice is not at all new. The classic speedball is a mixture of heroin and cocaine. It was referred to as such by the heroin-using community as early as the 1930s, and as whizbang as far back as 1918.[58] Whether the user's primary drug of choice is cocaine or heroin, the speedball intensifies the euphoric effect. It can also be quite dangerous: speedballing killed actor-comedian John Belushi in 1982.

---

[x] Perhaps the most extravagant complications associated with the intraurethral administration of cocaine were reported from New York Hospital/Cornell Medical Center in 1988. The patient was a 34-year-old male, and his use of cocaine in this manner touched off a series of chain reactions in his body that caused blood abnormalities, skin and muscle deterioration, and gangrene. The eventual consequences included the amputation of his penis, both of his legs above the knees, and 9 fingers. See John C. Mahler, Samuel Perry, and Bruce Sutton, "Intraurethral Cocaine Administration," *Journal of the American Medical Association*, 259 (3 June 1988), p. 3126.

[y] When cocaine was first introduced during the latter part of the nineteenth century, intramuscular injections were frequently employed. This mechanism, however, is not reported among contemporary users.

Whether the pattern of use involves snorting, freebasing, shooting, speedballing, or smoking (see Chapter 4), the hazards of cocaine use can go well beyond those already noted. Some individuals, likely few in number, are hypersensitive to cocaine, and as little as 20 milligrams can be fatal. Since cocaine is a potent stimulant that rapidly increases the blood pressure, sudden death can also occur from only small amounts among users suffering from coronary artery disease or weak cerebral blood vessels. Cocaine is also a convulsant that can induce major seizures and cause fatalities if emergency treatment is not immediately at hand. Postcocaine depression, if intense, can lead to suicide. If the dose is large enough, cocaine can be toxic and result in an overdose. For the majority of users, this can occur with as little as one gram, taken intravenously. When injecting cocaine, furthermore, the user is also at high risk of exposure to all that can result from the use of unsterile needles—hepatitis, infections, and even AIDS (see Chapter 6).[z]

Many different mechanisms have been used to classify cocaine users into different groups. Some classifications have been based on frequency and amount of use, whereas others have focused on motivations, routes of administration, or context of use.[59] Perhaps the most practical way of differentiating types of cocaine users is the simple four-fold classification of *experimenters, social-recreational users, involved users,* and *dysfunctional abusers*—a general classification that has been widely applied in the drug field for quite some time.

The experimenters are by far the largest group of cocaine users. They most frequently try cocaine a time or two in a social setting, but the drug does not play a significant role in their lives. They use cocaine experimentally because their social group relates the drug's effects as being pleasurable. Experimenters do not seek out cocaine but may use it when someone presents it to them in an appropriate setting. In this situation, they may snort the drug once or twice because it does something to them. As a University of Delaware senior commented in 1985:

> I generally don't use drugs, except maybe a little grass now
> and then. My only experience with coke was a few weeks ago

---

[z] Numerous cocaine-related deaths have resulted from body packing, a smuggling method. Small amounts of cocaine are packed into condoms, which are then swallowed or secreted in the rectum or vagina. Unless the carrier is a suspected cocaine courier or mule, the drug's detection by Customs agents is difficult. On many occasions one or more of these condoms have ruptured, releasing lethal amounts of pure cocaine into the carrier's body. In one case, more than five dozen cocaine-packed condoms were found in the stomach of a smuggler. See the *Wall Street Journal,* 5 Aug. 1982, pp. 1, 8; Kano (Nigeria) *Triumph,* 21 Aug. 1986, p. 16; Hong Kong *South China Morning Post,* 18 Sept. 1987, p. 4; Lisbon *Tal & Qual,* 7 Feb. 1986, p. 3; London *Sunday Times,* 26 Oct. 1986, p. 3; Dakar (Senegal) *Le Soleil,* 26 June 1990, p. 7; Richard Mackenzie, ''Borderline Victories in Drug War's Front Line,'' *Insight,* 14 Jan. 1991, pp. 8–17.

> in the dormitory. My roommate came in with a couple of other
> guys and started getting high on it. They kept trying to get me
> to do some, and finally I snorted some just for the heck of it.
> When I did, it was quite a blast at first, from my head all the
> way down, and then I felt like I was floating. After, I felt a little
> weird. . . . It was good.

Social-recreational users differ from experimenters primarily in
terms of frequency and continuity of consumption. For example, they
may use cocaine when they are at a party and someone presents the
opportunity. Cocaine still does not play a significant role in these users'
lives. They still do not actively seek out the drug but use it only because
it does something to them—it makes them feel good. A 28-year-old
Miami woman related:

> Partying can be even more fun with a few lines of coke. I
> never have any of my own, but usually I'll tie in with some
> guy who does. We'll get a little stoned and maybe go to bed.
> It's all in good fun. . . . Another time I was on a double date
> and this guy had some good toot. We drove up to Orlando and
> went into Disney World. Do you know what it's like goin'
> through the haunted mansion stoned like that? It's a whole
> different trip. . . .

For involved users, a major transition has taken place since the
social-recreational use. As users become involved with cocaine, they
also become drug seekers, and cocaine becomes significant to their
lives. Although they are still quite able to function—in school, on the
job, or as a parent or spouse—their proficiency in many areas begins
to decline markedly. Personal and social functioning tends to be
inversely related to the amount of time involved users spend with
cocaine. They still have control over their behavior, but their use of
the drug occurs with increasing frequency for some adaptive reason;
cocaine does something for them.

Involved cocaine users are of many types. Some use the drug to
deal with an unbearable work situation, indulging in controlled
amounts several times a day. Others use cocaine to enhance performance or bolster their self-esteem. And still a third group regularly
uses cocaine to deal with stress, anxiety, or nagging boredom. As one
involved user, a self-employed accountant, put it:

> I seem to be always uptight these days with almost everything
> I do. Everybody seems to always want something—my clients,
> my wife, the bank, the world. . . . A few lines [of cocaine]
> every two–three hours gets me through the day—through
> the tax returns, the tension at home, the bills, sex, whatever.

. . . Without the coke I'd probably have to be put away somewhere. . . .

The dysfunctional abusers are what have become known as the cokeheads, cokeaholics, and cokewhores. For them, cocaine has become the significant part of their lives. They are personally and socially dysfunctional and spend all of their time in cocaine-seeking, cocaine-taking, and other related activities. Moreover, they no longer have control over their cocaine use.

Although dysfunctional cocaine use is the least common pattern, it is nevertheless widespread. The list of those acknowledging such dysfunctional use to the media tends to sound like an excerpt from the Who's Who in entertainment and sports. A number of these have squandered as much as $1,000 a day on the drug—John Phillips, founder of The Mamas and the Papas singing group; his daughter Mackensie Phillips, who once starred in TV's "One Day at a Time"; guitarist Keith Richards of the Rolling Stones; John Lucas of the Washington Bullets; Carl Eller of the Minnesota Vikings; Thomas "Hollywood" Henderson of the Dallas Cowboys; David Crosby of The Byrds and Crosby, Stills and Nash, and Stacy Keach, TV's Mike Hammer. To a lesser extent there was Lawrence Taylor of football's New York Giants, and New York Mets pitcher Dwight Gooden. And at the extreme there was Academy Award winner Julia Phillips, producer of *The Sting* and *Close Encounters of a Third Kind,* who spent more than $1 million on cocaine over a 10-year period. Phillips became a dedicated cocaine user during the 18-hour days of filming *Close Encounters;* in a Time magazine interview, she commented:

> It didn't do much for personal relationships, and a lot of this business is personal relationships. I could stay up all night thinking up ideas, but I wasn't likely to present them in the nicest fashion possible. I mean tact goes out the window. . . . I looked like someone out of Dachau. I had terrible hallucinations, particularly when night fell. There was always a prowler outside my front door with evil in his heart and a gun in his hand. I thought I had bugs coming out of my skin. My little girl used to follow me around the house with a deodorant can spraying behind me because she hated the smell from freebasing.[60]

POSTSCRIPT

For how many more years pervasive heroin and cocaine use will persist in the United States is difficult to predict. In all likelihood, it will be for quite some time. Heroin use has been around for almost a century, and cocaine use for an even longer period. Treatment, prevention, and law-enforcement efforts have had some positive effects, but the problems are stubborn and recurring. The legalization of heroin and cocaine would not appear to be the answer, for both drugs are far too seductive to place uncontrolled on the open market.

Looking toward the future, one scenario might be plausible. The research, treatment, education, prevention, and law-enforcement efforts with respect to heroin use have not solved that problem, although to a great extent they seem to have contained it. As noted earlier, the number of estimated heroin users hit a level of 500,000 during the mid-1970s and has remained there ever since—more or less. The education and prevention initiatives targeting marijuana seem to have had some impact, and its use has been declining at a steady rate. It, too, may level off and remain at a plateau at some point in the near future. Perhaps the same situation will occur with cocaine.

Notes

1. Ruth R. Levine, *Pharmacology: Drug Actions and Reactions* (Boston: Little, Brown, 1973), p. 336.
2. Erich Goode, *Drugs in American Society*, 3rd ed. (New York: Alfred A. Knopf, 1989), pp. 25–26.
3. *New York Times*, 17 Aug. 1972, p. 16.
4. Alfred W. McCoy, *The Politics of Heroin in Southeast Asia* (New York: Harper & Row, 1972); Editors of Newsday, *The Heroin Trail* (New York: New American Library, 1974); Jon A. Wiant, "Narcotics in the Golden Triangle," *Washington Quarterly*, 8 (Fall 1985), pp. 125–140.
5. For an examination of the hill tribes that populate the Golden Triangle and how opium cultivation impacts on their culture, see Paul Lewis and Elaine Lewis, *Peoples of the Golden Triangle: Six Tribes in Thailand* (London: Thames and Hudson, 1984); Claudia Simms and Thomas Tarleton, "The Lisu of the Golden Triangle," *The World & I*, Oct. 1987, pp. 461–473.
6. Bureau of International Narcotics Matters, *International Narcotics Control Strategy Report* (Washington, DC: Department of State, Mar. 1990), p. 18.
7. For perspectives on the history of opium, the opium culture, and the processing of opium into heroin, see Dean Latimer and Jeff Goldberg, *Flowers in the Blood: The Story of Opium* (New York: Franklin Watts, 1981); Joseph Westermeyer, *Poppies, Pipes, and People: Opium and Its Use in Laos* (Berkeley: University of California Press, 1982); Peter W. White, "The Poppy," *National Geographic*, Feb. 1985, pp. 142–189.
8. *Newsweek*, 10 Oct. 1984, p. 29. See also, Nicosia (Cyprus) *Ta Nea*, 8 June 1986, p. 11; Copenhagen (Denmark) *Berlingske Tidende*, 3 May 1990, p. 4.
9. *New York Times*, 21 May 1984, p. B4.
10. *U.S. News & World Report*, 11 Mar. 1985, p. 47; and White, p. 155.
11. Dan J. Lettieri, Mollie Sayers, and Helen Wallenstein, eds., *Theories on Drug Abuse: Selected Contemporary Perspectives* (Rockville, MD: National Institute on Drug Abuse, 1980).

12. David P. Ausubel, "Causes and Types of Drug Addiction: A Psychosocial View," *Psychiatric Quarterly*, 35 (1961), 523–531; Jonathan D. Cowan, David C. Kay, Gary L. Neidert, Frances E. Ross, and Susan Belmore, "Drug Abusers: Defeated and Joyless," in *Problems of Drug Dependence*, ed. Louis S. Harris (Rockville, MD: National Institute on Drug Abuse, 1979), pp. 170–176.
13. Calvin J. Frederick, "Drug Abuse: A Self-Destructive Enigma," *Maryland State Medical Journal*, 22 (1973), pp. 19–21.
14. Alfred R. Lindesmith, *Opiate Addiction* (Bloomington, IN: Principia Press, 1947); reprinted edition, *Addiction and Opiates* (New York: Aldine, 1968).
15. Lettieri, Sayers, and Wallenstein.
16. Sandra B. Coleman, "The Family Trajectory: A Circular Journey to Drug Abuse," *Family Factors in Substance Abuse*, ed. B. Ellis (Rockville, MD: National Institute on Drug Abuse, 1978).
17. Kenneth Chapman, "A Typical Drug Addict," *New York State Health News*, 28 Aug. 1951.
18. Orin Ross Yost, *The Bane of Drug Addiction* (New York: Macmillan, 1964), pp. 68–69, 82.
19. See Harvey B. Milkman and Howard J. Shaffer, eds., *The Addictions: Multidisciplinary Perspectives and Treatments* (Lexington, MA: Lexington Books, 1985).
20. Richard P. Rettig, Manual J. Torres, and Gerald R. Garrett, *Manny: A Criminal Addict's Story* (Boston: Houghton Mifflin, 1977), pp. 33–34.
21. Rettig, Torres, and Garrett, p. 35.
22. Lindesmith, pp. 28–31.
23. David P. Ausubel, *Drug Addiction* (New York: Random House, 1958), p. 26; see also Isidor Chein, Donald L. Gerard, Robert S. Lee, and Eva Rosenfeld, *The Road to H: Narcotics, Delinquency, and Social Policy* (New York: Basic Books, 1964), pp. 113, 248.
24. A. S. Tuchler, "The Narcotic Habit: Further Observations on the Ambulatory Method of Treatment," *California Eclectic Medical Journal*, 38 (1917), pp. 261–264.
25. See Alex W. Young, "Skin Complications of Heroin Addiction: Bullous Impetigo," *New York State Journal of Medicine*, 15 June 1973, pp. 1681-1684; B. W. Pace, W. Doscher, and I. B. Margolis, "The Femoral Triangle: A Potential Death Trap for the Drug Abuser," *New York State Journal of Medicine*, Dec. 1984, pp. 596–598; Wayne Tuckson and Bernard B. Anderson, "Mycotic Aneurysms in Intravenous Drug Abuse: Diagnosis and Management," *Journal of the National Medical Association*, 77 (1985), pp. 99–102; Glenn W. Geelhoed, "The Addict's Angioaccess: Complications of Exotic Vascular Injection Sites," *New York State Journal of Medicine*, Dec. 1984, pp. 585–586. For a comprehensive overview of medical complications associated with heroin addiction, see Jerome J. Platt, *Heroin Addiction: Theory, Research, and Treatment* (Malabar, FL: Robert E. Krieger, 1986), pp. 80–102.
26. For a discussion of the causes of heroin overdose, see Peter G. Bourne, ed., *Acute Drug Emergencies: A Treatment Manual* (New York: Academic Press, 1976); David M. Petersen and Earl L. Mahfuz, "Heroin Overdose Deaths: A Critical Examination of Deaths Attributed to Acute Reaction to Dosage," *Sandoz Psychiatric Spectator*, 10 (1977), pp. 5–8.

27. Paul J. Goldstein, Douglas S. Lipton, Edward Preble, Ira Sobel, Tom Miller, William Abbott, William Paige, and Franklin Soto, "The Marketing of Street Heroin in New York City," *Journal of Drug Issues*, 14 (Summer 1984), pp. 553–566.
28. Goldstein et al., p. 559.
29. K. W. Bentley and D. G. Hardy, "New Potential Analgesics in the Morphine Series," *Chemical Society Proceedings*, 1963, p. 220. See also B. T. Alford, R. L. Burkhart, and W. P. Johnson, "Etorphine and Diprenorphine as Immobilizing and Reversing Agents in Captive and Free-Ranging Mammals," *Journal of the American Veterinary Medical Association*, 164 (1974), pp. 702–705; Jerry McAdams, "Elephant Juice," *Quarter Horse Track*, Aug. 1981, pp. 6–9.
30. *Newsweek*, 5 Jan. 1981, p. 21.
31. *USA Today*, 15 Feb. 1985, p. 1A; *New York Times*, 24 Mar. 1985, p. 22; *Time*, 8 Apr. 1985, p. 61; *Business Week*, 24 June 1985, pp. 101–102; *U.S. News & World Report*, 5 Aug. 1985, p. 14; *NIDA Notes*, Spring/Summer 1989, pp. 40–41; *Drug Enforcement Report*, 25 Oct. 1988, p. 7; *Street Pharmacologist*, 11 (Mar. 1987), p. 3; *Substance Abuse Report*, 1 Mar. 1991, p. 8.
32. *New York Times*, 4 Feb. 1991, pp. 1, 30, B1, B2; *Substance Abuse Report*, 15 Feb. 1991, pp. 2–3; *Newsweek*, 18 Feb. 1991, p. 58; *Time*, 18 Feb. 1991, p. 45.
33. National Institute on Drug Abuse, *Data From the Drug Abuse Warning Network, Annual Trend Data* (Rockville, MD: National Institute on Drug Abuse, 1990).
34. John C. Ball and Carl D. Chambers, *The Epidemiology of Opiate Addiction in the United States* (Springfield, IL: Chs. C. Thomas, 1970), p. 147.
35. Leon Gibson Hunt, *Recent Spread of Heroin Use in the United States: Unanswered Questions* (Washington, DC: Drug Abuse Council, 1974). See also Joan D. Rittenhouse, ed., *The Epidemiology of Heroin and Other Narcotics* (Rockville, MD: National Institute on Drug Abuse, 1977).
36. *Active Narcotic Addicts as of December 31, 1967, Annual Report,* (Washington, DC: Bureau of Narcotics, 1968).
37. Zili Amstel, Carl L. Erhardt, Donald C. Krug, and Donald P. Conwell, "The Narcotics Register Development of a Case Register" (Paper presented at the Thirty-first Annual Meeting of the Committee on Problems of Drug Dependence, National Academy of Sciences, National Research Council, Palo Alto, California, 25 Feb. 1969).
38. Ball and Chambers, pp. 71–73.
39. For the first of these surveys, see Carl D. Chambers, *An Assessment of Drug Use in the General Population* (Albany: New York State Narcotic Addiction Control Commission, 1970). Whereas this first survey focused exclusively on New York, subsequent efforts conducted by the National Institute on Drug Abuse have examined the nation as a whole.
40. Carl D. Chambers, James A. Inciardi, and Harvey A. Siegal, *Chemical Coping: A Report on Legal Drug Use in the United States* (New York: Spectrum Publications, 1975), p. 2.
41. Heroin Indicators Task Force, *Heroin Indicators Trend Report, 1976–1978—An Update* (Rockville, MD: National Institute on Drug Abuse, 1979), p. 16.

42. The White House, Drug Abuse Policy Office, Office of Policy Development, *National Strategy for Prevention of Drug Abuse and Drug Trafficking* (Washington, DC: U.S. Government Printing Office, 1984); National Drug Enforcement Policy Board, *National and International Drug Law Enforcement Strategy* (Washington, DC: Government Printing Office, 1987); Edgar H. Adams, Ann J. Blanken, Joseph C. Gfroerer, and Lorraine D. Ferguson, *Overview of Selected Drug Trends* (Rockville, MD: National Institute on Drug Abuse, Division of Epidemiology and Statistical Analysis, 1988); Bureau of Justice Assistance, Office of Justice Programs, *FY 1988 Report on Drug Control* (Washington, DC: U.S. Department of Justice, 1989).

43. *Newsweek*, 25 Feb. 1985, p. 23.

44. Cited by H. Wayne Morgan, *Drugs in America: A Social History, 1800–1920* (Syracuse, NY: Syracuse University Press, 1981), p. 93.

45. See Nils Noya, "Cocaine Crisis in Bolivia" (Paper presented at What Works? International Perspectives on Drug Abuse Treatment and Prevention Research, New York City, October 22–25, 1989); *New York Times*, 2 Dec. 1986, pp. A1, A9; *Latin America Reports, Andean Group Report*, 4 Sept. 1986, p. 2; *Time*, 28 July 1986, pp. 12–14; *Miami Herald*, 9 Dec. 1985, pp. 1A, 6A; Robert B. South, "Coca in Bolivia," *Geographical Review*, 67 (Jan. 1977), pp. 22–23; Edmundo Morales, *Cocaine: White Gold Rush in Peru* (Tucson: University of Arizona Press, 1989); Rensselaer W. Lee, *The White Labyrinth: Cocaine and Political Power* (New Brunswick, NJ: Transaction Publishers, 1989); Donald J. Mabry, *The Latin American Narcotics Trade and U.S. National Security* (Westport, CT: Greenwood Press, 1989); Anthony Daniels, *Coups and Cocaine: Two Journeys in South America* (Woodstock, NY: Overlook Press, 1987); Bureau of International Narcotics Matters.

46. For more complete descriptions of Amazonia, see Brian Kelly and Mark London, *Amazon* (San Diego: Harcourt Brace Jovanovich, 1983); Roger D. Stone, *Dreams of Amazonia* (New York: Viking, 1985); Redmond O'Hanlon, *In Trouble Again: A Journey Between the Orinoco and the Amazon* (New York: Vintage Books, 1990); Joe Kane, *Running the Amazon* (New York: Alfred A. Knopf, 1989).

47. See Ronald Wright, *Cut Stones and Crossroads: A Journey into the Two Worlds of Peru* (New York: Viking, 1984), p. 42.

48. The coca leaf and paste trades are so visible in Tingo Maria that they have attracted the attention of the media throughout the Americas. For example, see Lima *Panamericana Television Network*, 0200 GMT, 8 June 1987; Santiago (Chile) *Que Pasa*, 8 Feb. 1990, pp. 41–43; Sao Paulo *O Estado Se Sao Paulo*, 29 Oct. 1989, p. 16; Lima *El Nacional*, 3 Apr. 1988, pp. IV–VII; *Miami Herald*, 17 Apr. 1987, p. 8A; *Newsweek*, 31 Mar. 1986, p. 32; Mark Maden, "The Big Push," *Sierra*, 73 (Nov./Dec. 1988), pp. 66–75; Lima *Television Peruana*, 0100 GMT, 8 Feb. 90.

49. Eduardo Crawley, *The Drugs Trade in Latin America* (London: Latin American Newsletters, Ltd., 1990), p. 10.

50. For descriptions of the structure and operations of the Colombian cocaine cartels, see United States Attorneys and the Attorney General of the United States, *Drug Trafficking: A Report to the President of the United States, August 3, 1989* (Washington, DC: U.S. Department of Justice, 1989); Guy Gugliotta

and Jeff Leen, *Kings of Cocaine* (New York: Simon and Schuster, 1989); Paul Eddy, Hugo Sabogal, and Sara Walden, *The Cocaine Wars* (New York: W.W. Norton, 1988). Of related interest here are Charles Nicholl, *The Fruit Palace: An Odyssey Through Colombia's Cocaine Underground* (New York: St. Martin's Press, 1985); Berkeley Rice, *Trafficking: The Boom and Bust of the Air America Cocaine Ring* (New York: Charles Scribner's Sons, 1989); Alvaro Camacho Guizado, *Droga y Sociedad en Colombia* (Cali: Universedad del Valle, 1988).

51. See *U.S. News & World Report*, 22 Mar. 1982, pp. 27–29; *Wall Street Journal*, 22 Sept. 1983, pp. 1, 22; *Time*, 2 Apr. 1984, p. 87; *USA Today*, 3 July 1984, p. 3A; *New York Times*, 28 Nov. 1984, p. A 18; *Miami Herald*, 14 Mar. 1985, p. 7A; *Psychology Today*, Jan. 1985, p.20.

52. Sidney Cohen, "Recent Developments in the Use of Cocaine," *Bulletin on Narcotics*, Apr.–June 1984, p. 9.

53. Lawrence Gould, Chitra Gopalaswamy, Chandrakant Patel, and Robert Betzu, "Cocaine-Induced Myocardial Infarction," *New York State Journal of Medicine*, Nov. 1985, pp. 660–661; R. Fishel, G. Hamamoto, A Barbul, V. Niji, and G. Efron, "Cocaine Colitis: Is This a New Syndrome?" *Colon and Rectum*, 28 (1985), pp. 264–266; Louis Cregler and Herbert Mark, "Relation of Stroke to Cocaine Abuse," *New York State Journal of Medicine*, Feb. 1987, pp. 128–129; A. Naveen Rao, "Brain Abscess: A Complication of Cocaine Inhalation," *New York State Journal of Medicine*, Oct. 1988, pp. 548–550; Frank H. Gawin and Everett H. Ellinwood, "Cocaine and Other Stimulants: Actions, Abuse, and Treatment," *New England Journal of Medicine*, 318 (5 May 1988), pp. 1173–1182; John Grabowski, ed., *Cocaine: Pharmacology, Effects, and Treatment of Abuse* (Rockville, MD: National Institute on Drug Abuse, 1984).

54. See Maria-Elena Rodriguez, "Treatment of Cocaine Abuse: Medical and Psychiatric Consequences," pp. 97–111 in Knife K. Redda, Charles A. Walker, and Gene Barnett, eds., *Cocaine, Marijuana, Designer Drugs: Chemistry, Pharmacology, and Behavior* (Boca Raton, FL: CRC Press, 1989).

55. "Cocaine Abuse," *NIDA Capsules*, November 1989, p. 2.

56. Diana B. Petitti and Charlotte Coleman, "Cocaine and the Risk of Low Birth Weight," *American Journal of Public Health*, 80 (Jan. 1990), pp. 25–28; Ira J. Chasnoff, Dan R. Griffith, Scott MacGregor, Kathryn Dirkes, and Kayreen A. Burnes, "Temporal Patterns of Cocaine Use in Pregnancy," *Journal of the American Medical Association*, 261 (24/31 Mar. 1989), pp. 1741–1744; *NIDA Notes*, 3 (Aug. 1986), pp. 3–4; James N. Hall, "Impact of Mother's Cocaine Use," *Street Pharmacologist*, 11 (Oct. 1987), p. 1.

57. Patrick T Macdonald, Dan Waldorf, Craig Reinarman, and Sheigla Murphy, "Heavy Cocaine Use and Sexual Behavior," *Journal of Drug Issues*, 18 (Summer 1988), pp. 437–455.

58. See Eric Partridge, *A Dictionary of the Underworld* (New York: Bonanza Books, 1961), pp. 665, 770; Harold Wentworth and Stuart Berg Flexner, *Dictionary of American Slang* (New York: Thomas Y. Crowell, 1975), p. 507; Richard A. Spears, *Slang and Euphemism* (Middle Village, NY: Jonathan David, 1981), p. 369.

59. See, for example, Nannette Stone, Marlene Fromme, and Daniel Kogan, *Cocaine: Seduction and Solution* (New York: Pinnacle, 1984).

60. *Time*, 6 July 1981, p. 63.

CHAPTER FOUR

HURRICANE CRACK!

The earliest accounts of coca are contained in the writings of historians who chronicled both the Spanish conquests in South America in the sixteenth century and the Spanish travelers and Jesuit missionaries who followed in their wake. Perhaps the first in this regard was the Spanish soldier and historian Pedro de Cieza de Leon (1518–1560), who commented in 1552:

> I have observed in all parts of the *West Indies*, where I have been, that the natives delight in holding herbs, roots, or twigs of trees in their mouths. Thus, in the territory of *Antiocha*, they use a small Herb called *Coca*. . . .
>
> Throughout all *Peru*, from the time they rise in the morning till they go to bed at night, they are never without this *Coca* in their mouths. The reason some *Indians* to whom I put the question, gave me for so doing, was, that it made them insensible to hunger, and added to them strength and vigor.
>
> This *Coca* is planted in the Mountains *Andes*, where it grows up to little trees, which they cherish and nurse up carefully. So highly was this *Coca* valued in Peru in the years 1548, '49, '50, and '51, that I believe that no plant in the world, except Spice could equal it.[1]

Cieza de Leon attributed the popularity of coca among the natives of Peru to be the result of an "ill habit," as he put it, "and fit for such people as they are." He also noted coca's economic value, reporting that many plantations yielded coca crops valued at "80,000 pieces-of-eight a year," and that "several *Spaniards* got estates by buying and selling *Coca*, or bartering for it in the Indian markets." What Cieza de Leon likely never imagined was the impact that coca and coca products

105

would eventually have on the state of world affairs and the eventual course of history during the closing decades of the twentieth century.

THE "DISCOVERY" OF CRACK

The first mention of crack-cocaine in the major media occurred on November 17, 1985.[a] Buried within the pages of that Monday edition of the prestigious *New York Times,* journalist Donna Boundy, in writing about a local drug abuse treatment program, unceremoniously commented: "Three teenagers have sought this treatment already this year . . . for cocaine dependence resulting from the use of a new form of the drug called 'crack' or rock-like pieces of prepared 'freebase' (concentrated) cocaine."[2]

Although Boundy, like so many after her, had erred in describing crack as "freebase" or "concentrated" cocaine,[b] her mere mentioning of what was ostensibly an old drug initiated a major media event. Crack suddenly took on a life of its own, and in less than 11 months the *New York Times,*[c] the *Washington Post,* the *Los Angeles Times,* the wire services, *Time, Newsweek,* and *U.S. News & World Report* had among them served the nation with more than 1,000 stories in which crack had figured prominently. Or as social critic Malcolm Gladwell recalled the episode: ". . . coverage feeding coverage, stories of addiction and squalor multiplying across the land."[3] And then CBS capped their reporting with "48 Hours on Crack Street," a prime-time presentation that reached 15 million viewers and became one of the highest-rated documentaries in the history of television. Not to be outdone, NBC offered "Cocaine Country," culminating a six-month stretch in which the network had broadcast more than 400 reports on drug abuse.

As the crack hysteria was mounting during the summer of 1986, a number of researchers in the drug community were somewhat perplexed. While *Newsweek* claimed that crack was the biggest story

---

[a] The media story of crack can actually be traced to the latter part of 1984 when the Los Angeles dailies began reporting on local "rock houses" where small pellets of cocaine could be had for as little as $25 (for example, *Los Angeles Times,* 25 Nov. 1984, pp. CC1, CC8. *Newsweek* (11 Feb. 1985, p. 33) later gave a half page to the Los Angeles item, but the term crack was never used, and little attention was given to the matter.

[b] Rather than "concentrated" or "purified" cocaine, crack might be better described as the "fast-food" analog of cocaine.

[c] Following Boundy's brief mention of crack earlier in November, it was likely that the front page story in the November 29, 1985 issue of the *Times,* headlined "A New Purified Form of Cocaine Causes Alarm as Abuse Increases," represented the beginning of the drug's concentrated media attention.

since Vietnam and the fall of the Nixon presidency,[4] and other media giants compared the spread of crack with the plagues of medieval Europe, researchers were finding crack to be not a national epidemic but a phenomenon isolated to a few inner city neighborhoods in less than a dozen urban areas. By late August, crack hysteria had reached such proportions that the Drug Enforcement Administration (DEA) felt compelled to respond. Based on reports from its field agents and informants in cities throughout the country, a DEA report concluded:

> Crack is readily available in Atlanta, Boston, Detroit, Houston, Kansas City, Miami, New York City, Newark, San Diego, San Francisco, Seattle, and St. Louis. Availability at some level has also been reported in Dallas, Denver, Los Angeles, Minneapolis, Phoenix, and Washington, D.C. Crack generally is not available in Chicago, New Orleans, and Philadelphia.
>
> Crack is currently the subject of considerable media attention. The result has been a distortion of the public perception of the extent of crack use as compared to the use of other drugs. With multi-kilogram quantities of cocaine hydrochloride available and with snorting continuing to be the primary route of cocaine administration, *crack presently appears to be a secondary rather than primary problem in most areas.*[5]

Curiously, most of the major newspapers, networks, and weekly magazines ignored the DEA report. And crack media coverage experienced significant declines only after the revelations about Lt. Col. Oliver L. North and the Iran-contra connection toward the close of 1986 took up most of the front-page space.

In contrast with the media contention that crack was everywhere, observations in Miami during the summer of 1986 tended to concur with DEA's position.[6] Additional support in this regard came from New York City. Throughout 1986 crack seemed to be concentrated in the city's Washington Heights section, a neighborhood at the northern end of Manhattan Island. Many of the streets in Washington Heights had been transformed into outdoor drug marketplaces. One of the more curious aspects of the situation was that the streets were invariably clogged with cars—cars from other parts of New York City, from its suburbs, its neighboring states, and other locations.[7] If you lived outside of Washington Heights at that time, crack was generally unavailable. And as Dr. Sidney H. Schnoll of Northwestern University Medical School commented about Chicago late in the summer of 1986: "It's a hoax! There's just no crack in Chicago!"[8]

In an alternative direction, *Newsweek* described the crack scene as "an inferno of craving and despair."[9] *Time* stated it somewhat differently: "In minutes the flash high is followed by a crashing low that can leave a user craving another hit.''[10] And then there was the story of Katrina Linton in *USA Today:*

> Katrina Linton was 17 when she first walked into a crack house in the Bronx. By then she was selling her body to crack dealers just to support her $900-a-day habit.[11]

In these and other stories the implication was clear: crack led the user almost immediately into the nightmare worlds of Charles Adams, Stephen King, and Rod Serling, from which there was little chance of return. But to researchers and clinicians in the drug field who remembered the media's portrayal of the PCP ''epidemic'' a decade earlier, reports of the pervasiveness of crack were looked upon with skepticism. And interestingly, both the media and drug professionals were right about what they were saying. But at the same time, both were wrong as well. During the summer and fall of 1986, contrary to media claims, crack indeed had not been an epidemic drug problem in the United States. Crack was there all right, but it was not until the beginning of 1987 that it began to assert itself, eventually becoming perhaps the most degrading drug of the century.

UNRAVELING CRACK-COCAINE

The history of crack dates back to at least the early 1970s, to a time when cocaine was still known as charlie, corrine, bernice, schoolboy, and the ''rich man's drug.'' But to fully understand the evolution of crack-cocaine, a short diversion into a few other products of the coca leaf is warranted. More specifically, freebase and coca paste, both addressed briefly in Chapter 3, are prominent players in the story of crack.

From Powder-Cocaine to Freebase-Cocaine

During the late 1960s when cocaine had begun its initial trek from the underground to mainstream society, most users viewed it as a relatively safe drug. They inhaled it in relatively small quantities, and use typically occurred within a social-recreational context.[12] But as the availability of cocaine increased in subsequent years, so too did the number of users and the mechanisms for ingesting it. Some began sprinkling street cocaine on tobacco or marijuana and smoking it as a cigarette or in a pipe, but this method did not produce effects distinctly different from inhalation or snorting.[13] But a new alternative soon became available, freebasing, the smoking of freebase cocaine.

Freebase cocaine is actually a different chemical product than cocaine itself. As detailed in Chapter 3, in the process of freebasing, cocaine hydrochloride is transformed to the base state in a crystalline form. The crystals are then crushed and used in a special glass pipe. By 1977 it was estimated that there were some 4,000,000 users of cocaine in the United States,[14] with as many as 10% of these freebasing the drug exclusively.[15] Yet few outside of the drug-using and drug research and treatment communities were even aware of the existence of the freebase culture. And too, an even lesser number had an understanding of the new complications that freebasing had introduced to the cocaine scene.

The complications are several. First, cocaine in any of its forms is highly seductive. With freebasing, the euphoria is more intense than when the drug is inhaled. Moreover, this profound euphoria subsides into irritable craving after only a few minutes, thus influencing many users to continue freebasing for days at a time—until either they, or their drug supplies, are fully exhausted. Second, the practice of freebasing is expensive. When snorting cocaine, a single gram can last the social user an entire weekend or longer. With street cocaine ranging in price anywhere from $40 to $120 a gram depending on availability and purity, even this method of ingestion can be an expensive recreational pursuit. Yet with freebasing, the cost factor can undergo a geometric increase. Habitual users have been known to freebase continuously for three or four days without sleep, using up to 150 grams of cocaine in a 72-hour period.[16] Third, one special danger of freebasing is the proximity of highly flammable ether (or rum when it is used instead of water as a coolant in the pipe) to an open flame. This problem is enhanced since the user is generally suffering from a loss of coordination produced by the cocaine or a combination of cocaine and alcohol. As such, there have been many freebasing situations where the volatile concoction has exploded in the face of the user.

By 1980 reports of the problems associated with cocaine freebasing had begun to reach a national audience, crystallized by the near death by explosion of comedian-actor Richard Pryor, presumably the result of freebasing.[d]

From Cocaine and Freebase to Pasta Basica de Cocaina

Common in the drug-using communities of Colombia, Bolivia, Venezuela, Ecuador, Peru, and Brazil is the use of coca paste, known to most South Americans as basuco, susuko, pasta basica de cocaina, or just simply pasta.[17] Perhaps best known as basuco, and as detailed

---

[d] Although Pryor denied that he had been using cocaine at the time of the June 1980 explosion, he later admitted that he had been freebasing for three days prior to the event (see *Time*, 6 July 1981, p. 63). It might also be noted that in a 1986 interview with Barbara Walters, Pryor once again changed his story, claiming that the fire was the result of a suicide attempt, because he couldn't overcome his dependence on freebase.

in Chapter 3, coca paste is one of the intermediate products in the processing of the coca leaf into cocaine. It is typically smoked straight or in cigarettes mixed with either tobacco or marijuana.

The smoking of coca paste became popular in South America beginning in the early 1970s. It was readily available, inexpensive, had a high cocaine content, and was absorbed quickly. As the phenomenon was studied, however, it was quickly realized that paste smoking was far more serious than any other form of cocaine use. In addition to cocaine, paste contains traces of all the chemicals used to initially process the coca leaves—kerosene, sulfuric acid, methanol, benzoic acid, and the oxidized products of these solvents, plus any number of other alkaloids that are present in the coca leaf.[18] One analysis undertaken in Colombia in 1986 found, in addition to all of these chemicals, traces of brick dust, leaded gasoline, ether, and various talcs.[19]

When the smoking of paste was first noted in South America it seemed to be restricted to the coca processing regions of Bolivia, Colombia, Ecuador, and Peru, appealing primarily to low-income groups because of its cheap price compared with that of refined cocaine.[20] By the early 1980s, however, it had spread to other South American nations and to numerous segments of the social strata. Throughout the decade paste smoking further expanded to become a major drug problem for much of South America.[21] At the same time, coca paste made its way to the United States, first to Miami, its initial smuggling port of entry, and then elsewhere.[22] Interestingly, the paste quickly became known to young North American users as ''bubble gum,'' likely because of the phonetic association of the South American *basuco* with the American Bazooka bubble gum.[e]

The Coca Paste/Crack-Cocaine Connection

Contrary to popular belief, crack is not a new substance, first having been reported in the literature during the early 1970s.[23] At that time, however, knowledge of crack, known then as base or rock (not to be confused with rock cocaine—a cocaine hydrochloride product for

---

[e] During the latter part of the 1980s, a new form of coca paste smoking was noticed, principally in Brazil. For years in the nations of Peru, Bolivia, Ecuador, Argentina, and Brazil, the term pitillo (also petilho, and pitilio in Portuguese) had referred to a marijuana cigarette, or marijuana laced with coca paste. The new pitillo, however, also referred to in parts of Brazil as Bolivian crack, was marijuana and coca paste residue— the dregs left in the processing drum after coca paste precipitate had been removed. Although no analyses of this residue have been reported in the literature, it is suspected that the product has even higher concentrations of sulfuric acid and petroleum products than does coca paste. See Sao Paulo *Folha de Sao Paulo*, 30 July 1986, p. 15; Cochabamba *Los Tiempos*, 13 Oct. 1986, p. 5; Sao Paulo *O Estado de Sao Paulo*, 10 Nov. 1990, p. 5; Rio de Janeiro *O Globo*, 30 Nov. 1986, p. 18; Buenos Aires *La Prensa*, 20 June 1987, p. 9; Sao Paulo *Veja*, 12 Dec. 1990, pp. 22-23.

intranasal snorting), seemed to be restricted to segments of cocaine's freebasing subculture. Crack is processed from cocaine hydrochloride by using ammonia or baking soda and water, and heating it to remove the hydrochloride. The result is a pebble-sized crystalline form of cocaine base.

Crack is neither freebase cocaine nor purified cocaine. Part of the confusion about what crack actually is comes from the different ways that the word freebase is used in the drug community. Freebase (the noun) is a drug, a cocaine product converted to the base state from cocaine hydrochloride after adulterants have been chemically removed. Crack is converted to the base state without removing the adulterants. Freebasing (the act) means to inhale vapors of cocaine base, of which crack is but one form. Finally, crack is not purified cocaine, for during its processing, the baking soda remains as a salt, thus reducing its homogeneity somewhat. Informants in the Miami drug subculture indicate that the purity of crack ranges as high as 80% but generally contains much of the filler and impurities found in the original cocaine hydrochloride, along with some of the baking soda (sodium bicarbonate) and cuts (expanders for increasing bulk) from the processing. And interestingly, crack gets its name from the fact that the residue of sodium bicarbonate often causes a crackling sound when the substance is smoked.[f]

Crack was available in the drug communities of the early 1970s for only a short period of time before it was discarded by freebase-cocaine aficionados as an inferior product. Many of them referred to it as "garbage freebase" because of the many impurities it contained. In this regard, a 42-year-old Miami cocaine user commented in 1986:

> Of course crack is nothing new. The only thing that's new is the name. Years ago it was called rock, base, or freebase, although it really isn't true freebase. It was just an easier way to get something that gave a more potent rush, done the same way as now with baking soda. It never got too popular among the 1970s cokeheads because it was just not as pure a product as conventional freebase.

The rediscovery of crack seemed to occur simultaneously on the East and West Coasts early in the 1980s. As a result of the Colombian

---

[f] Some comment seems warranted on the practice of referring to crack as smokable cocaine. Technically, crack is not smoked. Smoking implies combustion, burning, and the inhalation of smoke. Tobacco is smoked. Marijuana is smoked. Crack, on the other hand, is actually inhaled. The small pebbles or rocks, having a relatively low melting point, are placed in a special glass pipe or other smoking device and heated. Rather than burning, crack vaporizes and the fumes are inhaled.

government's attempts to reduce the amount of illicit cocaine production within its borders, it apparently, at least for a time, successfully restricted the amount of ether available for transforming coca paste into cocaine hydrochloride. The result was the diversion of coca paste from Colombia through Central America and the Caribbean into South Florida for conversion into cocaine. Spillage from shipments through the Caribbean corridor acquainted local island populations with coca paste smoking. They developed the forerunner of crack-cocaine in 1980.[24] Known as baking-soda base, base-rock, gravel, and roxanne, the prototype was a smokable product composed of coca paste, baking soda, water, and rum. Migrants from Jamaica, Haiti, Trinidad, and locations along the Leeward and Windward Islands chain introduced the crack prototype to Caribbean inner-city populations in Miami's immigrant undergrounds, where it was ultimately produced from powder-cocaine rather than paste. As a Miami-based immigrant from Barbados commented in 1986 about the diffusion of what he referred to as "baking-soda paste":

> Basuco and baking-soda paste seemed to come both at the same time. There was always a little cocaine here and there in the islands, but not too much, and it wasn't cheap. Then 'bout five, maybe six, years ago, the paste hit all of the islands. It seemed to happen overnight—Barbados, Saint Lucia, Dominica, and [Saint] Vincent and [Saint] Kitts—all at the same time.[8]
>
> . . . Then I guess someone started to experiment, and we got the rum-soda-paste concoction. We brought it to Miami when we came in '82, and we saw that the Haitians too were into the same combination.

Apparently, at about the same time, a Los Angeles basement chemist rediscovered the rock variety of baking-soda cocaine, and it was initially referred to as cocaine rock.[25] It was an immediate success, as was the East Coast type, and for a variety of reasons. First, it could be smoked rather than snorted. When cocaine is smoked, it is more rapidly absorbed and crosses the blood-brain barrier within six seconds, hence, an almost instantaneous high. Second, it was cheap. While a gram of cocaine for snorting may cost $60 or more depending on its

---

[8] For those unfamiliar with the geography of the Caribbean, the locations spoken of by this informant are part of the Leeward and Windward Islands. The Leeward Islands are the northern segment of the Lesser Antilles and stretch some 400 miles in a southerly arc from the Virgin Islands to Dominica. The Windward Islands are the southern part of the Lesser Antilles, stretching some 200 miles from Martinique south to Grenada. Barbados is located just west of the southern half of the Windward chain but is not geographically part of it. The Leeward and Windward Islands are illustrated in Chapter 7, Figure 7.1 (Drug-Trafficking Sea Routes in the Caribbean).

purity, the same gram can be transformed into anywhere from 5 to 30 rocks. For the user, this meant that individual rocks could be purchased for as little as $2, $5 (nickel rocks), $10 (dime rocks), or $20. For the seller, $60 worth of cocaine hydrochloride (purchased wholesale for $30) could generate as much as $100 to $150 when sold as rocks. Third, it was easily hidden and transportable, and when hawked in small glass vials, it could be readily scrutinized by potential buyers. And as a South Miami narcotics detective described it during the summer of 1986:

> Crack has been a real boon to both buyer and seller. It's cheap, real cheap. Anybody can come up with $5 or $10 for a trip to the stars. But most important, it's easy to get rid of in a pinch. Drop it on the ground and it's almost impossible to find; step on it and the damn thing is history. All of a sudden your evidence ceases to exist.

By the close of 1985 when crack had finally come to the attention of the national media, it was predicted to be the "wave of the future" among the users of illegal drugs.[26] And too, there were media stories that crack was responsible for rising rates of street crime. As a cover story in *USA Today* put it:

> Addicts spend thousands of dollars on binges, smoking the contents of vial after vial in crack or "base" houses—modern-day opium dens—for days at a time without food or sleep. They will do anything to repeat the high, including robbing their families and friends, selling their possessions and bodies.[27]

As the media blitzed the American people with lurid stories depicting the hazards of crack, Congress and the White House began drawing plans for a more concerted war on crack and other drugs. At the same time, crack use was reported in Canada, most European nations, Hong Kong, South Africa, Egypt, India, Mexico, Belize, Bermuda, Barbados, Colombia, Brazil, and the Philippines.[28]

BRICKS, BOULDERS, BACKS, AND BOARDS: SKETCHES FROM THE CRACK HUSTLE

Although the use of crack-cocaine became evident in most major cities across the United States during the latter half of the 1980s, cocaine and crack tend to be associated more often with Miami than other urban areas. In part, this is due to Miami's association with the cocaine wars of the late 1970s and early 1980s, and with South Florida's reputation for cocaine importation and distribution.[29] No doubt the image of the city as the Casablanca on the Caribbean presented in TV's "Miami Vice" contributed as well. But whatever the reasons, crack is indeed a significant facet of Miami street life, and the Miami experience is targeted here to illustrate the players, the situations, the adventures, the degradation, and the tragedies associated with crack use.[h]

Crack was already part of the street scene in Miami by 1982,[30] and according to several informants, the drug could be purchased at several inner-city get-off houses (shooting galleries) as early as mid-1981. A long-time heroin user and resident of Miami's Overtown community recalled in 1989:

> I remember it clear like it was yesterday, 'cause I remember my brother Freddie and me were out celebrating. He had just finished doin' 18 months for a B & E [breaking and entering] and this was the first I had seen him since he was out. That was the last time he done any hard time, and he got out in May of '81.
>
> Anyway, there was this place on 17th Street, near a little park. It was a get-off house, you know, a shooting gallery. Freddie wanted some white boy [heroin], so since he was just out an' all that I told him it was on me. So we go to this place on 17th. After we're there a few minutes the house man [shooting gallery owner] shows me these small cocaine rocks. I forget exactly what he called them, but later on we know'd it as crack. Said they were comin' down every day from Little Haiti and he'd been dealin' them out of his place for three months for the smokin' cokeys [cocaine users]. I remember Freddie laughin' about it, that with there bein' coke there and the kind of people it attracted the place wouldn't be respectable much longer.

The use of crack and the existence of crack houses proliferated in Miami and elsewhere throughout the 1980s. Subsequent to the initial media sensationalism, press coverage targeted the involvement of youths in crack distribution, the violence associated with struggles to control the crack marketplace in inner city neighborhoods, and the child abuse, child neglect, and child abandonment by crack-addicted

[h] Much of the information presented here is based on the author's almost 20 years of street research in Miami, supported in part by grants RO1-DAO1827 and RO1-DAO4862, and contract #271888248/1 from the National Institute on Drug Abuse, and cooperative agreement U64-CCU404539 from the Centers for Disease Control.

mothers.[31] And in Miami, although the violence associated with crack distribution never reached the proportions apparent in other urban centers,[32] crack use was nevertheless a major drug problem.[33] By 1989 the Drug Enforcement Administration had estimated that there were no less than 700 operating crack houses in the greater Miami area.[34] And as in other urban locales, the production, sale, and use of crack,[35] as well as prostitution and sex for drugs exchanges,[36] became prominent features of the Miami crack scene.

Cracks, Hard White, and Eight-Ball

Crack is known by many pseudonyms. Most commonly, it might be cracks, hard white, white, or flavor. Furthermore, there are bricks, boulders, and eight-ball (large rocks or slabs of crack), doo-wap (two rocks), as well as crumbs, shake, and kibbles and bits (small rocks or crack shavings). And too, there is the dope man or bond man (crack dealer) who can deliver a cookie (a large quantity of crack, sometimes as much as 90 rocks), which he carries in his bomb bag (any bag in which drugs are conveyed for delivery) to any crack house in his neighborhood territory. The dope man may also deal (sell) or juggle (sell, for double what it is worth) his crack on the street.

In many crack houses, the drug might be displayed on boards (tables, mirrors, or bulletin boards), whereas in the street crack is hawked in small glass veils or plastic bags. In a few locales, these bags are sealed or stamped with a brand name. Like heroin labeling, such a practice affords the illusion of quality control and gives the buyer a specific name to ask for. In New York City, crack labeling has included such brands as White Cloud, Conan, and Handball, and in Miami, the better-known labels of the early 1990s included Cigarette (named after the high-performance racing boat), Biscayne Babe (an epithet for prostitutes who stroll Miami's Biscayne Boulevard), Olympus (perhaps from Greek mythology), Bogey (of *Key Largo*), and Noriega's Holiday (after a former Panamanian dictator).

"Beam Me Up, Scotty!"

Many crack users are uncertain as to what crack-cocaine actually is. Some know it as cocaine that has been cooked into a hard, solid form called a rock. Exactly what is in crack, in addition to street cocaine, is also debated: some say baking soda, while others say ether. Actually, most users don't know or care. A few will argue that crack is the purest form of cocaine, but others hold that freebase is. And still others believe that crack is freebase.

The rocking up (preparation) of crack-cocaine is done in a variety of ways, all of which require a cut of some sort to increase the volume and weight of the crack, and hence, the profits. Typical in this behalf are such things as comeback, swell up, blow up, and rush, all of which are cocaine analogs (novocaine, lidocaine, and benzocaine) which will bind with the cocaine when cooked. A popular recipe for a substantial quantity of crack is called *Miami Magic.*

Ingredients for Miami Magic

4 oz. cocaine hydrochloride
4 oz. comeback
2 oz. Arm & Hammer baking soda water
ice cubes

Preparation

Mix the cocaine, baking soda, and comeback with enough water to cover it. Bring to a boil, mixing constantly, and watch the blend draw together. Place the resulting gel in ice water. Let cool into a solid mass. Remove the crack from water. Let it stand until completely dry and hard. Break into pieces. Serves 1,000.

Other recipes are less formal. As one Miami crack user suggested:

> You put cocaine in a pyrex tube and boil your water; put baking soda about one third of the amount of cocaine . . . and add a couple of tablespoons of hot water, boiling water. And you just hold it in the pan with your boiling water and it will form a rock. It cooks two minutes, three minutes. And you just pour it out.

Although conventional cooking is most common, microwaves are becoming popular:

> In the microwave I have a little water, little tap water, I put my coke, which was half coke, half baking soda, and I pour it into the glass and I put it in the microwave. And let it start cooking, take the jar and let it start forming into a rock.

Crack is smoked in a variety of ways—special glass pipes, makeshift smoking devices fabricated from beer and soda cans, jars, bottles, and other containers, known as stems, straight shooters, skillets, tools, ouzies, or more directly, the devil's dick. A beam (from ''Beam me up, Scotty'' of TV's original ''Star Trek'') is a hit of crack, as is a bubb, backs (a single hit), and back up (a second hit). Crack is also smoked with marijuana in cigarettes, called geek joints, lace joints, and pin joints. Some users get high from a shotgun—secondary smoke exhaled from one crack user into the mouth of another.

Users typically smoke for as long as they have crack or the means to purchase it—money or sex, stolen goods, furniture, or other drugs. It is rare that smokers have but a single hit. More likely they spend $50 to $500 during a mission—a three- or four-day binge, smoking almost constantly, 3 to 50 rocks per day. During these cycles, crack users rarely eat or sleep. And once crack is tried, for many users it is not long before it becomes a daily habit. For example, a recovering crack user indicated:

> I smoked it Thursday, Friday, Saturday, Monday, Tuesday, Wednesday, Thursday, Friday, Saturday on that cycle. I was working at that time. I would spend my whole $300 check. Everyday was a crack day for me. My day was not made without a hit. I could smoke it before breakfast, don't even have breakfast or I don't eat for three days.

And a current crack user/dealer reported:

> For the past five months I've been wearing the same pants. And sneakers are new but with all the money you make a day at least $500/$600 a day you don't want to spend a $100 in clothes. Everything is rocks, rocks, rocks, rocks, rocks. And to tell you the truth I don't even eat well for having all that money. You don't even want to have patience to sit down and have a good dinner. I could tell you rock is . . . I don't know what to say. I just feel sorry for anyone who falls into it.

HUTS, CRIBS, AND JUNGLES: AN ASSORTMENT OF CRACK HOUSE STYLES

In 1989 a Miami crack house operator reported:

> The crack house is a carnival of vice. It is one hell of a nasty place where the kingrats and pay masters rule, where the gut buckets give slow necks for a penny, and where the freaks, rock monsters, and blood suckers will do anything for a hit on the stem.[i]

---

[i] In the Miami crack scene, kingrats are crack house owners. Owners are also known as rock masters and house men.

Pay masters are male crack house customers who purchase the sex from female crack users. A scrug is a man who tries to get sex for free.

The term crack house can mean a number of different things—a place to use crack, a place to sell or do both, a place to manufacture and package crack; and the location may be a house, an apartment, a small shack at the back of an empty lot, an abandoned building, or even the rusting hulk of a discarded automobile. There are no less than seven different types of crack houses in the Miami area. In addition to what might be called organized crack houses, there are numerous others locally known as castles, base houses, brothels, residence houses, resorts, and graveyards.[j]

Castles

Reportedly few in number, castles are fortified structures where large quantities of crack are manufactured from powder-cocaine, packaged in plastic bags or glass veils, and sold both wholesale and retail. Crack users are not permitted inside the walls of castles. Typical fortifications include barred windows, reinforced door and window frames, steel doors with heavy slide bolts, and walls reinforced from the inside with steel mesh and/or a layer of concrete blocks. Such heavy fortifications are for the purpose of making police raids difficult. As an 18-year-old former lookout for a crack house reported in 1990:

> The whole idea [of the fortifications] is to keep the cops off yer backs long enough to dump the stuff [crack] before they get in. This one rock castle I was in had all the doors and walls

---

Gut buckets are women who trade sex for crack in crack houses, while guts refer to a vagina.

A slow neck is oral sex during which the penis is sucked very slowly, as compared to a fast head where the intent is to bring the customer to a climax as quickly as possible. Slow necks typically cost more than fast heads.

A penny is a single hit on a crack pipe, typically in exchange for sex.

A freak was originally a crack whore who would engage in group sex, oral sex with another woman, or participated in any sexual activities other than fallatio or vaginal intercourse, and men who had bizarre sexual requests or publically engaged in gay sex. However, freak now refers to anyone who trades any type of sex for crack, and the freak room in a crack house is the locus of much of the sex.

Rock monsters, also known as base heads, base whores, crackies, strawberries, toss-ups, favor girls, rockstitutes, crack whores, head hunters, rock stars, skeeter heads, and skeezers, are women who trade sex for crack.

A blood sucker is a type of female freak, who will engage in oral sex with a woman who is menstruating.

Stems refer to crack smoking paraphernalia.

[j] The following descriptions are based on 22 observations in 7 Miami crack houses, combined with data from more than 70 informants collected during the period January 1988 through February 1991. For a discussion of the methods of entree, see James A. Inciardi, "Kingrats, Chicken Heads, Slow Necks, Freaks, and Blood Suckers: A Glimpse at the Miami Sex for Crack Market," paper presented at the 50th Annual Meeting of the Society for Applied Anthropology, Charleston, South Carolina, 13–17 March 1991.

braced with steel bars drilled into the floor and ceiling. It had
TV cameras lookin' up and down the street. Nothin' could go
down without them knowin' about it. The only time the DEA
[Drug Enforcement Administration] got in was when they came
with a tow truck to pull down the door and a battering ram
to get past a concrete barrier. It took them 15 minutes to get
in, and by then we had the place clean [free of drugs].

In addition to fortifications, most castles are well-armed, with
workers typically carrying automatic or semi-automatic weapons at all
times. Crack sales are accomplished with little or no interaction. In some
houses of this type, exchanges are made through a slot or hole in the
fortified door, with the money passed in and the crack passed out.
In others, the transaction is accomplished by means of a basket or pail
lowered from a second floor or attic window.

Base Houses

The base house seems to be an ''all-purpose drug joint,'' as one informant put it. Base houses are used by many kinds of drug users,
especially intravenous users. A variety of drugs are available, including
crack. However, smoking crack is not the primary activity. Intravenous
drug use (typically cocaine) is more commonly seen and accepted here
than in other types of crack houses, but sex for drugs exchanges rarely
occur. In this regard, a 35-year-old crack-using prostitute commented
in February, 1990:

> You can go there and shoot drugs and she [the owner] shoot,
> but she didn't smoke crack. She'll let you smoke there as
> long as you . . . give her $2. If you was a smoker, a rock
> smoker, you can give her $2 to smoke. If you was a cocaine
> shooter you give her cocaine to shoot or buy her some wine
> or something. The only thing she didn't let us do there is
> bring customers [johns].

Resorts

The resort is one of the more customary types of crack house in Miami.
The physical layout is that of a small apartment adapted for crack
use. The kitchen is used for cooking rock, at least one bedroom is set
aside for sex, and the living space is used for selling and smoking. As
one crack user described the resort:

> One of them was his main room and the other two he would
> rent out, one for sexuals and one for just smoking. And

sometimes there wouldn't be nobody smoking and they just come to have sex in both of them. Inside, candles burning, pillows on the floor, it wouldn't be very good for a person in his right mind.

The owners of these crack houses seem to be concerned about two things—money and crack. Many of them were addicted to crack and operating the house is to support a drug habit. Almost anything, furthermore, can happen in these crack houses. They were described and observed as filthy, chaotic, and crowded. The crack smokers got into fights, attempted to steal each other's drugs, and exhibited extreme paranoia. Several informants noted:

> I only went there to do my drugs. But I actually see some people stay there, you know, in that shit. You know, crawling around roaches, you know, like they have a dog, the fucking dog poop is all over the floor.
>
> You see people looking at the floors, looking at their chairs, picking up little things and putting them in a pipe and smoking them and turning green and coughing because its not crack and people falling on the floor and untying their shoes, and people hiding in closets and getting paranoid, peeking out windows and looking out the doors.
>
> He [a customer] was in the room with one of the tricks, right, one of the house ladies. She worked for the guy that was selling drugs in the house. She smoked too, and she tried to rob him, and he caught her. And he hit her. He didn't know she was working for the people in the place where they was. And he hit her and she went screaming and ran back down to the pimp, right. And she told the story that the mother fucker tried to take his money back. And the man [the customer] said: ''No, this bitch went in my pocket, man, the bitch went in my pocket.'' So he started out hitting his head, the pimp did. I guess he didn't want to shoot him so he took the torch and stuck right in that man's dick. You know they told him they were going to kill him. You don't go around there and beat their girl. When they say they will kill you I believe they will.
>
> One time I saw a girl raped beside me but I couldn't do nothing because I was all high and tripping you know, they tied her down to a bed and one got in front of her and the other got in back of her, and she was hollering and screaming you know and while he was doing it to her he was beating her you know, because she was trying to steal one of the guy's drugs.

A characteristic of the resort is easy access to crack, although each house has slightly different sales procedures. Some charge an entrance fee and customers are free to smoke and have sex. Crack is usually on a table and purchases are informal. In other houses, the crack may not be on display, and customers pay a worker to bring them a rock. For example:

> They just have it there on the table, whatever you want, give them the money for it and go in the back and then if you want another you go right to the front and buy a nickel [$5 rock] and then you smoke that.
>
> You have to buy your stuff from them. There was one where you could bring your stuff, but you would have to pay, pay them to use their equipment.

In resorts, there are numerous exchanges of sex for crack, the bartering occurs between the head hunter (prostitute) and her/his customer (john). The owner of the crack house receives a fee (crack or money) from the john for the use of the freak room. As such, the customer pays both the owner of the house and the prostitute.

And finally, the crack houses known in Miami as resorts are termed as such because of the variety of activities that occur there. A cocaine dealer reported in this behalf:

> That they call it a rock resort has nothin' to do with music. Ha, ha. It's because you can really get into it there—drugs, sex, rock 'n roll, all three at once, whatever. You can smoke your brains out, fuck your brains out, get sexed any way you want, watch sex, get paranoid, fight, watch fights, cut somebody, get cut, get high, get killed, whatever the fuck you want.

Brothels

Although prostitution and trading sex for crack are among the primary activities of many crack houses, in the brothel the owner is a dealer/ pimp and the sex/drugs exchange system is unique. The prostitute is a house girl (and/or house boy), and is not involved in the payment process. For the sexual services she provides, she receives payment from the house man in the form of crack, room, and board.

Several respondents reported having actually lived in a crack house brothel, with many more having visited such establishments. In August 1990 a 26-year-old crack addict with a ten-year career in drugs detailed the following:

> Bein' that I been workin' the streets since I was 11 and don't really mind sexin' a lot of different guys, I thought it would

> be a real easy deal for gettin' all the cracks that I needed. So this bond man [drug dealer] that I'd know'd real well takes me in. He says all it is givin' a lot a brains [oral sex]. Well man, I know'd a lot a brains. I probably done more FELLATIO [her emphasis] than any lady on the street.
>
> . . . I really got myself into somethin' bad. It wasn't just brains like he said. It was everything. . . . Most of the time I just didn't care, 'cause I was gettin' all the rock I wanted. But times I just wanted to be left alone, but I couldn't. One time they raped me man, they raped me, 'cause I wouldn't fuck 'em just that minute. They held me down and beat me and did all kind of terrible things. . . .
>
> And I tried to leave but I was a prisoner there. After the rape I tried to leave but the man at the door says he's got his orders and I can't go. So when I try to get out he slapped me around and they rape me again. . . . An' then to teach me another lesson they hold back on the pipe. . . .
>
> After a while I got sick, and I was all bruised and looked so bad that they threw me out. They just threw me out like I was just some piece of shit!

In addition to the sexual services available in the brothels, some street prostitutes use them solely as places to have sex with their customers. For example, a 25-year-old woman who had been exchanging sex for money and drugs for eight years reported:

> One of the rooms is for base [crack], the other three rooms are for tricking and one of the first rooms inside the door, that's where the dude sit, that's where the G-man [security man, bouncer] sit. When you come in the house he pat you down. They pat you down, and when you come in you say "date." That means pat you down and let you go and have a date. See anyone was allowed to bring a date, anyone was allowed to bring a trick. When you go in you can bring a date in from the outside and use the room and get money from him and you got to do what you gotta do—$5 to use the room, $5 one hour, they say an hour but they only give you forty-five minutes with that mother fucker. . . .

Residence Houses

Residence houses are quite numerous in the Miami area and are likely the most common form of crack house. They are houses or apartments where small groups of people gather regularly to smoke crack. The operators are reluctant to call these places crack houses because they are used as such only by their friends. However, the activities are the same as those in other crack houses, including sex for crack exchanges. The major differences revolve around the payment system. Crack is not sold in residence houses, it is only smoked. In the more traditional crack house, such as a brothel or resort, payment for using the house can be made either with money or crack; money being preferred. In the residence house, payment is made only with crack. Visitors give crack or more often share crack with the owner of the house or apartment, in return for having a place to smoke or turn a trick. There are usually fewer people in these crack houses than in others—5 or 6 compared to 15 or 20. They are also the same 5 or 6 individuals, whereas in other types there is a greater turnover of people. Finally, whereas the visitors to other types of crack houses are customers, only friends are invited to residence houses.

Graveyards

Graveyards are rooms in abandoned buildings, and the designation has an interesting genesis. At the corner of Northeast Second Avenue and 71st Street in Miami stands a housing project. As a journalist described it in 1987:

> Sure, there always were problems. Its official name is Site 5, Project FL527-B, but residents began calling it The Graveyard years ago. Poverty breeds crime, and crime bred more of itself. But when a tidal wave of cocaine rocks descended on the place two years ago, crime seemed to put The Graveyard in a stranglehold. The pulse of the community grew faint. Residents began moving out of The Graveyard and prospective tenants refused to move in. So basers [crack users and dealers] claimed the vacant apartments for themselves. . . . [37]

In time The Graveyard's abandoned apartments became overrun by crack dealers and users, so much so that the county government began boarding up the project's vacant rooms.[38] But the name took on a life of its own, and by the end of 1987 every abandoned building in Miami that was used for smoking crack became known as a graveyard. As a methadone client and active crack user reported in 1988:

> Now there are lots of graveyards in almost every part of the city—Liberty City, Overtown, Miami Beach, South Miami— every neighborhood where there's empty buildings and lots of crack. Crack, and lots of crack . . . that's what makes it a graveyard.

According to most informants, no one actually owns a particular graveyard, although there do seem to be turf issues associated with their use based on squatters' rights. Crack users bring their own crack. Sex for money and/or drugs is performed in these buildings. For example:

> I know'd this one place off Miami Avenue where this lady set up in a burned-out house. She was sort of a whore-crack-head-skeezer-bag lady who'd do anythin' for crack and for food for her trick baby [a prostitute's child fathered by a john], her base baby [a child conceived and gestated by a crack-using mother]. For a hit on yer pipe or for some food or money or drugs or cigarettes she'd let you smoke in her digs. . . .

And finally, somewhat related to graveyards are base cars—abandoned automobiles that serve as places to smoke crack, and to have sex, or to exchange sex for crack.

Organized Crack Houses

Organized crack houses are reportedly few in number in Miami. The environment in these establishments is far more controlled than any other type of crack house. The owners are more visible, closely monitoring all activities. Violence and general chaos are uncommon occurrences. The ambience is described as calm, and children are not permitted. They have more workers than other crack houses, most of whom maintain order inside or watch for police. Purchasing crack in organized houses is more structured than elsewhere. Several have specific hours of operation. Upon arrival, a customer is sold crack, seated with a pipe, and strict order is maintained. And finally, direct sex for crack exchanges do not occur in the organized houses.

CRACK IS MY PIMP

The following quotation, provided by a 28-year-old crack user legally employed as a shipping clerk, clearly illustrates characteristic aspects of both the compulsive nature of crack use and the sex for crack phenomenon. This woman had been a marijuana user since age 15, a cocaine user since age 18, and a crack user since age 26. In her comments below, she details her first exchange of sex for crack and how it came about.

> I had my last paycheck, that was $107. That day I went straight from there [work] with a friend guy and copped some drugs. I bought $25—5 nickel rocks. I walked up to the apartment, me and the same guy. We drunk a beer, we needed the can to

smoke on. So we sat there and we smoked those five rocks and you know like they say, one is too much and a thousand is never enough. And that's the truth. Those five rocks went like this [snaps fingers] and I immediately, I had maybe about $80 left. I had intentions of takin' my grandmother some money home for the kids. But I had it in my mind you know I was, I was just sick. I wanted to continue to get high so push come to shove I smoked up that—that whole day me and him we smoke up. It didn't last till maybe about 8 PM cause we started maybe about 12 that afternoon.

Okay all the money was gone, all the drugs was gone. About nine we went and sat in the park. Usually when we set in the park people will come over and they'll have drugs. Some friends came over and they had drugs. He walked home. I stayed out because I couldn't give an account for what I had did with the money. My grandmother done thought that I was goin' to pick up my check and comin' back. So I walked around and I walked down this street, you know you got people that will pick you up. So this guy stopped and I got in the car, and I never did any prostituting but I wanted more drugs. So this guy he stopped and he picked me up and he asked me: "How much would you charge me for a head?" That's oral sex. And I told him $40. And so he say how much would you charge me for two hours to have just sex not oral sex? And so I told him $40 so he say: "Okay get in," and he took me to this hotel.

He had about six rocks. I didn't wanna sex. I wanted to get high so we smoked the rocks and durin' the time I sexed with him. So after I sexed him he gave me the money and after the rocks was gone I still wanted to get high. So this man he gave his car and his keys and gave me more money to go get more drugs. We went into another hotel. By that time it was maybe six in the morning. He ended up leaving me in the hotel. By that time I done spent all my $40. It wasn't nothing I had done wasted the money. So later on that afternoon, my grandmother done let me get sleep and everything. I think later on that day and the next day I went to my godfather's house and I earned $15, I helped him do some work around the house so he gave me $15.

So I went and stayed home with the kids and waited till they got ready to go to bed that night. I went and got three rocks with that $15. I started off smokin' by myself, but when you sittin' in the park people come to know you and they be tryin' to horn in on what you doin'. So ended up smokin' I think about a rock and a half with somebody that was sittin' in the park. Later on I ended up walkin' down the main strip again and this guy came by and he say: ''Well how much money would do you want for a head?'' So I told him $10. I was really desperate this time around so I told him $10. He say: ''Well I don't have but $5.'' I say okay I'll take that you know I settle for little or nothin'. So we went down the street and parked in this parkin' lot and I gave him a head. And I immediately went to the drug house, and bought a nickel rock.

It would appear that most of the sex in Miami crack houses is oral and frequent. At the same time, the majority of the respondents reported performing sexual acts that they would do only while on crack and/or for crack. For example, a 31-year-old male prostitute reported:

As a matter of fact, when you are high on crack you'll do almost anything. We [the respondent and his boyfriend] had sex in front of other people, and one male joined us. Usually I gave the other guy head while we had anal intercourse.

Similarly, a male customer of sex for crack exchanges commented:

The next time I ran into this prostitute man dressed like a woman and I paid her/him $10 to have sex. I thought it was a woman. So she bend over and I got in from behind and hey it was just like a woman. And if I wasn't on crack I'm for sure I wouldn't have been doing that.

A 24-year-old woman who had been a prostitute for two years and had used cocaine in one form or another since age 17 noted:

I had a date that wanted me to find a girl friend that enjoys females. I said sure, I knew a girl that enjoyed females so I got her. We set a date and time where I was supposed to meet this guy and we did and it was $30 apiece. Just for him to watch us. . . . I was tryin' not to do it but then it was like he wanted to watch. He was like right there on top. So I had no choice but to do it if I wanted my money because I was high at the time. Still high coming, I was coming down and I wanted to get back out so I went ahead and done it. But I didn't enjoy it. I like men.

And finally, although the majority of the sexual activities take place in a separate room, in many crack houses they occur in the common area where everyone else is smoking. In this regard, one informant reported:

It was like a sex show or somethin' like that. Everybody's sittin' and layin' around smokin' and this lady starts takin' her clothes off, says she's burnin' up. And a guy goes over to her, hands her his pipe in one hand and his meat [penis] in the other. And she starts givin' him a blow job right there.

And similarly:

There was this one place where just nobody cared what they did and where they did it. And let's see, I was giving heads for everybody to see 'cause since they didn't care so I didn't either. So I givin' heads all around the room for hits. Even another lady.

POSTSCRIPT

Crack has been called the fast-food variety of cocaine. It is cheap, easy to conceal, it vaporizes with practically no odor, and the gratification is swift: an intense, almost sexual euphoria that lasts less than five minutes. Given these attributes, it would appear that crack-cocaine might be a safer alternative to powder-cocaine. But such a conclusion is far from accurate. In addition to all of the problems associated with cocaine discussed in Chapter 3, there are additional complications with crack use. Smoking cocaine as opposed to snorting it results in more immediate and direct absorption of the drug, producing a quicker and more compelling high, greatly increasing both the abuse liabity and dependence potential. Moreover, there is increased risk of acute toxic reactions, including brain seizure, cardiac irregularities, respiratory paralysis, paranoid psychosis, and pulmonary dysfunction.

The tendency to binge on crack for days at a time, neglecting food, sleep, and basic hygiene, severely compromises physical health. Crack users appear emaciated most of the time. They lose interest in their physical appearance. Many have scabs on their faces, arms, and legs, the results of burns, and picking on the skin (to remove bugs and other insects believed to be crawling under the skin). Crack users tend to have burned facial hair from carelessly lighting their smoking paraphernalia; they have burned lips and tongues from the hot stems of their pipes; and they seem to cough constantly. And the tendency of both male and female crack users to engage in high frequency, unprotected sex with numerous anonymous partners increases their risk for any variety of sexually transmitted diseases, including AIDS.

According to national surveys, crack never caught on too well in the general population, and where it did, usage rates began to decline at the close of the 1980s.[39] But for reasons difficult to understand, crack's appeal in the majority of the nation's inner cities has endured, and will likely remain so for some time. Perhaps the best explanation of crack's appeal in the inner city comes from anthropologist Philippe Bourgois:

> Substance abuse in general, and crack in particular, offers the equivalent of a born-again metamorphosis. Instantaneously, the user is transformed from an unemployed, depressed high school dropout, despised by the world—and secretly convinced that his failure is due to his own inherent stupidity and disorganization. There is a rush of heart-palpitating pleasure, followed by a jaw-gnashing crash and wide-eyed alertness that provides his life with concrete purpose: Get more crack—fast![40]

As a final note, it would appear that crack is initiating heroin use among a number of its devotees. Snorted in conjunction with crack smoking, or smoked with crack in a combination known as moonrock, parachute, and speedball rock,[k] heroin can not only mediate some of the unpleasant stimulant effects of crack, but prolong the high as well.[41] What this will likely result in is scores of drug users with concurrent addictions to stimulants and narcotics, and inevitably, a whole new generation of intravenous heroin users and yet another population at risk for AIDS.

Notes

1. Pedro de Cieza de Leon, *The Seventeen Years' Travels of Pedro de Cieza de Leon Through the Mighty Kingdom of Peru,* p. 211 (English translation, London: 1709), cited by William Martindale, *Coca and Cocaine* (London: H. K. Lewis, 1894), pp. 2–3.
2. *New York Times,* 17 Nov. 1985, p. B12.
3. Malcolm Gladwell, "A New Addiction to an Old Story," *Insight,* 27 Oct. 1986, pp. 8–12. See also Adam Paul Weisman, "I Was a Drug-Hype Junkie," *New Republic,* 6 Oct. 1986, pp. 14–17; Crain Reinarman and Harry G. Levine, "Crack in Context: Politics and Media in the Making of a Drug Scare," *Contemporary Drug Problems,* 16 (Winter 1989), pp. 535–577.
4. *Newsweek,* 16 June 1986, p. 15.
5. Drug Enforcement Administration, *Special Report: The Crack Situation in the United States,* unpublished release from the Strategic Intelligence Section, Drug Enforcement Administration, Washington, D.C., 22 Aug. 1986.
6. See James A. Inciardi, "Beyond Cocaine: Basuco, Crack, and Other Coca Products," *Contemporary Drug Problems,* 14 (Fall 1987), pp. 461–492.
7. *New York Times,* 21 Jan. 1987, p. B1.

---

[k] In early 1991, street informants in Miami also noted the smoking of karachi, a combination of heroin, methaqualone, and phenobarbital (a barbiturate sedative-hypnotic).

8. Personal communication, August 1986. It should be added here that even by the end of the 1980s, crack had still not become a major problem in Chicago. Clinicians, researchers, and representatives of federal and local police agencies generally agreed that this was due to the widespread availability in Chicago of high quality powder-cocaine at a relatively low cost. See *New York Times*, 10 Feb. 1989, p. A14.
9. *Newsweek*, 16 June 1986, p. 18.
10. *Time*, 2 June 1986, p. 16.
11. *USA Today*, 16 June 1986, p. 1A.
12. See Ronald K. Siegel, "Cocaine: Recreational Use and Intoxication," in Robert C. Petersen and Richard Stillman, eds., *Cocaine: 1977* (Rockville, MD: National Institute on Drug Abuse, 1977), pp. 119–136.
13. Lester Grinspoon and James B. Bakalar, *Cocaine: A Drug and Its Social Evolution* (New York: Basic Books, 1985), p. 279.
14. H. Abelson, R. Cohen, R. Schrayer, and M. Rappaport, "Drug Experience, Attitudes and Related Behavior Among Adolescents and Adults," in *Annual Report* (Washington, DC: Office of Drug Abuse Policy, 1978).
15. Ronald K. Siegel, "Cocaine Smoking," *Journal of Psychoactive Drugs*, 14 (1982), pp. 271–359.
16. Ronald K. Siegel, "Cocaine Smoking Disorders: Diagnosis and Treatment," *Psychiatric Annals*, 14 (1984), pp. 728–732.
17. F. Raul Jeri, "Coca-Paste Smoking in Some Latin American Countries: A Severe and Unabated Form of Addiction," *Bulletin on Narcotics*, Apr.–June, 1984, pp. 15–31.
18. M. Almeida, "Contrabucion al Estudio de la Historia Natural de la Dependencia a la Pasta Basica de Cocaina," *Revista de Neuro-Psiquiatria*, 41 (1978), pp. 44–45.
19. Bogota (Colombia) *El Tiempo*, 19 June 1986, p. 2-D.
20. F. R. Jeri, C. Sanchez, and T. Del Pozo, "Consumo de Drogal Peligrosas por Miembros Familiares de la Fuerza Armada y Fuerza Policial Peruana," *Revista de la Sanidad de las Fuerzas Policiales*, 37 (1976), pp. 104–112.
21. See Caracus (Venezuela) *El Universal*, 4 Oct. 1985, pp. 4, 30; Caracus *Zeta*, 12–23 Sept. 1985, pp. 39–46; Manaus (Brazil) *Jornal Do Comercio*, 20 May 1986, p. 16; Bogota (Colombia) *El Tiempo*, 1 June 1986, p. 3-A; Medellin (Colombia) *El Colombiano*, 22 July 1986, p. 16-A; Bogota *El Tiempo*, 6 Oct. 1986, p. 7-A; Lima (Peru) *El Nacional*, 14 Nov. 1986, p. 13; La Paz (Bolivia) *Presencia*, 3 March 1988, Sec. 2, p. 1; Sao Paulo (Brazil) *Folha de Sao Paulo*, 11 June 1987, p. A29; Buenos Aires (Argentina) *La Prensa*, 20 June 1987, p. 9; Sao Paulo *O Estado de Sao Paulo*, 8 March 1988, p. 18; Bogota *El Espectador*, 2 Apr. 1988, pp. 1A, 10A; La Paz *El Diario*, 21 Oct. 1988, p. 3; Cochabamba (Bolivia) *Los Tiempos*, 13 June 1989, p. B5; Sao Paulo *O Estado de Sao Paulo*, 18 June 1989, p. 32; Rio de Janeiro (Brazil) *Manchete*, 28 Oct. 1989, pp. 20–29; Philadelphia *Inquirer*, 21 Sept. 1986, p. 25A; Timothy Ross, "Bolivian Paste Fuels Basuco Boom," *WorldAIDS*, Sept. 1989, p. 9.
22. Curiously, coca paste was reportedly available in Italy during 1987. See Milan *Corriere Della Sera*, 26 Oct. 1987, p. 8.
23. Anonymous, *The Gourmet Cokebook: A Complete Guide to Cocaine* (White Mountain Press, 1972), cited by M. Schatzman, A. Sabbadini, and L. Forti,

"Coca and Cocaine," *Journal of Psychedelic Drugs,* 8 (Apr.–June 1976), pp. 95–128.

24. James N. Hall, "Hurricane Crack," *Street Pharmacologist,* 10 (Sept. 1986), pp. 1–2.
25. *U.S. News & World Report,* 11 Feb. 1985, p. 33.
26. See, *New York Times,* 29 Nov. 1985, p. A1.
27. *USA Today,* 16 June 1986, p. 1A.
28. Windsor (Canada) *Windsor Star,* 26 June 1986, p. A13; Toronto (Canada) *Globe and Mail,* 2 Sept. 1987, p. A5; Ottawa (Canada) *Citizen,* 13 Feb. 1988, p. A15; Belfast (Ireland) *News Letter,* 9 July 1986, p. 3; Helsinki (Finland) *Uusi Suomi,* 28 July 1986, p. 8; Rio de Janeiro (Brazil) *O Globo,* 24 May 1986, p. 6; Hong Kong *South China Morning Post,* 2 Aug. 1986, p. 16; Johannesburg (South Africa) *Star,* 23 Sept. 1986, p. 1M; Cape Town (South Africa) *Argus,* 10 March 1987, p. 13; Johannesburg *City Press,* 7 Jan. 1990, p. 5; Milan (Italy) *Panorama,* 3 May 1987, pp. 58–59; Oslo (Norway) *Arbeiderbladet,* 4 June 1987, p. 13; Madrid (Spain) *El Alcazar,* 14 Sept. 1986, p. 11; Nuevo Laredo (Mexico) *El Diario de Nuevo Laredo,* 12 Oct. 1986, Sec. 4, p. 1; Calcutta (India) *Statesman,* 16 Oct. 1986, p. 1; Belize City (Belize) *Beacon,* 25 Oct. 1986, pp. 1, 14; London *Al-Fursan,* 13 Sept. 1986, pp. 51–53; London *Sunday Telegraph,* 12 Apr. 1987, p. 1; Geneva (Switzerland) *Journal de Geneve,* 26 Dec. 1986, p. 1; Brussels (Belgium) *Le Sori,* 10/11 Nov. 1986, p. 3; Munich (West Germany) *Sueddeutsche Zeitung,* 18/19 Oct. 1986, p. 12; Lisbon (Portugal) *O Jornal,* 30 Jan./5 Feb. 1987, p. 40; Hamburg (West Germany) *Die Zeit,* 24 Apr. 1987, p. 77; Hamilton (Bermuda) *Royale Gazette,* 3 Dec. 1987, p. 3; Bridgetown (Barbados) *Weekend Nation,* 15–16 Jan. 1988, p. 32; Stockholm (Sweden) *Dagens Nyheter,* 2 Jan. 1988, p. 6; Grand Cayman (Bahamas) *Caymanian Compass,* 20 Jan. 1988, pp. 1–2; Paris *Liberation,* 12 Jan. 1990, p. 33; Bangkok (Thailand) *Siam Rat,* 13 Aug. 1988, p. 12.
29. See T. D. Allman, *Miami: City of the Future* (New York: Atlantic Monthly Press, 1987); David Rieff, *Going to Miami: Exiles, Tourists, and Refugees in the New America* (Boston: Little, Brown, 1987); Patrick Carr, *Sunshine States* (New York: Doubleday, 1990); Edna Buchanan, *The Corpse Had a Familiar Face: Covering Miami, America's Hottest Beat* (New York: Random House, 1987); John Rothchild, *Up for Grabs: A Trip Through Time and Space in the Sunshine State* (New York: Viking Press, 1985).
30. James A. Inciardi, "*Crack*-Cocaine in Miami," National Institute on Drug Abuse Technical Review Meeting on the Epidemiology of Cocaine Use and Abuse, Rockville, Maryland, 3–4 May 1988.
31. See, Ron Rosenbaum, "Crack Murder: A Detective Story," *New York Times Magazine,* 15 Feb. 1987, pp. 29–33, 57, 60; *Newsweek,* 22 Feb. 1988, pp. 24–25; *Time,* 7 Mar. 1988, p. 24; *Newsweek,* 28 Mar. 1988, pp. 20–29; *Newsweek,* 27 Apr. 1988, pp. 35–36; *Time,* 9 May 1988, pp. 20–33; *New York Times,* 23 June 1988, pp. A1, B4; *Time,* 5 Dec. 1988, p. 32; *New York Doctor,* 10 Apr. 1989, pp. 1, 22; *U.S. News & World Report,* 10 Apr. 1989, pp. 20–32; *New York Times,* 1 June 1989, pp. A1, B4; *New York Times* (National Edition), 11 Aug. 1989, pp. 1, 10; Andrew C. Revkin, "Crack in the Cradle," *Discover,* Sept. 1989, pp. 62–69.
32. James A. Inciardi, "The Crack/Violence Connection Within a Population of Hard-Core Adolescent Offenders," in Mario DeLaRosa, Elizabeth Y.

Lambert, and Bernard Gropper, eds., *Drugs and Violence: Causes, Correlates, and Consequences* (Rockville, MD: National Institute on Drug Abuse, 1990), pp. 92–111.

33. *Miami Herald* ("Neighbors" Supplement), 24 Apr. 1988, pp. 21–25; James A. Inciardi and Anne E. Pottieger, "Kids, Crack, and Crime," *Journal of Drug Issues*, 21 (Spring 1991), pp. 257–270.

34. *Crack/Cocaine: Overview 1989* (Washington, DC: Drug Enforcement Administration, 1989).

35. James N. Hall, "Cocaine Smoking Ignites America," *Street Pharmacologist*, Fall 1988/Winter 1989, pp. 28–30; *Substance Abuse Report*, 20 (15 June 1989), pp. 1–5; Michael Massing, "Crack's Destructive Sprint Across America," *New York Times Magazine*, 1 Oct. 1989, pp. 38–41, 58–59, 62; Steven Belenko and Jeffrey Fagen, *Crack and the Criminal Justice System* (New York: New York City Criminal Justice Agency, 1987); *Newsweek*, 28 Nov. 1988, pp. 64–79; Barbara Wallace, "Psychological and Environmental Determinants of Relapse in Crack Cocaine Smokers," *Journal of Substance Treatment*, 6 (1989), pp. 95–106; Tom Mieczkowski, "Crack Distribution in Detroit," *Contemporary Drug Problems*, 17 (Spring 1990), pp. 9–30; Jeffrey Fagen and Ko-Lo Chin, "Initiation into Crack and Cocaine: A Tale of Two Epidemics," *Contemporary Drug Problems*, 16 (Winter 1989), pp. 579–617; Philippe Bourgois, "In Search of Horatio Alger: Culture and Ideology in the Crack Economy," *Contemporary Drug Problems*, 16 (Winter 1989), pp. 619–649; Paul J. Goldstein, Henry H. Brownstein, Patrick J. Ryan, and Patricia A. Bellucci, "Crack and Homicide in New York City: A Conceptually Based Event Analysis," *Contemporary Drug Problems*, 16 (Winter 1989), pp. 651–687.

36. See, "Sex for Crack: How the New Prostitution Affects Drug Abuse Treatment," *Substance Abuse Report*, 19 (15 Nov. 1988), pp. 1–4; "Syphilis and Gonorrhea on the Rise Among Inner-City Drug Addicts," *Substance Abuse Report*, 20 (1 June 1989), pp. 1–2; "Syphilis and Crack Linked in Connecticut," *Substance Abuse Report*, 20 (1 Aug. 1989), pp. 1–2; *New York Times*, 20 Aug. 1989, pp. 1, 36; *New York Times*, 9 Oct. 1989, pp. A1, A30; *U.S. News & World Report*, 23 Oct. 1989, pp. 29–30; *Newsweek*, 25 Sept. 1989, p. 59; *Miami Herald*, 22 Oct. 1989, pp. 1G, 6G; James A. Inciardi, "Trading Sex for Crack Among Juvenile Drug Users: A Research Note," *Contemporary Drug Problems*, 16 (Winter 1989), pp. 689–700; Mary Ann Forney and T. Holloway, "Crack, Syphilis and AIDS: The Triple Threat to Rural Georgia," *Georgia Academy of Family Physicians Journal*, 12 (1989), pp. 5–6; Robert T. Rolfs, Martin Goldberg, and Robert G. Sharrar, "Risk Factors for Syphilis: Cocaine Use and Prostitution," *American Journal of Public Health*, 80 (July 1990), pp. 853–857.

37. Lynne Duke, "The Graveyard," Miami Herald *Tropic*, 5 Apr. 1987, pp. 12–28.

38. See, *Miami Herald*, 9 Apr. 1987, pp. 1D, 2D; *Miami Herald*, 22 Apr. 1987, p. 1B.

39. Edgar H. Adams, Ann J. Blanken, Lorraine D. Ferguson, and Andrea Kopstein, *Overview of Selected Drug Trends* (Rockville, MD: National Institute on Drug Abuse, Division of Epidemiology and Prevention Research, 1990).

40. Philippe Bourgois, ''Just Another Night on Crack Street,'' *New York Times Magazine,* 12 Nov. 1989, pp. 52–53, 60–65, 94.
41. *Drug Enforcement Report,* 23 Feb. 1989, p. 7; *U.S. News & World Report,* 14 Aug. 1989, pp. 31–32; Stephen Brooks, ''The Perilous Swim in Heroin's Stream,'' *Insight,* 5 Feb. 1990, pp. 8–17; *Newsweek,* 19 Feb. 1990, pp. 74, 77; *New York Times,* 21 July 1990, pp. 1, 26.

LEGENDS OF THE LIVING DEAD
Unraveling the Drugs/Crime Connection

Myth is a body of lore regarded as roughly true. It implies collective fantasy, drawing its fabulous plots from notions based more on traditions and convenience than on fact. Myth guides conduct by orienting, sustaining, or suppressing aspects of social behavior.

The chronicle of the American nation, from its earliest pages, reflects a noticeable dependence on myth in its perception and understanding of the use of drugs for the enhancement of pleasure or performance. Remarkably, this phenomenon seems to persist despite any contradictions by science and logic. For indeed, many people typically seem to ignore the treasuries of evidence descriptive of drugs, drug users, and drug taking that the fields of pharmacology, medicine, and the social sciences have provided in favor of many prevailing mythical systems.

It is generally believed, for example, that all drug users are degenerate and dependent people, that heroin and cocaine are the most dangerous substances on earth, that PCP is a Jekyll and Hyde drug that immediately changes mild-mannered users into raving maniacs, that crack is at the base of all inner city problems, that the use of marijuana invariably leads to heroin addiction, that more effective policing can eliminate drug use and drug-related crime, that severe punishment of drug users will prevent others from using drugs, that life sentences for drug dealers will curtail drug selling, that heroin addicts are enslaved to their drugs and are forced to commit crimes in order to support their habits, and that legalizing drugs will solve the drug problem and eliminate the crime associated with illegal drug distribution and use.

This brief listing reflects but a sampling of the mythical images that characterize popular drug awareness. Yet even these few have managed to galvanize the perceptions and responses of the legislature, the media, systems of law enforcement, armchair policy makers, civil libertarians, the public at large, and to some extent, even the scientific community. The curiosity, however, is the way in which many of the drug myths came into being, managing to persist for years.

RELIGIOUS ALCHEMY, D. B. COOPER, AND THE GENESIS OF THE DRUG MYTHS

Myth descends from a process—a series of actions and responses. It passes directly from both literary and folk traditions into belief. The art form of myth is drama, with plot, characters, and dialogue. The performance displays a collection of themes and events, and their interpretation invariably becomes understood as real. Many myths are the result of simple misunderstanding, reinterpretations of fact or deliberate misdirection to suit one's own needs or beliefs and erroneous or quasi-scientific methods of inquiry. This spirit of mythmaking is apparent, for example, in the journalistic sensationalism of the nineteenth-century American dime novelists, the approximations of fact by armchair historians, and the religious alchemy of generations of Christian writers and contemporary television evangelists.

Among the more curious myths that endured for centuries in much of the world was that of the unicorn, a product of the Holy Bible. The books of the Old Testament were first written in Hebrew and Aramaic, but circa 250 B.C. a group of Hellenistic Jews translated the Scriptures into Greek, producing a version of the Bible known as the Septuagint. In the original Scriptures, the Hebrew writers had mentioned with some awe an animal they called Re'em. In Job 39:9–12 and Num. 23:22, the Re'em was noted as having great strength. It was characterized as fleet, fierce, indomitable, and especially distinguished by the armor of its brow, but it was never actually described. Later studies discovered that Re'em was *Bos primigenius,* or the urus, a wild ox believed to be the feral ancestor of European domestic cattle. But the urus, now extinct, had never been seen by the translators since it no longer existed where they lived. Yet the traits of the Re'em awakened dim recollections of another beast that was believed to be as fierce, mysterious, strange, and remote. They used the Greek word $\mu o\nu\acute{o}\varkappa\epsilon\rho\omega\varsigma$ or *monokeros.*

The monokeros of the ancient Greeks came from the writings of Ctesias, the historian and one-time physician of the Persian King Artaxerxes II. In 398 B.C. he had produced a volume on India, based primarily on the tales and hearsay of travelers. In it he described a "wild ass of India" that had all the characteristics of the mythical unicorn. Zoologists have determined that Ctesias' monokeros or "wild ass of

India'' was actually the Indian rhinoceros, with admixtures of features of some other animal. But in English, monokeros means unicorn. Re'em was translated into monokeros with one main result: for many centuries to come, the existence of the unicorn would be reiterated, and it could not be doubted, for it was repeatedly mentioned in the Holy Bible.[1]

More entertaining is the myth of D. B. Cooper, the skyjacker who jumped from a Northwest Orient Airlines jetliner on Thanksgiving Eve in 1971 with a $200,000 ransom that he had demanded from airline officials. After he parachuted from the plane over Ariel, Washington, the FBI launched a massive manhunt. Cooper was never found, and almost immediately he became a modern-day folk hero—a twentieth-century Robin Hood. Popular mythology holds that he got away, that he beat the system. Every year on the Saturday after Thanksgiving in Ariel the festivities of D. B. Cooper Day are held. Hundreds of people, some from as far away as England, clog the town's only street to pay tribute to the perpetrator of America's only unsolved skyjacking. It is an article of faith among them that somehow, somewhere, Cooper is managing to live a discreetly decadent life on his marked money.[2] What the cultists do not understand is that when Cooper jumped from the 10,000-foot altitude into 200-mph freezing rain and air, dressed only in a light business suit and raincoat, it is likely that his body was thrown into immediate shock and that he did not stay conscious long enough even to open his parachute.

By contrast to the tales of the unicorn and D. B. Cooper, the genesis of drug myths is considerably more complex, having come from numerous medical, political, legislative, scientific, and moral postures of American society. They emerged, in part, from:

- the rural creeds of nineteenth-century Methodism, Baptism, Presbyterianism, and Congregationalism that emphasized individual human toil and self-sufficiency while designating the use of intoxicants as an unwholesome surrender to the evils of an urban morality;

- the medical literature of the late 1800s that arbitrarily designated the use of opium, morphine, and cocaine as a vice, a habit, an appetite, and a disease;

- the early association of opium smoking with the Chinese—a cultural and racial group that had been legally defined as alien, a designation that endured until around 1943;

- the effects of American narcotics legislation that effectively defined heroin users as criminal offenders;

- nineteenth- and twentieth-century police literature that stressed the involvement of professional and other habitual criminals with the use of drugs;

- the initiatives of moral crusaders who described drug use as evil and, in so doing, influenced national opinion makers and rule creators;

- the publicized findings of misguided research efforts, those contaminated by the use of biased samples, impressionistic data, and methodological errors;

- cultural and intellectual lag—that vast and ecumenical gap that stretches between the publication of new discoveries and the ultimate dismissal of earlier proclamations;

- the theoretical interpretations of the drug problem offered by armchair observers, academics, and politicians who have had little or no exposure to, or experience with, the dynamics and intricacies of drug-taking and drug-seeking phenomena.

And, too, the drug myths are a product of the mass media, where sentimentalized melodramas and/or irresponsible reporting—*The Man with the Golden Arm, Valley of the Dolls,* "Miami Vice," *People Weekly, Atlantic Monthly,* "Hill Street Blues," "60 Minutes," *Reader's Digest, The New Republic, Rolling Stone, High Times*—provide uninformed audiences with misshapen portraits of the worlds of drug use.

A TALE OF A TERRIBLE VICE

Although opium and its derivatives had been available as general remedies in patent medicines well before the Revolutionary War, it was not until the mid-nineteenth century that concern over their "evil effects" began to surface. Among the earliest to focus on opiate use as a growing social problem was physician George B. Wood in 1856.[3] Although Wood noted the range of physical impairments that could be attributed to chronic opium intoxication, his treatise focused on evil. Opiate use led to a loss of self-respect, Wood argued; it was a yielding to seductive pleasure, a form of moral depravity, and a vice that led "to the lowest depths of evil." Many of Wood's colleagues quickly agreed, and much of the medical literature that examined the opium problem during the next three decades more often stressed the moral rather than the medical issues.[4] As one commentator put it: "The morbid craving of morphia ranks amongst the category of other human passions, such as smoking, gambling, greediness for profit, and sexual excesses."[5]

To this collection of testimonials ascribing varying levels of stigma to the opiate user, a number of other medical commentators borrowed ideas suggested by the recently introduced theories of biological determinism and criminal anthropology. At the time, the writings of Charles Darwin had become prominent, and Italian physician Cesare Lombroso had just presented his thesis of "criminal man."[6] Lombroso argued that there is a "born criminal type"; that the criminal is an "atavism"—a throwback to an earlier stage in human evolution, a more apelike evolutionary ancestor. There was also Richard L. Dugdale's publication of *The Jukes,* a study which held that crime is caused by "bad heredity," and that criminality, degeneracy, and feeblemindedness are biologically transmitted through poor germ plasm.[7] Applying such notions to the drug-using population, it was claimed that addiction is the result of inherited predispositions: therefore morphine-takers will likely also indulge excessively in alcohol, absinthe drinking, and cocaine use.[8]

Public concern was also mounting over opium smoking in American cities. When gold was discovered in California in 1848, migrants from the Atlantic states as well as from Europe, Australia, and Asia contributed to the gold-seeking population. Among them were some 27,000 Chinese. With the lure of work in the mines and in the construction of railroads across the trans-Mississippi West, by the 1870s the Chinese population had expanded to more than 70,000. The new Asian immigrants had imported their cultural tradition of opium smoking, and they quickly established smoking parlors that were frequented by Orientals and Americans alike.[9]

With a Chinatown beginning in 1872 in New York City, a city at the very center of the nation's publishing capitals, knowledge of the Chinese way of life and the practice of opium smoking became readily disseminated. Common in mass-market publishing during that time were antiurban exposés, lurid guidebooks describing the many "evils" of the "great metropolis."[10] Chinatown was a popular subject, and the customs of orientals as well as the evil nature of the opium joints were often highlighted. In one volume, published in 1892 under the title *Darkness and Daylight; or, Lights and Shadows of New York Life,* the descriptions of the opium dens offered clear reflections of the Victorian moral climate of the era. For example:

> Near the farther end of the room was a bunk occupied by four white women, three of them apparently being adept in the vice, and the fourth a novice. Four persons crowd a bunk very closely; two recline their heads upon pillows or headrests, and the other two make use of their companions for the same purpose. A party may consist of either men or women, or it may be made up of both sexes; opium smokers do not stand on ceremony with each other, and strangers will recline on the same bunk and draw intoxication from the same pipe without the least hesitation. The old adage says "Misery loves

company"; this is certainly the case with debauchery, and especially of debauchery with opium.[11]

Although the use of opium was not a crime during those years, it was illegal in New York City to operate an opium-smoking parlor. Police efforts to close the establishments were vividly presented in the urban guidebooks. Moreover, descriptions of the opium habit and its consequences were dramatized as evil in the police literature of the day, directly associating drug-taking behavior with criminality. In 1884, for example, in a lengthy volume written and published by A. E. Costello, New York's chief of police, the dynamics of opium smoking were related with numerous vivid illustrations. In the commentary, Costello stated:

> A comparatively new criminal agency has been at work in certain sections of the city, spreading the fruitful seeds of contamination, and throwing additional responsibilities on the already overburdened shoulders of the police. The agency in question is what is known as "the opium habit." In a remarkably short space of time this terrible vice has taken deep root, and it is very much to be feared that it will not [slow] down, but that it has come to stay. . . . Unfortunately, this pernicious habit is not confined to the children of the flowery kingdom; a legion of opium smokers to the manner born, and many of them people of respectability and refinement, are slaves of the habit. . . . The most debased and wretched practice of the habit is smoking, which is now engaged in in scores of "joints" in New York.[12]

And finally, by 1896, the term dope fiend had made its way into popular slang usage, implying that drug-taking was, or at least resulted in, an evil obsession.[13]

MRS. W. K. VANDERBILT, CAPTAIN R. P. HOBSON, AND "THE LEGEND OF THE LIVING DEAD"

To suggest that during the late nineteenth century a fully committed effort was under way to criminalize the drug user would be an overstatement. Commentaries were in the medical and police literature. Also, occasional writers linked drug use with sexual license. Some authorities reported that "old smokers" of opium used the drug to seduce innocent girls;[14] that "female smokers, if not already lost in the point of virtue, soon become so"; [15] and that "rapes, seductions, and other criminal acts occur, sometimes boldly, or with secretiveness and cunning." [16] These sordid links of drug taking with vice and crime did have their impact on the shaping of public attitudes. In the main, however, people had many ambivalent views about drug abuse.

Experts knew that opium and morphine did not create sexual psychotics, and they were quite vocal about it. [17] Medical, pharmaceutical, and other organizations understood what they considered to be the threats that addiction posed for women and youth. Yet while loathing and fearing addiction, at the same time they had sympathy for addicts. They condemned the use of drugs for escape or sensual pleasure, but they also felt that morphinism was a form of physiological slavery that ought to be treated with pragmatic therapy rather than moralism. A growing body of confessional literature also revealed that addicts led lives of despair, that they sought freedom from the superhuman forces of addiction and repeatedly underwent rigorous cures. [18]

None of this should suggest, however, that there was no such thing as a criminal addict at this time, for indeed there was. Many contemporary commentators have argued that drug abuse and addiction are social problems created by such unenforceable laws as the Harrison Act of 1914. [19] Evidence of the existence of the pre-Harrison criminal addict appears in the writings of Dr. Perry Lichtenstein, a physician in charge of narcotic addiction treatment at City Prison, Manhattan. [20] Just weeks before the Harrison Act was signed into law, Lichtenstein noted that some 5% of the 16,000 prisoners that year were "narcotic habitues," and that the numbers had been increasing dramatically since the beginning of the decade. He added that the vast majority of his patients had become addicted not through prescription medications but had obtained their drugs through access to underworld black market sources. Moreover, they engaged in prostitution and petty crimes to maintain their supplies.

After the passage of the Harrison Act, however, the criminalization process began in earnest. By that time, concerned people viewed heroin use with increasing alarm. Heroin was considered the most threatening drug in history, appealing to a new youthful generation that seemed indifferent to the standards of conduct of the wider society. In addition, as more and more users were arrested for the illegal possession of the drug, the association of heroin with crime became more firmly entrenched.

Chronologically first among the post–Harrison Act crusaders was Mrs. William K. (Anna) Vanderbilt of New York society's elite Four Hundred. Jousting for prominence in the society pages of the New York press, the ladies of Gotham's best families pursued causes in the name of social reform. To keep up with her rivals who had become famous as suffragettes during these pre–World War I years, Anna Vanderbilt set out on a campaign against heroin. She wanted to prevent the drug from adding to its already engorged prison of "lost souls." She organized antinarcotics committees, led marches down Fifth Avenue, and warned New Yorkers of the armies of dangerous "fiends" roaming Harlem and the Bronx. Her endeavors resulted in a series of newspaper accounts that described an epidemic of heavy addiction within the youth culture and more than 1.5 million violent and dangerous addicts at large in the streets. The propaganda also included rumors of fiendish enemy agents prowling through the school yards of urban America passing out candy laced with heroin, seducing innocent children and teenagers into lives of addiction, vice, crime, and despair.[21] The reports quickly spread from the New York dailies to popular national magazines, and the *Literary Digest* offered commentaries on "American enslavement to drugs";[22] *The Outlook* described how drugs were being trafficked by gamblers, cabdrivers, domestics, vagrants, lunchroom helpers, poolroom employees, porters, and laundrymen;[23] and the *American Review of Reviews* stated that there were 5 million addicts nationwide, that the trafficker was a criminal of the worst type, and that the "drug menace" had to be stamped out.[24] All of that was only the beginning. In the 1920s Captain Richmond Pearson Hobson entered the crusade.

Described by one of his biographers as a man of "virtually unlimited moral indignation,"[25] Hobson was one of the most celebrated heroes of the Spanish-American War. He was also an adept temperance lecturer, but when national Prohibition went into effect he became a reformer without a cause. Hobson soon realized the potential of the addiction issue and began an unprecedented campaign of sensationalism. Through newspaper columns, magazine articles, and national radio broadcasts, he popularized the notion that addicts are "beasts" and "monsters" who spread their disease like medieval vampires.

Hobson launched his effort by forming the International Narcotic Education Association, and almost immediately his views were seen in popular magazines and press reports all across the nation. In the May 24, 1924 issue of the *Literary Digest,* he was quoted as saying:

> Every heroin addict, because of the drug's action on his brain, has a mania to spread his addiction to others, the drug is four times as powerful as morphine and comes in a convenient deceptive form of a white powder called "snow," which is generally "whiffed" into the nostrils.
>
> One "snow party" a day for a week makes a youth an addict. Organized efforts are directed at the young. Besides the professional peddlers we have a million young recruiting agents in our midst insanely trapping our youth into addiction. A sure symptom of the activities of this organization is seen in the rising tide of crime.[26]

The problem of "1 million heroin addicts" was an idea that Hobson pushed heavily, incorporating it into a pamphlet he entitled *The Peril of Narcotics—A Warning to the People of America.* He urged Congress to publish 5 million copies of the little booklet so that every home in the nation would have one on hand. Even government antidrug forces, well aware of Hobson's sensationalism and exaggeration, opposed the request. The Federal Narcotics Control Board found the warnings in *The Peril of Narcotics* fantastic: that 1 ounce of heroin will cause 2,000 addicts; that "in using any brand of face powder regularly, it is a wise precaution to have a sample analyzed for heroin."[27]

Undaunted, Hobson continued his drive. He managed to have *The Peril of Narcotics* read into the *Congressional Record,* and he sent copies under a congressional frank to 5,000 superintendents of education, hundreds of college and university presidents, officials of parent-teacher associations, and distinguished citizens listed in *Who's Who in America.*[28]

Captain Hobson ultimately achieved his greatest visibility on March 1, 1928, when NBC donated time for the radio broadcast of an emotionally charged address in which addicts were depicted as an army of the "living dead." In part:

> To get his heroin supply the addict will not only advocate public policies against the public welfare, but will lie, steal, rob, and if necessary, commit murder. Heroin addiction can be likened to a contagion. Suppose it were announced that there were more than a million lepers among our people. Think what a shock the announcement would produce! Yet drug addiction is far more incurable than leprosy, far more tragic to its victims, and is spreading like a moral and physical scourge.
>
> There are symptoms breaking out all over the country and now breaking out in many parts of Europe which show that individual nations and the whole world is menaced [sic] by this appalling foe . . . marching . . . to the capture and destruction of the whole world.
>
> Most of the daylight robberies, daring holdups, cruel murders, and similar crimes of violence are now known to be committed chiefly by drug addicts, who constitute the primary cause of our alarming crime wave.
>
> Drug addiction is more communicable and less curable than leprosy. Drug addicts are the principal carriers of vice diseases, and with their lowered resistance are incubators and carriers of the streptococcus, pneumococcus, the germ of flu, of tuberculosis, and other diseases.
>
> *Upon the issue hangs the perpetuation of civilization, the destiny of the whole world and the future of the human race!*[29]

Hobson's descriptions of addicts suggested to his readers and listeners images of wicked-looking denizens of the urban slime—ugly, scarred, and having all the stereotypic characteristics of the mugger and rapist. Yet the typical heroin user was hardly that. Most were young white males from the slums of eastern cities. They were citizens by birth, although their parents were typically immigrants. Moreover, they were poorly educated, and if they were employed they worked at unskilled or semiskilled jobs. Most addicts spent much of their time on the city streets, running with juvenile gangs.[30] In short, the heroin users of Hobson's time were indistinguishable from most of urban America's second-generation immigrant children—almost all were poor, uneducated, unemployed, and running in the streets. The only differentiating characteristic—if at all observable—was their narcotics use, which usually began with opium smoking within the context of their gang activities. They were indeed vagabonds and petty thieves, but so too were their nondrug-using peers in the Irish, Italian, Jewish, German, and Polish ghettos of the cities. Some heroin users were indeed gamblers and professional criminals, but these generally represented a small minority.

By the middle of the 1930s Captain Hobson had shifted his energies. He moved to the forefront with Harry J. Anslinger's fight against the evil weed of the fields. As for heroin, Hobson's dementia was no longer needed. There were others who carried on the crusade. He died in 1937, but by then the image of the addict had been well established. "Dope fiends," as they were called, were sex-crazed maniacs, degenerate street criminals, and members of the "living dead." "Narcotics," including marijuana and cocaine, reportedly ravaged the human body; they destroyed morality; addicts were sexually violent and criminally aggressive; they were weak and ineffective members of society; addiction was contagious since users had a mania for perpetuating the social anathema of drug taking; and finally, once addicted, the user entered into a lifetime of slavery to drugs. Then came the war years and more pressing concerns. The problems of addiction were set aside, at least temporarily, not to be resurrected for almost a decade.

JAILBAIT STREET, ROCK 'N ROLL, AND WHITE AMERICAN RESPECTABILITY

The United States entered the mid-century as the most powerful nation on earth. World War II had ended the Great Depression and unleashed a prosperous postwar era; unemployment had stabilized at a uniquely low level, and most Americans reveled in a new economic privilege. The period has been called the "Fabulous Fifties," for retrospective glances have characterized it as a golden age of simplicity and innocence—the thrilling days of bobby socks and soda fountains, of hot rods and Elvis Presley. There were no real wars, no riots, and no protests. But all was not well.

Along with the postwar prosperity, heroin addiction once more became visible. Having seemingly diminished when the draft sent the young white users off to war, it moved underground into the black ghetto, where it began to spread. The 1950s were also a time of youthful rebellion, and many adults in mainstream America feared that heroin use would become epidemic among the children of white society.

Of the many forms of youth rebellion, however, it appeared that juvenile delinquency, not heroin addiction, became the most visible. Education reporter Benjamin Fine of the *New York Times* predicted in the early 1950s that by the middle of the decade the number of youths being processed by the police would exceed 1 million. His estimates were quickly realized, and property crimes and car theft were the major juvenile offenses. The young were also committing acts of inexplicable and pointless violence—beatings, rape, and murder. Although statistically few of America's teenage groups were involved in violent crime, those that were had seemingly terrorized entire cities.[31] These were the fighting gangs of the 1950s—the Roman Lords, Young Stars, Pigtown, Scorpions, and other urban street gangs as portrayed in Irving Shulman's *The Amboy Dukes* and Hal Ellson's *Jailbait Street*.[a]

Curiously, however, although street crime was heavily tied to delinquency, at least as far as the media were concerned, juvenile drug use seemed to be absent from the gang culture. Isidor Chein's

---

[a] Throughout New York City during the 1950s, rumor had it that up in the far reaches of the East Bronx was the most fearsome gang of all, the Fordham Baldies. So terrible were they, with shaved heads as a mark of their membership, that the mere mention of their presence in a local neighborhood would clear the streets of youths—both gang and nongang members alike. But no one ever seemed actually to encounter the Baldies face to face—ever. In the years hence, many concluded that they were a myth, and in all of the literature descriptive of the New York ganglands of the 1950s, the Baldies are never mentioned. Even in the 3,652 issues of the rigorously indexed *New York Times* their name never appears. Yet in an autobiography of a heroin addict, written during the 1970s, its author makes one brief mention of the Baldies, and his remarks suggest how the myth may have started:

> The gangs we used to rumble with mostly were the Hoods, of course, and then the Seven Crowns, the Scorpions, occasionally the Mau Maus, and then the Fordham Baldies. The Baldies were a group of guys made up of the sons of racketeers from the Fordham Road area. The Godfather up Fordham way used to be known as Baldie. So naturally the kids took that name. They were a pretty tough group so we mostly left them alone.

See Richard P. Rettig, Manual J. Torres, and Gerald R. Garrett, *Manny: A Criminal-Addict's Story* (Boston: Houghton Mifflin, 1977), p. 27.

The Road to H, a pioneering, although theoretically problematic, study of narcotics use among juveniles, reflected what most other informed efforts had found. Adolescent drug use was concentrated in the ghetto, most widespread where income and education were lowest. Drug use, was not, however, intrinsically tied to gang activities. Some drug users were in organized juvenile gangs, yet these were less often involved in gang fighting.[32]

Extensive gang involvement or not, drug use, and particularly heroin addiction in the central cities, was indeed spreading at an unprecedented rate.[b] Although the media may have over-sensationalized their reporting,[33] researchers, clinicians, and law-enforcement groups working in the drug field were well aware of the growing problem. There were, after all, many indicators of the new trend. At New York's Bellevue Hospital during the years 1940–1948, no adolescents had been admitted for treatment with a diagnosis of drug addiction: in 1949 there was 1, followed by 6 in 1950, and 84 during the first two months of 1951.[34] In port cities around the nation, the number of heroin seizures had dramatically increased.[35] At the federal drug-treatment centers in Lexington, Kentucky, and Fort Worth, Texas, the proportion of youths

---

[b] It should be noted here that common gateway drugs (drugs of initiation) for youths then and now are the organic solvents and inhalants. These include a series of highly volatile compounds that act in a central nervous system depressant capacity. Chemically they exist either in a gaseous state at room temperature, or they rapidly evaporate from a liquid state when exposed to air. The more common organic solvents sought by drug abusers are generally of three varieties:

1. Coal tar derivatives: lacquers, paint thinners and removers; quick-drying glue and cements; gasoline, kerosene, and other petroleum products; lighter and cleaning fluids; nail polish remover; and various aerosols. Their active ingredients include toluene, acetone, benzene, carbon tetrachloride, chloroform, ethyl ether, and various alcohols and acetates.

2. Freon: a flurocarbon gas used as a refrigerant and commonly used as a propellant for aerosols prior to 1978 when flurocarbons were banned from use in household consumer products.

3. Nitrous oxide and related nitrites: derivatives of nitric acid, including amyl nitrate.

With the exceptions of ether, nitrous oxide (laughing gas), and chloroform, which are used for anesthesia, and amyl nitrate, which has been employed in the treatment of heart pain and asthma, the vast majority of organic solvents and inhalants have no general medical use. Furthermore, most of these compounds are not drugs and therefore are not subject to control.

As central nervous system depressants, these organic solvents and inhalants tend to have effects similar in many respects to those of alcohol and the sedatives. Reported effects at low dosage levels include mood elevation and mild euphoria, feelings of sociability, and a lessening of inhibitions. Higher dose levels produce laughing, dizziness, feelings of floating, perceptual distortions, illusions, confusion, blurred vision and slurred speech, and motor incoordination. With even further increases in dosage levels, the general effects of sedation and anesthesia may predominate, with respiratory depression, stupor, and unconsciousness in some cases. Acute intoxication may result in a lack of behavioral control, impaired judgment, or fear. Acute psychoses have been reported, as have abnormalities in kidney and liver functioning.

being admitted was expanding at a geometric rate.[36] In New York and other major cities, the number of youths coming to the attention of the police, the courts, and social-work and other human-service agencies on drug-related matters was also advancing. Finally, although it could be effectively argued that public pressure to do something about the heroin problem had encouraged selective enforcement of the narcotics laws, drug-related arrests were up in most large American cities.

In terms of the reasons for the new heroin epidemic, *Life* magazine felt it had the answer:

> What had come over today's 15-year-olds? One answer was the brazen pusher, who, needing customers, was now cynically making them among naive youngsters, usually, but not always, from poor homes. Another answer was marijuana, widely available and publicized as nonaddictive—which is scientifically true but tragically misleading since it is usually the first step toward ultimate enslavement by heroin.[37]

Harry J. Anslinger of the Bureau of Narcotics had a different answer. He blamed parents. In the October 1951 issue of the *Reader's Digest* he argued that most juvenile addicts come from families in which there is no proper parental control or training in decent personal habits. "Rarely," he added, "does a boy or girl from a normally balanced family in any income bracket become an addict."[38] In other words, Anslinger was suggesting that decent people just don't use drugs! Finally, the Crime Investigating Committee of the U.S. Senate had the solution to the problem: stiffer penalties for narcotics violators, "for no penalty is too severe for a criminal of such character"; increase the number of agents assigned to narcotics work; cancel the sailing papers of any seaman convicted of a narcotics violation; and initiate a worldwide ban on the growing of the opium poppy.[39]

Although it seemed clear from both media and scientific reports that heroin use was almost exclusively a problem of the urban inner city, there was considerable concern within segments of the white middle class as to "contaminating factors" that might induce drug using and other undesirable behaviors among the more socially privileged youth. A prime target of the parental establishment was the new "rock 'n roll" music.

When Alan Freed, a disk jockey for Cleveland radio station WJW, introduced the term in 1954, little did he imagine what the impact of rock 'n roll would be on American life and world social patterns.[c]

---

[c] Various accounts have Alan Freed introducing the term *rock 'n roll* in 1951, 1952, and 1954. The latter date is likely correct, as 1954 saw the release of what has since been almost universally agreed to be the first rock 'n roll record, "Sh-Boom" by The Chords

The new music had elements of the country and western sounds of the rural white working class, but it was primarily made up of the rhythm and blues of an urbanizing black America. As a product principally of the black community, it clearly had a racial stigma attached to it.[40] American racism condemned black tastes in general and "race records" in particular. When Freed presented rock 'n roll—a ghetto euphemism for both dancing and sex—to white youth, it was an immediate success.[d] Some whites had already been listening to the all-black rhythm and blues radio shows, but it was not a taste that the majority cultivated. Freed, a white DJ, put the music in a more familiar and acceptable format, reassuring the majority of repressed and nervous white kids. His framework encouraged them to make the effort to overcome their bland, stereotyped musical background.[41]

The acceptance of rock 'n roll was part of the new youth rebellion. At the same time it served to threaten every phobia of white American respectability—particularly when children were heard chanting, "rock 'n roll is here to stay!" Parents, congresspeople, and social commentators of the period claimed that it had infected white teenagers all across the country. It introduced them to their sexuality, to interracial contacts, to bizarre dance rituals, and most seriously, to drugs. As authors Jack Lait and Lee Mortimer articulated in their 1952 best-seller *U.S.A. Confidential:*

> Like a heathen religion, it is all tied up with tom-toms and hot jive and ritualistic orgies of erotic dancing, weed smoking and mass mania, with African jungle background. Many music shops purvey dope. White girls are recruited for colored lovers. Another cog in the giant delinquency machine is the radio disc jockey. We know that many platter spinners are hopheads. Many others are Reds, left-wingers, or hecklers of social convention. Through disc jocks, kids get to know colored and other hit musicians; they frequent places the radio oracles plug, which is done with design . . . to hook jives and guarantee a new generation subservient to the Mafia.[42]

(a black group) on Cat Records. A "white cover" (same song, white group) of "Sh-Boom" was recorded by The Crew Cuts the same year and released on Mercury with an almost identical rendering (with the exception that the "sha-na-na-na-na-na" bridge was a Crew Cut creation).

[d] The term *rock 'n roll* originally referred to the motions a car makes when two lovers were going at it in the back seat. Hence, rock 'n roll music became what poured out of the car radio while Johnny B. Goode was trying to mess up Peggy Sue's ponytail or Long Tall Sally's chantilly lace.

Lait and Mortimer went on to describe how marijuana use led to addiction and generated orgies of interracial sex.[e]

Yet regardless of the white phobias of the 1950s, rock 'n roll endured, and its relationship to drugs was never established.[f] In spite of media contentions about a connection between drug use and middle-class delinquency, throughout the decade heroin addiction appeared to remain at a relatively low level in white neighborhoods. Yet narcotics use continued to grow at an alarming rate in the inner city, particularly among the youths of black America and other minority populations. For many of them, drug use had become a way of life, and street crime was typically a part of their drug-taking and drug-seeking activities.[43]

---

[e] For more widely read observers, what appeared in *U.S.A. Confidential* was no surprise, for authors Lait and Mortimer had already established their general ignorance and prejudice. In *New York Confidential* (New York: Viking, 1948), a piece of popular reportorial carrion they had written a few years earlier stated:

> . . . from the days of earliest slavery in the United States and West Indies, Negroes have swept away their heavy inhibitions, forgotten the burn of the lash and the clank of the shackles with an age-old drug, hashish.
>
> Hashish was used among the ancients to stimulate armies for killing. . . .
>
> There are about 500 apartments in Harlem, known as "tea pads," set up exclusively for marijuana addicts.

[f] Although rock 'n roll survived and evolved, Alan Freed did not. As depicted in *American Hot Wax*, a 1978 Paramount Pictures release, he was destroyed by the violence of the 1950s mainstream. At a show promoted by Freed in Boston, police interrupted the performance. Later, members of the audience spread through the city, fighting. One person was killed, several were beaten, and Freed was charged with anarchy and inciting to riot. It took him many years and a considerable sum of money before the charges were finally dismissed. Then he was charged in investigations of *payola*—a standard practice in the record industry where bribes were given to disk jockeys to secure air time for certain records. Only the rock 'n roll industry was targeted, and Freed received only a $300 fine, but his career was ruined. He moved from station to station, drinking heavily and continually pursued by harassing indictments. He died in 1965 at the age of 43.

Contemporary rock has also experienced some repression. Perhaps best known in this behalf was the federal court decision in 1990 which ruled that rap group 2 Live Crew's album *As Nasty As They Wanna Be* was obscene. The decision was an unfortunate one, for not only did it compromise the integrity of the First Amendment, but it awarded fame and fortune to a less than average rap group. Rap is rhythmic chant, rhyme set to drums or the thundering cacophony of heavy metal, a musical culture filled with self-assertion, with cartoonish stories marked with exaggeration, and often with sex, anger, violence, and hate. What was declared obscene in *As Nasty As They Wanna Be* were lyrics about tearing and damaging vaginas, forcing anal sex on a young girl, and then forcing her to lick excrement. For an examination of the rap and 2 Live Crew controversy, see David Mills, "Rap Music That Guns for Violence," *Insight*, 25 Sept., 1989, pp. 54–56; *Newsweek*, 19 Mar. 1990, pp. 56–63; *U.S. News & World Report*, 19 Mar. 1990, p. 17; *Miami Herald*, 7 June 1990, pp. 1A, 10A; *New York Times*, 8 June 1990, p. A10; 11 June 1990, p. A14; 17 June 1990, pp. E1, E5.

THE RIDDLE OF THE SPHINX

The Sphinx was a monster of Greek mythology that had the face of a woman, the body of a lion, and the wings of a bird. For years she perched on Mount Phicium, near the ancient city of Thebes, posing a riddle to all passersby. "What goes on four feet," she would ask, "on two feet, and three, but the more feet it goes on the weaker it be?" Those who could not answer her riddle were promptly devoured— which were all, save one. Oedipus answered her directly. "It is man," he stated, "for he crawls as an infant, walks upright as an adult, and totters with a staff in old age." Upon hearing this, the Sphinx slew herself. Oedipus was made king of Thebes and went on to other adventures.

In the drug field, for as long as commentators were sensationalizing crimes allegedly the maniacal handiwork of heroin, cocaine, and marijuana users, researchers argued a corresponding riddle. Is criminal behavior antecedent to addiction; or, does criminality emerge subsequent to addiction? More specifically, is crime the result of or a response to a special set of life circumstances brought about by the addiction to narcotic drugs? Or conversely, is addiction per se a deviant tendency characteristic of individuals already prone to offense behavior? Moreover, and assuming that criminality may indeed be a pre-addiction phenomenon, does the onset of chronic narcotics use bring about a change in the nature, intensity, and frequency of deviant and criminal acts? Does criminal involvement tend to increase or decrease subsequent to addiction? There were also related questions. What kinds of criminal offenses do addicts engage in? Do they tend toward violent acts of aggression? Or are their crimes strictly profit oriented and geared toward the violation of the sanctity of private property? Or is it both?

As early as the 1920s researchers had been conducting studies— many studies—seeking answers to these very questions. Particularly, Edouard Sandoz at the Municipal Court of Boston and Lawrence Kolb at the U.S. Public Health Service examined the backgrounds of hundreds of heroin users, focusing on the drugs-crime relationship.[44] Their conclusions were relatively informed ones, however ignored. Basically what they found within criminal justice and treatment populations were several different types of cases. Some drug users were habitual criminals, and likely always had been; others were simply violators of the Harrison Act, having been arrested for no more than the illegal possession of narcotics. Moreover, with both types a record of violent crimes was absent.

The analyses provided by Sandoz, Kolb, and others established the parameters of several points of view:

- Addicts ought to be the object of vigorous law-enforcement activity, since the majority are members of a criminal element and drug addiction is simply one of the later phases of their deviant careers.

- Addicts prey upon legitimate society, and the effects of their drugs do indeed predispose them to serious criminal transgressions.

- Addicts are essentially law-abiding citizens who are forced to steal to adequately support their drug habits.

- Addicts are not necessarily criminals but are forced to associate with an underworld element that tends to maintain control over the distribution of illicit drugs.[45]

The notion that addicts ought to be the objects of vigorous police activity, a posture that might be called the criminal model of drug abuse, was actively and relentlessly pursued by the Federal Bureau of Narcotics and other law enforcement groups. Their argument was fixed on the notion of criminality, for on the basis of their own observations, the vast majority of heroin users encountered were members of criminal groups. To support this view, the Bureau of Narcotics pointed to several studies that demonstrated that most addicts were already criminals before they began using heroin.[46] Addicts, the bureau emphasized, represent a destructive force confronting the people of America. Whatever the sources of their addiction might be, they are members of a highly subversive and antisocial group. For the bureau, this position did indeed have some basis in reality. Having been charged with the enforcement of a law that prohibited the possession, sale, and distribution of narcotics, what bureau agents were confronted with were criminal addicts, often under the most dangerous of circumstances. It was not uncommon for agents to be wounded or even killed in arrest situations, and analyses of the careers of many addicts demonstrated that their criminal records were lengthy. Moreover, there was the matter of professional underworld involvement with narcotics, a point that Commissioner Anslinger himself commented on in 1951:

> It is well established that a larger proportion of the pickpocket artists, the shoplifters, the professional gamblers and card sharks, the confidence men operating fake horse race or fake stock sale schemes, the "short con" men such as the "short-change artists" or the coin matchers, are addicted to the use of narcotic drugs.[47]

Anslinger was referring to the world of professional thieves, and studies have demonstrated that predators of this kind are involved not only in the use of narcotics but in trafficking as well.[48] Anslinger was wrong, however, in his belief that all heroin users are from the same mold. Studies of drug-using populations of his time have referenced the existence of numerous and alternative patterns of narcotic addiction. The professional thieves about which Anslinger spoke were a group of highly skilled yet essentially nonviolent criminals who made a regular business of stealing. Crime was their occupation and means of livelihood, and as such, they devoted their entire time and energy to stealing. They operated with proficiency; they had a body of skills and knowledge that was utilized in the execution and planning of their work; and they were graduates of an informal developmental process that included the acquisition of specialized skills, knowledge, attitudes, and experience. Finally, in identifying themselves with the world of crime, professional thieves were members of an exclusive fraternity that extended friendship, understanding, sympathy, security, safety, recognition, and respect.[49] Their pattern of addiction revolved around the use of heroin or morphine by needle, or the smoking of opium. Spree use of drugs was also common, generally to reduce the boredom associated with incarceration, or as part of pleasure-seeking activities.

By contrast, during the years between 1900 and 1960, there was a pattern of addiction characteristic of a core of middle-aged white southerners. Identified through patient records at federal drug-treatment facilities, they were usually addicted to morphine or paregoric, and their drugs had been obtained from physicians through legal or quasi-legal means. As patients under treatment for some illness, these addicts were not members of any deviant subcultures and did not have contacts with other addicts.[50]

There were also groups of hidden addicts who, because of sufficient income and/or access to a legitimate source of drugs, had no need to make contacts with visibly criminal cultures to obtain drugs. Among these were musicians, physicians, and members of other segments of the health professions.[51]

Finally, there was the stereotyped heroin street addict—the narcotics user of the American ghetto of whom the mass media spoke. Heroin street addicts were typically from the socially and economically deprived segments of the urban population. They began their careers with drug experimentation as adolescents for the sake of excitement or thrills, to conform with peer-group activities and expectations, and/or to strike back at the authority structures which they opposed. The use of alcohol, marijuana, codeine, or pills generally initiated them into substance abuse, and later drug intake focused primarily on heroin. Their status of addiction was often said to have emerged as a result of an addiction-prone personality, and they supported their habits through illegal means. Also among this group were poly-drug users—those who concurrently abused a variety of drugs.[g]

---

[g] This listing of patterns of addiction is by no means exhaustive; there were, and still are, many more types.

Most law-enforcement agencies focused their attention and their commentary on those who manifested the pattern of heroin street addiction. In what may be one of the most scientifically prejudiced and ignorant studies targeting this group, FBI agent James P. Morgan, a former detective in the narcotics bureau of the New York City Police Department, compiled data in 1965 to "prove conclusively" that addiction was indeed a criminal problem.[52] His population included 135 narcotics users he had personally arrested during preceding years. Playing the roles of both police officer and scientific researcher, Morgan extensively questioned his quarries regarding their careers in crime and addiction. In terms of the validity and reliability of the responses received, Morgan was quite confident that his information was accurate. In fact he said so himself: "I do not believe that any false answers were given to the questions." Morgan's analysis indicated that "only 15 of the addicts studied were able to prove that they were lacking a criminal background." So logically, and with apparent confidence, he concluded:

> The statistical results of this study revealed that those addicts studied become what they are, not by accident, but as a result of criminal tendencies which they had already exhibited.

Reading on in Morgan's essay and in more serious works that address the issue of criminal tendencies, one could not avoid recalling Cesare Lombroso's thoughts on "born criminals" and "atavisms" and "inherited predispositions to crime" of a century earlier. Aside from Morgan's problems with sample bias and misguided interpretation, perhaps if given more time he might have resurrected Lombroso's ideas. After all, if his addicts did indeed have criminal tendencies, maybe their head shapes and sizes could have been significant in understanding their behaviors, as Lombroso had argued.

What Agent Morgan and company were responding to in their commentaries were the clinicians and social scientists of the 1950s and early 1960s who had put forth the notion of what might be called a medical model of addiction, as opposed to the criminal view of law enforcement. The medical model, which physicians first proposed in the late nineteenth century, held that addiction was a chronic and relapsing disease. The addict, it was argued, should be dealt with as any patient suffering from some physiological or medical disorder. At the same time, numerous proponents of the view sought to mitigate addict criminality by putting forth the "enslavement theory of addiction." The idea here was that the monopolistic controls over the heroin black market forced "sick" and otherwise law-abiding drug users into lives of crime to support their habits.

PRICE DANIELS, THE PRESIDENT'S COMMISSION, RICHARD NIXON, AND THE FIRST "WAR ON DRUGS"

For the better part of a half century, hundreds of studies of the relationship between crime and addiction were conducted.[53] Invariably, when one analysis would appear to support the medical model of addiction, the next would affirm the criminal model. Given these repeated contradictions, something had to be wrong—and indeed there was. The theories, hypotheses, conclusions, and other findings generated by almost the entire spectrum of research were actually of little value, for there were awesome biases and deficiencies in the very nature of their designs. Data-gathering enterprises on criminal activity had usually restricted themselves to drug-users' arrest histories, and there can be little argument about the inadequacy of official criminal statistics as measures of the incidence and prevalence of offense behavior.[54] Those studies that did manage to go beyond arrest figures to probe self-reported criminal activity were invariably limited to either incarcerated heroin users or addicts in treatment settings. The few efforts that did manage to locate active heroin users in the street community typically examined the samples' drug-taking behaviors to the exclusion of their drug-seeking behaviors. Given the many methodological difficulties, it was impossible to draw many reliable conclusions about the nature of drug-related crime—about its magnitude, shape, scope, or direction. Moreover, and perhaps most importantly, the conclusions being drawn from the generations of studies were not taking a number of important features of the drug scene into account: that there were many different kinds of drugs and drug users; that the nature and patterns of drug use were constantly shifting and changing; that the purity, potency, and availability of drugs were dynamic rather than static; and that both drug-related crime and drug-using criminals were undergoing continuous metamorphosis.

Meanwhile, in 1956, while mainstream America was persecuting Alan Freed, and the Fordham Baldies were terrorizing the imaginations of New York youth, Senator Price Daniels of Texas was repeating an oft quoted message:

> Addiction is bad enough in itself. But with it goes crime, committed to pay for the habit. This combination of addiction and crime is a very communicable disease.[55]

If one had not known otherwise, one might have thought the words had come from the ghost of Captain Richmond Hobson, echoing lines from his enthusiastic "living dead" sermon of almost three decades earlier. Senator Daniels, however, did Hobson one better. He claimed that he had established a startling fact: that narcotic addiction was directly responsible for one fourth of all the crimes committed in the United States. His declaration was an interesting one, for not only was the nature and extent of drug-related crime virtually unknown but, further, absolutely no one had even the vaguest idea of how much crime of any kind there was in the nation.

Then came the 1960s, a decade that occupies an individual summit in Americans' jagged images of the crime and violence in their midst. It began with the assassination of John Fitzgerald Kennedy, the fourth president of the United States to die by such violent means. But Kennedy's death was only the beginning. His alleged assassin, Lee Harvey Oswald, was shot to death within 36 hours of the president. In 1965 Black Muslim leader Malcolm X died violently in New York City. In 1967 American Nazi leader George Lincoln Rockwell was murdered by one of his followers. The next year the lives of civil-rights leader Dr. Martin Luther King, Jr. and Senator Robert Kennedy were taken by assassination. Of less political renown, the 1960s also saw the cold-blooded murders of three young civil-rights workers by members of the Ku Klux Klan in Mississippi, with the connivance of local law-enforcement officers; the fire bombing of the "freedom riders" in Alabama; the bloody battles at Kent State, "Ole Miss," and other campuses across the nation spurred by America's involvement in the Vietnam War; the ghetto riots in Los Angeles, Newark, Detroit, and numerous other densely populated urban areas; and the police riot at the 1968 Democratic Convention when Chicago's Mayor Richard Daley unleashed a force of 18,000 law-enforcement officers, Illinois National Guardsmen, and regular Army troops armed with rifles, flamethrowers, and bazookas against peace marchers demonstrating their opposition to the Vietnam war. There was also street crime.

During the first half of the decade alone, reported crimes of violence had increased by one half, property crimes by two thirds, and the overall crime rate by almost one half. In response, newly elected President Lyndon Johnson announced a "war on crime" during an address to the 89th Congress on March 8, 1965. The visible army in his war was the President's Commission on Law Enforcement and Administration of Justice, established by Johnson to study the problems of crime and justice.[56] A major task of the commission, at a time when politicians, parents, and the press were claiming that addiction was responsible for up to half the crime in the nation, was to examine the drug problem and its relation to crime.

When the commission's work was complete, the task force assigned to study narcotics and drug abuse made the following embarrassing, however honest, announcement:

> The simple truth is that the extent of the addict's or drug abuser's responsibility for all nondrug offenses is unknown.

Obviously it is great, particularly in New York City, with its
heavy concentration of users; but there is no reliable data to
assess properly the common assertion that drug users or addicts
are responsible for 50% of all crime.[57]

Professionals in the drug field applauded the announcement,
hoping that, finally, resources would be made available to measure
the phenomenon in question. To their chagrin, however, no federal
funds were earmarked for focused studies of the drugs-crime nexus,
and on into the next decade the issue remained unresolved. By that
time, common assertions had pushed the amount of crime presumed
to have been committed by addicts up to 90%.

Then, when Richard M. Nixon assumed the presidency of the
United States, he spoke of a "war on drugs" and a "war on heroin."
He established a Special Action Office for Drug Abuse Prevention, but
according to investigative reporter Edward Jay Epstein, the real purpose
of the war was to increase the power of the White House bureaucracy.
Epstein maintained that under the aegis of a war on heroin, Nixon had
established two new agencies—the Office of Drug Abuse Law Enforcement and the Office of National Narcotics Intelligence—created for the
purpose of investigating his political enemies.[58] Whether or not this
was really so, Nixon's war seemed to accomplish little.

Yet there was Nixon's "screwworm" project.[59] It was an effort by
the White House, the Department of Agriculture, and NASA to create
a wonderfully wicked weevil that, when released in Turkey and the
Golden Triangle, would eat the plants that produced the pod that gave
the opium that supplied the drug that obsessed poor Richard Nixon.
A screwworm as such was actually created, but its developers feared
that if released, it might start eating rice, wheat, and other plants once
it had devoured the world's poppy crop. That, combined with the
possibility of its crossing international boundaries to attack Soviet
poppies, ultimately led to the little bug's demise.

In 1972 the fear of crime climbed to new heights. According to a
Gallup Poll in that year, almost half of those surveyed were afraid to
walk in their neighborhoods at night, and drug addiction was cited
among the major reasons for the high crime rate.[60] By January 1973
crime was ranked highest among the nation's urban problems, with
drug use ranking third.[61] President Nixon, by that time in his second
term and all too busy denying his complicity in the Watergate cover-
up, nevertheless responded with a statement reemphasizing his war
on drugs:

No single law-enforcement problem has occupied more time,
effort, and money in the past four years than that of drug abuse
and drug addiction. We have regarded drugs as "public enemy

number one," destroying the most precious resource we have—our young people—and breeding lawlessness, violence and death.[62]

Although often accused of exaggeration, the President this time made many claims that were quite accurate. Estimated federal expenditures for drug-abuse prevention and law enforcement were indeed staggering—increasing from $150.2 million in 1971 to $654.8 million just two years later.[63] But Nixon's descriptions of the drug problem and its relation to crime often went beyond the parameters of reasonable estimate. He referred to heroin use as a plague that threatened every man, woman, and child in the nation with the "hell of addiction," and maintained that addict crime—largely in the form of "crime in the streets"—cost the nation roughly $18 billion a year. Yet the billions of dollars of losses from thefts and robberies that Nixon claimed addicts were committing to buy their heroin supplies was actually more than 25 times greater than the value of all property stolen and unrecovered throughout the United States in 1971.[64]

HEROIN, COCAINE, AND CRIME IN THE STREETS

In the aftermath of Watergate and Nixon's resignation, the Pittsburgh Steelers' victory over the Minnesota Vikings in Super Bowl IX, Evel Knievel's unsuccessful attempt to leap across Idaho's 1,600-foot-wide Snake River Canyon on a motorcycle, and five decades of banter about the nature and extent of drug-related crime, the National Institute on Drug Abuse (NIDA) convened a one-day workshop in 1975 for the purpose of establishing a federal drugs-crime research agenda. Subsequently, a panel of experts was assembled to examine any available data and prior research on the topic, to determine what questions could be readily addressed, and to recommend research approaches for studying questions that remained unanswered.

The ultimate conclusion of the panel was politically disturbing to at least a few government drug officials at any rate. Many studies had heretofore demonstrated a statistical correlation between drug use and crime. From such data, policy makers had drawn an "inference of causality"—that is, that drug use causes crime. Yet the panel, on the basis of existing data and prior research, called the inference of causality into question, suggesting that the "drug use causes crime" conclusion could not be drawn from what was known. Moreover, in holding that any such linkage could not be demonstrated, the panel was questioning a fundamental assumption of American drug-control policy—that by reducing the demand for drugs through prevention and treatment initiatives, the criminality of the addict could be eliminated.[65] Nevertheless, NIDA established a federal drugs-crime research agenda. In the years hence, both NIDA and the National Institute of Justice funded a series of studies in many parts of the nation that began the building of a more meaningful data base on the elusive drugs-crime connection.

On the basis of extensive follow-up studies of addict careers in Baltimore, for example, John C. Ball of Temple University and David N. Nurco of the University of Maryland School of Medicine found that there were high rates of criminality among heroin users during those periods that they were addicted and markedly lower rates during times of nonaddiction.[66] This finding was based on the concept of the ''crime-days per year at risk.'' The crime-day was defined as a 24-hour period during which an individual committed one or more crimes. Thus crime-days per year at risk was a rate of crime commission that could vary anywhere from 0 to 365. Over the addiction careers of the Baltimore addicts studied, the average crime-days per year at risk was 230, suggesting that their rates of criminality were not only persistent on a day-to-day basis but also tended to continue over an extended number of years and periods of addiction.[67]

In a series of New York studies, the investigators operated from a storefront. During their many projects, they conducted interviews with hundreds of criminally active drug users recruited from the streets of east and central Harlem. The findings on drug-related criminality tended to confirm what was being learned elsewhere and provided insights as to how addicts functioned on the streets—how they purchased, sold, and used drugs; the roles that drugs played in their lives; and how the street-level drug business was structured.[68]

A series of studies conducted in Miami demonstrated that the amount of crime drug users committed was far greater than anyone had heretofore imagined, that drug-related crime could at times be exceedingly violent, and that the criminality of heroin and cocaine users was far beyond the control of law enforcement.[69] Other research investigations were arriving at similar conclusions.[70] What most seemed to be saying was that although the use of heroin and other drugs did not necessarily initiate criminal careers, it tended to intensify and perpetuate them. In that sense, it might be said that drug use freezes its devotees into patterns of criminality that are more acute, dynamic, unremitting, and enduring than those of other offenders.

THE DRUGS/VIOLENCE CONNECTION

It has been a recurring theme over the years that drugs instigate users to acts of wanton violence. Richmond Pearson Hobson and many others before and after him said it about heroin; Harry J. Anslinger and members of other anti-marijuana contingents made a similar proclamation about the evil weed of the fields; and at various times the same has been said about cocaine, the amphetamines, and PCP. More recently, the same arguments are made about cocaine and crack. There is a lengthy literature on the issue, with inconsistencies and contradictions on both sides of the argument.

During the 1920s, after Captain Hobson had launched his ravings against the quagmire of heroin use, Dr. Lawrence Kolb of the U.S. Public Health Service responded with what turned out to be one of the most often-quoted statements in the literature on drugs and violence:

> There is probably no more absurd fallacy prevalent than the notion that murders are committed and daylight robberies and holdups are carried out by men stimulated by cocaine or heroin which has temporarily distorted them into self-imagined heroes incapable of fear. . . . Violent crime would be much more prevalent if all habitual criminals were addicts who could obtain sufficient morphine or heroin to keep themselves fully charged with one of these drugs at all times.[71]

Kolb's argument was based on his belief that all preparations of opium capable of producing addiction tend to inhibit aggressive impulses, and furthermore that the soothing narcotic properties of the opiates have the effect of making psychopaths less likely to commit crimes of violence. From a strictly pharmacological point of view Kolb was correct, for the opiates do indeed depress the central nervous system. In the decades hence, others reiterated his position. In 1957, for example, the Council on Mental Health of the American Medical Association clearly stated that the belief that opiates per se directly incite otherwise normal people to violent assaultive criminal acts, including sexual crimes, is not tenable.[72] During the 1960s the President's Commission on Law Enforcement and Administration of Justice reached the same conclusion.[73]

What the American Medical Association and the president's commission were reacting to was the growing body of studies that were empirically documenting that drug users were not coming to the attention of the criminal justice system for the commission of violent crimes. In 1957 sociologist Harold Finestone's study of a jail population found that heroin users engaged primarily in nonviolent property crimes.[74] The perspective that developed from the work of Finestone and others was that narcotics users tended toward burglary and prostitution—low-risk activities that generated the income necessary to purchase drugs. Thus, noneconomically productive crimes, such as assault, were avoided. Other studies have argued that individuals who are involved in violent crime become less so after initiation into drug use.[75] Perhaps all of that was so in the 1920s through the 1960s. Perhaps the addict was indeed nonviolent. Or perhaps the findings were the result of the long-standing tradition in drug abuse research to study only captured populations and to assess criminality on the basis of arrest records alone.

In 1972 in an obscure paper published in what may be the most remote corner of the social science-criminology literature, a New York University graduate student challenged the position that heroin users were nonviolent.[76] Based on the growing number of studies of poly-drug abusers, an emergent cohort of multiple drug users that had evolved from the drug revolution of the 1960s, it was argued that a new and different breed of heroin user was living on the streets of American cities. They not only used heroin but other drugs as well. Most importantly, their criminality was situational in nature. Rather than repeatedly committing burglaries, they lacked any type of criminal specialization. They engaged in a wide variety of crimes—including assaults, muggings, and armed robberies—selected according to the nuances of situational opportunity. Shortly thereafter other research studies began reporting on the same phenomenon.[77] And all of this was some time before the research literature began examining the criminality of cocaine users and well before the rediscovery of crack-cocaine.

Paul J. Goldstein of New York's Narcotic and Drug Research, Inc., conceptualized the whole phenomenon of drugs and violence into a useful theoretical framework.[78] The *psychopharmacological model of violence* suggests that some individuals, as the result of short-term or long-term ingestion of specific substances, may become excitable, irrational, and exhibit violent behavior. The *economically compulsive model of violence* holds that some drug users engage in economically oriented violent crime to support costly drug use. The *systemic model of violence* maintains that violent crime is intrinsic to the very involvement with any illicit substance. As such, systemic violence refers to the traditionally aggressive patterns of interaction within the systems of illegal drug trafficking and distribution.

The early statements attributing violent behavior to drug use generally focused on the psychopharmacological argument. More recently this model has been applied to cocaine, barbiturates, and PCP, with a major focus on the amphetamines, crank, and crack. In study after study, it was reported that the chronic use of amphetamines produced paranoid thought patterns and delusions that led to homicide and other acts of violence.[79] The same was said about cocaine. The conclusion is a correct one, although it did not apply to every amphetamine and cocaine user. Violence was most typical among the hard-core, chronic users.

Contrary to everything that has been said over the years about the quieting effects of narcotic drugs, recent research has demonstrated that there may be more psychopharmacological violence associated with heroin use than that of any other illegal drug. Goldstein's studies of heroin-using prostitutes in New York City during the 1970s found a link between the effects of the withdrawal syndrome and violent crime.[80] The impatience and irritability caused by withdrawal motivated a number of prostitutes to rob their clients rather than provide them with sexual services. This phenomenon was found to be common in Miami, and not only among prostitutes but with other types of criminals as well. For example, one prostitute declared:

> . . . there are lots of shortcuts to get the john's money without having to go down on him. Sometimes you can con him out of it. Sometimes you just rob them outright. . . . Most of the time when me and the other girls are feeling sick and we just want to get back out in the street to fix . . . somethin' just seems to come over us. More than one time we felt so bad that I just cut a guy just to get out'a there and get straight. One time I was so crazy I just cut this guy and didn't even take his money.

A methadone patient stated:

> Many times when you're sick you might do things you don't normally [do] . . . you can get so desperate and uptight that you don't see straight. . . . I cut a connection more than once just so I didn't have to argue over the price of shit.

A low-level street dealer added:

> I'm just talkin' to this guy and all of a sudden, bam! He hits me. I know he wasn't feelin' too good, but the cocksucker just hits me and walks away.

To these can be added the many incidents of violence precipitated by the irritability and paranoia associated with crack use.[81]

The economically compulsive model of violence best fits the aggressive behavior of contemporary heroin, cocaine, and crack users. Among 573 narcotics users interviewed in Miami, for example, more than a third engaged in a total of 5,300 robberies over a one-year period as a source of income.[82] Some of these were strong-arm robberies or muggings with the victim attacked from the rear and overpowered, whereas the majority occurred at gunpoint. In fact, more than a fourth of the respondents in this study used a firearm in the commission of a crime. A similar phenomenon was found among a cohort of 429 nonnarcotics users in Miami, with weapon use most common among those who were primarily cocaine users.[83] Also, of 611 adolescent drug (primarily crack) users in Miami, 59% had participated in more than 6,000 robberies during the one-year period prior to interview.[84]

In the systemic model, acts of drug-related violence can occur for a variety of reasons: territorial disputes between rival drug dealers; assaults and homicides committed within dealing and trafficking hierarchies as means of enforcing normative codes; robberies of drug dealers, often followed by unusually violent retaliations; elimination of informers; punishment for selling adulterated, phony, or otherwise "bad" drugs; retribution for failing to pay one's debts; and general disputes over drugs or drug paraphernalia.

Most street drug users report having been either the perpetrator or victim of drug-related violence. In this regard, a Miami heroin dealer made the following comment about one of his street-level sellers:

> Just the other day we caught this dumb junky nigger stiff with his hand in the till messin' with the money. We took care of him outright so as the word would get around quick. . . . We cut three of the stupid motherfucker's fingers off and fed them to his dog.

Many women drug users reported over the years that they were the victims of rape at the hands of drug dealers. One 24-year-old cocaine and marijuana user stated:

> In the last few years I've been beaten and raped at least 10 times when I was trying to make a buy. One time this Cuban pimp drug dealer smacked me across the mouth, tied me to a bed, and then had all his friends try to fuck me to death—all the time sayin', "pretty white girl, ya just love it don't ya." If I ever find the bastard I'll blow his fucking brains out.

Violence associated with disputes over drugs has been common to the drug scene probably since its inception. Two friends come to blows because one refuses to give the other a taste. A husband beats his wife because she raided his stash. A woman stabs her boyfriend because he didn't cop enough drugs for her too. A kingrat beats and rapes his house girl because she asks for too much crack. A cocaine injector kills another for stealing his only set of works. In short, systemic violence seems to be endemic to the parallel worlds of drug dealing, drug taking, and drug seeking.

POSTSCRIPT

Researchers in the drug field have maintained that narcotics addicts are responsible for tens of millions of crimes each year in the United

States.[85] In addition, an unknown and perhaps greater level of crime is committed by cocaine, crack, and other drug users. Contemporary data and analyses tend to support such contentions.[86] Significant in this behalf are the findings of Drug Use Forecasting (DUF) program.

The Drug Use Forecasting program was established by the National Institute of Justice to measure the prevalence of drug use among those arrested for serious crimes.[87] Since 1986 the DUF program has used urinalysis to test a sample of arrestees in selected major cities across the United States to determine recent drug use. Urine specimens are collected from arrestees anonymously and voluntarily and tested so as to detect the use of 10 different drugs, including cocaine, marijuana, PCP, methamphetamine, and heroin. What the DUF data have consistently demonstrated is that drug use is pervasive among those coming to the attention of the criminal justice system.[88] As indicated in Table 5.1, for example, of the male arrestees sampled in 20 major cities during the first quarter of 1990, a clear majority in every city tested positive for at least one illegal drug. Similarly, of female arrestees, in all but one city the majority tested positive for at least one illegal drug. Typically, this drug was cocaine (or crack).[89]

In the final analysis, then, are drug users—and particularly cocaine, crack, heroin, and other narcotics users—driven to crime, driven by their enslavement to expensive drugs that can be afforded only through continuous predatory activities? Or is it that *drugs drive crime*, that careers in drugs intensify already existing criminal careers? Contemporary data tend to support the latter position more than any other explanation.

Notes

1. For a more complete analysis of the unicorn myth, see James A. Inciardi, Alan A. Block, and Lyle A. Hallowell, *Historical Approaches to Crime: Research Strategies and Issues* (Beverly Hills: Sage, 1977), pp. 11–13.
2. Robert J. Trotter, "Psyching the Skyjacker," *Science News,* 101 (12 Feb. 1972), pp. 108–110; *New York Times,* 25 Nov. 1979, p. 45; *People,* 3 Mar. 1980, pp. 45–46; *Newsweek,* 26 Dec. 1983, p. 12; *USA Today,* 18 Nov. 1988, p. 3A; *USA Today,* 28 Nov. 1988, p. 3A.
3. George B. Wood, *A Treatise on Therapeutics and Pharmacology of Materia Medica* (Philadelphia: J. B. Lippincott, 1856).
4. See, for example, F. E. Oliver, "The Use and Abuse of Opium," in *Third Annual Report,* Massachusetts State Board of Health (Boston: Wright and Potter, 1872), pp. 162–177; J. M. Hull, "The Opium Habit," in *Third Biennial Report,* Iowa State Board of Health (Des Moines: George E. Roberts, 1885), pp. 535–545.
5. E. Levinstein, "The Morbid Craving of Morphia," cited in Charles E. Terry and Mildred Pellens, *The Opium Problem* (New York: Bureau of Social Hygiene, 1928), p. 139.

Drug use by MALE arrestees*

% Positive any drug*

City	0	20	40	60	80	100
Philadelphia					80	
San Diego					80	
New York					79	
Chicago				75		
Houston				70		
Los Angeles				70		
Birmingham				69		
Dallas				66		
Cleveland				65		
Portland				64		
San Antonio				63		
St. Louis				62		
Ft. Lauderdale				61		
New Orleans				60		
Phoenix				60		
Indianapolis				60		
Wash., D.C.				59		
Denver				59		
San Jose				58		
Kansas City			57			

Drug use by FEMALE arrestees*

% Positive any drug*

City	0	20	40	60	80	100
Cleveland					88	
Wash., D.C.					85	
Philadelphia					81	
Ft. Lauderdale					79	
Kansas City				76		
Portland				76		
Los Angeles				73		
New York				71		
Dallas				71		
San Diego				70		
St. Louis				69		
Phoenix				69		
Houston				65		
Birmingham				66		
New Orleans				65		
San Jose				64		
Denver				62		
Indianapolis			56			
San Antonio			44			

Source: National Institute of Justice/Drug Use Forcasting Program

* Positive urinalysis, January through March 1990. Drugs tested for include cocaine, opiates, PCP, marijuana, amphetamines, methadone, methaqualone, benzodiazepines, barbiturates, and propoxyphene.
** Less than 1%.

During the first quarter of 1990, the majority of arrestees in major cities across the United States tested positive for at least one illegal drug.

6. Cesare Lombroso, *Crime, Its Causes and Remedies* (Boston: Little, Brown, 1911).
7. Richard L. Dugdale, *The Jukes* (New York: Putnam, 1911).
8. W. G. Thompson, *Textbook of Practical Medicine* (Philadelphia: Lea Brothers, 1902).
9. See Frank Soulé, John H. Gilran, and James Nisbet, *The Annals of San Francisco* (San Francisco: A. L. Bancroft, 1878); Herbert Asbury, *The Barbery Coast* (Garden City, NY: Garden City, 1933).
10. J. W. Buel, *Sunlight and Shadow of America's Great Cities* (Philadelphia: West Philadelphia Publishing Co., 1891); Edward Crapsey, *The Nether Side of New York* (New York: Sheldon, 1872); Gustav Lening, *The Dark Side of New York Life and Its Criminal Classes* (New York: Fred'k Gerhard, 1873); Edward Winslow Martin, *Sins of the Great City* (Philadelphia: National, 1868).

11. Helen Campbell, Thomas Knox, and Thomas Byrnes, *Darkness and Daylight; or, Lights and Shadows of New York Life* (Hartford: A. D. Worthington, 1892), p. 570.

12. A. E. Costello, *Our Police Protectors* (New York: Author's Edition, 1884), pp. 516–524. See also Thomas Byrnes, *Professional Criminals of America* (New York: G. W. Dillingham, 1895), pp. 39–40.

13. Harold Wentworth and Stuart Berg Flexner, *Dictionary of American Slang* (New York: Thomas Y. Crowell, 1960), p. 161.

14. Alonzo Calkins, *Opium and the Opium Appetite* (Philadelphia: J. B. Lippincott, 1871), pp. 324–330.

15. H. H. Kane, *Opium Smoking in America and China* (New York: G. P. Putnam's, 1881), p. 81.

16. Thomas D. Crothers, *Morphinism and Narcomaniacs from Other Drugs* (Philadelphia: W. B. Saunders, 1902), pp. 88, 112–113.

17. For example, see J. B. Mattison, "The Impending Danger," *Medical Record*, 22 Jan. 1876, pp. 69–71.

18. H. Wayne Morgan, *Yesterday's Addicts: American Society and Drug Abuse: 1865–1920* (Norman: University of Oklahoma Press, 1974), p. 28.

19. For example, see the "Forward" by Walter C. Bailey in James W. Brown, Roger Mazze, and Daniel Glaser, *Narcotics Knowledge and Nonsense* (Cambridge: Ballinger, 1974), p. xiii.

20. Perry Lichtenstein, "Narcotic Addiction," *New York Medical Journal*, 100 (14 Nov. 1914), pp. 962–966.

21. See Rufus King, *The Drug Hang-Up: America's Fifty-Year Folly* (New York: W. W. Norton, 1972), pp. 23–27.

22. *Literary Digest*, 26 Apr. 1919, p. 32.

23. *The Outlook*, 25 June 1919, p. 315.

24. *American Review of Reviews*, July 1919, pp. 331–332.

25. Cited in David T. Courtwright, *Dark Paradise: Opiate Addiction in America before 1940* (Cambridge: Harvard University Press, 1982), p. 33.

26. *Literary Digest*, 24 May 1924, p. 32.

27. Committee on Education of the House of Representatives, Conference on Narcotic Education, *Hearings on HJR 65*, 69th Cong., 1st sess., 16 Dec. 1925, pp. 2–3.

28. David F. Musto, *The American Disease: Origins of Narcotic Control* (New Haven: Yale University Press, 1973), p. 322.

29. National Broadcasting Company, "The Struggle of Mankind Against Its Deadliest Foe," radio broadcast, 1 Mar. 1928.

30. Courtwright, p. 91.

31. Douglas T. Miller and Marion Nowak, *The Fifties: The Way We Really Were* (Garden City, NY: Doubleday, 1977), pp. 279–287.

32. Isidor Chein, Donald L. Gerard, Robert S. Lee, and Eva Rosenfeld, *The Road to H: Narcotics, Delinquency, and Social Policy* (New York: Basic Books, 1964). See also Harold Alksne, *A Follow-up Study of Treated Adolescent Narcotics Users* (New York: Columbia University School of Public Health and Administrative Medicine, 1959); Isidor Chein and Eva Rosenfeld, "Juvenile Narcotic Use," *Law and Contemporary Problems*, Winter 1957, pp. 52–68; A. S. Meyer, *Social and Psychological Factors in Opiate Addiction* (New York: Columbia University Bureau of Applied Social Research, 1952).

33. *Newsweek,* 25 June 1951, pp. 19–20; 11 June 1951, pp. 26–27; 17 Sept. 1951, p. 60; *Life,* 25 June 1951, pp. 21–24; *The Survey,* July 1951, p. 328; *Time,* 26 Feb. 1951, p. 24; 7 May 1951, pp. 82, 85; 3 Oct. 1955, pp. 63–64; *Reader's Digest,* Dec. 1957, pp. 55–58; *The Nation,* 31 Aug. 1957, pp. 92–93; *Ladies' Home Journal,* Mar. 1958, pp. 173–175.
34. *Newsweek,* 13 Aug. 1951, p. 50.
35. *Newsweek,* 11 June 1951, p. 26.
36. *Newsweek,* 20 Nov. 1950, pp. 57–58.
37. *Life,* 11 June 1951, p. 116.
38. *Reader's Digest,* Oct. 1951, pp. 137–140.
39. *Time,* 10 Sept. 1951, p. 27.
40. Ian Whitcomb, *After the Ball: Pop Music from Rag to Rock* (New York: Viking, 1974), pp. 219–241.
41. Miller and Nowak, p. 295.
42. Jack Lait and Lee Mortimer, *U.S.A. Confidential* (New York: Crown, 1952), pp. 37–38.
43. David M. Wilner, Eva Rosenfeld, Donald L. Gerard, and Isidor Chein, "Heroin Use and Street Gangs," *Journal of Criminal Law, Criminology and Police Science,* Nov.–Dec. 1957, pp. 399–409.
44. Edouard C. Sandoz, "Report on Morphinism to the Municipal Court of Boston," *Journal of Criminal Law and Criminology,* 13 (1922), 10–55; Lawrence Kolb, "Drug Addiction and its Relation to Crime," *Mental Hygiene,* 9 (1925), pp. 74–89.
45. James A. Inciardi, "The Vilification of Euphoria: Some Perspectives on an Elusive Issue," *Addictive Diseases: An International Journal,* 1 (1974), p. 245.
46. U.S. Treasury Department, Bureau of Narcotics, *Traffic in Opium and Dangerous Drugs for the Year Ended December 31, 1939* (Washington, DC: U.S. Government Printing Office, 1940).
47. Harry J. Anslinger, "Relationship Between Addiction to Narcotic Drugs and Crime," *Bulletin on Narcotics,* 3 (1951), pp. 1–3.
48. James A. Inciardi and Brian R. Russe, "Professional Thieves and Drugs," *International Journal of the Addictions,* 12 (1977), pp. 1087–1095.
49. For detailed descriptions and analyses of the history, social organization, occupational structure, and criminal activities of professional thieves, see Edwin H. Sutherland, *The Professional Thief* (Chicago: University of Chicago Press, 1937); James A. Inciardi, *Careers in Crime* (Chicago: Rand McNally, 1975).
50. John C. Ball, "Two Patterns of Narcotic Addiction in the United States," *Journal of Criminal Law, Criminology and Police Science,* 52 (1965), pp. 203–211; John A. O'Donnell, "The Rise and Decline of a Subculture," *Social Problems,* Summer 1967, pp. 73–84.
51. Charles Winick, "Physician Narcotic Addicts," *Social Problems,* Fall 1961, pp. 174–186; Charles Winick, "The Use of Drugs by Jazz Musicians," *Social Problems,* Winter 1961, pp. 240–253.
52. James P. Morgan, "Drug Addiction: Criminal or Medical Problem," *Police,* July–Aug. 1966, pp. 6–9.
53. For bibliographies and analyses of the literature on drug use and crime, see Harold Finestone, "Narcotics and Criminality," *Law and Contemporary Problems,* Winter 1957, pp. 72–85; Florence Kavaler, Donald C. Krug, Zili

Amsel, and Rosemary Robbins, "A Commentary and Annotated Bibliography on the Relationship between Narcotics Addiction and Criminality," *Municipal Reference Library Notes*, 42 (1968), 45–63; Jared R. Tinklenberg, "Drugs and Crime," in *Drug Use in America: Problem in Perspective*, Appendix, vol. I, National Commission on Marihuana and Drug Abuse (Washington, DC: U.S. Government Printing Office, 1973), pp. 242–267; Gregory A. Austin and Dan J. Lettieri, *Drugs and Crime: The Relationship of Drug Use and Concomitant Criminal Behavior* (Rockville, MD: National Institute on Drug Abuse, 1976); Research Triangle Institute, *Drug Use and Crime: Report of the Panel on Drug Use and Criminal Behavior* (Springfield, VA: National Technical Information Service, 1976); Stephanie W. Greenberg and Freda Adler, "Crime and Addiction: An Empirical Analysis of the Literature, 1920–1973," *Contemporary Drug Problems*, 3 (1974), pp. 221–270; Robert P. Gandossy, Jay R. Williams, Jo Cohen, and Henrick J. Harwood, *Drugs and Crime: A Survey and Analysis of the Literature* (Washington, DC: United States Department of Justice, National Institute of Justice, 1980); David N. Nurco, John C. Ball, John W. Shaffer, and Thomas Hanlon, "The Criminality of Narcotic Addicts," *Journal of Nervous and Mental Disease*, 173 (1985), pp. 94–102.

54. For a review essay on the unreliability of official criminal statistics, see James A. Inciardi, "The Uniform Crime Reports: Some Considerations on Their Shortcomings and Utility," *Public Data Use*, 6 (Nov. 1978), pp. 3–16.

55. *Reader's Digest*, June 1956, p. 21.

56. President's Commission on Law Enforcement and Administration of Justice, *The Challenge of Crime in a Free Society* (Washington, DC: U.S. Government Printing Office, 1967).

57. Task Force on Narcotics and Drug Abuse, President's Commission on Law Enforcement and Administration of Justice, *Task Force Report: Narcotics and Drug Abuse* (Washington, DC: U.S. Government Printing Office, 1967), p. 11.

58. Edward J. Epstein, *Agency of Fear* (New York: G. P. Putnam's, 1977), p. 8.

59. Epstein, pp. 148–151.

60. *New York Times*, 23 Apr. 1972, p. 23.

61. *Washington Post*, 16 Jan. 1973, p. A3.

62. Cited by Carl D. Chambers and James A. Inciardi, "Forecasts for the Future: Where We Are and Where We Are Going," in *Drugs and the Criminal Justice System*, eds. James A. Inciardi and Carl D. Chambers (Beverly Hills: Sage, 1974), p. 221.

63. Chambers and Inciardi, p. 222.

64. Epstein, pp. 179–181.

65. For a complete discussion of the operations of the drugs/crime "panel" and the structuring of the federal drugs-crime research agenda, see Richard R. Clayton, "Federal Drugs-Crime Research: Setting the Agenda," In *The Drugs-Crime Connection*, ed. James A. Inciardi (Beverly Hills: Sage, 1981), pp. 17–38.

66. John C. Ball, Lawrence Rosen, John A. Flueck, and David N. Nurco, "The Criminality of Heroin Addicts: When Addicted and When Off Opiates," in James A. Inciardi, ed., *The Drugs-Crime Connection* (Beverly Hills: Sage, 1981), pp. 39–65; John C. Ball, John W. Shaffer, and David N. Nurco,

"The Day-to-Day Criminality of Heroin Addicts in Baltimore—a Study in the Continuity of Offense Rates," *Drug and Alcohol Dependence,* 12 (1983), pp. 119–142.

67. David N. Nurco, John C. Ball, John W. Shaffer, and Thomas E. Hanlon, "The Criminality of Narcotic Addicts," *Journal of Nervous and Mental Disease,* 173 (1985), p. 98.

68. See Bruce D. Johnson, Paul J. Goldstein, Edward Preble, James Schmeidler, Douglas S. Lipton, Barry Spunt, and Thomas Miller, *Taking Care of Business: The Economics of Crime by Heroin Abusers* (Lexington, MA: Lexington, 1985). See also Paul J. Goldstein, "Getting Over: Economic Alternatives to Predatory Crime Among Street Heroin Users," in Inciardi, pp. 67–84.

69. See James A. Inciardi, "Heroin Use and Street Crime," *Crime and Delinquency,* July 1979, pp. 335–346; Susan K. Datesman and James A. Inciardi, "Female Heroin Use, Criminality, and Prostitution," *Contemporary Drug Problems,* 8 (1979), pp. 455–473; James A. Inciardi, "Women, Heroin, and Property Crime," in *Women, Crime, and Justice,* ed. Susan K. Datesman and Frank R. Scarpitti (New York: Oxford University Press, 1980), pp. 214–222; James A. Inciardi, "The Impact of Drug Use on Street Crime" (Paper presented at the 33rd Annual Meeting of the American Society of Criminology, Washington, D.C., 11–14 Nov. 1981); Anne E. Pottieger and James A. Inciardi, "Aging on the Street: Drug Use and Crime Among Older Men," *Journal of Psychoactive Drugs,* Apr.–June 1981, pp. 199–211; Charles E. Faupel, "Drugs and Crime: An Elaboration of an Old Controversy" (Paper presented at the Thirty-third Annual Meeting of the American Society of Criminology, Washington, D.C., 11–14 Nov. 1981); Susan K. Datesman, "Women, Crime, and Drugs," in Inciardi, ed., *The Drugs-Crime Connection,* pp. 85–105; Carl D. Chambers, Sara W. Dean, and Michael Pletcher, "Criminal Involvements of Minority Group Addicts," in Inciardi, ed., pp. 125–154; Anne E. Pottieger, "Sample Bias in Drugs/Crime Research: An Empirical Study," in Inciardi, ed., pp. 207–238; James A. Inciardi, Anne E. Pottieger, and Charles E. Faupel, "Black Women, Heroin and Crime: Some Empirical Notes," *Journal of Drug Issues,* Summer 1982, pp. 241–250; James A. Inciardi, "The Production and Detection of Fraud in Street Studies of Crime and Drugs," *Journal of Drug Issues,* Summer 1982, pp. 285–291; James A. Inciardi and Anne E. Pottieger, "Drug Use and Crime Among Two Cohorts of Women Narcotics Users: An Empirical Assessment," *Journal of Drug Issues,* 16 (Winter 1986), pp. 91–106; Leon Pettiway, "Partnership in Crime Partnerships by Female Drug Users: The Effects of Domestic Arrangements, Drug Use, and Criminal Involvement," *Criminology,* 25 (Aug. 1987), pp. 741–766.

70. Charles E. Faupel and Carl B. Klockars, "Drugs-Crime Connections: Elaborations From the Life Histories of Hard-Core Heroin Addicts," *Social Problems,* 34 (Feb. 1987), pp. 54–68; Marcia R. Chaiken and Bruce D. Johnson, *Characteristics of Different Types of Drug-Involved Offenders* (Washington, DC: National Institute of Justice, 1988); Jose E. Sanchez and Bruce D. Johnson, "Women and the Drugs-Crime Connection: Crime Rates Among Drug Abusing Women at Rikers Island," *Journal of Psychoactive Drugs,* 19 (Apr.–June 1987), pp. 205–216; Eric D. Wish, Kandace A. Klumpp, Amy H. Moorer, Elizabeth Brady, and Kristen M. Williams,

An Analysis of Drugs and Crime Among Arrestees in the District of Columbia (Washington, DC: National Institute of Justice, 1981); George Speckart and M. Douglas Anglin, "Narcotics Use and Crime: An Overview of Recent Research Advances," *Contemporary Drug Problems,* Winter 1986, pp. 741–769; M. Douglas Anglin and Yih-Ing Hser, "Addicted Women and Crime," *Criminology,* 25 (May 1987), pp. 359–397.

71. Lawrence Kolb, "Drug Addiction and Its Relation to Crime," *Mental Hygiene,* 9 (1925), p. 78.
72. American Medical Association, Council on Mental Health, "Report on Narcotic Addiction," *Journal of the American Medical Association,* 7 Dec. 1957, p. 1834.
73. Task Force on Narcotics and Drug Abuse, pp. 10–11.
74. Harold Finestone, "Use of Drugs Among Persons Admitted to a County Jail," *Public Health Reports,* 90 (1957), pp. 553–568.
75. For a review of the issues and early research on drugs and violence, see Duane C. McBride, "Drugs and Violence," in Inciardi, ed., *The Drugs-Crime Connection,* pp. 105–123.
76. James A. Inciardi, "The Poly-Drug Abuser: A New Situational Offender," in *Politics, Crime and the International Scene: An Inter-American Focus,* ed. Freda Adler and G. O. W. Mueller (San Juan: North-South Center for Technical and Cultural Exchange, 1972), pp. 60–68.
77. Richard C. Stephens and Rosalind D. Ellis, "Narcotics Addicts and Crime: Analysis of Recent Trends," *Criminology,* 12 (1975), pp. 474–488; Margaret A. Zahn and Mark Bencivengo, "Violent Death: A Comparison Between Drug Users and Non-Drug Users," *Addictive Diseases: An International Journal,* 1 (1974), pp. 283–296.
78. Paul J. Goldstein, "The Drugs/Violence Nexus: A Tripartite Conceptual Framework," *Journal of Drug Issues,* 15 (Fall 1985), pp. 493–506.
79. See Everett H. Ellinwood, "Assault and Homicide Associated with Amphetamine Abuse," *American Journal of Psychiatry,* 127 (1971), pp. 1170–1175; Roger C. Smith, "Speed and Violence: Compulsive Methamphetamine Abuse and Criminality in the Haight-Ashbury District," in *Proceedings of the International Conference on Drug Abuse,* ed. Chris Zarafonetis (Philadelphia: Lea & Febiger, 1972), pp. 435–448; S. Asnis and Roger C. Smith, "Amphetamine Abuse and Violence," *Journal of Psychedelic Drugs,* 10 (1978), pp. 317–378.
80. Paul J. Goldstein, *Prostitution and Drugs* (Lexington, MA: Lexington, 1979), p. 126.
81. See Duane C. McBride and James A. Swartz, "Drugs and Violence in the Age of Crack Cocaine," in Ralph Weisheit, ed., *Drugs, Crime and the Criminal Justice System* (Cincinnati: Anderson Publishing Co., 1990), pp. 141–169.
82. James A. Inciardi, *The War on Drugs: Heroin, Cocaine, Crime, and Public Policy* (Palo Alto, CA: Mayfield, 1986), pp. 122–132.
83. Ibid.
84. James A. Inciardi, "The Crack/Violence Connection Within a Population of Hard-Core Adolescent Offenders," in Mario DeLaRosa, Elizabeth Y. Lambert, and Bernard Gropper, eds., *Drugs and Violence: Causes, Correlates, and Consequences* (Rockville, MD: National Institute on Drug Abuse, 1990), pp. 92–111.

85. John C. Ball, Lawrence Rosen, John A. Flueck, and David N. Nurco, "The Lifetime Criminality of Heroin Addicts in the United States," *Journal of Drug Issues,* 12 (1982), 225–239.

86. The most recent analyses of the drugs/crime equation appear in Michael Tonry and James Q. Wilson, eds., *Drugs and Crime* (Chicago: University of Chicago Press, 1990); David N. Nurco, Timothy Kinlock, and Thomas E. Hanlon, "The Drugs-Crime Connection," in James A. Inciardi, ed., *Handbook of Drug Control in the United States* (Westport, CT: Greenwood Press, 1990), pp. 72–90.

87. *Leading Drug Indicators,* ONDCP White Paper (Washington, DC: Office of National Drug Control Policy, 1990); National Institute of Justice, *Drug Use Forecasting* (Washington, DC: National Institute of Justice, 1988); Eric D. Wish and Bernard A. Gropper, "Drug Testing by the Criminal Justice System: Methods, Research, and Applications," pp. 321–391 in Tonry and Wilson; Eric D. Wish, "Drug Testing and the Identification of Drug-Abusing Criminals," pp. 230–244 in Inciardi, *Handbook of Drug Control in the United States;* Bernard R. Gropper, "Drug Detection: Developing New Approaches for Criminal Justice Questions" (Paper presented at the annual meeting of the Academy of Criminal Justice Sciences, San Francisco, April 1988); Eric D. Wish, "Identifying Drug–Abusing Criminals," in Carl G. Leukefeld and Frank M. Tims, eds., *Compulsory Treatment of Drug Abuse: Research and Clinical Practice* (Rockville, MD: National Institute on Drug Abuse, 1988), pp. 139–159.

88. For trend data, see National Institute of Justice, *DUF: 1989 Drug Use Forecasting Annual Report* (Washington, DC: National Institute of Justice, 1990).

89. National Institute of Drug Abuse, *Drug Use Forecasting, January to March 1990, Arrestee Drug Use* (Washington, DC: National Institute of Justice, 1990).

CHAPTER SIX

MAINLINING IN
THE SHADOW OF DEATH
Probing the AIDS/Drugs Connection

George Gordon Byron, the nineteenth-century English poet better known as Lord Byron, is credited with having coined the phrase about truth being stranger than fiction. So often that seems to be the case. Some two decades ago there was the best-selling science fiction novel by Michael Crichton, *The Andromeda Strain.* It was a gripping story of a space-borne organism that wiped out an entire American town before mutating into a harmless germ. Little would the readers of Crichton's book have believed what was about to begin in their country, and across the globe.

AIDS: A STRANGE DISEASE OF UNCERTAIN ORIGINS

Acquired Immune Deficiency Syndrome (AIDS) has been called many things.[1] In 1986 the United States Surgeon General referred to the disease as the most serious health issue since the bubonic plague of the fourteenth century.[2] Or similarly in 1988 the Secretary of Health and Human Services called AIDS America's "Number One" public health problem.[3] By contrast, however, both God and nature have also been brought into discussions of the disease. To some, AIDS is "nature's revenge" for the "crime" of homosexuality, or God's retribution for the perversions committed by "junkies, perverts, queers and whores."[4] And to many more, AIDS has become like syphilis, leprosy, and plague—the contemporary metaphor for corruption, decay, and consummate evil.

The linking of AIDS with homosexual practice and drug use makes it easily susceptible to these and perhaps many other metaphorical interpretations, as are other diseases that are transmitted through taboo behaviors or those with unknown causes. But these should not distract from the seriousness of the disease. AIDS confronts everyone with a variety of concerns about such things as risk factors and disease vectors, as well as susceptibility, contagion, and the spread of a disorder that would appear to kill virtually all of its victims.

The Emergence of AIDS

Acquired Immune Deficiency Syndrome was first described as a new and distinct clinical entity during the late spring and early summer of 1981.[5] First, clinical investigators in Los Angeles reported five cases to the Centers for Disease Control (CDC) of *Pneumocystis carinii* pneumonia (PCP) among homosexual men. None of these patients had an underlying disease that might have been associated with the PCP, or a history of treatment for a compromised immune system. All, however, had other clinical manifestations and laboratory evidence of immunosuppression. Second, and within a month, 26 cases of Kaposi's sarcoma (KS) were reported among homosexual men in New York and California.

What was so unusual was that prior to these reports, the appearance of both PCP and KS in populations of previously healthy young men was unprecedented. PCP is an infection caused by the parasite *P. carinii*, previously seen almost exclusively in cancer and transplant patients receiving immunosuppressive drugs.[a] KS, a cancer or tumor of the blood vessel walls and typically appearing as blue-violet to brownish skin blotches, had been quite rare in the United States, occurring primarily in elderly men, usually of Mediterranean origin. Like PCP, furthermore, KS had also been reported among organ

---

[a] Prior to the age of AIDS, *Pneumocystis carinii* pneumonia was one of the perhaps thousands of malevolent microorganisms that always lurked on the fringes of human existence. PCP was first observed in guinea pigs and identified in 1910 by a Brazilian scientist known in the literature only as Dr. Carini. Three years later, physicians at the Pasteur Institute in France found that the same microbe lived quite comfortably in the lungs of Parisian sewer rats. Dr. Carini's discovery of the organism combined with its cystlike makeup resulted in its designation of *Pneumocystis carinii*. As one of the tens of thousands of creatures that exist in almost every corner of the world's inhabited terrain but easily held in check by a normally functioning immune system, *P. carinii* was identified in human lungs during World War II in Europe. In 1956, it was diagnosed in the United States for the first time among immunosuppressed patients. See Randy Shilts, *And the Band Played On: Politics, People, and the AIDS Epidemic* (New York: St. Martin's Press, 1987), p. 34; Jeffrey A. Golden, "Pulmonary Complications of AIDS," in Jay A. Levy, ed., *AIDS: Pathogenesis and Treatment* (New York: Marcel Dekker, 1989), pp. 403–447; W. T. Hughes, "Pneumosystis Carinii," in G. L. Mandell, R. G. Douglous, and J. E. Bennett, eds., *Principles and Practices of Infectious Diseases* (New York: John Wiley, 1979), pp. 2137–2142.

transplant recipients and others receiving immunosuppressive therapy.[b] This quickly led to the hypothesis that the increased occurrences of the two disorders in homosexual men were due to some underlying immune system dysfunction. This hypothesis was further supported by the incidence among homosexuals of opportunistic infections—infections caused by microorganisms that rarely generate disease in persons with normal immune defense mechanisms. It is for this reason that the occurrence of KS, PCP, and/or other opportunistic infections in a person with unexplained immune dysfunction became known as "acquired immune deficiency syndrome," or more simply, AIDS.[c]

With the recognition that the vast majority of the early cases of this new clinical syndrome involved homosexual men, it seemed logical that the causes might be related to the life-style unique to that population. The sexual revolution of the 1960s and 1970s was accompanied not only by greater carnal permissiveness among both heterosexuals and gays but also by a more positive social acceptance of homosexuality. The emergence of commercial bathhouses and other outlets for sexual contacts among gays further increased promiscuity, with self-selected segments of the male gay population viewing promiscuity as

---

[b] Sarcoma is a medical term describing a tumor that is often malignant, and Kaposi's sarcoma has been observed in a number of non-AIDS populations. First described in 1872 by the Viennese dermatologist Moritz Kaposi as a "multiple pigmented sarcoma of the skin," it was an extremely rare malignancy for more than a century in both the United States and Europe. Elderly men, particularly of Mediterranean or Jewish origin, would occasionally develop this variety of cancer. Clinically it appeared most frequently as a tumor of the feet and lower extremities. It was not accompanied by immune depression, other than the expected immunological attrition associated with aging.

During the early 1960s, studies in Uganda revealed that KS was a common cancer—up to 9% of all cancers in the region. But again, no associated immunodeficiency was determined, although a few reports of particularly aggressive cases, often in the young, were recorded.

The only non-AIDS population to develop KS with parallels to current AIDS-related cases were patients receiving immunosuppressive therapy following kidney transplants. As with many AIDS patients, the cancer was often aggressive. However, KS in transplant patients often regressed completely after the withdrawal of the immunosuppressive drugs. See P. A. Volberding, M. A. Conant, R. B. Strickler, and B. J. Lewis, "Chemotherapy in Advanced Kaposi's Sarcoma: Implications for Current Cases in Homosexual Men," *American Journal of Medicine* 74 (1983), pp. 652–656; Bureau of Hygiene and Tropical Diseases, "Kaposi's Sarcoma: More Questions Than Answers," *WorldAIDS.* Nov. 1990, p. 11.

[c] By early 1982 the disease was known by a variety of names and acronyms. The most popular of these was G.R.I.D., for Gay-Related Immune Deficiency. But staff members at the Centers for Disease Control despised the GRID acronym and refused to use it, particularly since they were well aware that the disease was not restricted to homosexuals. When someone finally suggested the sexually neutral yet snappy acronym "AIDS" during the middle of 1982, it immediately replaced all others. See Randy Shilts, *And the Band Played On: Politics, People, and the AIDS Epidemic* (New York: St. Martin's Press, 1987), p. 171.

a facet of gay liberation. In fact, among early patients diagnosed with AIDS, their sexual recreation typically occurred within the anonymity of the bathhouses with similarly promiscuous men. Some had had as many as 20,000 sexual contacts and more than 1,100 sex partners. And to complicate matters, active homosexual men with multiple sex partners were manifesting high rates of sexually transmitted diseases— gonorrhea, syphilis, genital herpes, anal warts, and hepatitis B.[6] And to this could be added the matter of enteric diseases. As journalist Randy Shilts described it:

> Another problem was enteric diseases, like amebiasis and giardiasis, caused by organisms that lodged themselves in the intestinal tracts of gay men with alarming frequency. At the New York Gay Men's Health Project . . . 30 percent of the patients suffered from gastro intestinal parasites. In San Francisco, incidence of the ''Gay Bowel Syndrome,'' as it was called in medical journals, had increased by 8,000 percent since 1973. Infection with these parasites was a likely effect of anal intercourse, which was apt to put a man in contact with his partner's fecal matter, and was virtually a certainty through the then-popular practice of rimming, which the medical journals politely called oral-anal intercourse.[7]

Because of this, it is not surprising that such factors as frequent exposure to semen, rectal exposure to semen, the body's exposure to amyl nitrate and butyl nitrate (better known as ''poppers,'' and used to enhance sexual pleasure and performance), and/or a high frequency of sexually transmitted diseases were themselves considered potential causes of AIDS. Yet while it was apparent that AIDS was a new disease, most of the gay life-style factors were not particularly new, having changed only in a relative sense. As such, it was difficult to immediately single out specific behaviors that might be related to the emerging epidemic.

Within a brief period of time, the notion that AIDS was some form of ''gay plague'' was quickly extinguished. The disease was suddenly being reported in other populations, such as intravenous and other injecting drug users, blood transfusion patients, and hemophiliacs.[8] And what these reports suggested to the scientific community was that an infectious etiology for AIDS had to be considered.

Tracking the Epidemic

Almost immediately after the first cases of AIDS were reported in 1981, researchers at the Centers for Disease Control began tracking the disease backward in time to discover its origins. They ultimately determined that the first cases of AIDS in the United States probably occurred in 1977. By early 1982 AIDS had been reported in 15 states, the District of Columbia, and two foreign countries, but the total remained extremely low—158 men and 1 woman. Although more than 90% of the men were either homosexual or bisexual, interviews with all of the patients failed to provide any definite clues about the origin of the disease.

Although it was suspected that AIDS might be transmitted through sexual relations among homosexually active men, the first strong evidence for the idea did not emerge until the completion of a case control study in June 1982 by epidemiologists at the Centers for Disease Control.[9] In that investigation, data were obtained on the sexual partners of 13 of the first 19 cases of AIDS among homosexual men in the Los Angeles area. Within five years before the onset of their symptoms, nine had had sexual contact with people who later developed Kaposi's sarcoma or *P. carinii* pneumonia. The nine were also linked to another interconnected series of 40 AIDS cases in 10 different cities by one individual who had developed a number of the manifestations of AIDS and was later diagnosed with Kaposi's sarcoma. Overall, the investigation of these 40 cases indicated that 20% of the initial AIDS cases in the United States were linked through sexual contact—a statistical clustering that was extremely unlikely to have occurred by chance.

Yet even in the face of this evidence, there were those who doubted that AIDS was caused by some transmissible agent. However, when AIDS cases began to emerge in other populations—among individuals who had been injected with blood or blood products but had no other expected risk factors—the transmission vectors for the disease became somewhat clearer. Such cases were confirmed first among people with hemophilia, followed by blood transfusion recipients and intravenous drug users who shared hypodermic needles. Then, when there were documented cases of AIDS among the heterosexual partners of male injecting drug users, it became increasingly evident that AIDS was a sexually transmitted disease, and that sexual preference was not necessarily the only risk factor.[10]

In 1983 and 1984 scientists at the Institute Pasteur in Paris and the National Institutes of Health in the United States identified and isolated the cause of AIDS—Human T-Cell Lymphotropic Virus, Type III (HTLV-III), or Lymphadenophy-Associated Virus (LAV).[d] Later, this virus would be renamed human immunodeficiency virus, more

---

[d] HTLV-III was the name given by researchers at the National Cancer Institute to the isolates of the virus that caused AIDS. LAV was the name given by French researchers.

commonly known as HIV.[e] More specifically, HIV is a retrovirus, a type of infectious agent that had previously been identified as causing many animal diseases. The designation of retrovirus derives from the backward (or retro-) flow of genetic information from RNA to DNA, which reverses the normal flow of genetic messages.[f] Subsequent studies demonstrated that HIV is transmitted when virus particles or infected cells gain direct access to the bloodstream. This can occur through all forms of sexual intercourse, the sharing of contaminated needles, blood, and blood products, and the passing of the virus from infected mothers to their unborn or newborn children.[g] Within this context, HIV is a continuum of conditions associated with immune dysfunction, and AIDS is best described as a severe manifestation of infection with HIV.[h]

---

[e] The HTLV-III/LAV distinction was the result of a dispute as to whether the virus that caused AIDS had been discovered by Robert Gallo of the National Cancer Institute in 1984 (HTLV-III) or by Luc Montagnier of the Pasteur Institute in Paris a year earlier (LAV). The conflict had economic implications involving royalty rights associated with the blood tests developed by Gallo and Montagnier. It appeared to be settled in 1987, giving both scientists credit for the discovery. In the meantime the virus was renamed HIV by an international team of virologists. See S. Connor and S. Kingman, *The Search for the Virus: The Scientific Discovery of AIDS and the Quest for a Cure* (London: Penguin, 1989); *Chicago Tribune,* 7 Oct. 1990, Section 1, pp. 4, 19. In early 1991, the Office of Scientific Integrity of the National Institutes of Health determined that HIV had been discovered by the French in 1983 and that the similarities between the Gallo and Montagnier viral cultures were the result of the inadvertent contamination of each other's specimens. See Robert Gallo, *Virus Hunting: AIDS, Cancer and the Human Retrovirus* (New York: New Republic/ Basic Books, 1991); Judith Colp, "Taking Credit for AIDS," *Insight,* 13 May 1991, pp. 35–37; Robert P. Charrow, "The Mystery of the Migrating Virus," *Journal of NIH Research,* 3 (May 1991), pp. 87–89. Shortly thereafter, Gallo dropped his claim to have discovered the virus (*New York Times,* 3 May 1991, p. A12).

[f] DNA is the carrier of genetic information for all organisms, except the RNA viruses. See Institute of Medicine, National Academy of Sciences, *Mobilizing Against AIDS: The Unfinished Story of a Virus* (Cambridge: Harvard University Press, 1986), pp. 62–63.

[g] HIV has been isolated from blood, semen, vaginal secretions, urine, cerebrospinal fluid, saliva, tears, and breast milk of infected individuals. Transmission could theoretically occur from contact with any of these fluids, but the concentration of HIV found in saliva and tears is extremely low. Moreover, no cases of HIV infection have been traced to saliva or tears. Virus is found in greater concentration in semen than vaginal secretions, which supports the hypothesis that transmission occurs more readily from male to female than from female to male.

[h] There is more than one strain of human immunodeficiency virus (HIV). HIV-1 is the most common form. A second variety, discovered in late 1985 and subsequently termed human immunodeficiency virus type 2 (HIV-2), was isolated from two West African patients with AIDS. In evolutionary terms, HIV-2 is clearly related to HIV-1. The two viruses are similar in their overall structure and both can cause AIDS. Although differences in the relative infectiousness of HIV-1 and HIV-2 have not yet been determined, it would appear that HIV-2 is a less virulent pathogen. For the sake of simplicity, all references to HIV-1 throughout this chapter are designated as HIV.

Subsequent to the discovery of HIV, an early priority was to fully verify its association with the diseases in question.[i] Using a variety of laboratory tests, researchers in virology and molecular biology searched for antibodies against HIV in the blood of AIDS patients. Ultimately they found that almost 100% of AIDS patients had HIV antibodies.[11] The presence of specific antibodies in the blood indicates that a previous infection registered on the body's immune system. The antibody molecules that remain in the bloodstream act as scouts, so to speak: if the virus appears again, the scouts recognize it immediately and attempt to prevent it from getting a foothold.

This research led in 1985 to the widespread availability of a commercial test for antibodies to HIV. The basic test is an enzyme-linked immunosorbent assay. More commonly known as ELISA or EIA, it is not a test for AIDS, nor does it even detect the presence of the virus itself. What the test does indicate is whether HIV has been noticed by an individual's immune system.

The Origins of HIV and AIDS

As to where AIDS and HIV actually originated, the matter remains unsettled. However, there is considerable agreement that the source may have been Central Africa. The AIDS problem in Africa first became evident in 1982 when physicians in Belgium began seeing patients from Zaire and Burundi.[12] Prior to gaining their independence in the early 1960s, Zaire and Burundi were part of the Belgian Congo for many years, and citizens with financial means traveled to Belgium for major medical care. They had signs and symptoms virtually identical to what was being called AIDS in the United States. Further investigation led to a number of different theories. The first was that HIV existed for decades, nestled in remote regions of Africa and limited to small, relatively isolated populations.[13] The social mores of those populations may not have been conducive to the rapid spread of the disease, and the few cases that did develop could likely have escaped detection against the backdrop of multiple life-threatening infections that are common to the region.

---

[i] HIV manifests itself in a variety of conditions, which has complicated efforts to define AIDS. The Centers for Disease Control formulated an initial definition of AIDS in 1982 that relied on the presence of certain opportunistic infections and malignancies. Opportunistic infections in this original case definition included pneumonia, meningitis, and encephalitis caused by nine different viruses, bacteria, fungi, and protozoa; esophagitis (inflammation of the esophagus) caused by candidiasis, cytomegalovirus, or herpes simplex; progressive brain disease with multiple lesions; chronic inflammation of the intestine caused by certain protozoan parasites (lasting more than four weeks); and unusually persistent herpes simplex infections of the mouth or rectum (lasting more than five weeks).

There were a number of factors that eventually changed this pattern. African cities grew dramatically after World War II, principally the result of many African countries gaining their independence. As in other parts of the world, the urbanization of Africa was accompanied by social changes and family disruptions, combined with the anonymity of urban life—all of which increased the likelihood of behaviors (multiple sex partners and prostitution) that contributed to the spread of sexually transmitted diseases. In time the prevalence of HIV increased sufficiently to make AIDS visible as a new clinical entity in Africa and elsewhere.

An alternative theory suggests that the natural home of the AIDS virus is in an animal. The African green monkey has been singled out as a prime suspect, with the hypothesis that somehow, the virus mutated and jumped species, entering the human population when monkeys bit hunters who were attempting to capture them for food.[14] Several investigations have also suggested that AIDS and HIV may have made their way to North America from Africa via Haiti. More specifically, from the early 1960s through the mid-1970s there was considerable migration from Zaire to Haiti, and many of these immigrants are believed to have settled in the United States.[15] In addition, several commentators have argued that African green monkeys were imported to Haiti from Zaire and kept as pets in male houses of prostitution.[16] And finally, there is the point of view that Haiti was a popular vacation spot for gay Americans, who brought the disease home with them and infected the mainland population.[17]

There were a number of conspiratorial theories as well about the origins of AIDS. Perhaps the most widely circulated was an opinion that was introduced by the Soviet press. During the summer months of 1987 a number of Soviet-sponsored articles stated that the AIDS virus had been created by Pentagon experiments; that the experiments had been carried out at Fort Detrick, Maryland; and that they were initiated to develop a subtle biological weapon. The articles appeared not only in Soviet outlets but in newspapers in Kenya, Peru, Sudan, Nigeria, Mexico, and Senegal as well. On November 4, 1987, however, members of the Soviet Academy of Sciences distanced themselves from the rumor, and their disavowals were published in *Izvestia*, the Soviet government newspaper.[18]

Then, in a letter dated February 25, 1987, written and widely circulated by Frances Cress Welsing, a Washington, D.C. psychiatrist, an alternative theory of AIDS as a man-made virus was forcefully presented. Reminding readers of the Tuskegee syphilis experiments,[j]

---

[j] The Tuskegee Study, as it has come to be known, involved a sample of some 400 syphilitic black men in Macon County, Alabama, who were deliberately denied treatment. The purpose of the study was to determine the course and complications of

Dr. Welsing implied that AIDS was an instrument of genocide likely introduced into black and other "undesirable" populations for the purpose of a systematic depopulation agenda.[19]

As "proof" of her contention, Dr. Welsing went on to quote the following paragraph from *A Survey of Chemical and Biological Warfare:*

> The question of whether new diseases could be used [for biological warfare] is of considerable interest. Vervet monkey disease may well be an example of a whole new class of disease-causing organisms. Handling of blood and tissues without precautions causes infection. It is unaffected by any antibiotic substance so far tried and is unrelated to any other organism. It causes fatality in some cases and can be venereally transmitted in man.[20]

As apparent proof of her thesis, Dr. Welsing pointed out that the vervet monkey was none other than the African green monkey.

Dr. Welsing's theory is easily refuted, for the disease of which she spoke is of a category known as viral hemorrhagic fever.[k] In 1967 an outbreak of a particular strain of hemorrhagic fever occurred in Germany and Yugoslavia among laboratory workers engaged in processing kidneys from African green monkeys for cell culture production. Additional cases involved medical personnel attending these patients. There were a total of 31 cases, including 6 secondary cases, and there were 7 deaths. A virus was isolated from the blood and tissues of the patients. The virus, named *Marburg virus* after the town in Germany where the first cases were described, was found to be unique and unrelated to any other known human pathogen.[21]

In subsequent years there were a few small and short-lived outbreaks of the disease, and clinical studies found that the secondary spread occurred through close contact with infected persons or contact

---

untreated latent syphilis in black males and to ascertain whether it differed from the course of the disease in whites. Syphilitic men chosen for the Tuskegee sample were told that they were ill and were promised free care. Unaware that they were participants in an experiment, all subjects believed that they were being treated for "bad blood"—a rural South colloquialism for syphilis. The project endured from 1932 through 1972, undertaken with the complicity of the United States Public Health Service. For the full story of the Tuskegee Study, see, Molly Selvin, "Changing Medical and Social Attitudes Toward Sexually Transmitted Diseases: A Historical Overview," in King K. Holmes, Per-Anders Mardh, P. Frederick Sparling, and Paul J. Wiesner, eds., *Sexually Transmitted Diseases* (New York: McGraw-Hill, 1984), pp. 13–14; J. H. Jones, *Bad Blood: The Scandalous Story of the Tuskegee Experiment* (New York: Free Press, 1981).

[k] The term viral hemorrhagic fever refers to the illness associated with a number of geographically restricted viruses. It is characterized by fever and, in the most severe cases, shock and hemorrhage. See S. P. Fisher-Hoch and D. I. H. Simpson, "Dangerous Pathogens," *British Medical Journal*, 41 (1985), pp. 391–395.

with infected blood or body secretions or excretions.[22] Sexual transmission of the disease has occurred, and the virus has been isolated from seminal fluid up to two months after illness.[23] Although this would suggest some similarities with HIV infection, the incubation period for Marburg virus ranges from only 3 to 9 days—a marked difference with the months to years between initial HIV infection and the appearance of AIDS.[1]

Whatever the source or sources, by 1983 it was clear that AIDS was an epidemic disease with a virtual 100% mortality rate.

AIDS in the Pre-AIDS Era

Any new epidemic begins as an enigma wrapped in subtle clues that sometimes ends in a mystery worthy of Agatha Christie, P. D. James, or even Arthur Conan Doyle. And that certainly seems to have been the case with AIDS. And although medical epidemiologic research and conventional wisdom dates the beginnings of the epidemic in Africa, Europe, and the United States to the late 1970s, there is evidence that the disease appeared earlier in several locales, thus contributing further to this medical mystery.

Several reports of cases resembling AIDS both clinically and immunologically have appeared in the literature.[24] Typically, however, conclusive evidence of HIV infection in these cases has not been (or cannot be) documented. In other cases the evidence is more convincing. A previously healthy, 32-year-old, heterosexual Canadian man who received a blood transfusion in Zaire in 1976 represents an interesting example.[25] Twelve days after his plane crashed in a remote section of Zaire, he was found by a group of villagers and transported to Kisingani University. Having suffered a compound fracture in his right leg, his treatment included a blood transfusion. After his transfer to a hospital in Canada, he began to manifest symptoms of a variety of opportunistic infections. He died in June 1980, and postmortem examination revealed findings similar to those described in cases of AIDS.[26] Serologic testing in 1983 of stored blood drawn several months before his death repeatedly had positive results for antibody to HIV. When the physician who treated this patient in Zaire was contacted,

---

[1] For the longest time, AIDS researchers believed that people exposed to HIV developed antibodies within six months of infection. In June, 1989, however, researchers from the U.C.L.A. Medical Center reported that one fourth of a group of 133 homosexual men who engaged in high risk sexual behavior were infected but for long periods did not produce HIV antibodies, thus causing some uncertainties about the test. See, D. T. Imagawa, H. L. Moon, S. M. Wolinsky, K. Sano, F. Morales, S. Kwok, J. J. Sninsky, P. G. Nishanian, J. Giorgi, J. L. Fahey, J. Dudley, B. R. Visscher, and R. Detels, "Human Immunodeficiency Virus Type 1 in Homosexual Men Who Remain Seronegative for Prolonged Periods," *New England Journal of Medicine*, 320 (1989), pp. 1458–1462.

he reported that local villagers had come to the hospital to donate blood for his transfusion, suggesting that transfusion-related AIDS cases date to the mid-1970s, and that HIV was present in Zaire prior to the known beginnings of the epidemic.

An even earlier case involved a Norwegian child and her parents.[27] The father, born in 1946, exhibited clinical and immunological manifestations of AIDS beginning in 1966; the mother, born in 1943, had similar manifestations starting in 1967; and the child, born in 1967, became ill with bacterial and other recurring infections at the age of two years. All three members of the family died in 1976, and subsequent assays of stored blood samples were found to be HIV positive. The child would appear to be the first recorded case of pediatric AIDS, and the family as a whole represent the first proven case of AIDS in Europe. The case history of the father suggests that he may have contracted the infection in Africa. He was a sailor and had visited a number of African ports several times prior to 1966. He had contracted sexually transmitted diseases on at least two occasions during his travels, and no other known risk factors for HIV were present in his family.

The first AIDS case in the United States may also date back to the 1960s. It involved a 15-year-old who had been admitted to St. Louis City Hospital suffering from extensive swelling of his legs, penis, and scrotum.[28] He had no history of intravenous drug use, blood transfusions, or travel outside the Midwest. He did admit to being sexually active, engaging in anal intercourse, and it was suspected that he may have been homosexual. In addition to the swelling, he was suffering from a number of infections, and he continued to deteriorate. He died 16 months later. The postmortem examination revealed that he had Kaposi's sarcoma—at that time an extremely rare cancer in the United States. Because the physicians at the St. Louis hospital were at a loss to explain the cause and course of the youth's condition, blood and tissue samples were frozen for later analysis. Subsequent study of the samples found a retrovirus related to HIV.

What all of these cases suggest is that HIV or a genetically related virus may have entered several communities before the current epidemic. In each case, however, the virus failed to gain a foothold in a large, sexually active or needle-sharing population. When each lone carrier died, the chain of infection was broken.

THE EPIDEMIOLOGY OF AIDS AND HIV

From analyses of AIDS reports combined with data from HIV testing, it appears that there are at least three distinct patterns of AIDS across the globe.[29]

Pattern-I seems to be typical of industrialized nations with relatively large numbers of AIDS cases, such as the United States, Canada and Mexico, many Western European countries, Australia and New Zealand, Brazil, and a few regions of South Africa (which are not industrialized). In pattern-I nations, HIV probably began to spread extensively during the late 1970s. Most cases occur among homosexual and bisexual males and urban intravenous drug users. Heterosexual transmission of the virus, although increasing, is responsible for only a small proportion of cases. There was transmission of HIV through some transfusions of blood and blood products in pattern-I countries between the late 1970s and 1985. However, that route of transmission has been practically eliminated in some countries and drastically reduced in others by convincing members of high risk groups not to donate blood and by the testing of potential blood donors for the presence of HIV antibodies. Unsterile needles, aside from those used by IV drug users, are not a significant factor in the transmission of HIV in pattern-I nations. Finally, relatively few women are infected in these countries, and as a result, perinatal transmission (from mother to infant) is also low.

The current male-to-female ratio of reported AIDS cases in pattern-I countries ranges from 10-to-1 to 15-to-1. This is rapidly changing, however, as is the incidence of perinatal transmission, because of the growing spread of the virus within populations of injecting drug users and their sex partners.

Pattern-II can be observed in Haiti, a few other parts of the Caribbean, and several countries in central, eastern, and southern Africa. As in the pattern-I nations, pattern-II areas saw the initial spread of the virus during the late 1970s. Unique to this pattern, however, the male-to-female ratio is almost 1-to-1, with most cases occurring among heterosexuals. Transmission through homosexual activity or injecting drug use is either absent or at a low level, whereas perinatal transmission is common.

In the developing nations of Central and West Africa, the epidemic character of AIDS is related in part to existing health-care practices. Many such practices tend to be unsanitary, such as the reuse of unsterilized hypodermic needles for transfusions in bush hospitals and in mass inoculations.[30] In addition, a strong link exists in this part of the world between AIDS and prostitution. As one observer explained the situation:

> A study of Nairobi's Kenyatta Hospital shows just how fast a virus can spread in a society where sexual partners change frequently. Within 6 years, 60% of all prostitutes examined were carriers [of HIV]. In the slums of Nairobi today, there is almost no prostitute who is not infected with the virus. The women,

most of whom were forced by poverty to leave their native villages, have about 1,000 customers a year. After spending awhile in the slums, the women return to their families on the land. They bring the plague with them.[31]

An additional element in the AIDS-Africa connection is that the disease has been compounded by other infections—malaria, yellow fever, tuberculosis, and leprosy—and by undernourishment and pregnancy. All of these burdens weaken the immune system, making it easier for human immunodeficiency virus to establish itself.

During the early years of the AIDS epidemic, given the prevalence of AIDS among Haitian immigrants, the Centers for Disease Control classified them as a separate risk group for the disease. Focused study of the Haitian cases in Miami and New York determined, however, that being Haitian was not necessarily a risk factor for AIDS. Rather, as in Africa, there were other variables—prostitution, malnutrition, and a complex of sexually transmitted and other diseases that compromised the immune system.[32]

Pattern-III prevails in sections of Eastern Europe, North Africa, the Middle East, Asia, and the majority of the Pacific. In these areas, HIV was likely introduced during the early and mid-1980s. Only small numbers of cases have been observed, and primarily in people who have traveled to pattern-I or pattern-II countries and had sexual contacts during their visits. Indigenous homosexual, heterosexual, and intravenous drug transmission patterns have been documented only recently. Finally, some cases have been caused from imported blood products that were contaminated by HIV.

In addition to patterns I, II, and III, there are several other configurations of AIDS transmission that may be unique to specific areas. Recent research in Brazil suggests that the transmission of HIV in parts of that country incorporates aspects of patterns I and II.[33] The authors suggest a pattern of HIV infection from an initially male homosexual population to the larger heterosexual population by means of bisexuals rather than injecting drug users. Such a pattern indeed seems plausible, particularly since anal intercourse, which is an extremely efficient mechanism for HIV transmission, is not uncommon among some heterosexual populations in Brazil.[34]

By contrast, what would appear to be a wholly unique pattern was uncovered in Rumania during the early weeks of 1990. After the fall of dictator Nicolae Ceausescu, Western physicians revealed a mysterious epidemic of AIDS among segments of Rumania's infant population. Continuing tests of children at hospitals and orphanages identified 706 of 2,184 examined to be infected with HIV. Two theories were posed to explain the phenomenon. The first relates to the traditional practice in Rumania of injecting minute quantities of adult blood

into infants who appear anemic. The blood supply used for this purpose
was likely contaminated. The second pathway of infection was the reuse
of dirty needles. As was the case in most Eastern European countries
at the time, disposable syringes were in short supply, and hospital staff
were not always trained properly in effective sterilizing techniques.[35]

In terms of the national dimensions of AIDS, as of December 31,
1990, there were a total of 161,073 diagnosed cases of AIDS in the
United States that were reported to the Centers for Disease Control.[36]
The majority of these were concentrated in the states of New York,
California, Florida, New Jersey, and Texas, which collectively accounted
for some two thirds of all cases. Homosexual and bisexual men
accounted for some 59% of the adult and adolescent cases, followed
by female and heterosexual male injecting drug users (22%), and then
homosexual/bisexual male injecting drug users (7%). Collectively,
homosexual and bisexual men and intravenous drug users accounted
for almost 90% of the known cases of AIDS in the United States.
Importantly, however, although injecting drug users (including those
who are also homosexual and bisexual men) ranked a distant second
as a major risk group for AIDS, their numbers were, and still are,
proportionately increasing.

The next exposure category in the adult/adolescent age cohort
includes those infected through heterosexual contacts and accounts for
some 5% of all diagnosed cases. The number of individuals in this
group is relatively small—8,440 since June of 1981. However, this group
also appears to be growing rapidly, and persons who have had sex
with an injecting drug user or with an individual born in a pattern-II
country account for the overwhelming majority.

Of interest is the distribution of pediatric cases—persons under
13 years of age. Not surprisingly, there are comparatively few—2,786
since June 1981, representing only 1.7% of all reported cases in the
United States. However, the overwhelming majority (84%) were
the result of perinatal (occurring prior to or at birth) transmission. And
most importantly, some 59% of these perinatal cases were the result
of the mother's injecting drug use or her sexual contacts with an
injecting drug user.

From 1981, when AIDS was first recognized, through 1990, more
than 100,000 persons in the United States died from AIDS.[37] In
addition, an estimated 1 million persons are infected with HIV. As the
disease has spread, it has changed from an epidemic once overwhelmingly identified with homosexual men to one that strikes with increasing frequency low income, inner city blacks and Hispanics—primarily
drug users, their sex partners and babies.[38]

Regarding the global dimensions of AIDS, some 307,379 cases had
been reported to the World Health Organization (WHO) by the close of
February 2, 1990.[39] The United States ranked first among the 177 nations

Table 6.1 Possible Routes of HIV-1 Acquisition and Transmission Among Injecting Drug Users

Blood
Contaminated needles, syringes, spoons, cookers, and cottons
Needle sharing, booting, frontloading, and backloading
Use of contaminated drug paraphernalia in shooting galleries

Sexual
Sex partner of injecting drug user
Intravenous drug-using prostitute
Homosexual male injecting drug user

Perinatal
Prepartum transplacental
Peripartum HIV-infected genital secretions or blood
Postpartum HIV-infected breast milk

reporting to WHO, with more than 152,000 cases, followed by Uganda (15,569), Brazil (12,405), Zaire (11,732), and France (9,718). Important in these data is the consideration that reporting in many nations is neither complete nor timely. In 1990, WHO estimated that there were 700,000 AIDS cases worldwide, that 5 million to 6 million people were infected with HIV, and that by the year 2000 the number infected may approach 20 million.[40]

MAINLINING DEATH

The ready transmission of HIV and AIDS among intravenous and other injecting drug users is the result of needle-sharing practices combined with the presence of cofactors. Cofactors include any behavioral practices or microbiological agents that facilitate the transmission of HIV. The risk factors that relate to injecting drug users are summarized in Table 6.1.

The sharing of hypodermic needles and syringes is the most likely route of HIV transmission among injecting drug users. The mechanism is the exchange of the blood of the previous user that is lodged in the needle, the syringe, or some other part of the works (drug paraphernalia).

Levels of risk vary, however, depending on the particular injection practice. Of lesser risk, for example, is skin-popping—the subcutaneous (under the skin) injection of narcotics and other drugs. Skin-popping (or simply popping) is a common method of heroin use by experimenters and tasters (novice and casual users) who mistakenly believe that addiction cannot occur through this route.[41] At the opposite end of the risk spectrum is booting, a process involving the use of a syringe to draw blood from the user's arm, the mixing of the drawn blood with the drug already taken into the syringe, and then mainlining—intravenous injection (and in the case of booting, the injection of the blood/drug mixture directly into the vein). Many injecting users believe that this practice potentiates a drug's effects. Importantly, however, booting leaves traces of blood in the needle and syringe, thus placing subsequent users of the injection equipment at risk.[42] And although most injecting drug users are generally aware of the risks associated with booting and needle sharing, they are often ignored. Moreover, little thought is typically given to the risks associated with other aspects of the injection process.

Virological studies have indicated that HIV can survive in ordinary tap water for extended periods of time.[43] Injecting drug users require water to both rinse their syringes and mix with their drugs to liquify them for injection. Rinsing, for example, is not for hygienic purposes, but to make sure a syringe does not become clogged with blood and drug residue so that it can be used again. And the rinse water is often shared. As one user explained:

> People don't clean their works before they shoot dope, they clean them afterward, and they clean them out of the same cup of water that everyone is using. So, while somebody is rinsing their syringe out in a cup of water, another person is pulling water out into their spoon to cook their dope in.[44]

As such, water contaminated through the rinsing of a syringe is used for rinsing other syringes and for mixing the drug. Similarly, spoons, cookers, and cottons are parts of the injecting kit that also represent potential reservoirs of disease. Spoons and cookers are the bottle caps, spoons, baby food jars, and other small containers used for mixing the drug; cottons refer to any materials placed in the spoon to filter out undissolved drug particles. Filtering is considered necessary since undissolved particles tend to clog injection equipment. The risks of HIV infection from spoons and cottons are due to their frequent sharing, even by drug users who carry their own syringes.

Viral contamination might also result from frontloading and backloading, techniques for distributing a drug solution among a drug-injecting group.[45] When frontloading, the drug is transferred from the syringe used for measuring by removing the needle from the receiving syringe and squirting the solution directly into its hub. Common in Miami shooting galleries is the intercontamination of drug doses through the mixing and frontloading of speedball (heroin and cocaine). Since heroin is cooked (heated in an aqueous solution), whereas cocaine is not during its preparation for injecting, separate containers are used for the mixing process. Those who share speedball draw the heroin into one syringe and the cocaine into another; remove the needle from the cocaine syringe and discharge the heroin into it through its hub; and return half the speedball mixture back into the syringe that originally contained the heroin. If either syringe contains virus at the start of such an operation, both are likely to contain it afterward.[46]

The backloading of speedball has also been observed in Miami galleries. Backloading involves essentially the same process, but the plunger rather than the needle is removed from the receiving syringe. Frontloading seems to be the preferred mixing/sharing method, with backloading as a substitute when syringes with detachable needles are unavailable.

Both frontloading and backloading have been reported by inmate informants in Delaware, Florida, New York, Maryland, and Ohio penitentiaries. Illicit drugs are generally available in most American prisons but typically in limited quantities and at considerable cost, often resulting in the sharing of injectable heroin, cocaine, and speedball by groups of three to four prisoners. Backloading is the preferred mixing/ measuring technique. Since hypodermic syringes are closely controlled in prisons, makeshift injection equipment is manufactured from securable materials. The most common works in the penitentiary is an eye dropper, with the glass or plastic end sharpened to an angular point. Backloading is accomplished by removing the squeeze bulb. Regarding the practice, an inmate in Miami's Dade County Stockade indicated in 1989:

> There's times when a backloaded dose is all you can get, with drugs bein' so scarce and all inside. They'll be someone with some dope and a few droppers with sharpened ends. You get your share by havin' yours pointed down with your finger covering the tip while someone loads it in.

An alternative method of drug sharing is referred to by some injecting drug users as shooting back and drawing up. This practice has been observed in instances when every member of the drug-sharing group has a syringe. After the heroin, cocaine, or speedball is thoroughly mixed, it is discharged from the mixing syringe into a common spoon, cap, or container. Each member of the sharing group then draws a specific amount.

Booting, frontloading, and backloading are not the only aspects of injecting drugs that place users at risk for HIV infection. The street subculture of illegal drug use is characterized by exploitation and danger. Moreover, it is a perpetually embattled subculture conditioned by scarcity—scarce money, scarce drugs, scarce needles, scarce places in which to be safe. Within this relentless context, users must temper trust with street-wise wariness and vigilance. Deals gone sour, bad drugs, bad deals, bogus sterilized needles, rip-offs, and outright violent assaults combine with the omnipresent threat of arrest, worry about drug availability, and the generalized anxiety associated with poverty and the inner city to create an environment which is bleak and harrowing, threatening and exciting.

But within this subculture can be found fragile threads of social support and bonding—structures necessary to sustain users in the face of external hostility and internal danger. Ironically, it is these very patterns of social support that increase the pathways for HIV contamination. The issue is this: All forms of needle sharing tend to occur among running partners (or running buddies)—injecting drug users who are lovers, good friends, crime partners, or live together. They serve as lookouts for one another—one watching for police and other intruders while the other cops (purchases the drugs), prepares the drugs, or injects. Running partners also provide other elements of safety, such as monitoring each other's responses to the drugs they use in order to prevent overdoses or other acute reactions. And in this regard, as a 32-year-old former heroin-using prostitute in Miami related in late 1990, for some injecting drug users having a running partner can mean the difference between life and death:

> Without my partner I'd be dead. He was big, and more than once he saved my ass from being beat on. . . . We weren't lovers or anything like that, although we did sleep together a few times when I was really down. He was no pimp either. We were just really good friends. We could depend on each other.
>
> One time I was cut up pretty bad and he got me patched up. One of my dates had really worked me over—one of them sado-blood freaks, tied me to a bed and worked over my change purse [vagina] with a coat hanger. Another time when I was bein' ripped off by a bunch of street kids who wanted all of my shit [money and drugs] he came to the rescue, like the fucking Lone Ranger.

For many decades, needle sharing has been a prominent aspect of the subculture of the street drug scene, and all of its associated practices are generally learned during initiation to drug use.[47] A user's first episode of sharing is typically unplanned. Since novice injecting users rarely have their own fit (injection kit or works), they often borrow a more experienced user's equipment. After becoming a regular user, a person may begin an association with a running partner, and sharing both drugs and needles serves as a convenience and a symbol of friendship and trust. And since a running partner is often a lover, a surrogate family member, or a replacement family, refusing to share a needle would be viewed as an indication of mistrust. For running partners who are also sex partners, injecting drugs as a pair can serve as an even deeper symbol of emotional bonding. In addition, the mixing of blood while injecting and the booting of each other's blood is not uncommon, symbolizing a brotherhood or bond between running partners. The risks of such ritual blood exchanges are obvious and are likely responsible for scores of HIV and other infections.

SHOOTING GALLERIES AND INJECTING DRUG USE

In most urban locales where rates of intravenous drug use are high, common sites for injecting drugs (and sometimes purchasing drugs) are the neighborhood shooting galleries, typically referred to in some locales as safe houses and in Miami as get-off houses. After purchasing heroin, cocaine, amphetamines, or some other injectable substance in a local copping (drug selling) area, users are faced with three logistical problems: how to get off the street quickly to avoid arrest for possession of drugs, where to obtain a set of works with which to administer the drugs, and where to find a safe place to get off (inject the drugs). As such, shooting galleries occupy a functional niche in the world of injecting drug use, where for a fee of two or three dollars users can rent a set of works and relax while getting off. After using a syringe and needle, the user generally returns them to a central storage place in the gallery where they are held until someone else rents them. On many occasions, however, these works are just passed to another user in the gallery.

Shooting galleries are situated in basements and backrooms in the rundown sections of cities where drug-use rates are high. Typically, they are only sparsely furnished, and cleanliness is absent. Moreover, they are run by drug users, drug dealers, and drug user/dealers. Neighborhood heroin and/or cocaine dealers may operate shooting galleries as a service to customers—providing them for just a few dollars with a nearby location to safely shoot up (inject). More often, however, gallery operators are drug users who provide a service for a small fee or a taste (sample) of someone else's drugs.[m]

For the majority of injecting drug users, shooting galleries are considered to be the least desirable places to patronize. Most prefer to

---

[m] It should be noted here that there are many less formally structured shooting galleries located in darkened hallways and empty rooms in abandoned buildings. Characterized by the stench of urine and littered with trash, human feces, garbage, and discarded injection paraphernalia, the conditions are extremely unsanitary and rarely is there heat, running water, or functional plumbing.

use their own homes or apartments or those of drug-using friends. These are considered safer than galleries, and there are few users who appreciate having to pay a fee to use someone else's drug paraphernalia. And for a minority of hard-core users, there is also the matter of personal hygiene. As one heroin user summed it up:

> Galleries ain't where it's at. We wasn't brought up like that. They be definitely hardcore junkies and they don't give a damn no more about how their appearance is or nothing like that. Ain't nobody want to give another two dollars. Their works . . . all dirty, man. An' people be shootin' blood all over you.[48]

For many injecting drug users, however, the use of shooting galleries is routine and commonplace. Moreover, there are repeated occasions in the lives of all injecting users, including the most hygienically fastidious types, when galleries become necessary. If they have no works of their own, or if friends or other running partners have no works, then a neighborhood gallery is the only recourse. Similarly, users who purchase drugs far from home also gravitate toward the galleries. This tendency is based on the heightened risk of arrest when carrying drugs and drug paraphernalia over long stretches. Moreover, the gallery operator often serves as a middleman between drug user and drug dealer, thus making the get-off house the locus of exchange. For example, as one Miami heroin user explained the situation in 1988:

> OK, so let's say I'm white, but the only place I can cop some smack [heroin] is in the black neighborhoods, but I'm afraid that I'll be ripped off [robbed] there. But, then there's this gallery an' I know the man there, he's right [trusted] by the buyers and sellers. So I go there an' he cops for me for a few dollars and maybe a taste. For another $3 I can use his works and house to lay up in for a little while.

And finally, there are a few injecting users who actually prefer local galleries because of the opportunities they provide to socialize with other drug users. In short, despite their unsavory character, shooting galleries do indeed occupy a functional role in the street worlds of drug taking and drug seeking along the mainline.

While systematic research and clinical observation suggest that the use of shooting galleries, the sharing of needles and other drug paraphernalia, and the practice of booting combine to explain the increasing proportion of injecting drug users infected with HIV, little is known about the prevalence of HIV antibodies in needle/syringe combinations utilized by injecting users. In this behalf, samples of needle/syringe combinations from major shooting galleries in Miami were collected for the sake of analyzing their contents for the presence of HIV antibodies. Of a total of 148 needle/syringe combinations collected and tested, 15 (10.1%) were found to be seropositive—positive for HIV antibodies—133 were seronegative, and in two cases serostatus was indeterminate.[49] As such, it would appear that shooting galleries represent a significant health problem as far as the spread of the HIV infection is concerned.

THE DILEMMAS OF DRUGS, SEX, AND HIV

In addition to themselves, injecting drug users also represent a group primarily at risk for transmitting HIV infection to non-injecting heterosexuals and perinatal cases. As indicated earlier in this chapter, sex with an injecting drug user accounts for more than half of all reported AIDS cases through heterosexual contacts in the United States. And similarly, well over half of all reported pediatric AIDS cases have some association with injecting drug use—mothers at risk of HIV infection through injecting drug use and/or sex with an injecting drug user. Furthermore, there are estimates that 23% to 60% of the heterosexual partners of injecting drug users, depending on the locale, have contracted HIV infection.[50] Transmission occurs most often from male to female, and the majority of those infected are non-injecting women.[51]

Many of the issues surrounding the spread of HIV infection to sex partners are rooted in subcultural issues of trust, since the lives of most injecting users are beset with insecurity, apprehension, fragile relationships, and minimal kinship. As such, the kinds of behavioral changes appropriate for HIV risk reduction have the potential for introducing elements of suspicion into a relationship. It has been argued, for example, that to ask a sex partner to use a condom is in direct contradiction to the gender roles existing in the injecting drug street culture.[52] More specifically, a woman's request of her man to use a condom not only compromises her prescribed role in the relationship but also suggests that she believes her partner to be contaminated in some way. The reverse could also be the case when a male injecting user begins using condoms with his partner. Quite clearly, there is a substantial asymmetry of power and risk in sexual relationships between male drug users and female partners who do not inject drugs.

The existence of shooting galleries across the urban landscape combined with the drug-taking and sexual behaviors of injecting drug users pose a dilemma. Although most, if not virtually all, injecting drug users are aware of AIDS and the risk of infection through needle sharing and unprotected sex, in many instances the prevention messages are either not heard or are not listened to.

The problem is this. Heroin and cocaine are highly seductive drugs. For those dependent on them, heroin and cocaine become life consuming. They become mother, father, spouse, lover, counselor, confessor, and confidant. Since they are short-acting drugs, they must be taken regularly and repeatedly. Because there is a more rapid onset and a more powerful euphoric high when taken intravenously, most heroin users and a growing number of cocaine users inject their drugs. Collectively, these attributes result in a majority of chronic users more concerned with drug taking and drug seeking than with careers, relationships, or health. As such, it would appear that altering the risk behaviors of drug users might be difficult. Or as one intravenous cocaine-using prostitute summed it up at the close of 1988:

> Every day I risk my health, and my life for that matter, when I shoot up. Every time I go out to cop [buy drugs] I risk getting cut [stabbed] or even killed. Every time I'm strolling [walking the streets soliciting clients] at night, there are all kinds of crazies, geeks, thugs, and death freaks out there just waiting to carve up my ass. Now they say that if I use some dirty needle I can get sick, even die in a few years. So I care? I'm probably already dead. Why should I care?

In other words, it is difficult to prevent behavior that may cause sickness and death in two or five years or more when the injecting drug user is confronted with violence, sickness, and death almost every day; it is difficult to motivate behaviors aimed at preventing death in the future within a population already at high risk of imminent death.

POSTSCRIPT

By the mid-1980s risk reduction efforts geared toward injecting drug users were focusing on issues of needle contamination and sexual behavior. During the latter half of the decade, however, some programs included not only education, but such proactive intervention techniques as distributing needle cleaning supplies, latex condoms, and establishing needle exchange centers.

According to most reports, outreach workers and intervention and treatment programs succeeded in educating drug users on the risks of infection and prevention methods.[53] A number of these evaluations also noted some positive changes in needle sterilizing practices.

In Europe, many needle exchange programs were organized early in the AIDS epidemic. Several of them have been evaluated and were found to be somewhat effective.[54] The first needle exchange program began in the Netherlands during 1984. According to its founders, the rate of infection among intravenous drug users did not rise significantly after its inception.[55] Positive evaluations have also been reported for a British program initiated two years after the Dutch piloted their experiment.[56] Other needle exchange programs have reported similar successes.[57]

In the United States, government-approved needle exchange programs did not begin until 1988, the delay due mainly to the illegal status of needles and syringes in most parts of the country. In the overwhelming majority of state jurisdictions, injection equipment may not be legally purchased without a doctor's prescription. However, privately funded activist groups began distributing sterile equipment as early as 1986. Among the first was that operated by John Parker, a graduate student at Yale University. In 1986, Parker founded the Boston AIDS Brigade and began distributing needles in those neighborhoods with high rates of injecting drug use.[58] He secured his needles legally in Vermont and transported them to Boston for distribution.

Since then, several legally sanctioned needle exchange schemes have been implemented in the United States, beginning with a pilot program in New York City.[59] Other cities commenced similar operations, such as that developed in Tacoma, Washington. In January 1989 the Tacoma-Pierce health department added a needle exchange component to its drug education, counseling, and treatment programs.[60] Both the New York and Tacoma programs were designed to provide injecting drug users with sterile needles in exchange for their used ones and to monitor client samples to measure program effectiveness.

From their outset the needle exchange programs were mired in controversy.[61] Some observers feared a repeat performance of the black market diversion incidents that plagued methadone maintenance programs.[62] In April 1989 New York Congressman Charles Rangel introduced a bill banning federal funds or assistance to exchange programs and others that dispensed sterilizing materials.[63] Rangel argued that "addicts . . . think that their habit is safe [when the government provides the needles] . . . this lends an air of approval to a practice that prolongs drug addiction." Also there were claims that distribution of sterile needles enabled addicts to keep their habits, which—given their higher rates of injecting drug use—amounts to genocide of blacks and Hispanics.[64] In response to these accusations, exchange advocates pointed to statistics from the apparently successful projects elsewhere in the world which suggested that since the exchanges began, treatment entries increased and the rate of AIDS infection stabilized.[65]

The effectiveness of some needle exchange schemes were called into serious question, however, often an outgrowth of program policies. New York City's exchange program required that clients participating in the project carry identification cards, be in drug treatment, and travel significant distances to the program center. Participants received only one free needle at each visit to the center. This eliminated injecting drug users with no money for transportation or no desire to enter treatment. Or as one intravenous drug user in New York remarked in late 1988:

> Who the hell are they trying to attract? There are what you could call your good junkies, and there are your average run-of-the-mill New York dope fiends. The good junkies who might be interested in the [needle] exchange already clean their needles, or don't mix blood in them, or don't share, and stuff like that. But then there are your street dope fiends, which are probably 99% of New York's junk heads. They want to be out in the street shooting and hustling, and that's why they're not in treatment. And besides, they wouldn't even cross the street to get a clean needle, no less cross town to get one. And then if from some miracle they did, they'd probably use it 'till it got dull, and then wrap it up in cellophane and sell it as new.[66]

And as a final note here, one must not forget the sexual activities associated with crack use—risk behaviors that are unaffected by needle exchange initiatives. As pointed out in Chapter 4, sex for crack exchanges are commonplace in crack houses. Given the frequency of unprotected sex with multiple, anonymous sex partners, crack users represent significant players in the secondary spread of HIV and AIDS.

Notes

1. Segments of this chapter were adapted from Dale D. Chitwood, James A. Inciardi, Clyde B. McCoy, Duane C. McBride, H. Virginia McCoy, and Edward J. Trapido, *A Community Approach to AIDS Intervention* (Westport CT: Greenwood Press, 1991).
2. C. Everett Koop, *Surgeon General's Report on Acquired Immune Deficiency Syndrome* (Washington, DC: Department of Health and Human Services, 1986).
3. O. R. Bowen, "In Pursuit of the Number One Public Health Problem," *Public Health Reports*, 103 (May–June 1988), pp. 211–212.
4. David Black, *The Plague Years: A Chronicle of AIDS, the Epidemic of Our Times* (New York: Simon and Schuster, 1986).
5. Centers for Disease Control "Pneumocystis Pneumonia-Los Angeles," *Morbidity and Mortality Weekly Report*, 30 (5 June 1981), pp. 250–252; Centers for Disease Control, "Kaposi's Sarcoma and Pneumocystis Pneumonia Among Homosexual Men—New York City and California," *Morbidity and*

Mortality Weekly Report, 30 (3 July 1981), pp. 305–308; M. S. Gottlieb, R. Schroff, H. Schanker, J. D. Weismal, P. T. Fan, R. A. Wolf, and A. Saxon, "Pneumocystis Carinii Pneumonia and Mucosal Candidiasis in Previously Healthy Homosexual Men: Evidence of a New Acquired Cellular Immuno-deficiency," *New England Journal of Medicine,* 305 (10 Dec. 1981), pp. 1425–1431; H. Masur, M. A. Michelis, J. B. Greene, I. Onorato, R. A. Vande Stouwe, R. T. Holzman, G. Wormser, L. Brettmen, M. Lange, H. W. Murray, and S. Cunningham-Rundles, "An Outbreak of Community-Acquired Pneumo-cystis Carinii Pneumonia: Initial Manifestation of Cellular Immune Dysfunc-tion," *New England Journal of Medicine,* 305 (10 Dec. 1981), pp. 1431–1438.

6. Anne Rompalo and H. Hunter Handsfield, "Overview of Sexually Trans-mitted Diseases in Homosexual Men," in Pearl Ma and Donald Armstrong, eds., *AIDS and Infections of Homosexual Men* (Boston: Butterworths, 1989), pp. 3–11.

7. Randy Shilts, *And the Band Played On: Politics, People, and the AIDS Epidemic* (New York: St. Martin's Press, 1987), pp. 18–19.

8. Centers for Disease Control, "Epidemiologic Aspects of the Current Out-break of Kaposi's Sarcoma and Opportunistic Infections," *New England Journal of Medicine,* 306 (28 Jan. 1982), pp. 248–252.

9. D. M. Auerbach, W. W. Darrow, H. W. Jaffe, and J. W. Curran, "Cluster of Cases of Acquired Immune Deficiency Syndrome: Patients Linked by Sexual Contact," *American Journal of Medicine,* 76 (March 1984), pp. 487–492.

10. For a discussion of the early history of AIDS, see Ann Giudici Fettner, "The Discovery of AIDS: Perspectives from a Medical Journalist," in Gary P. Wormser, Rosalyn E. Stahl, and Edward J. Bottone, eds., *AIDS and Other Manifestations of HIV Infection* (Park Ridge, NJ: Noyes Publications, 1987), pp. 2–17.

11. Institute of Medicine, National Academy of Sciences, *Mobilizing Against AIDS: The Unfinished Story of a Virus* (Cambridge: Harvard University Press, 1986), p. 20.

12. N. J. Clumeck, H. Sonnet, and H. Taelman, "Acquired Immunodeficiency Syndrome in African Patients," *New England Journal of Medicine,* 210 (1984), pp. 492–497.

13. Institute of Medicine, National Academy of Sciences, *Mobilizing Against AIDS* (Cambridge: Harvard University Press, 1989), p. 107.

14. See Max Essex and Phyllis J. Kanki, "The Origins of the AIDS Virus," in Jonathan Piel, ed., *The Science of AIDS* (New York: W. H. Freeman, 1989), pp. 27–37; *New York Times,* 21 Nov. 1985, p. A1.

15. Vincent T. DeVita, Samuel Hellman, and Steven A. Rosenberg, *AIDS: Etiology, Diagnosis, Treatment, and Prevention* (Philadelphia: J.B. Lippincott, 1985), p. 304.

16. Dennis Altman, *AIDS in the Mind of America: The Social, Political, and Psychological Impact of the New Epidemic* (Garden City, NY: Doubleday, 1987), p. 72; *Newsweek,* 7 May 1984, pp. 101–102.

17. Altman, p. 72.

18. See *New York Times,* 5 Nov. 1987, p. A31.

19. Frances Cress Welsing, Unpublished letter, Washington, DC, 25 Feb. 1987.

20. J. Cookson and J. Nottingham, *A Survey of Chemical and Biological Warfare* (New York: Monthly Review Press, 1969), pp. 322–323.

21. Frederick A. Murphy, "Marburg and Ebola Viruses," in Bernard N. Fields, ed., *Virology* (New York: Raven Press, 1985), pp. 1111–1118; G. A. Martini and R. Siegert, *Marburg Virus Disease* (Berlin: Springer-Verlag, 1971).

22. J. P. Luby and C. V. Sanders, "Green Monkey Disease (Marburg Virus' Disease): A New Zoonosis," *Annals of Internal Medicine*, 17 (1969), pp. 657–660; F. W. Van der Walls, K. L. Pomeroy, J. Goudsmit, D. M. Asher, and D. C. Gajdusek, "Hemorrhagic Fever Virus Infections in an Isolated Rainforest Area of Central Liberia: Limitations of the Indirect Immuno-fluorescence Slide Test for Antibody Screening in Africa," *Tropical and Geographical Medicine*, 38 (1986), pp. 209–214; J. S. S. Gear, G. A. Cassel, A. J. Gear, B. Trappler, L. Clausen, A. M. Meyers, M. C. Kew, T. H. Bothwell, R. Sher, G. B. Miller, J. Schneider, H. J. Koornhof, E. D. Gomperts, M. Isaacson, and J. H. S. Gear, "Outbreak of Marburg Virus Disease in Johannesburg," *British Medical Journal*, 29 (1975), pp. 489–493.

23. D. H. Smith, B. K. Johnson, and M. Isaacson, "Marburg Virus Disease in Kenya," *Lancet*, 1 (1982), pp. 816–820.

24. H. P. Katner and G.A. Pankey "Evidence of a Euro-American Origin of Human Immunodeficiency Virus (HIV)," *Journal of the National Medical Association*, 79 (1987), pp. 1068–1072; D. Huminer and S. D. Pitlik, "Further Evidence for the Existence of AIDS in the Pre-AIDS Era," *Reviews of Infectious Diseases*, 10 (Sept.–Oct. 1988), p. 1061.

25. E. Rogan, L. D. Jewell, B. W. Meilke, D. Kunimoto, A. Voth, and D. L. Tyrrell, "A Case of Acquired Immune Deficiency Syndrome Before 1980," *Canadian Medical Association Journal*, 137 (1 Oct. 1987), pp. 637–638.

26. C. Reichert, T. Giliary, and D. Levens, "Autopsy Pathology in the Acquired Immune Deficiency Syndrome," *American Journal of Pathology*, 112 (1983), pp. 357–382.

27. S. S. Froland, P. Jenum, C. F. Lindboe, K. W. Wefring, P. J. Linnestad, and T. Bohmer, "HIV-1 Infection in Norwegian Family Before 1970," *Lancet*, (11 June 1988), pp. 1344–1345.

28. R. F. Garry, M. H. Witte, A. Gottleib, M. Elvin-Lewis, M. S. Gottlieb, C. L. Witte, S. S. Alesander, W. R. Cole, and W. L. Drake, "Documentation of an AIDS Virus Infection in the United States in 1968," *Journal of the American Medical Association*, 260 (14 Oct. 1988), pp. 2085–2087.

29. Jonathan M. Mann, James Chin, Peter Piot, and Thomas Quinn, "The International Epidemiology of AIDS," pp. 51–61 in Piel.

30. Thomas C. Quinn, "AIDS in Africa: Evidence for Heterosexual Transmission of Human Immunodeficiency Virus," *New York State Journal of Medicine*, 87 (1987), pp. 286–287; *New York Times*, 24 Nov. 1985, p. 34.

31. *World Press Review*, February 1987, p. 57.

32. Collaborative Study Group of AIDS in Haitian-Americans, "Risk Factors for AIDS Among Haitians Residing in the United States," *Journal of the American Medical Association*, 257 (1987), pp. 636–639.

33. E. Cortes, R. Detels, D. Aboulafia, X. L. Li, T. Moudgil, M. Alam, C. Bonecker, A. Gonzaga, L. Oyafuso, M. Tondo, C. Boite, N. Hammershlak, C. Capitani, D. J. Slamon, and D. D. Ho, "HIV-1, HIV-2, and HTLV-I Infection in High-Risk Groups in Brazil," *New England Journal of Medicine*, 320 (1989), pp. 953–958.

34. R. Parker, "Acquired Immunodeficiency Syndrome in Urban Brazil," *Medical Anthropology Quarterly*, 1 (1987), pp. 155–175.

35. See *Time*, 10 Feb. 1990, p. 74; *Newsweek*, 19 Feb. 1990, p. 63; *U.S. News & World Report*, 19 Feb. 1990, pp. 11–12.

36. Centers for Disease Control, *HIV/AIDS Surveillance*, January 1991.

37. Centers for Disease Control, "Mortality Attributable to HIV Infection/ AIDS—United States, 1981–1990," *Morbidity and Mortality Weekly Report*, 40 (25 Jan. 1991), pp. 41–44.

38. See Jacob A. Gayle, Richard M. Selik, and Susan Y. Chu, "Surveillance for AIDS and HIV Infection Among Black and Hispanic Children and Women of Childbearing Age, 1981–1989," *Morbidity and Mortality Weekly Report*, 39, No. SS-3 (July 1990), pp. 23–30; Leigh E. Krueger, Robert W. Wood, Paula H. Diehr, and Clare L. Maxwell, "Poverty and HIV Seropositivity: The Poor are More Likely to be Infected," *AIDS*, 4 (1990), pp. 811–814; Steven J. Schleifer, Steven E. Keller, John E. Franklin, Stephanie LaFarge, and Sheldon I. Miller, "HIV Seropositivity in Inner-City Alcoholics," *Hospital and Community Psychiatry*, 41 (Mar. 1990), pp. 248–249, 254; Ciro V. Sumaya and Maurine D. Porto, "AIDS in Hispanics," *Southern Medical Journal*, 82 (Aug. 1989), pp. 943–945; *Miami Herald*, 14 Dec. 1988, pp. 1A, 19A; *New York Times*, 5 Feb. 1989, pp. 1, 28.

39. World Health Organization, *Weekly Epidemiological Record*, 65 (7 Dec. 1990), pp. 377–378.

40. J. Chin, P. A. Sato, and J. M. Mann, "Projections of HIV Infections and AIDS Cases to the Year 2000," *Bulletin of the World Health Organization*, 68 (1990), pp. 1–11. See also William B. Johnston and Kevin R. Hopkins, *The Catastrophe Ahead: AIDS and the Case for a New Public Policy* (New York: Praeger, 1990).

41. Michael M. Baden, "Methadone Related Deaths in New York City," *International Journal of the Addictions*, 5 (1975), pp. 489–498; John Kaplan, *The Hardest Drug: Heroin and Public Policy* (Chicago: University of Chicago Press, 1983), p. 10.

42. Don C. Des Jarlais and Samuel R. Friedman, "Intravenous Cocaine, Crack, and HIV Infection," *Journal of the American Medical Association*, 259 (1988), pp. 1945–1946; Don C. Des Jarlais and Samuel R. Friedman, "HIV Infection Among Persons Who Inject Illicit Drugs: Problems and Prospects," *Journal of the Acquired Immune Deficiency Syndromes*, 1 (1988), pp. 267–273; Don C. Des Jarlais, Samuel R. Friedman and William Hopkins, "Risk Reduction for Acquired Immunodeficiency Syndrome Among Intravenous Drug Users," *Annals of Internal Medicine*, 103 (1985), pp. 755–759.

43. L. Resnick, L. K Veren, S. Z. Salahuddin, S. Tondreau, and P. D. Karkham, "Stability and Inactivation of HTLV-III/LAV Under Clinical and Laboratory Environments," *Journal of the American Medical Association*, 255 (11 Apr. 1986), pp. 1887–1891.

44. Stephen Koester, Robert Booth, and Wayne Wiebel, "The Risk of HIV Transmission from Sharing Water, Drug Mixing Containers and Cotton Filters Among Intravenous Drug Users," *International Journal On Drug Policy* 1 (1990), pp. 28–30.

45. Jean-Paul Grund, Charles Kaplan, and Nico F. P. Adriaans, "Needle Exchange and Drug Sharing: A View from Rotterdam," *Newsletter of the International Working Group on AIDS and IV Drug Use,* 4 (1989), pp. 4–5; Jean-Paul C. Grund, Charles D. Kaplan, Nico F. P. Adriaans, Peter Blanken, and Jan Huismanm, "The Limitations of the Concept of Needle Sharing: The Practice of Frontloading," *AIDS* 4 (Aug. 1990), pp. 819–821.

46. James A. Inciardi and J. Bryan Page, "Drug Sharing Among Intravenous Drug Users," *AIDS,* 5 (June 1991), pp. 772–773.

47. Don C. Des Jarlais and Dana Hunt, *AIDS and Intravenous Drug Use,* National Institute of Justice AIDS Bulletin (Feb. 1988); Richard C. Stephens and Duane C. McBride, "Becoming a Street Addict," *Human Organization,* 15 (1976), pp. 87–93.

48. Bill Hanson, George Beschner, James M. Walters, and Elliott Bovelle, *Life With Heroin: Voices from the Inner City* (Lexington, MA: D.C. Heath, 1985), p. 43.

49. Dale D. Chitwood, Clyde B. McCoy, James A. Inciardi, Duane C. McBride, Mary Comerford, Edward Trapido, H. Virginia McCoy, J. Bryan Page, James Griffin, Mary Ann Fletcher, and Margarita A. Ashman, "HIV Seropositivity of Needles from Shooting Galleries in South Florida," *American Journal of Public Health,* 80 (1990), pp. 1–3.

50. J. A. Wiley and M. C. Samuel, "Prevalence of HIV Infection in the USA," *AIDS* 3 (1989), Supplement 3, pp. S71–S78.

51. M. Marmor, K. Krasinsky, M. Sanchez, H. Cohen, N. Dubin, L. Weiss, A. Manning, N. Saphier, C. Harrison, and D. J. Ribble, "Sex, Drugs, and HIV Infection in a New York City Hospital Population," *Journal of Acquired Immune Deficiency Syndromes,* 3 (1990), pp. 307–318.

52. R. Conviser and J. H. Rutledge, "The Need for Innovation to Halt AIDS Among Intravenous Drug Users and Their Sexual Partners," IV International Conference on AIDS, Stockholm, June 12–16, 1988.

53. J. Sorensen, J. Guydish, and M. Constantini, "Changes in Needle Sharing and Syringe Cleaning Among San Francisco Drug Abusers," *New England Journal of Medicine,* 320 (1989), p. 807; Jeffrey A. Kelly and Janet S. St. Lawrence, *The AIDS Health Crisis: Psychological and Social Interventions* (New York: Plenum Press, 1988); *AIDS Education: Reaching Populations at Higher Risk* (Washington, DC: United States General Accounting Office, 1988); John C. Ball, W. Robert Lange, C. Patrick Myers, and Samuel R. Friedman, "Reducing the Risk of AIDS Through Methadone Maintenance Treatment," *Journal of Health and Social Behavior,* 29 (September 1988), pp. 214–226; Robert L. Hubbard, Mary Ellen Marsden, Elizabeth Cavanaugh, J. Valley Rachal, and Harold M. Ginzburg, "Role of Drug-Abuse Treatment in Limiting the Spread of AIDS," *Reviews of Infectious Diseases,* 10 (Mar.–Apr. 1988), pp. 377–384; Sandra Baxter, "AIDS Education in the Jail Setting," *Crime and Delinquency,* 37 (Jan. 1991), pp. 48–63; Des Jarlais and Friedman; Chitwood et al., *A Community Approach to AIDS Intervention.*

54. C. A. Raymond, "U.S. Cities Struggle to Implement Needle Exchanges Despite Apparent Successes in European Cities," *Journal of the American Medical Association,* 260 (1988), pp. 2620–2621.

55. E. Buning, T. Reid, H. Hagan, and L. Pappas, "Needle Exchange V: Update on the Netherlands and the United States," *Newsletter of the International*

Working Group on AIDS and IV Drug Use, 4 (June 1989), pp. 9–10; C. Hartgers, E. C. Buning, G. W. Van Santen, A. D. Verster, and R. A. Coutinho, "The Impact of the Needle and Syringe-Exchange Programme in Amsterdam on Injecting Risk Behavior," *AIDS* 3 (1989), pp. 571–576; *Alcoholism and Drug Abuse Week,* 26 Apr. 1989, p. 5; Grund, Kaplan, and Adriaans.

56. *New York Times,* 29 Feb. 1988, p. A4; *Alcoholism and Drug Abuse Week,* 26 April 1989, p. 5.

57. G. V. Stimson, "Editorial Review: Syringe-Exchange Programmes for Injecting Drug Users," *AIDS,* 3 (1989), pp. 253–260; M. C. Donoghoe, G. V. Stimson, K. Dolan, and L. Alldritt, "Changes in HIV Risk Behavior in Clients of Syringe-Exchange Schemes in England and Scotland," *AIDS,* 3 (1989), pp. 267–272; G. J. Hart, A. L. M. Carvell, N. Woodward, A. M. Johnson, P. Williams, and J. V. Parry, "Evaluation of Needle Exchange in Central London: Behaviour Change and Anti-HIV Status Over One Year," *AIDS,* 3 (1989), pp. 261–265; *World Press Review,* June 1988, pp. 31–32.

58. *International Journal On Drug Policy,* Sept./Oct. 1989, p. 5.

59. C. A. Raymond, "First Needle Exchange Program Approved: Other Cities Await Results," *Journal of the American Medical Association,* 259 (1988), pp. 1289–1290.

60. *Alcoholism and Drug Abuse Week,* 12 July 1989, p. 7; *New York Times,* 23 Jan. 1989, p. A12.

61. See, "Needle Exchange Goes on Trial," *International Journal On Drug Policy,* 1 (1989), p. 5.

62. B. T. Farid. "AIDS and Drug Addiction Needle Exchange Schemes: A Step in the Dark," *Journal of the Royal Society of Medicine,* 81 (1988), pp. 375–376.

63. *Alcoholism and Drug Abuse Week,* 26 Apr. 1989, p. 5.

64. *Drug Abuse Report,* 22 Nov. 1988, p. 1.

65. Hartgers et al.

66. For a full commentary and chronology of the New York program, see *New York Times,* 1 Jan. 1988, p. A1; *Time,* 15 Feb. 1988, p. 81; *New York Times,* 6 June 1988, p. B3; *New York Times,* 8 Nov. 1988, pp. B1, B5; *New York Times,* 13 Nov. 1988, p. E6; *New York Times,* 30 Jan. 1989, p. A1; C. Gilman, "After One Year: New York City's Needle Exchange Pilot Programme." *International Journal On Drug Policy,* 1 (1990), pp. 18–21.

CHAPTER SEVEN

FROM MIAMI TO MANDALAY AND TINGO MARIA TO KATMANDU

The Domestic and International
Implications of Drug Trafficking

Drug dependence is generally understood in terms of a limited number of issues. First, there are public health considerations. Illicit drugs, whether they be narcotics, stimulants, depressants, or hallucinogens, have been found to cause a range of physical and/or psychosocial complications. As such, the use of drugs can place the productivity and well-being of a potentially large segment of the population at risk. The second issue is the connection between substance abuse and crime, a link that has become better understood in recent years. The drug-taking and drug-seeking activities of cocaine, crack, heroin, and other types of users have indeed affected rates of burglaries, larcenies, robberies, and other crimes. Too, the drug-trafficking and drug-distribution marketplace has increased the profits and power of organized criminal syndicates. Furthermore, violent death has come to be associated with the competition that exists at all levels of drug selling and drug distribution networks.

To foreign observers, particularly those in South America where U.S. antidrug efforts have been politically visible since the late 1970s, these health and safety issues facing U.S. citizens seem to represent the overwhelming public conception of the international drug scene. Too, since the flow of North American narcodollars into drug producing countries has seemingly bettered the economic lot of many local farmers and peasants, there has been considerable opposition to most U.S.-backed drug-control initiatives. For example, as one Bolivian media representative phrased the question not too long ago:

Drug abuse is a North American problem, a U.S. vice that Bolivia has no responsibility for. Therefore, Bolivia has no

203

responsibility for drug control. There is no drug problem here. It is in the United States. Why, then, does your DEA come down here?[a]

Similarly, a military police official in Lima, Peru, commented:

The North American appetite for cocaine has done more to feed the children of Simon Bolivar and the descendants of the Inca empire than most government programs. Why not just let it be?

And in 1990 President Cesar Gaviria Trujillo of Colombia commented to reporters after a meeting with President George Bush:

It doesn't matter how much we work against the trafficking of drugs, how many lives we loose. It doesn't matter how great our effort, the problem will be there. The United States and other industrialized countries need a way to reduce the consumption of drugs.[1]

Finally, numerous local politicians, media representatives, educators, and concerned citizens in many cities in the coca-growing and cocaine-trafficking nations of South America have expressed the sentiment that the United States should solve its drug problem within its borders. Why, they ask, should they and their governments cooperate with control efforts that will only hurt their interests? These same questions have been asked in other parts of the world when U.S. proposals to limit the cultivation of the opium-poppy have been advanced over the years.

The reasons for the United States-supported drug-control efforts in South America and Asia are no doubt numerous: in behalf of the stateside public health and crime problems; in the interests of appropriate foreign policy considerations and effective international relations; in response to the long-range needs of many developing nations; and for the sake of various other political and economic considerations. More specifically:

1. Attempts have been made to reduce both the demand and the supply of illegal drugs in the United States. The effectiveness of these demand-and-supply-reduction strategies has only been minimal. To many, a seemingly logical alternative is to

---

[a] Note here that all undocumented quotations and observations were drawn from the author's field research in Colombia, Bolivia, Ecuador, Peru, and Brazil during the 1980s and early 1990s.

combine these initiatives with an assault on drug production at its source.

2. Many have held that when drug production and trafficking become pervasive problems in nations with weak governments and faltering economic systems, both politics and economics become further destabilized. Those who support this position maintain that these conditions can lead to the emergence of dictatorships, aggressive and/or communistic governments, guerrilla insurgent activities, and even war.

3. As developing countries, many nations of the Third World receive aid from the United States in the interests of stimulating agricultural and industrial growth and upgrading standards of living. Drug production and trafficking can have counterproductive effects on any potential for growth.

There are likely other political, economic, and even humanitarian grounds as well. Yet, whatever the reasons, the intention here is neither to decipher nor defend U.S. international drug-control policies, nor to preach to foreign governments regarding any benefits of a broad-based support of American interests. Perhaps that is best left to the politicians, diplomats, and specialists in foreign affairs who have a better understanding of such matters. Rather, the idea is to identify and examine the implications of drug trafficking at both broad and discrete levels and to illustrate how these can have an impact on the economic, social, political, and other sectors of life in both drug-producing and "corridor" nations and communities.[b] The primary focus here is on South America, the continent from which virtually all the cocaine consumed in the United States originates.

BACK TO AMAZONIA AND THE ANDES

Historically, the chewing of coca leaves has been a dominant cultural pattern among the Indian peasant laborers of the Andes Mountains of South America. The mild stimulation engendered by the low cocaine-content leaves enables workers to endure the burdens of their 12-to-14-hour days at hard labor in the mines and in the fields.[2] Both

[b] Corridor, as it refers to foreign nations, is a U.S. State Department term. It relates to those countries in which the cultivation of the raw materials for illicit drugs plays only a limited role in the trafficking complex. Rather, the major effort is directed at the conveyance of raw materials from one producer to another, or the transportation of the intermediate or final product to some port of embarkation.

Bolivian and Peruvian law permits controlled licit production of coca for domestic consumption—about 12,000 kilograms in Bolivia and 14,000 kilograms in Peru (which also includes production for international pharmaceutical use). As such, a substantial part of the Andean economy has always depended on the cultivation, transport, and sale of coca leaves. The growers of illegal coca are the thousands of farm families who have shifted away from the cultivation and harvest of more traditional crops. One can readily understand the reasons for such a transition given the realities of the economic, political, and geographical conditions that dominate South American life.

Bolivia

Straddling the Andes, Bolivia is a land of gaunt mountains, cold desolate plains, and semitropical lowlands. Its 424,165 square miles occupy an area about the size of Texas and California combined. It is a big country but with a population of only 6.7 million. About 14% are of European heritage; the balance are Aymara (25%) and Quechua Indians (30%), and mestizos (mixed Indian and European ancestry).

Much of the Bolivian population lives on the bleak, treeless, wind-swept Altiplano (high plain), a lofty plateau more than 13,000 feet above sea level. The Altiplano is a harsh, strange land. An arid expanse of red earth, it appears to be a great void—some 40,000 square miles of emptiness. The Altiplano is also a cold and haunting stretch of ground, where horizons and distant mountains seem to melt into the sky or into each other; where phantom lakes seem to appear and disappear or suddenly change size. The entire impression is one of grave solitude, with observers left wondering what they're actually seeing.

There are llamas, sheep, some cows, and homesteads widely scattered across the Altiplano. The houses, small and often windowless, are of a mud-brick architecture that makes them look not only sullen, but depressingly tentative as well. One gets the impression that a clap of thunder, or even a slammed door or a raised voice, would cause them to crumble. When the residents of the Altiplano die, it is seldom from old age. More typically, it is either alcoholism or the afflictions of altitude and rarified air: enlarged heart, excess red cells, cerebral and pulmonary edema, and perhaps intensified exposure to solar and cosmic radiation. Despite the fact that the Altiplano is a trackless waste, giving the impression of some forbidden zone in the apocalyptic nightmare worlds of *Mad Max* and *The Road Warrior*, it is also the most livable part of the country, with 70% of the population residing along its western quarter.

Rising from the floor of a shallow canyon in the middle of the Altiplano is the city of La Paz, Bolivia's capital and major urban area. Living in La Paz is in many ways like living on the moon. The city rests in a barren crater of naked land at an altitude of more than two miles, where the air is so thin that newcomers find it difficult to breathe.[c] In fact, there is so little oxygen in the city's rarified atmosphere that fires rarely occur. It might be added that La Paz is a city with only two directions, up and down, and where "over there" is invariably at the top of a 20% gradient.

La Paz is unusual in other ways as well. The city's 1.1 million residents are packed into a few square miles. There is a small population of financial elites—merchants, professionals, and politicians who see to the needs of the city and country; executives and landowners made affluent by Bolivia's rich mineral resources; and "narcotraficantes," whose extravagant wealth has come from the cultivation of the coca leaf and its processing into cocaine. The majority of the people of La Paz are impoverished Aymara Indians. The men wear work clothes, often the type that laborers in the United States wear, but the few who can find jobs are typically employed at the most menial of tasks. The Aymara women present a striking contrast. Jamming the streets and sidewalk stalls to sell the few fruits and vegetables that can be grown on the Altiplano wasteland, they are always dressed in the most colorful of costumes. Their typical dress includes a large skirt of brilliant color under which there are six or more *polleras* (petticoats), a striped or embroidered shawl in an infinite rainbow of pinks, blues, reds, and yellows, crowned with either bowlers or white top hats. Many carry babies, each tied into a bundle of striped blankets on their backs.

For the Indians and mestizos of Bolivia life is spare and bitter, with almost no comforts. Those who reside in La Paz actually live in the surrounding hills where the air is even thinner.[d] Their homes are shanties made of discarded signboards, doors, and other debris, or of mud shaped into bricks and dried in the sun, Altiplano style. The houses have no windows, electricity, or plumbing; they are dark, dank, musty, and unpleasant. The life expectancy of the Indians in some parts of Bolivia is only 33 years; there is never any financial security; and tuberculosis and other diseases take a tremendous toll on children and adults. Most Indian mothers expect to have two or three children die in their first few years of life.

---

[c] When arriving by air in La Paz (whose airport is above the city on the Altiplano), many travelers are immediately stricken with altitude sickness, generally characterized by an intense headache. The typical remedy is a cup of maté de coca, or coca tea, which increases the oxygen flow to the brain.

[d] Curiously, the higher a Bolivian's social standing, the lower he or she lives in La Paz, since oxygen is at a premium. The president's mansion is in a viewless gully, while the poorest Aymara or Quechua Indian climbs tortuously to the top of the cliff to live in an airless hovel with a heavenly view. For an engaging description of La Paz, see Celia Wakefield, *High Cities of the Andes* (San Carlos, CA: World Wide Publishing/Tetra, 1988).

Although Bolivia is rich in natural resources—petroleum, natural gas, tin, lead, zinc, copper, and gold—it is in a state of economic chaos. Most of the population works in agriculture, which is generally unrewarding. Those who do toil in the mines spend much of their time on strike. The country had a national debt of $4.1 billion at the close of 1989,[3] a trifling sum compared to the staggering U.S. budget deficits, but Bolivia's annual gross national product barely exceeded $4 billion at the close of the 1980s (as compared with $5.2 trillion for the United States in 1989).[e] In an attempt to pay its debts, in years past the Bolivian government printed more pesos. The results were catastrophic. Whereas the official exchange rate in 1982 was 44 *pesos bolivianos* to 1 American dollar, by March 1986 a $1 bill could buy 1,552,950 pesos— and that was the official rate. On the black market, the dollar was valued at more than double the official rate.[4] This level of currency devaluation reminds one of complaints about the double-digit inflation at the beginning of the Reagan administration. But the American citizen has little understanding of what real inflation can be. There was such an inflationary spiral in Bolivia during the mid-1980s that by the end of 1985 the annual inflation rate had averaged almost 12,000%.[5] Although severe austerity measures dropped inflation to 15.9% by the close of 1990,[6] Bolivia has remained in a debt crisis and depression that is likely to endure for at least the balance of the century. In view of such vast natural resources amidst apparently uncontrollable economic chaos, it is no wonder that many Bolivians refer to their country as "a beggar sitting on a throne of gold."[f]

Bolivia is also in a shambles politically. Since gaining its independence from Spain in 1825 under the leadership of Simon Bolivar, the country has had more than 60 revolutions, 70 presidents, and 16 constitutions; the government has changed hands some 250 times (189 times by coup); and from 1978 through the early 1990s there have been 14 presidents, with the 11th resigning out of sheer frustration. Part of the difficulty has been corruption, a problem endemic to many regimes. Another has been poor economic planning and management at times when world markets were unfavorable to Bolivian production.[7] Many citizens of Bolivia feel, however, that they have difficulties

---

[e] How much is $5.2 trillion ($5,200,000,000,000)? Five trillion two hundred billion dollars in $1 bills placed end to end would stretch 485 million miles—from earth to the sun and back almost three times. A 5.2-trillion-dollar spending spree, at a rate of $1,000 a minute would take more than 10,000 years.

[f] The sparse living standards in Bolivia have spawned other sayings as well. Many Bolivians speak of their land as a poor place, where the soil is poor, the grass is poor, and even the air is poor, adding that if everyone is to have something, no one can have very much. "A little is enough for us," the Indians say, "for if it weren't, we all would perish."

because their people just cannot seem to get along with one another. In fact, indicative of this self-denigrating attitude, there are stories in Bolivian folklore which hold that the quarrelsome nature of the peoples of that country is the result of a deliberate act of God.

Peru

Situated in western South America, Peru extends nearly 1,500 miles along the Pacific Ocean. In land area, it is almost the size of Alaska, with a population of some 22 million. Peru is divided by the Andes Mountains into three sharply differentiated zones. To the west are the coastal plains, mostly arid and extending 50 to 100 miles inland. The central area is mountains, some reaching to heights of 20,000 feet, and plateaus and deep valleys. Beyond the mountains to the east lie the high and low jungles—the heavily forested slopes leading to Amazonia.

Economically, Peru is not much better off than Bolivia. Large segments of its predominantly Indian and mestizo population are either unemployed or underemployed; triple-digit inflation has plagued the economy for years; there is a rapidly declining per capita income; and the value of the currency has declined drastically—from 289 *soles* to the dollar in 1980 to almost 14,000 by late 1985, placing the country on the verge of bankruptcy.[8] During the second half of the 1980s, the *inti*, a new currency, was established. But it too ran into difficulty, ranging widely in value: from 265 to U.S.$1 in 1988, to 13,100 to U.S.$1 by the beginning of the 1990s.[9]

Peru's precarious condition is due partially to natural disasters and world economic trends but primarily to inappropriate political and economic decisions. Agriculture, which accounts for 40% of the country's working population, suffered a variety of setbacks during the early 1980s when there were heavy rains and flooding in northern Peru, landslides in central Peru, and drought in the south. The prosperous mining sector was affected by widespread strikes and declining silver and copper prices on world markets. Moreover, at one time Peru's fishing catch—primarily anchovy—was the fourth largest in the world. In 1976, however, it was virtually halted because of depleted stocks; it resumed in 1982 but was suspended again when the meandering El Niño current brought exceptionally warm waters to the Peruvian fishing grounds.[8]

---

[8] El Niño is an infrequent counterflow of Pacific equatorial water. In addition to bringing heat, humidity, and flooding to coastal lowlands, it is a threat to the fragile marine ecosystem. In 1982–1983, the El Niño climactic phenomenon brought storms to California, drought to the southeastern United States, floods and landslides to coastal Ecuador and Peru, and death to billions of anchovies off Peru. See T. Y. Canby, "El Niño's Ill Wind," *National Geographic*, Feb. 1984, pp. 144–183.

In the political sphere, a military coup in 1968 gave power to a pro-Marxist military government. In its attempt to create a nationalist-socialist system, the military took over many locally and foreign-owned industries and large agricultural estates. The result was inefficient and low-output production. Moreover, rather than using the national treasury for economic development, the ruling junta used much of it for the purchase of Soviet fighter planes.[10]

When Peru changed back to democratic rule in 1980 another set of problems were added. President Fernando Belaunde Terry, apparently a well-meaning visionary who had hoped to build a "new Peru," shifted the country's development emphasis from the nation's somewhat thriving Pacific coast to the jungle-covered Amazonia. The effort, after consuming the country's limited savings and billions of dollars borrowed from abroad, proved to be a costly failure.[11]

The most visible signs of the economic changes over the last three decades can be seen in Lima. Once a quiet city of impressive Spanish-style buildings, stately museums, and world-class restaurants, its 2 million residents seemed to feel confident about the future of their city and country. After the military junta took power and began to dismantle the rural economy, Lima experienced explosive urbanization—accumulating more than 3 million additional residents over a 25-year period. Most were displaced peasants in search of work. Now, the streets are broken and littered with garbage. Many new business and residential structures, although occupied on their first and second floors, remain unfinished, their construction halted for lack of funds. Also, as in La Paz, there are the *pueblos jovenes*—the squalid shantytowns.

On July 28, 1990, Alberto Keinya Fujimori was inaugurated President of Peru. His election had been greeted with a festive atmosphere, for it was believed that this son of humble Japanese immigrants (and the first person of East Asian descent to lead an American republic) could solve Peru's economic crisis. Immediately, Fujimori ended all price controls and subsidies, quadrupled the minimum wage, ordered the payment of bonuses to all public and many private-sector employees, fashioned an emergency relief program for the poor—all to be financed by a temporary export tax and a one-time levy on corporate equity and the private holdings of the wealthy. What resulted was what has become known as "Fujishock," characterized by the steepest one-day price increases in the twentieth century.[12] Gasoline increased by 3,000%, electric rates quintupled, water charges in Lima rose more than eightfold, and food staples jumped upwards of 1,000%. Soup kitchens were overwhelmed by hungry people, there was rioting and looting on the streets of the capitol, and the price increases brought about inflation of 400% for the month of August 1990.[h] By the beginning of 1991 Fujishock had brought Peru to the brink of economic and social dissolution.

Adding to the problems of Peru is the *Sendero Luminoso*, or Shining Path, a corps of fanatic guerilla insurgents seeking to purify Peru by violence. The Sendero Luminoso emerged from a tangled web of Peruvian politics in 1970 in the ancient colonial city of Ayacucho—a community of 70,000 residents located some 200 miles southeast of Lima. The moving force behind Sendero's creation was Abimael Guzman, a philosophy professor at the San Cristobal de Huamanga University.[13] Noting the striking class differences in his society, Guzman concluded that as Peru approached the twenty-first century, it was still a semi-feudal and semi-colonial society. Moreover, the government embodied a fascist structure masquerading as democracy and engaging in the construction of a corporate state and the development of bureaucratic capitalism. Guzman's political ideology was predominantly Maoist, the militant communist philosophy of China's Mao Tse-Tung, which teaches "uninterrupted revolution" and the overwhelming role of the human will in history. As such, Guzman held that social reform could be had only by making revolutionaries out of Peruvian peasants for the purpose of overthrowing the established government.

Sendero Luminoso first came to widespread public attention after a full decade of dogmatic self-examination and rigorously selective recruitment. The violence against the government began in July 1980, and by the end of the year some 240 incidents had been recorded, including the destruction of local tax records, bombings of government offices, and sabotage of electricity pylons.[14] By 1981 the rate of incidents had increased, expanding to such activities as the raiding of banks, mines, and police posts. Kidnapping was added the following year. Sendero's most spectacular action took place early in 1982 when 150 guerrillas attacked the Ayacucho jail and set some 300 prisoners free.

The ideological politics of the Sendero Luminoso became most evident in the focus of its terrorist activities during 1986. In southern Peru, Sendero guerrillas captured plantations and haciendas, sometimes killing their owners and employees, and distributing cattle, sheep, alpacas, and other goods to local peasants.[15] At the time of Peru's national elections in 1990 the death toll from the country's guerrilla war approached 21,000 people. Property damage was estimated at $16 billion. A state of emergency, with constitutional guarantees in

---

[h] Although inflation fell to 10% from September to November, jumped to 23% in December, and back to 16% in January 1991, the annual rate remained in triple digits. See *New York Times*, 24 Feb. 1991, p. 2E.

abeyance, existed in almost two thirds of Peru, affecting half the population. Moreover, Sendero Luminoso was believed to have fielded some 5,000 guerrillas and 50,000 followers nationwide.[16]

Colombia

Situated in the northwestern part of South America and occupying a land area almost the size of Bolivia, Colombia is the only country on the continent that borders both the Atlantic and Pacific oceans. It has a population of almost 33 million, 98% of which is concentrated in the mountainous sections of the country. These highland regions, which account for 45% of the land, are composed mainly of high peaks, narrow valleys where many of the cities are clustered, and isolated intermont basins. The rest of the country is in the Orinoco Llanos, the almost uninhabited lowlands to the east.

The population of Colombia is considerably varied, ranging from pure white, pure Indian, and pure black to blood mixtures of all three. In fact Colombia as a whole is considerably varied, fitting few patterns that are typically associated with South America. Military coups have been infrequent, and many Colombian people are not poor, nor are they all coffee growers peripherally associated with the drug trade. Economically, the country is more prosperous than many of its neighbors. Agricultural products and natural resources are numerous, but its foreign debt has become unmanageable. Moreover, health and sanitation are growing problems that have resulted in high rates of infant mortality. With 50% of the population living in urban areas and a high birthrate, there are growing numbers of the inevitable *barrios clandestinos*—shantytowns. Although these are a common feature of city landscapes throughout South America, they seem to be more pronounced in Colombia—lacking drinking water, electricity, and sanitation facilities.

In general, the combination of at least the geography and economics of Bolivia, Peru, and Colombia has made them opportune for the development of the illicit drug trades. The topography and climate are the best in the world for the cultivation of coca, and the vast areas of almost inaccessible mountain slopes make these countries difficult to police. Their sliding economic situations provide further incentives to drug trafficking.

For many peasants, the cultivation of marijuana and coca, the refining of coca leaves into paste or cocaine hydrochloride, and the trafficking in these substances have served as a way out of poverty. In Bolivia, where the per capita income is but a few hundred dollars for the laborer working at traditional crops earning $5 a day, the opportunities in the coca fields are significant. Just caring for the crop and picking and hauling the leaves can bring a tripling of income. For the farm family that can actually grow and process the coca, there is the lure of modest wealth. For government leaders who see vast amounts of trafficking dollars infused into their faltering economies, it appears that the illicit drug trades have their positive qualities. Yet in the short run and the long run, these activities can have serious negative implications. In the economic sphere, there have been effects on inflation, government economic planning, wages and property values, and the availability of traditional goods and services. In the social sphere, there is drug use, violence, and street crime. In the political sphere, there is corruption and the destabilization of government power. There can also be effects on the cultural traditions of entire groups and on the ecology of entire regions.

NARCODOLLARS, COFFEE BEANS, AND AMERICA'S CASABLANCA: THE ECONOMIC IMPLICATIONS OF DRUG TRAFFICKING

The sudden infusion of large sums of money into any country or community can be inflationary. It has been estimated that in 1979 alone, more than $3 billion entered the Colombian economy as the result of illicit crop cultivation and drug trafficking. Almost one third of these funds entered directly in the form of U.S. dollars.[17] The investment of these drug dollars was generally limited to construction of luxury housing and resort hotels. The result was the bidding up of prices in the construction industry well beyond already inflationary levels, thus pushing lower- and middle-income families out of the housing market.

In the Peruvian jungle town of Tingo Maria, the effects of the drug-related inflationary spiral were of a different sort. As already noted in Chapter 3, the primary business activity of this remote town is the trafficking in coca products. The drug trades infused great sums of money into this little community over a short period of time, making many local peasants and farmers virtual millionaires. Along with the instant wealth came a sudden demand for automobiles, trucks, and various luxury items. Auto dealers moved in, but the demand was much greater than the supply. As a result, for a short period in 1981 Chevrolet Chevettes were selling for $25,000; small pickup trucks went for $35,000; Cadillacs and Lincolns were $100,000; and a Corvette or Mercedes could fetch as much as $350,000. Many legitimate business operators were either priced out of the market or drawn into trafficking in order to survive. Then a most curious thing happened. Since the auto dealers were more interested in sales than service, there were no facilities for parts or repair. Thus, when a vehicle broke down, it was simply abandoned in the jungle and replaced with a new one. A similar phenomenon occurred in parts of Bolivia.

Miami, the major cocaine-corridor community in the United States, also experienced inflated real estate values as the result of cocaine trafficking. As a real estate broker indicated during the early 1980s:

> Part of the problem was the South American economy as a whole. Legitimately wealthy families were flying up for the day just to invest their money in something safe, to protect their savings. They'd buy luxury condos almost sight unseen and then go home. That tended to push up prices. Then the cocaine cowboys would walk in with suitcases full of money. They'd buy a house for $1 million and pay all cash up front. . . . Canal-front houses that were selling a year earlier for $300,000 were suddenly $1 million.

And drug-related inflations in real estate have occurred most recently in Bolivia, Ecuador, and Peru.[18]

The sudden infusions of money into some communities have had their effects on currency exchange rates. During the 1980s in several cities throughout Colombia, there was a glut of American dollars on the streets and in the banks. To convert these into pesos, traffickers worked with black-market foreign-exchange entrepreneurs who would discount the value of the dollar. This had a ripple effect on legitimate businesses that had to accept U.S. currency. A Bogota hotel manager stated:

> Officially, the dollar was stable, but on the street it was constantly floating. We tried to get our U.S. customers to pay in pesos or credit card, which was fine. But every time they settled a bill with dollars or traveler's checks we took about a 5% loss on the transaction. After a few weeks of this, the owners insisted that we raise the rates for all visitors from the United States.

Trafficking has also had an economic impact on agriculture. As arable lands became more profitable from the cultivation of marijuana and coca, their value increased dramatically. Furthermore, traditional crops were replaced with coca, causing a decline in legitimate crop output. For example, from all over Bolivia during the 1970s and the early 1980s, Aymara and Quechua Indians crisscrossed the Andes with new trails leading to the coca-growing regions, leaving wheat and rice fields behind.[19] Most of the settlers living along the banks of Colombia's Putumayo, Cauca, and Caqueta rivers no longer planted yucca, corn, and pineapples. They abandoned their fields to work in the coca trade, eliminating economically significant crops from that part of the country.[20] A similar experience served to reduce the level of Colombian coffee exports.[21] Alternatively, in 1991 farmers in Ecuador, sandwiched between the world's largest coca leaf grower (Peru) and the world's largest cocaine refiner (Colombia), were complaining that cash-rich Colombian investors were bidding up farm land in border areas, sometimes paying three times the going value. One town, Santo Domingo de los Colorados, received so much Colombian investment that locals jokingly referred to it as "Santo Domingo de los Colombianos."[22]

In a number of corridor communities that historically have been known as major winter resorts, the presence of drug trafficking has resulted in significant declines in tourism. Miami, where tourism is a $10 billion annual industry, has been particularly affected in this way. The increased attention given to the drug scene since the late 1970s resulted in losses of billions of tourist dollars, capped by periodic drops in hotel occupancy rates. This problem is further compounded when the media features the Miami situation before national and international audiences. After *Time* magazine, with its weekly circulation of almost 5 million copies, published its "Trouble in Paradise" issue on September 23, 1981, which detailed the Miami drug-related violence,[23] hotel managers and travel agents were inundated with cancellations. A motel owner commented in 1984:

> The day after the "Trouble in Paradise" story hit the streets, I lost 10% of my bookings, followed by another 20% the following week. Some of my regular customers who have been staying here every winter since the 1960s have never come back. Now they go to the west coast of Florida where the drug scene is less visible.

But if "Trouble in Paradise" wasn't enough, the cover story of the July 19, 1987 issue of the *New York Times Magazine* was "Can Miami Save Itself?"[24] The *Times* story also targeted Miami's drugs/violence connection. And then in 1988 it was *Newsweek's* turn, with the cover story "Miami: America's Casablanca."[25] For *Newsweek* readers, Miami became not only a city of drugs and vice, but also one of wheelers and dealers, of exiles and refugees, and of ethnic tensions and foreign intrigue. Although crime, like nostalgia, isn't what it used to be in Miami, the media image of the city suggested something quite different.

A similar situation became apparent in Cartagena, Colombia, on the Caribbean coast. Cartagena's Bocagrande beach, one mile from the historic colonial city, is an expanse of restaurants, resort hotels, and picturesque markets that has lured North and South American tourists for decades. Although Cartagena is a safe city, seemingly untouched by Colombia's position in international drug trafficking, hotel managers no longer see tourists coming from the United States. In this regard, a tour director stated:

> . . . we still have the South Americans coming in year round, but most of the others [from the United States] don't come down any more. They see us as a nation of outlaws.

FROM AL PACINO TO CAPTAIN KIDD: THE SOCIAL IMPLICATIONS OF DRUG TRAFFICKING

So the feds in Miami ask this guy Tony Montana where he picked up his good English, and Tony says, "My father ta'e me to da movies. I watch da guys like Humphrey Bogart, James Cagney. I learn to spe' from dose guys. I li'e dose guys." And so begins Brian De Palma's *Scarface*, a 1983 intended epic, portraying the rise and fall of a Cuban refugee turned cocaine cowboy. Played by actor Al Pacino, Tony works his way through the violent world of the Miami cocaine-trafficking scene, making it to the top, for a while at least. Ultimately, like almost every other character in the film, Tony falls in a hailstorm of bullets.

The reviews of *Scarface* were decidedly mixed.[26] One critic called it "a limp allegory of impotence"; others praised it as a gruesome morality play that accurately depicted the violent world of cocaine trafficking. Good or bad, *Scarface* was an interesting oddity. It was one of the few times in motion-picture history that a major production received an "X" rating. The reasons for the poisonous rating were two. The first was the vulgar language. One common four-letter obscenity was uttered, by consecutive count, a total of 181 times. In that sense, the rating seemed to be a bad rap, for after all, that's no worse than Richard Pryor or Eddie Murphy, even on one of their good days. The second reason was the gruesome violence, chain-saw executions and all. On appeal, the rating was reduced to "R" and *Scarface* made it to the neighborhood picture show. What was curious here was that even with the grisly circus of horrors that was so furiously presented, the film did not even begin to approach the actual magnitude of violence that characterizes the real-life world of cocaine trafficking.[i]

---

[i] *Scarface* was a surprise hit in Miami. While it was being made, it had been denounced by every responsible civic, church, and Hispanic leader in town. But when it was released, all their kids went to see it, and *Scarface* quickly became a cult movie in Miami. Not surprisingly, when "Miami Vice" was being planned, the official response was to panic. Terrified of more bad publicity, there were efforts to keep it from coming to town. But like *Scarface,* "Miami Vice" became a revered institution. See David Rieff, *Going to Miami: Exiles, Tourists, and Refugees in the New America* (New York: Penguin, 1988); T. D. Allman, *Miami: City of the Future* (New York: Atlantic Monthly Press, 1987).

Described earlier as "systemic violence," drug trafficking and the large profits associated with it instigate brutal aggression against people, property, and institutions. Throughout the trafficking regions of South America, killings are quite common. A typical pattern involves the execution of not only the rival dealer but of his entire family, as well, to serve as a warning to others. A characteristic case in this behalf occurred in New York City during 1984. Years earlier, Enrique Bermudez, a low-level dealer in the East Coast drug world, had pleaded guilty to selling a half ounce of cocaine to an undercover police officer. Under the New York drug laws, the strongest in the nation, Bermudez could have received a life sentence. Instead, he chose to cooperate with the authorities in return for a shorter sentence. He served five years in prison, and his testimony resulted in the incarceration of several other dealers. However, Bermudez apparently failed to understand the laws of retribution in the Colombian cocaine industry. On Palm Sunday in 1984, while Bermudez was at work, several traffickers entered his home to exact their revenge. Two women and eight children, ranging in age from 2 to 14 years, were executed. All had been either held in their chairs while being shot in the head or later propped up into positions that made the scene resemble the house of horrors in London's famous Madame Tussaud's Wax Museum. As one investigator described the mode of execution:

> Colombian killers leave no witnesses. They kill the maid, the TV repairman, the child. They kill anyone who is around.[27]

An agent of the Drug Enforcement Administration, working in Medellin, Colombia, a major refining and exchange point in the South American cocaine network, described the two most common methods of execution in that city:

> The first way is by simple machine gunning. Two hit men will ride through the traffic on a motorcycle. When they get up to the victim's car, the guy on the back of the bike levels a cannon and sprays the car. The second way is a bit messy. They'll carve him up with hatchets and chain saws and feed the pieces of meat to pigs that run free in the neighborhood.

Moreover, a Colombian military official added:

> The Colombian drug-assassination ethic also features what some call the "necktie killing." The target's throat is slit open so his tongue can hang through it like a tie. . . . It is a gruesome sight to see this—men, women, and children, all lined up in chairs like soldiers with their tongues coming out their necks.

The violence is not restricted to traffickers. In Bolivia, Colombia, Peru, and Brazil, aborigines are murdered for their coca plantings; drug enforcement and other police agents are tortured, mutilated, and executed; and peasants who refuse to cooperate with drug traffickers are summarily disposed of.[28] Killings occur in other sectors as well. In Medellin and other Colombian drug centers, prosecutors and judges seeking convictions of traffickers have been systematically eradicated. One of the victims was that nation's justice minister, Rodrigo Lara Bonilla, assassinated in 1984 after he made the mistake of publicly demanding stronger measures against local ''narcotrafficantes.''[29] Others have included journalists and presidential candidates.[30]

Perhaps most notable in this regard was the assassination of candidate Luis Carlos Galan on August 18, 1989. The result was an all out war on the drug cartels declared by Colombian president Virgilio Barco Vargas.[31] Within a few weeks, some 10,000 people were detained, millions of dollars in cartel property and assets were seized, and the extradition of traffickers wanted in the United States was initiated.[32] Fearing extradition, the cartels responded with a war of their own, with killings, kidnappings, and bombings. As the wars moved through 1990 and into 1991, and while the violence, the raids, and the extraditions continued on course, los extraditables (the extraditables—those wanted for extradition to the United States) negotiated with the Colombian government for a more flexible anti-cartel policy.[33] But most importantly in terms of the implications of the cartel wars, foreigners stopped visiting Colombia, while others started leaving Colombia.[34] And perhaps most curiously, a new term—''Colombianization''—was added to the mass media lexicon around the globe. Or as an editorial in Pakistan explained it in 1990:

> Evidence grows daily that Pakistan is making a steady—if as yet slow—advance towards the ''Colombianisation'' of its society, with the drug mafia extending its poisonous tentacles to all parts of the country.[35]

Drug trafficking can also be credited with the recent rise of piracy in the Caribbean, the Bahamas, and the Gulf of Mexico. It was in these same waters that piracy in the grand manner of Captain Kidd and Henry Morgan flourished several centuries ago. The voyages of Columbus had provided Spain with an early start in seeking the treasures of the New World. The ensuing territorial conquests gave that nation an almost total claim on the Americas as well as the financial strength to construct the most powerful navy in Europe. Trade, often with cargoes in excess of $100 million per ship, found a natural right-of-way through the Caribbean, made highly navigable by the Gulf Stream currents, prevailing winds, and sheltering islands of the West

Indies. During the seventeenth and eighteenth centuries, the West Indies became a depository for transported convicts; social and political refugees from France, Spain, and Great Britain; and vagrant sailors when the Treaty of Utrecht in 1713 brought an end to the War of the Spanish Succession.[36]

The grand era of piracy began in 1714 when Captain Henry Jennings of Jamaica and 300 seamen descended upon the salvage crew of a grounded Spanish galleon, looting the vessel of some 300,000 pieces of eight. News of the event proved inspirational to the social pariah and displaced mariner on the Caribbean waterfronts, and ships were seized, manned, and turned pirate. It was the topography of the Indies that made piracy a lucrative pursuit. Located along the heavily traveled Gulf Stream routes, the islands provided landside strongholds close to the illicit maritime ventures. The endless number of coves offered natural opportunities for ambush, and with the area's scattered habitation and development, the marine bandits could swiftly retreat to the security and sanctuary of unobserved seclusion.

Many of the reasons that spawned piracy in the Caribbean during the 1700s also contributed to its reemergence in the contemporary era of drug trafficking. Much of the smuggling during the 1970s was by sea. According to the head of Colombia's *Guardacostas* (Coast Guard), the shuttles would begin along the Caribbean coast from secluded ports between the cities of Cartagena, Barranquilla, and Santa Marta. As illustrated on page 220, shipments bound for Key West and Gulf Coast ports followed a northwesterly bearing, passing to the west of the Cayman Islands and Cuba and through the Yucatan Channel into the Gulf of Mexico. Those heading toward Atlantic Coast ports went in a more northerly direction, selecting the Windward Passage between Cuba and Haiti and then sailing northwest in a straight line through the Bahamas. Another route was the Mona Passage between Puerto Rico and the Dominican Republic, followed by sea routes meandering through or along the east side of the Bahamas until their South Florida destinations were close at hand. These passages provided relative seclusion combined with relative ease of navigation. Moreover, with some 700 islands and no less than 2,000 cays (from the Spanish cayo, meaning a low island or reef) within the Bahama chain alone, there were many isolated locations where drug transactions could take place.

The piracy of pleasure craft, or "yachtjacking" as some have called it, began during the early 1970s. Some vessels were pirated and used for transporting drugs. Others were seized because they had come too close to drug-transaction areas or were mistaken as rival drug craft. In all instances, the passengers and crew of the stolen boats were killed, tossed overboard, and likely devoured by sharks and other sea creatures. So prevalent had the problem become that warnings

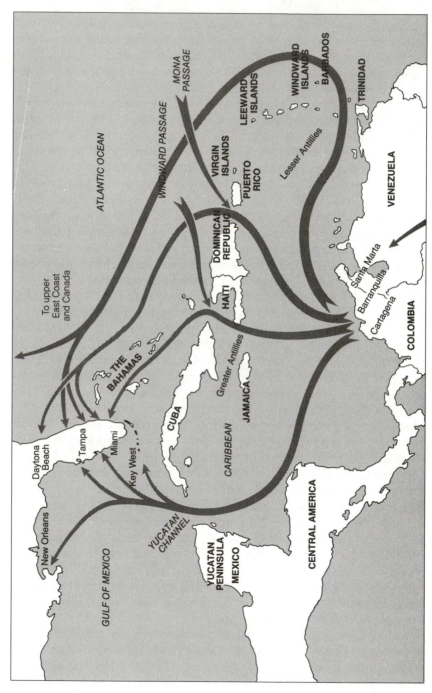

Drug-Trafficking Sea Routes in the Caribbean

to mariners repeatedly appeared in U.S. Coast Guard bulletins and respected yachting publications.[37]

By 1981 the problem seemed to have peaked. Aircraft had become a more popular form of smuggling transport. More effective enforcement efforts in Bahama and Caribbean waters had shifted traffickers' sea routes east through the Leeward Passage, well away from the areas frequented by recreational boaters. Drug trafficking as a whole had become better financed, and the theft of vessels was generally unnecessary. Perhaps most importantly, boat owners took more care in avoiding reported trouble spots and began to arm themselves heavily. Yet throughout the 1980s the piracy of pleasure craft in waters off the coast of Florida periodically surfaced, however infrequently.[38] At national boat shows and local exhibitions catering exclusively to Florida and Caribbean boaters, dealers in security equipment are prominent. As one Miami gun shop owner stated:

> Although the homeowner is the major buyer of guns here, yachtsmen and fishermen probably rank second. So many of them cruise those lonely waters from Grand Bahama Island and Bimini down through Andros, the Exumas, Deadman's Cay, and the Inagua islands that there's no way they're going without at least a .38 or .45 handgun. Corrosion-proof firearms are the most popular.

Similarly, the dockmaster at a Key West marina commented:

> Nobody seems to take any chances any more. Just about every serious boater crossing the Gulf Stream or headed for the Bahamas carries firearms.

Finally, a Miami firearms instructor added:

> I have two kinds of students—home owners and boat owners. The home owners want to know how to shoot pistols, while the boat owners are into heavy artillery. By and large, when they're out on the high seas in the no-man's-land of the cocaine cowboys, they want something that will let bullets fly like water spraying from a hose. In fact, they want training with the same things that the drug runners carry—automatics and semiautomatics like the UZI and MAC-10—something that can crank out at least 600 rounds per minute.

However, violence is not the only social problem that emerges as the result of trafficking in drugs. Through a natural-history process, as soon as trafficking becomes firmly established in drug-producing and corridor nations, these locales begin to develop drug-use and street-crime problems of their own. Producing countries initially export the raw materials they have cultivated, such as coca leaves, for refining and distribution elsewhere. In time, to maximize profits, refining operations begin to move closer to cultivation areas, and quickly, what was once only a growing area has suddenly been transformed into a refining and distributing area as well.

The presence of illicit drugs in any trafficking nation increases their availability to local citizens, not only because the drugs are readily at hand but also because any surpluses must be sold somewhere. Thus the emergence and growth of a local drug-use problem. Drug traffickers are very enterprising people. As soon as a drug culture has begun to develop, traffickers bring in other drugs not indigenous to the area. Nations that were once simple suppliers of drugs evolve into primary consumers. This historical pattern has repeated itself throughout the world in recent years, in South America and the Bahama and Caribbean Islands, throughout Eastern and Western Europe, the Soviet Union, India, Pakistan, Africa, and almost all of Southeast and Southwest Asia—just about everywhere, from New York to Miami and Mandalay and from Tingo Maria to Teheran and Katmandu.[39]

HOW ARE THINGS IN ZINAHOTA? THE POLITICAL IMPLICATIONS OF DRUG TRAFFICKING

It is a market like no other market in the world, and it thrives in Zinahota, Bolivia. This is a village of only 300 peasants in the heart of the Chapare coca-growing region, some 120 kilometers east of Cochabamba. As far as the rest of the world knows, a place by the name of Zinahota does not exist. It is so small and remote that even the most detailed maps of Bolivia fail to show it. Yet on almost any given day during the coca harvest season, Zinahota is a chaos of jostling pigs, chickens, children, traffic jams, and crowded alleys, where merchants hawk pots and pans, onions and peppers, shampoo, bicycle tires, and transistor radios. However, the most common items bought and sold are coca leaves and concentrated coca paste. Unlike other parts of the world where clandestine transfers of illicit drugs must take place in seclusion, far from probing law-enforcement agents, in Zinahota this is done in the public market, totally unmolested. The reason? The Bolivian government cannot ensure the safety of any drug agents working in the area.[40]

The situation in Zinahota, which illustrates a government's total loss of control over a region, is only one of the political implications of drug trafficking. In addition, there is the securing of power by traffickers or their representatives at all levels of government; there is the indirect control of government posts by corruption and violence; there is regime instability demonstrated through an unwillingness to arrest and imprison traffickers; and there are antigovernment threats when drug moneys are used to finance political terrorism or actual government takeovers.

Perhaps the most pervasive problem in the political arena is the wholesale corruption of individuals and institutions. In some trafficking areas, corruption is so widespread in the justice system, banking, the legal profession, military, the diplomatic corps, customs, and general government that it is often viewed as part of the natural order of things. In South Florida, drug-related corruption in law enforcement was so common during the 1980s that reports of new scandals received little press coverage. In South America, Central America, and the Caribbean, it would appear that politics is even further corrupted.[41]

Corruption has long since been a part of the banking industry in the form of money laundering. Money laundries have been used for decades by organized-crime figures and others wanting to keep large amounts of money from being taxed. Their widest use, however, has occurred in recent years among drug dealers and traffickers who accumulate millions of dollars each week, in cash. Because of the amount of funds involved, the dollars cannot be spent or invested without attracting government attention. Thus the "dirty" money must be "cleaned," giving it the appearance of legitimacy—hence the need for its "laundering" or "rinsing."

There are many ways to launder cash, with one of the more typical operations occurring through banks in Miami, Switzerland, Panama, Hong Kong, the Bahamas, Belize, the Cayman Islands, Singapore, and Gibralter to name but a few. The pattern involves the depositing of, say, $10 million, in a U.S. bank, in cash. Although the federal Bank Secrecy Act requires that banks must report deposits of $10,000 or more to the Internal Revenue Service, for a 2% fee some bankers will forget to file the proper notice with the IRS.[j] The American bank then wires the money to an account in the Cayman Islands, a country with strict banking laws that protect the privacy and identity of its depositors. The account to which the money is wired belongs to a bogus Cayman Islands corporation owned by the drug trafficker. The corporation, by way of the Cayman Islands bank, returns the money to the drug dealer

---

[j] Another common way around the Bank Secrecy Act is a practice known in the trade as smurfing. A trafficker will dispatch his or her couriers, the smurfs, to different banks to buy cashier's checks and money orders in values less than $10,000, which are than delivered to another agent who deposits them in one of the trafficker's accounts. See Stephen Brookes, "Drug Money Soils Cleanest Hands," *Insight*, 21 Aug. 1989, pp. 8–17.

in the form of a loan. Thus, the dealer gets his money back, clean, in an ostensibly lawful manner, and because it is a loan, it is not subject to taxation.

In a 1982 case Miami's Great American Bank of Dade County was charged with laundering $96 million in South American drug profits.[42] During the same year, more than 100 crime leaders, Bahamian government officials, and international financiers became the targets of a U.S. government inquiry into the laundering of billions of narcodollars.[43] In 1985 money laundering was found to be an $80-billion-a-year industry, with the majority of the money coming from illegal drug sales and involving major banks and brokerage houses throughout the United States.[44] By the beginning of the 1990s laundering operations were reportedly even more active.[45] Curiously, as the result of the extensive money-laundering operations involving Miami banks and with the widespread use and trafficking of cocaine in that city, virtually every piece of U.S. currency handled in South Florida and other cities where cocaine and crack use rates are high is likely contaminated with microscopic traces of cocaine.[46]

The most threatening political aspect of drug trafficking is its impact on government institutions. Through bribery and corruption, traffickers and/or their representatives have secured judgeships and administrative appointments. Moreover, weak governments can be the focus of direct takeovers by traffickers. There is a precedent for this. In 1980, for example, the presidential election in Bolivia yielded no clear winner. Before the congress could meet to decide between the main contenders, a military junta led by army commander General Luis Garcia Meza staged a coup. Ironically Garcia Meza was himself a major cocaine trafficker, and he proceeded to establish alliances between the government and civilian drug enterprises.[47] A year later Garcia Meza was ultimately forced to resign, not because of his involvement with the cocaine trades, but for his fiscal mismanagement. Three years later Bolivian President Hernan Siles Zuazo, the fourth person to hold that office since Garcia Meza's resignation, announced a war on cocaine. In 1984 Zuazo was kidnapped from the presidential palace by a group of cocaine traffickers. Although he was released unharmed and the attempted coup was aborted, the problem seems to be ever present in that nation.[k]

The final issue in the political arena is the link between drug trafficking and terrorism. Not too long after the Colombian cocaine

---

[k] And too, there was the Panamanian dictator General Manuel Antonio Noriega, indicted in 1988 on a variety of cocaine trafficking charges and ultimately captured and extradited to the United States in 1990. See *Miami Herald*, 1 Sept. 1989, pp. 1A, 10A; *Newsweek*, 4 Sept. 1989, p. 33; David Brock, "Washington's Long Tolerance Turns into Day of Reckoning," *Insight*, pp. 26–28; *Time*, 15 Jan. 1990, pp. 24–27.

entrepreneur, Carlos Lehder Rivas, was arrested and extradited to the United States during the early weeks of 1987, *U.S. News & World Report* published a rather dramatic feature.[48] Headlined ''NARCOTICS: TERROR'S NEW ALLY'' in bold red letters, the lead-in to the article commented:

> With cash from global drug trafficking bankrolling the agendas of governments and insurgents bent on destabilizing democracies, spawning anarchy and exporting revolution, the specter of narco-terrorism is a powerful threat on the international stage as dope becomes the newest political weapon.

Fraught with journalistic innuendo, the article presented a rather melodramatic discussion of the "deadly new threat on the international stage"—trafficking in drugs for the purpose of underwriting insurgencies on four continents. And there was more. The *U.S. News* report went on to speculate on the stake the Soviets, Bulgarians, and Cubans had in the international drug trades. The implication was that of a conspiracy with both strategic and tactical goals that were far more threatening than those of either illegal drug distribution or political terrorism alone. By fostering, and even supporting, the trafficking of heroin, cocaine, and other drugs to the United States and other Western countries, there was the potential for further spreading drug abuse and thereby weakening the very fabric of democratic society on a global scale.[49]

The *U.S. News* story offered no answers to its speculations, but for researchers and students of crime, drugs, and world affairs, it posed a variety of questions. What, first of all, is narco-terrorism? Is it a subspecies of terrorism, or some new form of political violence? Where is it concentrated and how is it manifested?

At the outset, it would appear that narco-terrorism, a term reportedly invented by former Peruvian President Fernando Belaunde Terry,[50] has never been properly defined but suggests some unholy alliance between drugs and terrorism, or at the very least a link between drug trafficking and the activities of terrorist groups. And the likely reason why narco-terrorism has remained undefined is because it applies to a number of different groups and activities.

One approach to unraveling the meaning of narco-terrorism is to point out that while terrorism is a political concept, narco-terrorism is an economic concept. As such, narco-terrorism is not some new form of terrorist activity, but rather, it is no more than a shorthand label used to identify the many different ways that the economics of illegal drug production and distribution can be tied to violence and terrorist activities.

Drugs and terrorism seem to be linked in two significant ways. First, there are the terrorist-like activities used by some drug trafficking groups for the sake of intimidation and deterrence. Although these violent activities have no connection with what is typically understood as terrorism, they have been labeled as narco-terrorism nevertheless. Second, there is the direct and indirect involvement in drug trafficking by insurgent groups and national governments for the purpose of financing their revolutionary ventures. In either case, narco-terrorism is an economic, rather than a political, concept.[51]

Although traditional criminal organizations continue to dominate the international heroin, cocaine, and other illegal drug trades, in recent years a growing number of insurgent and revolutionary groups have become involved in drug-related operations. These activities, all undertaken for economic purposes, have been referred to in the South American media as narco-terrorism and include (1) the extortion of money from low-level producers (such as peasants who grow opium poppies or coca leaves), (2) providing protection to refining and trafficking organizations, (3) direct involvement in illegal drug production and distribution, and (4) outright control over drug-producing regions. It is in these activities that the most direct links between drugs and terrorism exist. Moreover, it is from these insurgent activities that narco-terrorism likely gets its name.

The more visible involvement of revolutionary organizations in the drug trades is relatively recent, in part the result of expansions in the international demand for narcotics, cocaine, Quaalude tablets, and other illicit substances.[52] With greater demand came opportunities for non-traditional suppliers—ranging from presidents and sovereign governments to political parties, business entrepreneurs, law-enforcement agents, and insurgent-terrorist groups. Perhaps most associated with narco-terrorism is FARC, the Armed Revolutionary Forces of Colombia, a pro-Marxist revolutionary group with some 4,000–7,000 members and supporters, divided into perhaps two dozen guerrilla fronts, half of which operate in the regions of Colombia's marijuana and cocaine industries.[53] After its formation in 1966 FARC had little impact on the Colombian political scene for a number of years, limiting its activities to a symbolic occupation of some remote rural villages. In the mid-1970s, however, FARC went into the ransom kidnapping business. As its income grew, so too did its ambitions.

FARC's entry to the drug trades came in the early 1980s, and since that time its narco-terrorism has been focused in four areas, with payments received in the form of cash or armaments: (1) the regular collection of protection money from marijuana and coca growers in its operating territories; (2) the overseeing of drug trafficking in certain areas with collections based on specific quotas; (3) providing traffickers with guaranteed access to clandestine airfields; and (4) direct involvement in coca growing and refining.[54]

As a final note, the drug trafficking/terrorism connection is an important one primarily because one tends to facilitate the other. In addition, narco-terrorism can be a determinant of the direction that a guerrilla or insurgent movement will take, having impacts on both international drug trafficking and local government stability. And on this latter point, there is widespread opinion that the activities of the Palestine Liberation Organization, the Syrians in the Bakaa Valley, and the communist insurgents in Burma are financed and armed by the heroin, cocaine, marijuana, and hashish industries.[55]

POSTSCRIPT

Drug abuse, whether it involves heroin, cocaine, crack, or other drugs, is not simply the problem of the consuming community or nation. There are implications for trafficking nations as well in their political, social, and economic sectors of life. Moreover, the impact of trafficking tends to be circular. That is, whatever influences one sphere of activity seems to rebound on all others.

There are other effects as well. In Bolivia, for example, the centuries-old custom of coca chewing by laborers is repeatedly threatened by the often inflated price of leaves, brought on by trafficking. There are also consequences in the ecological sector. Throughout the United States and Mexico, paraquat, a potent herbicide, has been used to eradicate fields of marijuana plants. Environmentalists have questioned the safety of its use, but its effects on the general ecology of the areas where it has been introduced are immeasurable. However, a different situation exists in many coca-growing regions. On the slopes of the Andes in the high jungles of Peru, for example, coca growers use paraquat heavily. They apply it to the soil surrounding each bush to inhibit any weed growth that might draw nutrients away from the coca. Better coca plants have been one result, but so too have been widespread soil erosion and landslides.[56]

Finally, any number of unanticipated consequences have occurred in the diplomatic, financial, and social sectors for those nations and peoples whose economies depend on drug trafficking. A number of Latin American nations have lost U.S. economic aid, foreign investment, and international bank loans as a result of their unwillingness to better control drug trafficking within their borders. During the closing days of 1989 Panamanian dictator Manuel Antonio Noriega found himself at war with the United States because of cocaine trafficking. Moreover, there is a long-term implication that is potentially more drastic. Drug abuse in the United States and Western Europe has been characterized by change—change over the years in the preference of one drug over another. At present, cocaine in its various forms is the widespread drug of choice. Yet when cocaine becomes less appealing, or when the effects of drug enforcement, treatment, and prevention efforts begin to have a more significant impact, what will happen to those peasants who abandoned the coffee and sugar plantations to cultivate marijuana and coca? Cocaine use in the United States had already begun to decline by the 1990s, at least in some segments of society. It was inevitable. When coca products become passé, what will happen to those nations and communities whose economic systems are dependent on cocaine trafficking?

Notes

1. *Washington Post*, 14 July 1990, p. A10.
2. See June Nash, *We Eat the Mines and the Mines Eat Us: Dependency and Exploitation in Bolivian Tin Mines* (New York: Columbia University Press, 1979).
3. *Latin American Regional Reports, Andean Group Report*, 1 Feb. 1990, p. 7.
4. Bankers Trust, Foreign Exchange Division, 4 Mar. 1986.
5. *New York Times*, 5 Aug. 1985, p. A4; *Latin American Regional Reports, Andean Group Report*, 24 Jan. 1986, p. 2.
6. *Latin American Economy & Business*, Dec. 1990, p. 10.
7. *Christian Science Monitor*, 13 Aug. 1985, p. 14; Eric Lawlor, *In Bolivia* (New York: Vintage, 1989).
8. *U.S. News & World Report*, 15 July 1985, p. 49; *New York Times*, 18 Aug. 1985, p. F25.
9. *Latin American Regional Reports, Andean Group Report*, 1 Feb. 1990, p. 4.
10. Thomas S. Skidmore and Peter H. Smith, *Modern Latin America* (New York: Oxford University Press, 1984), pp. 187–224.
11. *U.S. News & World Report*, 11 Mar. 1985, p. 39.
12. David P. Werlich, "Fujimori and the 'Disaster' in Peru," *Current History*, 90 (February 1991), pp. 61–64, 81–83.
13. Michael Reid, *Peru: Paths to Poverty* (London: Latin America Bureau, 1985), p. 108.
14. Peter Janke, *Guerrilla and Terrorist Organizations: A World Directory and Bibliography* (New York: Macmillan, 1983), p. 505.
15. *Latin American Regional Reports, Andean Group Report*, 31 July 1986, pp. 2–3; *New York Times*, 15 June 1986, p. 7.
16. Werlich, p. 63.
17. Peter A. Lupsha, "The Political Economy of Drug Trafficking" (Paper presented at the Annual Meeting of the Latin American Studies Association, Bloomington, Ind., 16–20 Oct. 1980).
18. Melvin Burke, "Bolivia: The Politics of Cocaine," *Current History*, 90 (February 1991), pp. 65–68, 90; Lima *Caretas*, 19 Feb. 1990, pp. 40–41, 48; *New York Times*, 27 Jan. 1991, p. 11.
19. *New York Times*, 12 Sept. 1984, p. A16.
20. Bogota *El Tiempo*, 18 Apr. 1982, p. 1A.
21. Bogota *El Tiempo*, 29 May 1981, p. 1A.
22. *New York Times*, 27 Jan. 1991, p. 11.

23. *Time*, 23 Sept. 1981, pp. 22–32.
24. Robert Sherrill, "Can Miami Save Itself? A City Beset by Drugs and Violence," *New York Times Magazine*, 19 July 1987, pp. 18–26, 44, 68.
25. *Newsweek*, 25 Jan. 1988, pp. 22–29.
26. *New Statesman*, 3 Feb. 1984, p. 28; *New Yorker*, 26 Dec. 1983, pp. 50–53; *Time*, 5 Dec. 1983, p. 96; *Newsweek*, 12 Dec. 1983, p. 109; *Commonweal*, 24 Feb. 1984, p. 116.
27. *Newsweek*, 30 Apr. 1984, p. 24.
28. Bogota *El Tiempo*, 28 Apr. 1982, p. 3A; *Miami Herald*, 14 Nov. 1982, p. 24; *Miami Herald*, 17 Apr. 1983, p. 26A; *New York Times*, 19 Nov. 1984, p. 1A; Sao Paulo *O Estado de Sao Paulo*, 15 July 1990, p. 36; Bogota *El Espectador*, 26 Feb. 1989, p. 1D; Madrid *EFE*, 2120 GMT, 23 May 1989; Madrid *Cambio*, 7 Mar. 1988, pp. 68–75; La Paz *La Red Panamericana*, 1130 GMT, 7 Apr. 1988.
29. *USA Today*, 2 May 1984, p. 7A; *Newsweek*, 14 May 1984, p. 48.
30. John D. Marts, "Colombia at the Crossroads," *Current History*, 90 (February 1991), pp. 69–72, 80–81; Bruce M. Bagley, "Colombia and the War on Drugs," *Foreign Affairs*, 67 (Fall 1988), pp. 70–92; Larry Gurwin, "Latin America's Killing Fields," *The Economist*, 8 Oct. 1988, pp. 21–23.
31. *Miami Herald*, 27 Aug. 1989, pp. 1A, 16A, 1C, 6C; *Newsweek*, 11 Sept. 1989, pp. 30–32.
32. *New York Times*, 18 Sept. 1989, p. A12.
33. *Latin American Regional Reports, Andean Group Report*, 8 Mar. 1990, p. 7; *U.S. News & World Report*, 30 July 1990, p. 27; Christopher Caldwell, "Cocaine Violence is the Last Straw," *Insight*, 2 Apr., 1990, pp. 8–17; *Miami Herald*, 15 Feb. 1990, pp. 1A, 17A; *Time*, 28 May 1990, p. 39; *New York Times*, 9 Jan. 1991, p. A4; *Time*, 19 Feb. 1990, pp. 62–63; *New York Times*, 28 Jan. 1991, p. A2; *Latin American Regional Reports, Andean Group Report*, 31 Jan. 1991, p. 2.
34. *Washington Post*, 31 Aug. 1989, p. A41; *New York Times*, 1 Sept. 1989, p. A6.
35. Lahore *Viewpoint*, 4 Jan. 1990, p. 7.
36. See James Burney, *The History of the Buccaneers of America* (New York: W. W. Norton, 1950); Philip Gosse, *The History of Piracy* (New York: Tudor, 1932); P. A. Means, *The Spanish Main* (New York: Scribner's, 1935); Hugh F. Rankin, *The Golden Age of Piracy* (New York: Holt, Rinehart & Winston, 1969); George Woodbury, *The Great Days of Piracy in the West Indies* (New York: W. W. Norton, 1951); Robert C. Ritchie, *Captain Kidd and the War Against the Pirates* (Cambridge: Harvard University Press, 1986); Debra Baukney, "Back When the Seas Were Really Wild and Woolly: Pirates, New Providence, and the Ghosts in Bahamian Waters," *Southern Boating*, Dec. 1986, pp. 27–29, 62–63; *Ocean Reef Review*, May/June 1989, p. 7.
37. G. O. W. Mueller and Freda Adler, *Outlaws of the Ocean* (New York: Hearst Marine Books, 1985), p. 139. See also *Time*, 22 Sept. 1980, p. 24.
38. William H. MacLeish, *The Gulf Stream: Encounters With the Blue God* (Boston: Houghton Mifflin, 1989), pp. 68–74; Wilmington (Delaware) *News-Journal*, 25 Apr. 1985, p. A10; *Motor Boating & Sailing*, Aug. 1987, p. 28; *Ocean Navigator*, 19 (May/June 1988), pp. 67–70.
39. For example, see James A. Inciardi, "Narcotic Addiction in the Georgian SSR," *Journal of Psychoactive Drugs*, 19 (Oct./Dec. 1987), pp. 329–334; Rio

de Janeiro *O Globo*, 23 July 1982, p. 5; Lima *El Comercio*, 30 Dec. 1981, p. D-3; F. Raul Jeri, "Coca-Paste Smoking in Some Latin American Countries: A Severe and Unabated Form of Addiction," *Bulletin on Narcotics*, Apr.–June 1984, pp. 15–31; C. P. Spencer and V. Navaratnam, *Drug Abuse in East Asia* (New York: Oxford University Press, 1981); *U.S. News & World Report*, 24 May 1982, p. 49; *Time*, 19 Mar. 1984, p. 35; *Miami Herald*, 11 Oct. 1989, pp. 1A, 10A; Victoria *Seychelles Nation*, 19 Jan. 1990, pp. 1, 2; Jakarta (Indonesia) *Antara News Bulletin*, 13 Jan. 1990, p. A-3; Khartoum (Sudan) *Al-Sudan Al-Hadith*, 28 Nov. 1989, p. 5; London *Keyhan*, 18 Jan. 1990, p. 3; Hong Kong *Zhongguo Tongxun She*, 1023 GMT, 4 Apr. 1990; Lima *El Nacional*, 15 Feb. 1990, p. 15; Rio de Janeiro *Jornal do Brasil*, 13 Mar. 1990, p. 3; Athens *To Vima Tis Kiriakis*, 13 May 1990, p. 32; Kabul (Afghanistan) *Payam*, 30 Apr. 1990, p. 3; Sofia (Bulgaria) *Vecherni Novini*, 2 Apr. 1989, p. 5; Buenos Aires *La Nacion*, 2 Apr. 1989, p. 18; Kuala Lumpur (Malaysia) *Berita Harian*, 28 Apr. 1989, p. 6; Calcutta *Telegraph*, 21 Mar. 1989, p. 2; Bangkok (Thailand) *Nation*, 26 Apr. 1989, p. 2; Madrid (Spain) *Tiempo*, 29 May 1989, pp. 69–70, 72–73; Lagos (Nigeria) *African Guardian*, 25 Sept. 1989, pp. 12–15; La Paz (Bolivia) *Diario*, 26 Oct. 1989, p. 10; Moscow *Sovetskaya Yustitsiya*, No. 19, Oct. 1988, pp. 13–15; Dhaka *Bangladesh Observer*, 30 Nov. 1987, p. 2; Katowice (Poland) *Niedzielny*, No. 7, 14 Mar. 1988, p. 1; Madras (India) *Hindu*, 12 Mar. 1988, p. 8; Lisbon (Portugal) *Diario de Noticias*, 20 Apr. 1988, p. 13; Oslo (Norway) *Aftenposten*, 16 Apr. 1988, pp. 1, 8; Tel Aviv *Davar*, 3 May 1988, p. 11; Hanoi (Vietnam) *Van Hoa Nghe Thuat*, No. 8, Apr. 1988, p. 4; Karachi (Sri Lanka) *Dawn*, 21 Nov. 1986, p. v; Georgetown (Guyana) *Staboek News*, 5 Dec. 1986, p. 24.

40. La Paz *La Red Panamericana*, 1130 GMT, 4 July 1987.

41. Jamaica Kincaid, *A Small Place* (New York: New American Library, 1988); Port-of-Spain *Trinidad Guardian*, 18 Apr. 1990, pp. 12–13; Madrid *EFE*, 2009 GMT, 26 Oct. 1990; Bridgetown (Antigua) *Canaq*, 1852 GMT, 11 Nov. 1990; Bogota *El Espectador*, 26 Feb. 1989, p. 1D; Lima *El Comercio*, 16 Mar. 1989, p. 2; Nassau (Bahamas) *Tribune*, 18 Apr. 1988, p. 4.

42. *Miami Herald*, 14 Dec. 1982, p. 1.

43. *Miami Herald*, 7 Nov. 1982, p. 21A.

44. *American Banker*, 15 Feb. 1985, pp. 4–6; *American Banker*, 22 Feb. 1985, pp. 4–7; *American Banker*, 28 Feb. 1985, pp. 4–12; *Business Week*, 11 Mar. 1985, p. 37; *Wall Street Journal*, 12 Mar. 1985, pp. 1, 26; *USA Today*, 15 Mar. 1985, p. 3A; *Business Week*, 18 Mar. 1985, pp. 74–82; *World Press Review*, Nov. 1985, p. 58; *Christian Science Monitor*, 18 Oct. 1985, p. 21; *Newsweek*, 23 Sept. 1985, p. 52.

45. *Time*, 18 Dec. 1989, pp. 50–56; *Miami Herald*, 11 Feb. 1990, pp. 1A, 24A, 25A; *Drug Enforcement Report*, 23 Jan. 1991, pp. 6–7.

46. *Miami Herald*, 19 Feb. 1985, pp. 1–2C; *The Economist*, 15 Apr. 1989, p. 32.

47. Department of State, Bureau of International Narcotics Matters, *International Narcotics Control Strategy Report* (Washington, DC: Department of State, 1985), p. 49.

48. *U.S. News & World Report*, 4 May 1987, pp. 30–37.

49. Although there appears to be no serious evidence in support of this allegation, the thesis is nevertheless presented in considerable detail in Joseph D. Douglass, *Red Cocaine: The Drugging of America* (Atlanta: Clarion House, 1990).

50. Bogota *Chromos*, 22 July 1986, pp. 48–52.

51. James A. Inciardi, "Narcoterrorism: Cocaine, Insurgency, and the Links Between Political and Economic Violence in South America," Paper Presented at the Defense Academic Research Support Program Conference, "International Drugs: Threat and Response," National Defense College, Defense Intelligence Analysis Center, Washington, D.C., 2–3 June 1987.

52. Mark S. Steinitz, "Insurgents, Terrorists and the Drug Trade," *Washington Quarterly*, Fall 1985, pp. 141–153.

53. James Adams, *The Financing of Terror* (New York: Simon and Schuster, 1986), p. 259.

54. Santiago (Chile) *Ercilla*, 8 Oct. 1986, pp. 22–25; Bogota *Chromos*, 22 July 1986, pp. 48–52; Bogota *El Tiempo*, 24 May 1986, p. 2A.

55. Lauren Ayacucho, "Coca Link Embroils Antirebel War," *Insight*, 5 Feb. 1990, pp. 30–31; William A. Hazleton and Sandra Woy-Hazleton, "Terrorism and the Marxist Left: Peru's Struggle Against Sendero Luminoso," *Terrorism*, 11 (1988), pp. 471–490; Rachel Ehrenfeld, *Narco Terrorism* (New York: Basic Books, 1990).

56. *Lima Television Peruana*, 0100 GMT, 15 June 1990; La Paz *Presencia*, 8 Aug. 1989, p. 1.

THE GREAT DRUG WAR AND THE GREAT DRUG DEBATE
Wrangling Over Control Versus Legalization

Historically the federal approach to drug abuse and drug control has included a variety of avenues for reducing both the supply of and the demand for illicit drugs. At the outset the supply-and-demand reduction strategies were grounded in the classic deterrence model: through legislation and criminal penalties, individuals would be discouraged from using drugs; by setting an example of traffickers, the government would force potential dealers to seek out other economic pursuits. For most people who had a significant investment in the social system, the model worked—at least for a time. Other components were then added: treatment for the user; education and prevention for the would-be user; and research to determine how to best develop and implement plans for treatment, education, and prevention.

By the early 1970s when it appeared that the war on drugs had won few, if any, battles, new avenues for supply and demand reduction were added. There were the federal interdiction initiatives: the Coast Guard, Customs, and Drug Enforcement Administration operatives were charged with intercepting drug shipments coming to the United States from foreign ports; in the international sector there were attempts to eradicate drug-yielding crops at their source. On the surface, none of these strategies seemed to have any effect, and illicit drug use continued to spread.

The problems were many. Legislation and enforcement alone were not enough, and early education programs of the "scare" variety quickly lost their credibility. For social scientists, clinicians, and most other people who had humanitarian ideals—which probably included the majority of the American people—treating drug abuse as a medical problem seemed to be the logical answer. The difficulty was threefold. First, the medical model of treatment was structured around a belief in the addiction-prone personality—that deep-rooted personality disorder that was used to characterize just about everyone with a drug problem. However, all drug abusers were not the same. The result was high program-failure rates regardless of the method of treatment.[1] Second, from what is now known about the course of drug abuse treatment, back in the 1950s, 1960s, and much of the 1970s most treatment regimens just weren't long enough to have significant impacts. Third, research technologies for assessing program effectiveness were weak.

Even today, an overview of the various drug-abuse treatment strategies suggests that everything is working and everything is failing. This overview means that all therapeutic approaches—whether they involve residential therapeutic communities, methadone maintenance, individual and group therapy, psychotherapy, simple detoxification, or even penitence through prayer—seem to be working for somebody. However, the tactics of clinical and social science research do not seem to be capable of determining what rehabilitative technique is most effective for whom. The difficulty seems to be in the selection of drug abusers for the delivery of treatment services. Particularly poor achievements appear in the screening of patients into treatment, in the focusing of the most appropriate programs upon those who need them most, in the failure to admit there are some who cannot be helped, and in the determination of when a patient has received the maximum benefits from any given therapeutic technique.[2]

LAW, THE MILITARY, AND "ZERO TOLERANCE": EXPANDING THE WEAPONRY IN THE WAR ON DRUGS

Given the perceived inadequacy of the traditional approaches to drug-abuse control, during the late 1970s federal authorities began drawing plans for a more concerted legislative and technological assault on drugs. It began with the RICO (Racketeer-Influenced and Corrupt Organizations) and CCE (Continuing Criminal Enterprise) statutes. What RICO and CCE accomplish is the forfeiture of the fruits of criminal activities.[3] Their intent is to eliminate the rights of traffickers to their personal assets, whether these be cash, bank accounts, real estate, automobiles, jewelry and art, equity in businesses, directorships in companies, or any kind of goods or entitlements that are obtained in or used for a criminal enterprise.

Added to the perceived strength offered by RICO and CCE was a new extradition treaty between the United States and the Republic of Colombia, signed on September 14, 1979 and entered into force on March 4, 1982.[4] The treaty was notable in that it added to the list of extraditable crimes a whole variety of offenses related to drug trafficking, aircraft hijacking, obstruction of justice, and bribery. In addition, Article 8 of the treaty was a considerable innovation in international affairs in that it imposed an obligation on the government of Colombia to extradite all persons, including its nationals, when the offense was a punishable act in both countries and was intended to be consummated in the United States (e.g., the export of cocaine and/or marijuana into the United States from Colombia by Colombian citizens).

The new, evolving federal drug strategy considered it crucial to include the U.S. military in its war on drugs, but to do so, something then had to be done about the Posse Comitatus Act originally passed by the 45th Congress on June 18, 1878. The act had been a response to post–Civil War reconstruction policies that permitted U.S. marshals in occupied southern states to call upon federal troops to enforce local laws. It was the goal of southern congressmen to prevent such a practice, and the Posse Comitatus Act accomplished exactly that. It prohibited the army (and eventually other branches of the military) from enforcing federal, state, and local civilian law and from supplementing the efforts of civilian law-enforcement agencies.[5]

But the Posse Comitatus Act was never a constitutionally mandated statute. In fact its very wording permitted the assistance of the military if specifically authorized by an act of Congress.[a] As a result, when President Ronald Reagan signed the Department of Defense Authorization Act of 1982 into law, it included several amendments to the century-old Posse Comitatus Act. Although military personnel were still prohibited from physically intercepting suspected drug vessels and aircraft, conducting searches and seizures, and making arrests, the entire war chest of U.S. military power did become available to law enforcement—for training, intelligence gathering, and detection. Moreover, members of the U.S. Army, Navy, Air Force, and Marines could operate military equipment for civilian agencies charged with the enforcement of the drug laws.[b]

Beginning in 1982 the war on drugs had a new look. Put into force was the Bell 209 assault helicopter, more popularly known as the Cobra. There was none in the military arsenal that was faster, and in its gunship mode it could destroy a tank. In addition, there was the awesome Sikorsky Black Hawk assault helicopter, assigned for

---

[a] Over the years Congress has authorized the use of the military to control civil disorder. It was for this reason Chicago's Mayor Daley was able to call in the Illinois National Guard as well as regular army troops to control the perceived threat of disorder by antiwar protestors at the Democratic National Convention in 1968.

[b] It should be noted here that the Posse Comitatus Act never prevented the U.S. Coast Guard from intercepting and seizing vessels at sea that were transporting contraband to American ports. For an examination of Coast Guard antidrug activities, see Hans Halberstadt, *USCG* (Novato, CA: Presidio Press, 1986), pp. 31–47.

operation by U.S. Customs Service pilots. Customs also had the Cessna Citation, a jet aircraft equipped with radar originally designed for F-16 fighters. There was the Navy's EC-2, an aircraft equipped with a radar disk capable of detecting other aircraft from as far as 300 miles away. There were "Fat Albert" and his pals—aerostat surveillance balloons 175 feet in length equipped with sophisticated radar and listening devices. Fat Albert could not only pick up communications from Cuba and Soviet satellites but also detect traffic in Smugglers' Alley, a wide band of Caribbean sky that is virtually invisible to land-based radar systems. There were NASA satellites to spy on drug operations as far apart as California and Colombia, airborne infrared sensing and imaging equipment that could detect human body heat in the thickest underbrush of Florida's Everglades, plus a host of other high technology devices. The U.S. Coast Guard also strengthened its equipment, and U.S. Customs put into service Blue Thunder, a vessel specifically designed to outrun the high-performance speedboats that traffickers use in Florida waters. A 39-foot catamaran with 900 horsepower, Blue Thunder cut through 6-foot seas at speeds better than 60 mph.[c] In all, drug enforcement appeared well equipped for battle.[6]

The final component added to the drug war armamentarium was "zero-tolerance," a 1988 White House anti-drug policy that was never clearly articulated in the national media. It would appear that zero-tolerance is based on a number of premises: (1) that if there were no drug abusers there would be no drug problem; (2) that the market for drugs is created not only by availability, but also by demand; (3) that drug abuse starts with a willful act; (4) that the perception that drug users are powerless to act against the influences of drug availability and peer pressure is an erroneous one; (5) that most illegal drug users can choose to stop their drug-taking behaviors and must be held accountable if they do not; (6) that individual freedom does not include the right to self- and societal destruction; and (7) that public tolerance for drug abuse must be reduced to zero.[7] As such, the zero-tolerance policy expanded the war on drugs from suppliers and dealers to users as

---

[c] Blue Thunder had been designed by the late Don Aronow, the creator of such internationally recognized "go-fast boats" as Formula, Donzi, Magnum, and the most famous powerboat ever—the Cigarette. Nicknamed the "Ferrari of the open seas," the Cigarette became the boat desired by both the famous and infamous throughout the world, from former presidents Richard M. Nixon and Lyndon B. Johnson to the Shah of Iran, fugitive financier Robert Vesco, and likely every bandit and drug-runner that carried contraband across water. What distinguished Blue Thunder from the Cigarette was not its speed, but its ability to sustain high speeds in extremely heavy seas without breaking up. For an examination of the making of Blue Thunder and the gangland-style murder of Don Aronow in 1987, see Thomas Burdick and Charlene Mitchell, *Blue Thunder* (New York: Simon and Schuster, 1990).

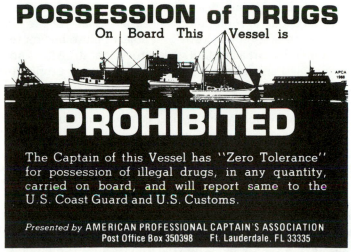

POSSESSION of DRUGS
On Board This Vessel is

PROHIBITED

The Captain of this Vessel has "Zero Tolerance" for possession of illegal drugs, in any quantity, carried on board, and will report same to the U.S. Coast Guard and U.S. Customs.

Presented by AMERICAN PROFESSIONAL CAPTAIN'S ASSOCIATION
Post Office Box 350398   Ft. Lauderdale, FL 33335

To protect themselves against vessel confiscation, many boat captains have "zero tolerance" policies of their own.

well—especially casual users—and meant that planes, vessels, and vehicles could be confiscated for carrying even the smallest amount of a controlled substance.

Not surprisingly, the policy quickly became unpopular, particularly with non-drug-using owners of confiscated boats. As a case in point, during May 1988 the Coast Guard seized the *Ark Royal,* a $2.5 million, 133-foot yacht that was in international waters between Mexico and Cuba. The on-board drug stash was one tenth of an ounce of marijuana, and because only the captain and crew were on board at the time of the raid, it was not even apparent that the drug had been used by the vessel's owner.[8] Similar incidents led to an easing of the zero-tolerance policy, and an "innocent owner's" defense was established to protect against vessel and vehicle confiscation when someone else's personal use drugs were found.[9] And to emphasize the notion of an innocent owner, fishing and charter boat captains began displaying zero-tolerance plaques on their vessels.[10]

DEBATING LEGALIZATION

By 1988, well after the newest war on drugs (including a war on crack and a war on drug-related violence) had been declared and put into operation, it had long since been decided by numerous observers that the 74 years of federal prohibition since the passage of the Harrison Act of 1914 were not only a costly and abject failure but represented a totally doomed effort as well. It was argued that drug laws and drug enforcement had served mainly to create enormous profits for drug dealers and traffickers, overcrowded jails, police and other government corruption, a distorted foreign policy, predatory street crime carried on by users in search of the funds necessary to purchase black market drugs, and urban areas harassed by street-level drug dealers and terrorized by violent drug gangs.[11]

Much of what these observers were remarking about indeed had been the case. To begin with, expenditures for the war on drugs had been considerable. For example, federal disbursements for supply and demand reduction from 1981 through 1988 totaled some $16.5 billion.[12] These figures, furthermore, did not include the many more billions spent by state and local governments on law enforcement and other criminal justice system costs and on drug prevention, education, treatment, and research. On the positive side of the equation, interdiction initiatives had resulted in a somewhat impressive set of figures. For example, from 1981 through 1987 some 5.3 million kilograms of marijuana had been seized. And even more importantly, cocaine seizures also increased dramatically, from 2,000 kilograms in 1981 to 36,000 in 1987.[13]

Yet there was a negative side to the equation as well. Customs, Coast Guard, and Drug Enforcement Administration (DEA) officials had readily admitted that these seizures likely reflected only 10% of the marijuana and cocaine entering the country.[14] Furthermore, DEA figures indicated that despite the seizures and increased expenditures on interdiction, the growing supply of cocaine in the United States had resulted in increased availability and a dramatic decline in price. To further complicate the picture, the purity of cocaine had increased substantially over this period of time.[15]

Intimidating as well for the war on drugs were the reported increases throughout the 1980s in the worldwide production of both marijuana and opium.[16] To this could be added the problem that many countries seemed to be unable, or unwilling, to take a stand against major drug traffickers. The extradition of Colombian trafficker Carlos Lehder Rivas to stand trial in the United States had been hailed as a courageous act when it occurred in 1987, but the subsequent intimidation of the Colombian justice system by traffickers and what appeared to be a de facto nullification in 1988 of the extradition treaty between the United States and the Republic of Colombia set back international efforts to curtail drug distribution significantly.[17] And there were other problems: the continued use of illegal drugs, with many cities seemingly overwhelmed with crack-cocaine; violence in the inner cities and elsewhere as drug trafficking gangs competed for distribution territories; street crime committed by users for the sake of supporting their drug habits; and corruption in law enforcement and other branches of government brought on by the considerable economic opportunities for those involved in drug distribution.

Within the context of the concerns, 1988 also marked the onset of renewed calls for the decriminalization, if not the outright legalization, of most or all illicit drugs.[d] Most vocal in this behalf were Ethan A. Nadelmann from the Woodrow Wilson School of Public and International Affairs at Princeton University;[18] free-market economist Milton Friedman;[19] and Professor Arnold S. Trebach of the American University.[20]

The arguments posed by the supporters of legalization seem all too logical. First, they argue, the drug laws have created evils far worse than the drugs themselves—corruption, violence, street crime, and disrespect for the law. Second, legislation passed to control drugs has failed to reduce demand. Third, you cannot have illegal that which a significant segment of the population in any society is committed to doing. You simply cannot arrest, prosecute, and punish such large numbers of people, particularly in a democracy. And specifically in this behalf, in a liberal democracy the government must not interfere with personal behavior if liberty is to be maintained. Fourth, they added, if marijuana, cocaine, crack, heroin, and other drugs were legalized, a number of very positive things would happen:

1. Drug prices would fall;

2. users could obtain their drugs at low, government-regulated prices and would no longer be forced to engage in prostitution and street crime to support their habits;

3. the fact that the levels of drug-related crime would significantly decline would result in less crowded courts, jails, and prisons and free law enforcement personnel to focus their energies on the real criminals in society;

---

[d] Although the terms legalization and decriminalization are often used interchangeably in discussions of drug policy, they clearly have different meanings. Legalizing a drug would serve to abolish the laws (and associated criminal penalties) that prohibit its production, sale, distribution, and possession. As such, alcohol is a legal drug, tobacco is a legal drug, aspirin is a legal drug. In contemporary usage, decriminalizing a drug is a lesser measure, serving only to remove the criminal penalties associated with possession. Under current marijuana decriminalization statutes, the criminal penalties associated with possession of small amounts for personal use have been removed. However, sale, distribution, production, importation, and certain levels of possession remain prohibited by the criminal law. See James A. Inciardi, "Marijuana Decriminalization Research: A Perspective and Commentary," *Criminology*, 19 (May 1981), pp. 145–159.

4. drug production, distribution, and sale would be removed from the criminal arena; no longer would it be within the province of organized crime, and as such, criminal syndicates like the Medellin Cartel and the Jamaican posses would be decapitalized, and the violence associated with drug distribution rivalries would be eliminated;

5. government corruption and intimidation by traffickers as well as drug-based foreign policies would be effectively reduced, if not eliminated entirely; and

6. the often draconian measures undertaken by police to enforce the drug laws would be curtailed, thus restoring to the American public many of its hard-won civil liberties.

To these contentions can be added the argument that legalization in any form or structure would have only a minimal impact on current drug use levels. Apparently there is the assumption on the part of the legalizers that given the existing levels of access to most illegal drugs, current levels of use closely match demand. Thus there would be no additional health, safety, behavioral, and/or other problems accompanying legalization. And finally, a few protagonists of legalization make one concluding point. Through government regulation of drugs, the billions of dollars spent annually on drug enforcement could be better utilized. Moreover, by taxing government-regulated drugs, revenues would be collected that could be used for preventing drug abuse and treating those harmed by drugs.

In the long and the short, the argument for legalization seems to boil down to the basic belief that America's prohibitions against marijuana, cocaine, heroin, and other drugs impose far too large a cost in terms of tax dollars, crime, and infringements on civil rights and individual liberties. And while the overall argument may be well intended and appear quite logical, it is highly questionable in its historical, socio-cultural, and empirical underpinnings, and demonstrably naive in its understanding of the negative consequences of a legalized drug market.[21]

SHOOTING FROM THE HIP

At the outset, it can be argued that current legalization of drugs proposals are not proposals at all. Although legalizing drugs has been debated ever since the passage of the Harrison Act in 1914, never has an advocate of the position structured a concrete proposal. Any attempt to legalize drugs would be extremely complex, but all proponents tend to proceed from simplistic shoot-from-the-hip positions without first developing any sophisticated proposals. Even amid the late 1980s and early 1990s clamor for legalization, specific proposals that addressed all of the complex control issues could not be found. And in this regard, there are many questions that would need to be addressed, including:

1. What drugs should be legalized? Marijuana? Heroin? Cocaine? And if cocaine is designated for legalization, should proposals include such coca products as crack and other forms of freebase cocaine? Should the list include basuco (coca paste), that potent and highly toxic processing derivative of the coca leaf discussed earlier in Chapter 4? There are other drugs to be considered as well. Which hallucinogenic drugs should be legalized? LSD? Peyote? Mescaline? What about Quaaludes? Should they be returned to the legal market? And let's not forget ecstasy and the various designer drugs. In short, which drugs should be legalized, according to what criteria, and who should determine the criteria?

2. Assuming that some rationally determined slate of drugs could be designated for legalization, what potency levels should be permitted? Like 80, 100, and 151 proof rum, should marijuana with 5%, 10%, and 14% THC content be permitted? Should legalized heroin be restricted to Burmese No. 3 grade, or should Mexican "black tar" and the mythical "China White" be added to the ledger?

3. As with alcohol, should there be age limits as to who can and cannot use drugs? Should those old enough to drive be permitted to buy and use drugs? And which drugs? Should it be that 16-year-olds can buy pot and Quaaludes but have to wait until 18 for cocaine and crack, and 21 for heroin?

4. Should certain drugs be limited to only those already dependent on them? In other words, should heroin sales be restricted to heroin addicts and cocaine sales limited to cocaine addicts? And if this approach is deemed viable, what do we say to the heroin addicts who want to buy cocaine? In other words, do we legalize heroin and cocaine sales but forbid speedballing? And then, what about drug experimenters? Should they be permitted access to the legal drug market? And assuming that these issues can be decided, in what amounts can users—regardless of their drugs of choice—purchase heroin, cocaine, marijuana, Quaaludes, and other chemical substances?

5. Where should the drugs be sold? Over the counter in drug and grocery stores as is the case with many pharmaceuticals? Through mail order houses? In special vending machines strategically located in public restrooms, hotel lobbies, and train and bus stations? In tax-supported "drug shacks" as Rep. Charles Rangel (D-NY) satirically asked?[22] Should some, or all, of the newly legalized drugs be available only on a prescription basis? And if this be the case, should a visit to a physician be necessary to get a prescription? And for how many tabs, lines, lids, bags, rocks, or whatever, should prescriptions be written for? How often should these prescriptions be refillable?

6. Where should the raw material for the drugs originate? Would cultivation be restricted to U.S. lands, or would foreign sources be permitted? Coca from Bolivia and Peru, or from all of South America and Java as well? Marijuana from Colombia and Jamaica? Opium from Mexico, Laos, Thailand, or from the Golden Crescent countries of Iran, Afghanistan, and Pakistan? Should trade restrictions of any type be imposed—by drug, amount, potency, purity, or by country? Should legalization policies permit the introduction of currently little-known drugs of abuse into the U.S. from foreign ports, such as *qat* from Yemen or *bekaro* from Pakistan.[e]

7. If drugs are to be legalized, should the drug market be a totally free one, with private industry establishing the prices as well as levels of purity and potency? What kinds of advertising should be permitted? Should advertisements for some drugs be allowed, but not others? Should Timothy Leary and Manuel Noriega be permitted to endorse certain drugs or brands of drugs as part of advertising programs?

8. If drugs are to be legalized, what types of restrictions on their use should be structured? Should transportation workers, nuclear plant employees, or other categories of workers be forbidden to use them at all times, or just while they are on duty?

---

[e] *Qat* (also known as khat, and described more fully in Chapter 9), is the evergreen shrub *Catha edulis*, whose leaves and buds are chewed or brewed as a beverage. Qat produces stimulant effects similar to, but milder than, those induced by the amphetamines, and psychic dependence has been known to develop. *Bekaro*, the seeds of the Tula tree (*Pterygota alata*), is well known in parts of India and Pakistan as an effective substitute for opiates. See Shelagh Weir, *Qat in Yemen: Consumption and Social Change* (London: British Museum Publications, 1985); William Emboden, *Narcotic Plants* (New York: Macmillan, 1979).

9. As is the case with alcohol, will certain establishments be permitted to serve drugs (and which drugs) to their customers? And similarly, as is the case with cigarettes, should there be separate drug-using and non–drug-using sections in restaurants, on planes and trains, and in the workplace? As with coffee and cigarette breaks, should users be permitted pot and coke breaks as part of their union contracts or employer policies?

10. For any restrictions placed on sales, potency levels, distribution, prices, quantity, and advertising in a legalized drug market, what government bureaucracy should be charged with the enforcement of the legalization statutes? The Federal Bureau of Investigation (FBI)? The Drug Enforcement Administration (DEA)? The Food and Drug Administration (FDA)? The Bureau of Alcohol, Tobacco, and Firearms (ATF)? State and local law enforcement agencies? Or should some new federal bureaucracy be created for the purpose? Going further, what kinds of penalties ought to be established for violation of the legalization restrictions?

There are likely many more questions. In short, the whole idea of even articulating a legalization policy is complex. Not only have legalization proponents failed to answer the questions, they have yet to even pose most of them. Moreover, anyone attempting to structure a serious proposal highlighting the beneficial expectations of a legalization policy would find little support for his or her arguments in either published research data or clinical experience. By contrast, there are numerous legitimate arguments against the legalization of drugs, all of which have considerable empirical, historical, pharmacological, and/or clinical support.

THE PUBLIC HEALTH AND BEHAVIORAL CONSEQUENCES ARGUMENT

There is considerable evidence to suggest that the legalization of drugs would create behavioral and public health problems to a degree that would far outweigh the current consequences of the drug prohibition. There are some excellent reasons why marijuana, cocaine, crack, heroin, and other drugs are now controlled and why they ought to remain so.

Marijuana

There is considerable misinformation about marijuana. To the millions of adolescents and young adults who were introduced to the drug during the social revolution of the 1960s and early 1970s, marijuana was a harmless herb of ecstasy. As the "new social drug" and a "natural organic product," it was deemed to be far less harmful than either alcohol or tobacco.[23] More recent research suggests, however, that marijuana smoking is a practice that combines the hazardous features of both tobacco and alcohol with a number of pitfalls of its own. Moreover, there are many disturbing questions about marijuana's effect on the vital systems of the body, on the brain and mind, on immunity and resistance, and on sex and reproduction.[24]

One of the more serious difficulties with marijuana use relates to lung damage. The most recent findings in this behalf should put to rest the rather tiresome argument by marijuana devotees that smoking just a few joints daily is less harmful than regularly smoking several times as many cigarettes. Researchers at the University of California (Los Angeles) reported early in 1988 that the respiratory burden in smoke particulates and absorption of carbon monoxide from smoking just one marijuana joint is some four times greater than from smoking a single tobacco cigarette.[25] Specifically, it was found that one toke (drag) of marijuana delivers three times more tar to the mouth and lungs than one puff of a filter-tipped cigarette; that marijuana deposits four times more tar in the throat and lungs and increases carbon monoxide levels in the blood fourfold to fivefold.

There seem to be three distinct sets of facts about marijuana its apologists tend to downplay, if not totally ignore—about its chemical structure, its persistence-of-residue effect, and its changing potency.

First, the *cannabis sativa* plant from which marijuana comes is a complex chemical factory. Marijuana contains 426 known chemicals which are transformed into 2,000 chemicals when burned during the smoking process. Seventy of these chemicals are *cannabinoids*, substances that are found nowhere else in nature. Since they are fat-soluble, they are immediately deposited in those body tissues that have a high fat content—the brain, lungs, liver, and reproductive organs.

Second, the fact that THC (delta-9-tetrahydrocannabinol), the active ingredient and most potent psychoactive chemical in marijuana, is soluble in fat but not in water has a significant implication. The human body has a water-based waste disposal system—blood, urine, sweat, and feces. A chemical such as THC that does not dissolve in water becomes trapped, principally in the brain, lungs, liver, and reproductive organs. This is the persistence-of-residue effect. One puff of smoke from a marijuana cigarette delivers a significant amount of THC, half of which remains in the body for several weeks. As such, if a person is smoking marijuana more than once a month, the residue levels of THC are not only retained, but also building up—in the brain, lungs, liver, and reproductive organs.

Third, the potency of marijuana has risen dramatically over the years. During the 1960s the THC content of marijuana was only 2/10ths of 1%. By the 1980s the potency of imported marijuana was up to 5%, representing a 25-fold increase. Moreover, California sinsemilla, a seedless, domestic variety of marijuana, has a THC potency of 14%. In fact, so potent is sinsemilla that it has become the pot of choice both inside and outside the United States. On the streets of Bogota, Colombia, sinsemilla has been traded for cocaine on an equal weight basis.[26]

Finally, aside from the health consequences of marijuana use, recent research on the behavioral aspects of the drug suggests that it severely affects the social perceptions of heavy users. Findings from the Center for Psychological Studies in New York City, for example, found that adults who smoked marijuana daily believed the drug helped them to function better—improving their self-awareness and relationships with others.[27] In reality, however, marijuana had served to be a buffer so to speak, enabling users to tolerate problems rather than face them and make changes that might increase the quality of their social functioning and satisfaction with life. The study found that the research subjects used marijuana to avoid dealing with their difficulties, and the avoidance inevitably made their problems worse—on the job, at home, and in family and sexual relationships.

What this research documented was what clinicians had been saying for years. Personal growth evolves from learning to cope with stress, anxiety, frustration, and the many other difficulties that life presents, both small and large. Marijuana use (and the use of other drugs as well, including alcohol), particularly among adolescents and young adults, interferes with this process, and the result is a drug-induced arrested development.[28]

Alternatively, it has been argued that for humanitarian reasons, a reclassification of marijuana under the scheduling provisions of the Controlled Substances Act is in order.[f] At present, marijuana is a Schedule I drug, which means that it has no recognized accepted medical use. Cocaine on the other hand is a Schedule II drug, meaning that it can be legally obtained on a prescription basis under special circumstances. As such, with many AIDS patients saying that marijuana alleviates the nausea and vomiting caused by the syndrome and the drugs used to treat it (an argument also made by cancer

[f] Schedules I through V of the Controlled Substances Act are outlined in Appendix II of this book.

chemotherapy patients), a reclassification of the drug into Schedule II would make it available for medical purposes.[29]

Cocaine and Crack

As already detailed in Chapter 3, the pleasure and feelings of power that cocaine engenders make its use a rather unwise recreational pursuit. Its euphoric lift, with feelings of pleasure, confidence, and being on top of things that comes from a few brief snorts is short-lived and invariably followed by a letdown. When the elation and grandiose feelings begin to wane, a corresponding deep depression is often felt, which is in such marked contrast to users' previous states that they are strongly motivated to repeat the dose and restore the euphoria. This leads to chronic, compulsive use. And when chronic users try to stop using cocaine, they are typically plunged into a severe depression from which only more cocaine can arouse them. Then there are the physiological consequences of cocaine use—convulsions, hyperstimulation, and overdose—also discussed in Chapter 3.

To these can be added what is known as the cocaine psychosis.[30] As dose and duration of cocaine use increase, the development of cocaine-related psychopathology is not uncommon. Cocaine psychosis is generally preceded by a transitional period characterized by increased suspiciousness, compulsive behavior, fault finding, and eventually paranoia. When the psychotic state is reached, individuals may experience visual and/or auditory hallucinations, with persecutory voices commonly heard. Many believe that they are being followed by police or that family, friends, and others are plotting against them. Moreover, everyday events tend to be misinterpreted in a way that support delusional beliefs. When coupled with the irritability and hyperactivity that the stimulant nature of cocaine tends to generate in almost all of its users, cocaine-induced paranoia may lead to violent behavior as a means of self-defense against imagined persecutors.

Finally, already examined at length in Chapter 4, what has been said about cocaine also applies to crack, and perhaps more so. Crack's low price (as little as $2 per rock in some locales) has made it an attractive drug of abuse for those with limited funds, particularly adolescents. Its rapid absorption brings on a faster onset of dependence than is typical with cocaine, resulting in higher rates of addiction, binge use, and psychoses. The consequences include higher levels of cocaine-related violence and all the same manifestations of personal, familial, and occupational neglect that are associated with other forms of drug dependence.

Heroin

As discussed in detail in Chapters 1 and 3, heroin is a highly addictive narcotic and the drug historically associated with addiction and street crime. Although heroin overdose is not uncommon, unlike alcohol, cocaine, tobacco, and many prescription drugs, the direct physiological damage caused by heroin use tends to be minimal. And it is for this reason that the protagonists of drug legalization include heroin in their arguments. By making heroin readily available to users, they argue, many problems could be sharply reduced if not totally eliminated, including: the crime associated with supporting a heroin habit; the overdoses resulting from problematic levels of heroin purity and potency; the HIV and hepatitis infections brought about by needle sharing; and the personal, social, and occupational dislocations resulting from the drug-induced criminal life-style.[31]

The belief that the legalization of heroin would eliminate crime, overdose, infections, and life dislocations is for the most part delusional, for it is likely that the heroin-use life-style would change little for most addicts regardless of the legal status of the drug. And there is ample evidence to support this argument—in the biographies and autobiographies of narcotics addicts, in the clinical assessments of heroin addiction, and in the treatment literature.[32] And to this can be added the many thousands of conversations conducted with heroin users over the past three decades.

The point is this. To reiterate what has been stated elsewhere in this book, heroin is a highly addicting drug. For the addict, it becomes life consuming: it becomes mother, father, spouse, lover, counselor, and confessor. Because heroin is a short-acting drug, with its effects lasting at best 4 to 6 hours, it must be taken regularly and repeatedly. Because there is a more rapid onset when taken intravenously, most heroin users inject the drug. Because heroin has depressant effects, a portion of the user's day is spent in a semi-stupefied state. Collectively, these attributes result in a user more concerned with drug taking than health, family, work, or anything else.

As a final and perhaps most important note to this section, recently completed research by professors Michael D. Newcomb and Peter M. Bentler of the University of California at Los Angeles has documented the long-term behavioral effects of drug use on teenagers.[33] Beginning in 1976 a total of 654 Los Angeles County youths were tracked for a period of eight years. Most of these youths were only occasional users of drugs and alcohol, using them moderately at social gatherings, whereas upwards of 10% were frequent, committed users. The impact of drugs on these frequent users was considerable. Drugs used by teenagers tend to intensify the typical adolescent problems with family and school. In addition, drugs contributed to such psychological difficulties as loneliness, bizarre and disorganized thinking, and suicidal thoughts. Moreover, frequent drug users left school earlier, started jobs earlier, and formed families earlier, and as such, they moved into adult roles with the maturity levels of adolescents. The consequences of this pattern included rapid family break-ups, job instability, serious crime, and ineffective personal relationships. In short, frequent drug use prevented the acquisition of the coping mechanisms that are part of maturing; it blocked teenagers' learning of interpersonal skills and general emotional development.

THE CRIME AND VIOLENCE ARGUMENT

Remember the ''enslavement theory of addiction,'' mentioned briefly in Chapter 5 (it will be examined in depth in Chapter 9)? Essentially, it involves the conviction that because of the high prices of heroin and cocaine on the drug black market, users are forced to commit crimes in order to support their drug habits. In this regard, supporters of drug legalization argue that if the criminal penalties attached to heroin and cocaine possession and sale were removed, three things would occur: the black market would disappear, the prices of heroin and cocaine would decline significantly, and users would no longer have to engage in street crime in order to support their desired levels of drug intake. But there has never been any solid empirical evidence to support the contentions of enslavement theory.

Yet as also pointed out in Chapter 5, research since the middle of the 1970s with active drug users from the streets of New York, Miami, Baltimore, and elsewhere has demonstrated that enslavement theory has little basis in reality, and that the contentions of the legalization proponents in this behalf are mistaken.[34] All of these studies of the criminal careers of heroin and other drug users have convincingly documented that while drug use tends to intensify and perpetuate criminal behavior, it usually does not initiate criminal careers. In fact, the evidence suggests that among the majority of street drug users who are involved in crime, their criminal careers were well established prior to the onset of either narcotics, cocaine, or crack use.

In terms of legalization drugs/violence connection, recall the three models of drug-related violence addressed in Chapters 5 and 7.[35] The psychopharmacologic model of violence suggests that some individuals, as the result of short-term or long-term ingestion of specific substances, may become excitable, irrational, and exhibit violent behavior. The paranoia and aggression associated with the cocaine psychosis fit into the psychopharmacological model, as does most alcohol-related violence. The economically compulsive model of violence holds that some drug users engage in economically oriented violent crime to support drug use. This model is illustrated in the many studies of drug use and criminal behavior which have demonstrated that while drug sales, property crimes, and prostitution are the primary economic offenses committed by users, armed robberies, and muggings do indeed occur. The systemic model of violence maintains that violent crime is intrinsic to the very involvement with illicit substances. As such, systemic violence refers to the traditionally aggressive patterns of inter-action within systems of illegal drug trafficking and distribution.

It is the systemic violence that has become associated with traf-ficking in cocaine and crack in the inner cities which has brought the most attention to drug-related violence in recent years. Moreover, it is concerns with this same violence that focused interest on the possibility of legalizing drugs.[36] And it is certainly logical to assume that if heroin, cocaine, and marijuana were legal substances, systemic drug-related violence would indeed decline significantly. But too, there are some very troubling considerations. First, to achieve the desired declines in systemic violence, it would require that crack be legalized as well. For after all, it is in the crack distribution system that much of the drug-related violence has occurred. Second, it is already clear that there is considerable psychopharmacologic violence associated with the cocaine psychosis. Moreover, research has demonstrated that there is far more psychopharmacologic violence connected with heroin use than is generally believed.[37] Given the fact that drug use would certainly increase with legalization, in all likelihood any declines in systemic violence would be accompanied by corresponding increases in psychopharmacologic violence. The United States already pays a high price for alcohol-related violence, a phenomenon well documented by recent research.[38] Why compound the problem with the legaliza-tion of additional violence-producing substances?

THE EXPANDED MARKET ARGUMENT

An often neglected argument revolves around the assumption that legalization will have minimal impact on use; that most or all those who would use drugs are now using. Such an assumption appears to ignore one of the most powerful aspects of American tradition: the ability of an entrepreneurial market system to create, expand, and maintain high levels of demand.

As noted previously, explicit legalization proposals are few, and there has yet to be a serious discussion of how the issues of adver-tising and marketing might be handled. However, if the treatment of such other legal drugs as alcohol and tobacco are used as models of regulatory control, then it is reasonable to assume an application of free speech rights to legalized drugs. And this indeed would be logical, for after all, the drugs would be legal products. And similarly it would not seem unreasonable to assume that the American market economy would become strongly involved in expanding and maintaining demand for the legalized substances. The successes of tobacco and alcohol advertising programs are eminently conspicuous. The linking of smoking with women's rights has been masterful. The linking of alcohol with the pursuit of happiness after work, in recreational activities, and in romantic liaisons has been so effective that Americans spend tens of billions of dollars each year on beer, wine, and distilled spirits.

In an America where drugs are legal, how far will advertisers go? Will they show students, executives, and truck drivers—overworked and faced with tight schedules and deadlines—reaching for a line of cocaine instead of a cup of coffee? Will cocaine be touted as the mark of success in an achievement oriented society? Will heroin be portrayed as the real way to relax after a harried day? Will the new Marlboro man be smoking marijuana or crack instead of tobacco? These are not fanciful speculations, for there are many controlled substances that are regularly advertised, even if only in medical journals. Regardless, the focus of advertising is to market a product by creating and maintaining demand.

The issue, then, of whether the market is saturated fails to recognize the ability of a free enterprise system to expand demand. And there are epidemiological data that confirm that there is considerable room for increasing the demand for drugs. Estimates projected from the National Institute on Drug Abuse's 1990 household survey of drug abuse suggest that less than 6% of the general population of the United States ages 12 years and older are current users (use during the past month) of marijuana, and less than 1% are current users of cocaine.[39] These are very small proportions. The survey also demonstrated, however, that a fourth of America's adolescents and the majority of young adults are current users of the major available legal drug—alcohol—and that in all, there are no less than 53.6 million current users of cigarettes and more than 102.9 million current users of alcohol. Such numbers represent very significant proportions. To assume that the legalization of drugs would maintain the current, relatively low levels of drug use when there are high rates of both alcohol and tobacco use seems rather naive. Moreover, it considerably underestimates the deterrent effect of the law as well as the advertising industry's ability to create a context of use that appears integral to a meaningful, successful, liberated life.

THE DECLINING DRUG USE TREND ARGUMENT

It would appear that agitation for such a drastic policy change as would be involved in the legalization of drugs is in great part an outgrowth

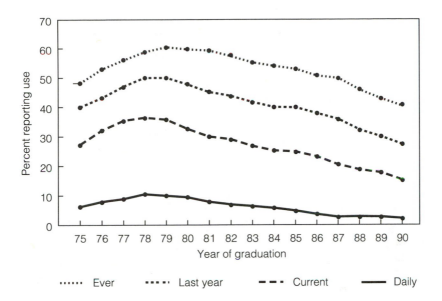

Trends in Marijuana Use Among American High School Students, 1975–1990

of frustration. "After having spent billions of dollars on interdiction, education, prevention, treatment, and research," many ask, "what do we have to show for it?" What indeed do we have to show for it?

To many, the response being offered here might seem a bit odd, but it would appear that to a very measurable extent America is beginning to show some very positive gains in its war on drugs, at least in the middle class. For example, consider the data. First, there is the National Institute on Drug Abuse's annual survey of high school seniors, conducted each year by the University of Michigan.[40] As indicated in the graph above, for example, marijuana use has been on a steady decline since its peak usage levels at the close of the 1970s. Whereas 60.4 percent of high school seniors in 1979 had used marijuana at least once in their lives, by 1990 that figure had dropped to 40.7. Even sharper declines are apparent with regard to use in the past year and current use (any use in the past 30 days). Perhaps the most significant drop was been in the daily use of marijuana, from a high of 10.7% in 1978 to 2.2% in 1990.

The results of the 1990 survey also reflected reductions in cocaine consumption. As indicated in the graph on the following page, the survey found a decrease from 6.2% in 1986 to 1.9% in 1990 in the proportion of seniors who they said were current users of cocaine, and a decline from 12.7% to 5.3% in seniors who had used the drug at least

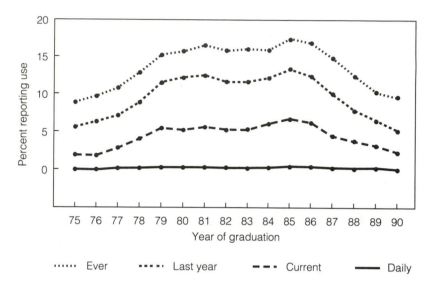

Trends in Cocaine Use Among American High School Students, 1975–1990

once in the past year. The proportion of seniors who had ''ever used'' and who used ''daily'' also declined.

There are other indicators of declining drug use. Since 1980 the University of Michigan survey team has been collecting data on drug use among college students. As indicated in Table 8.1, the proportion of college students reporting ''any use during the past year'' has also declined. Marijuana use has been on a steady decline in this population since 1980, and cocaine use experienced major declines since 1987. Moreover, the use of all other drugs declined when comparing 1980 with 1990. And going further, the National Household Surveys on Drug Abuse conducted by the National Institute on Drug Abuse tend to confirm the findings of the high school surveys.

POSTSCRIPT

It should be pointed out at this juncture that the logic used by those in favor of legalizing drugs is often both simplistic and sophist. They pose the argument, for example, that rates of injury and death from illegal drugs are relatively low when compared with those of alcohol and tobacco use. The logical deduction offered is that heroin and

Table 8.1 Drug Use in the Past Year Among American College Students, 1980–1990

	1980	1981	1982	1983	1984	1985	1986	1987	1988	1989	1990
							Percent Who Used in the Last 12 Months				
Marijuana	51.2	51.3	44.7	45.2	40.7	41.7	40.9	37.0	34.6	33.6	29.4
Cocaine	16.8	16.0	17.2	17.3	16.3	17.3	17.1	13.7	10.0	8.2	5.6
Crack	NA	NA	NA	NA	NA	NA	1.3	2.0	1.4	1.5	0.6
LSD	6.0	4.6	6.3	4.3	3.7	2.2	3.9	4.0	3.6	3.4	4.3
Heroin	0.4	0.2	0.1	0.0	0.1	0.2	0.1	0.2	0.2	0.1	0.1
Other Opiates	5.1	4.3	3.8	3.8	3.8	2.4	4.0	3.1	3.1	3.2	2.9
Barbituates	2.9	2.8	3.2	2.2	1.9	1.3	2.0	1.2	1.1	1.0	1.4
Methaqualone	7.2	6.5	6.6	3.1	2.5	1.4	1.2	0.8	0.5	0.2	NA
Tranquilizers	6.9	4.8	4.7	4.6	3.5	3.6	4.4	3.8	3.1	2.6	3.0
Alcohol	90.5	92.5	92.2	91.6	90.0	92.0	91.5	90.9	89.6	89.6	89.0

Note: For other opiates, barbituates, methaqualone, and tranquilizers, only use that was under a physician's orders is included here.

cocaine aren't really all that bad, and hence should be legalized. What is summarily ignored is that the death rates from alcohol and tobacco use are high because these substances are readily available and widely used, and that the death rates from heroin and cocaine use are low because these drugs are not readily available and not widely used. And indeed, as already demonstrated, illegal drugs are not widely used!

Another feature of the legalizers' circular thinking involves their portrayal of the drug enforcement establishment as an ineffective, inefficient, power hungry, and sometimes corrupt bureaucracy attempting to enforce impossible laws. Yet this cynical disdain for drug enforcement is replaced with a naive faith in the effectiveness of government regulation. Don't criminalize drugs, they argue, legalize and regulate them. While the specifics of regulation have yet to emerge, all of the legalization proposals actually involve increased regulation. Yet with alcohol and tobacco, it is clear that regulation doesn't work very well. Using the alcohol analogy, the legalizers seem to be suggesting that American society's best defense against the use of cocaine and crack by youths is to distribute the drugs to those 21 years and older but only after carefully explaining to them that they must not share their government-sanctioned-and-supplied drugs with adolescents. The point is that there is a real naivete to the belief that drug laws are unenforceable but drug regulations are.

Shifting to an alternative segment of the debate, many drug legalization proponents seem to believe that the willingness of political conservatives and free market economists to support their arguments somehow provides them with at least the appearance of broad-based social and even moral support. Yet the fact that a few free market economists support legalization should be seen for the purely material, or at least intellectual, self-interest that it is. Nineteenth-century capitalists were willing to fight a war in China to keep opiates legal. From a free market economic perspective, producing, distributing, and expanding the market for a product that is immediately consumed and readily addictive would appear to be a fantasy come true.

Under the free market arrangement, would there be the so-called market segmentation practices that the alcohol and tobacco industries use for targeting their products toward blacks and other minorities in America's inner cities? Even if this were prohibited, since research has documented that illegal drug use is concentrated in the inner city, under the free market system, drug use in all likelihood would expand dramatically in socioeconomically marginal communities. Urban ghettos are not particularly pleasant places in which to live. There are vice, crime, and littered streets. There is the desolation of people separated culturally, socially, materially, and politically from the mainstream. There are the disadvantages of a tangle of economic, family, and other problems—delinquency, teenage pregnancy, unemployment, child neglect, poor housing, substandard schools, inadequate health care, and limited opportunities. There are many modes of adaptation to ghetto life. One of them is drug use, perhaps the main cause of higher drug use rates in inner cities. And it is for this reason that a free market for heroin, cocaine, crack, and other drugs would be a nightmare.

The social fabric of the ghetto is already tattered, and drugs are further shredding what is left of the fragile ghetto family. A great number of inner city families are headed by women, and for reasons that are not at all clear, women seem to be more disposed to become dependent on crack-cocaine than men—further increasing the problems of child abuse and neglect. Within this context, in large part the legalization of drugs would function as a program of social management and control that would serve to legitimate the chemical destruction of an urban generation and culture. As such, legalization would be an elitist and racist policy supporting the old neocolonialist views of underclass population control.

In untangling the logic of the legalization thesis, a more focused look should be directed towards those who make up the pro-legalization lobby. In all likelihood their arguments are born of frustration—frustration with the lack of immediate major successes in the prevention and control of drug use. Part of the problem is reflected in the old saying about a little bit of knowledge being dangerous. As academics, economists, and civil libertarians from outside the drug field, their experiences have rarely, if at all, exposed them to the full dynamics of addiction, drug craving, and drug-taking and drug-seeking behaviors. It should be noticed as well that those who have spent their lives and careers in the trenches researching the drug problem, treating the drug problem, or otherwise coping with the drug problem feel that legalization would initiate a public health problem of unrestrained proportions.[41]

Notes

1. See Raymond Glasscote, James N. Sussex, Jerome H. Jaffe, John Ball, and Leon Brill, *The Treatment of Drug Abuse: Programs, Problems, Prospects* (Washington, DC: American Psychiatric Association, 1972); Marvin R. Burt, Sharon Pines, and Thomas J. Glynn, *Drug Abuse: Its Natural History and the Effectiveness of Current Treatments* (Cambridge: Schenkman, 1979); Barry S. Brown, ed., *Addicts and Aftercare: Community Integration of the Former Drug User* (Beverly Hills: Sage, 1979).
2. James A. Inciardi, "The Effectiveness of Addiction Treatment," *Addiction Therapist*, Autumn 1975, pp. 2–5.
3. See John Dombrink and James W. Meeker, "Beyond 'Buy and Bust': Non-traditional Sanctions in Federal Drug Law Enforcement," *Contemporary Drug Problems*, 13 (Winter 1986), pp. 711–740; John Dombrink and James W. Meeker, "Racketeering Prosecution: The Use and Abuse of RICO,"

Rutgers Law Journal, 16 (Spring/Summer 1985), pp. 632–654; James Meeker and John Dombrink, "Criminal RICO and Organized Crime: An Analysis of Appellate Litigation," *Criminal Law Bulletin*, 20 (July/Aug. 1984), pp. 309–320; *U.S. News & World Report*, 5 Dec. 1988, pp. 20–22; United States General Accounting Office, *Profitability of Customs Forfeiture Program Can be Enhanced* (Washington, DC: General Accounting Office, 1989); *New York Times*, 7 Jan. 1990, p. 13; *Drug Enforcement Report*, 23 Apr. 1990, p. 8.

4. *Extradition Treaty Between the United States of America and the Republic of Colombia*, Senate Treaty Document 97–98, 97th Congress, 1st Session. See also Committee on Foreign Relations, *Extradition Treaty with the Republic of Colombia*, Senate Report to Accompany Treaty Document 97–98, 20 Nov. 1981; Mary Ann Forney, "Extradition and Drug Trafficking," in James A. Inciardi, ed., *Handbook of Drug Control in the United States* (Westport, CT: Greenwood Press, 1990), pp. 327–338.

5. See *Drug Law Enforcement: Military Assistance for Anti-Drug Agencies* (Washington, DC: United States General Accounting Office, 1987); David C. Morrison, "The Pentagon's Drug Wars," *National Journal*, 6 Sept. 1986, pp. 13–19; Steven Zimmerman, "Posse Comitatus," *Drug Enforcement*, Summer 1982, pp. 17–22; *Drug Enforcement*, Summer 1984, p. 33; *United States Statutes at Large*, 45th Cong., 1877–1879, vol. 20, p. 152.

6. For descriptions of the military involvement and high technology approaches to drug enforcement, see *Wall Street Journal*, 5 Aug. 1982, pp. 1, 8; *Newsweek*, 9 Aug. 1982, pp. 14–15; *Motor Boating & Sailing*, Sept. 1982, pp. 46–49, 107–109; *National Law Journal*, 1 Nov. 1982, pp. 3, 17; *Miami Herald*, 23 Jan. 1983, p. 11A; *Miami Herald*, 17 July 1983, p. 1A; *National Law Journal*, 13 Feb. 1984, pp. 1, 27–28; *Time*, 13 May 1985, p. 27; *New York Times*, 30 June 1985, p. E4; *New York Times*, 10 Mar. 1990, pp. 1, 5; *Time*, 22 Jan. 1990, pp. 22–23; United States General Accounting Office, *DOD Counter-Drug Activities: GAO Review of DOD's Compliance With FY 1989 DOD Authorization Act* (Washington, DC: General Accounting Office, 1989); Richard Mackenzie, "Borderline Victories on Drug War's Front Line," *Insight*, 14 Jan. 1991, pp. 8–17.

7. For a discussion of the philosophy of zero-tolerance, see *Drug Abuse Report*, 19 Apr. 1988, p. 6; *Drug Abuse Report*, 3 May 1988, pp. 1–3; U.S. Department of Transportation, Office of Public Affairs, *Transportation Facts*, "Zero Tolerance Policy on Illegal Drugs," 6 June 1988; Department of the Treasury, U.S. Customs Service, "Zero Tolerance Made Plain," *Southern Boating*, Oct. 1988, pp. 86–88; *New York Times*, 12 Apr. 1988, pp. A1, A10; *Drug Enforcement Report*, 8 July 1988, pp. 1–2; *U.S. News & World Report*, 6 June 1988, p. 11.

8. *Time*, 23 May 1988, p. 55; *Boat/U.S. Reports*, XXIV (May 1989), pp. 1, 7.

9. *National Law Journal*, 7 Nov. 1988, pp. 3, 9; *In Command*, Fall 1989, p. 5; *Miami Herald*, 20 May 1988, pp. 1A, 24A; *Drug Enforcement Report*, 8 June 1988, p. 3; *Drug Enforcement Report*, 23 Sept. 1988, p. 6; *Drug Enforcement Report*, 8 Mar. 1989, p. 4; *Drug Enforcement Report*, 24 Apr. 1989, p. 4; *Drug Enforcement Report*, 8 Nov. 1989, p. 4; *Boat/U.S. Reports*, XXIII (Nov./Dec. 1988), pp. 1–2.

10. *In Command*, Aug. 1988, p. 5.

11. See, for example, Steven Wisotsky, *Breaking the Impasse in the War on Drugs* (Westport, CT: Greenwood Press, 1986); Arnold S. Trebach, *The Great Drug War* (New York: Macmillan, 1987); Louis Kraar, "The Drug Trade," *Fortune*, 20 June 1988, pp. 27–38.

12. See James A. Inciardi, "Debating the Legalization of Drugs," *American Behavioral Scientist*, 32 (Jan./Feb. 1989), pp. 233–242.

13. *New York Times*, 11 Apr. 1988, p. A12.

14. *Drug Smuggling: Large Amounts of Illegal Drugs Not Seized by Federal Authorities* (Washington, DC: United States General Accounting Office, 1987).

15. Maurice Rinfret, "Cocaine Price, Purity, and Trafficking Trends," National Institutional Institute on Drug Abuse Technical Review on the Epidemiology of Cocaine Use and Abuse, Rockville, Maryland, 3–4 May 1988.

16. United States Department of State, Bureau of International Narcotics Matters, *International Narcotics Control Strategy Report*, 1 March 1988.

17. For the most complete account of trafficker intimidation in Colombia, see Fabio Castillo, *Los Jinetes de la Cocaina* (Bogota: Editorial Documentos Periodisticos, 1987). See also, Paul Eddy, Hugo Sabogal, and Sara Walden, *The Cocaine Wars* (New York: W. W. Norton, 1988).

18. See Ethan A. Nadelmann, "U.S. Drug Policy: A Bad Export," *Foreign Policy*, 70 (Spring 1988), pp. 83–108; Ethan A. Nadelmann, "The Real International Drug Problem" (Paper presented at the *Defense Academic Research Support Conference*, "International Drugs: Threat and Response," National Defense College, Defense Intelligence Analysis Center, Washington, D.C., 2–3 June 1987); Ethan A. Nadelmann, "The Case for Legalization," *The Public Interest*, 92 (Summer 1988), pp. 3–31; Ethan A. Nadelmann, "Drug Prohibition in the United States," Costs, Consequences, and Alternatives," *Science*, 245 (1 Sept. 1989), pp. 939–947.

19. Milton Friedman and Rose Friedman, *Tyranny of the Status Quo* (San Diego: Harcourt Brace Jovanovich, 1984), pp. 132–141; Milton Friedman, "An Open Letter to Bill Bennett," *Wall Street Journal*, 7 Sept. 1989, p. A14.

20. Arnold S. Trebach, "Effects of the Drug War on Constitutional Guaranties," *Drug Law Report*, 2 (Jan.–Feb. 1989), pp. 248–258; Arnold S. Trebach, "A Bundle of Peaceful Compromises," *Journal of Drug Issues*, 20 (Fall 1990), pp. 515–531.

21. The arguments *against* legalization presented here are drawn from James A. Inciardi and Duane C. McBride, "Legalization: A High-Risk Alternative in the War on Drugs," *American Behavioral Scientist*, 32 (Jan./Feb. 1989), pp. 259–289; James A. Inciardi and Duane C. McBride, "Debating the Legalization of Drugs," in James A. Inciardi, ed., *Handbook of Drug Control in the United States* (Westport, CT: Greenwood Press, 1990), pp. 283–299.

22. See *Drug Abuse Report*, 17 May 1988, p. 7.

23. See Lester Grinspoon, *Marihuana Reconsidered* (Cambridge: Harvard University Press, 1971); David E. Smith, ed., *The New Social Drug: Cultural, Medical, and Legal Perspectives on Marijuana* (Englewood Cliffs, NJ: Prentice-Hall, 1970); Larry Sloman, *Reefer Madness: The History of Marijuana in America* (Indianapolis: Bobbs-Merrill, 1979).

24. For a thorough discussion and analysis of these points, see, Helen C. Jones and Paul W. Lovinger, *The Marijuana Question* (New York: Dodd, Mead, 1985).

25. Donald Ian Macdonald, ''Marijuana Smoking Worse for Lungs,'' *Journal of the American Medical Association*, 259 (17 June 1988), p. 3384; C. Nora Chiang and Richard L. Hawks, eds., *Research Findings on Smoking of Abused Substances* (Rockville, MD: National Institute on Drug Abuse, 1990).

26. *Street Pharmacologist*, May/June 1988, p. 5.

27. Herbert Hendin, Ann Pollinger Haas, Paul Singer, Melvin Ellner, and Richard Ulman, *Living High: Daily Marijuana Use Among Adults* (New York: Human Sciences Press, 1987).

28. See Robert L. DuPont, *Getting Tough on Gateway Drugs* (Washington, DC: American Psychiatric Press, 1984), pp. 80–83; John W. Spencer and John J. Boren, eds., *Residual Effects of Abused Drug on Behavior* (Rockville, MD: National Institute on Drug Abuse, 1990).

29. See Dina Van Pelt, ''AIDS Patients Seek a Legal High,'' *Insight*, 14 Jan. 1991, pp. 50–51.

30. Roger D. Weiss and Steven M. Mirin, *Cocaine* (Washington, DC: American Psychiatric Press, 1987), pp. 50–53.

31. This point of view is most thoroughly articulated in Arnold S. Trebach, *The Heroin Solution* (New Haven: Yale University Press, 1982).

32. See Anonymous, *Twenty Years in Hell, or the Life, Experience, Trials, and Tribulations of a Morphine Fiend* (Kansas City, MO: Author's Edition, 1903); William Burroughs, *Junkie* (New York: Ace, 1953); Seymour Fiddle, *Portraits From a Shooting Gallery* (New York: Harper & Row, 1967); Florrie Fisher, *The Lonely Trip Back* (New York: Bantam, 1972); Phil Hirsch, *Hooked* (New York: Pyramid, 1968); Leroy Street, *I Was a Drug Addict* (New York: Random House, 1953); Leroy Gould, Andrew L. Walker, Lansing E. Crane, and Charles W. Litz, *Connections: Notes from the Heroin World* (New Haven: Yale University Press, 1974); Richard P. Rettig, Manual J. Torres, and Gerald R. Garrett, *Manny: A Criminal-Addict's Story* (Boston: Houghton Mifflin, 1977); Marsha Rosenbaum, *Women on Heroin* (New Brunswick, NJ: Rutgers University Press, 1981); David E. Smith and George R. Gay, eds., *''It's So Good, Don't Even Try It Once''* (Englewood Cliffs, NJ: Prentice-Hall, 1971); Marie Nyswander, *The Drug Addict as a Patient* (New York: Grune & Stratton, 1956); Jerome J. Platt, *Heroin Addiction* (Malabar, FL: Robert E. Krieger, 1986); Stanton Peele, *The Meaning of Addiction* (Lexington, MA: Lexington Books, 1985); David Courtwright, Herman Joseph, and Don Des Jarlais, *Addicts Who Survived: An Oral History of Narcotic Use in America, 1923–1965* (Knoxville: University of Tennessee Press, 1989).

33. Michael D. Newcomb and Peter M. Bentler, *Consequences of Adolescent Drug Use: Impact on the Lives of Young Adults* (Newbury Park, CA: Sage, 1988).

34. See, James A. Inciardi, *The War on Drugs: Heroin, Cocaine, Crime, and Public Policy* (Palo Alto, CA: Mayfield, 1986), pp. 115–143; Bruce D. Johnson, Paul J. Goldstein, Edward Preble, James Schmeidler, Douglas S. Lipton, Barry Spunt, and Thomas Miller, *Taking Care of Business: The Economics of Crime by Heroin Users* (Lexington, MA: Lexington Books, 1985); David N. Nurco, John C. Ball, John W. Shaffer, and Thomas F. Hanlon, ''The Criminality of Narcotic Addicts,'' *Journal of Nervous and Mental Disease*, 173 (1985), pp. 94–102; Richard C. Stephens and Duane C. McBride, ''Becoming a Street Addict,'' *Human Organization*, 35 (1976), pp. 87–93; Duane C. McBride and Clyde B. McCoy, ''Crime and Drugs: The Issues and the

Literature," *Journal of Drug Issues*, Spring 1982, pp. 137–152; James A. Inciardi and Anne E. Pottieger, "Kids, Crack, and Crime," *Journal of Drug Issues*, 21 (Spring 1991), pp. 257–270.

35. Paul J. Goldstein, "Homicide Related to Drug Traffic," *Bulletin of the New York Academy of Medicine*, 62 (June 1986), pp. 509–516.

36. See *Time*, 30 May 1988, pp. 12–19; *USA Today*, 18 May 1988, p. 10A; *Drug Abuse Report*, 6 Apr. 1988, pp. 7–8; Wilmington (Delaware) *News-Journal*, 3 Apr. 1988, p. E2; *Newsweek*, 30 May 1988, pp. 36–38; *Fortune*, 20 June 1988, pp. 39–41; *New York Times*, 2 June 1988, p. A26.

37. See Paul J. Goldstein, *Prostitution and Drugs* (Lexington, MA: Lexington Books, 1979), p. 126; Duane C. McBride, "Drugs and Violence," in James A. Inciardi, ed., *The Drugs-Crime Connection* (Beverly Hills: Sage, 1981), pp. 105–123; James A. Inciardi, *The War on Drugs*, p. 135.

38. James J. Collins, ed., *Drinking and Crime: Perspectives on the Relationships between Alcohol Consumption and Criminal Behavior* (New York: Guilford Press, 1981).

39. *National Household Survey on Drug Abuse: Population Estimates 1990* (Rockville, MD: National Institute on Drug Abuse, 1991).

40. University of Michigan News and Information Services Release, January 23, 1991.

41. This point is shared elsewhere in the world. For example, see Madrid (Spain) *Cambia*, 2 Oct. 89, pp. 12–17; Windsor (England) *Star*, 27 Dec. 1989, p. A14; Paris *Match*, 25 Jan. 1990, pp. 102–103; Bogota (Colombia) *El Tiempo*, 19 Apr. 1990, p. 6B; Lausanne (Switzerland) *L'Hebdo*, 2 Aug. 1990, pp. 10–13; Brasilia (Brazil) *Correio Braziliense*, 1 Sept. 1990, p. 3; La Paz (Bolivia) *Presencia*, 16 Feb. 1989, p. 7; Peshawar (Pakistan) *Frontier Post*, 29 Jan. 1989, p. 5; *Vienna Domestic Service*, 0500 GMT, 8 Sept. 1989; Copenhagen (Denmark) *Berlingske Tidende*, 31 May 1988, p. 6; Buenos Aires (Argentina) *Clarin*, 10 Aug. 1988, p. 31.

雞馬

特選頂上道地原料拣
專門人材秘法精製
十足天良好信用昭著
承蒙光顧諸君愛
請認鷄馬老牌為難記
特此聲明以杜假冒
五九年本主人謹白

鷄馬牌辦真券

WHERE DO WE GO FROM HERE?
Some Considerations on Heroin, Cocaine, Crack,
Crime, AIDS, and American Drug Policy

In 1974 at a time when heroin and Quaaludes were the major drugs of abuse and cocaine was only in a starting phase of its takeover of the American drug scene, the noted psychiatrist Thomas Szasz commented in his book *Ceremonial Chemistry:*

> The plain historical facts are that before 1914 there was no "drug problem" in the United States; nor did we have a name for it. Today there is an immense drug problem in the United States, and we have lots of names for it. Which came first: "the problem of drug abuse" or its name? It is the same as asking which came first: the chicken or the egg? All we can be sure of now is that the more chickens, the more eggs, and vice versa; and similarly, the more problems, the more names for them, and vice versa. My point is simply that our drug abuse experts, legislators, psychiatrists, and other professional guardians of our medical morals have been operating chicken hatcheries: they continue—partly by means of certain characteristic tactical abuses of our language—to manufacture and maintain the "drug problem" they ostensibly try to solve.[1]

Szasz certainly does have a way with words. He was suggesting something that nominalists have been saying for centuries: that a thing does not exist until it is imagined and given a name. For Szasz, a hopeless believer in this position, the "drug problem" in the United States did not exist before the passage of the Harrison Act in 1914, but became a reality when the behavior under consideration was labeled as a problem. If one were to read Szasz's entire volume, despite the numerous errors of fact, poor scholarship, and his caustic abuse of the English language, his point would be clear: the drug problem in

America was created in great part by the very policies designed to control it. On the other hand, one could save a good bit of time by just glancing at the subtitle of the Szasz book: *The Ritual Persecution of Drugs, Addicts, and Pushers*—it seems to convey the same message.

MASTURBATION, ENSLAVEMENT THEORY, AND THE "BRITISH SYSTEM"

The position taken by Szasz has been fashionable for quite some time. Others have attacked American drug-control policies with equal vigor and zeal. Washington attorney Rufus King described the issue as a 50-year folly, a misguided and ineffective endeavor.[2] David F. Musto's classic *The American Disease* offered a similar perspective, although accomplished with considerable scholarship.[3] Then there were a number of early social scientists, among the first to speak out against the federal approach to drug control. Alfred R. Lindesmith, for example, who probably spent a good part of his professional career condemning federal policies, summed up his position in a 1956 issue of *The Nation:*

> For 40 years the United States has tried in vain to control the problem of drug addiction by prohibition and police suppression. The disastrous consequences of turning over to the police what is an essentially medical problem are steadily becoming more apparent as narcotic arrests rise each year to new records and the habit continues to spread, especially among young persons. Control by prohibition has failed; but the proposed remedies for this failure consist mainly of more of the same measures which have already proved futile.[4]

For Dr. Szasz the solution to the drug problem is simple. Ignore it, and it will no longer be a problem. After all, he maintained, there is precedent for it:

> What does this larger view show us? How can it help us? It shows us that our present attitudes toward the whole subject of drug use, drug abuse, and drug control are nothing but the reflections, in the mirror of "social reality," of our own expectations toward drugs and toward those who use them; and that our ideas about and interventions in drug-taking behavior have only the most tenuous connection with the

actual pharmacological properties of "dangerous drugs." The "danger" of masturbation disappeared when we ceased to believe in it: when we ceased to attribute danger to the practice and to its practitioners; and ceased to call it "self-abuse."⁵

What Szasz seems to be suggesting is that heroin, cocaine, and other "dangerous drugs" be legalized; hence, the problems associated with their use would disappear. Rufus King, Alfred Lindesmith, and most others who spoke out against American drug-control policies in the pre-crack era favored the so-called "British system" as the answer to the problem.⁶

The logic of the British system of drug control, as it would relate to the American drug scene at any rate, is grounded in an idea that has been referred to elsewhere in this volume as the enslavement theory of addiction. The whole notion of enslavement theory is intricately tied to the complex relationship between drug abuse and criminal behavior, for it suggests that essentially law-abiding individuals become criminals as the result of drug use. That is, the high price that the drug black market imposes forces users to commit crimes to support their habits. Thus, criminality is the result of enslavement to drugs and the drug black market.

Although the origins of the theory date back to nineteenth-century America with the early clinical writings about morphine dependence, its most complete statement appears in the work of David W. Maurer and Victor H. Vogel. In the third edition of their *Narcotics and Narcotic Addiction*, Maurer and Vogel stated:

> *First*, the potential addict begins to take very small doses of some addicting drug, let us say morphine, or heroin. He either does not realize what the drug will do to him, or he knows that others have become addicted but believes that it will never happen to him. . . .
>
> *Second*, the addict notices that the amount of the drug he has been taking does not "hold" him, and, if he is addiction-prone, he no longer experiences the intense pleasure which he felt in the very early stages of the use of the drug. If he has been "pleasure-shooting" (taking small doses at intervals of several days or several weeks) he notices that he must increase these in size to continue to get any pleasure from the drug; eventually, of course, he will also increase the frequency until he is taking a shot four to six times daily. . . .
>
> *Third*, as the habit increases in size over a period of weeks or months, the addict who must buy his drugs from bootleg sources finds that more and more of his wages go for drugs

and that he has less and less for the other necessities; in fact, other things come to mean less and less to him, and he becomes heavily preoccupied with simply supporting his habit. . . .

Fourth, it becomes obvious to him that he must have increasing amounts of money on a regular basis, and that legitimate employment is not likely to supply that kind of money. . . . *Therefore, some form of crime is the only alternative.*[7]

The theory, of course, is not without some logic. As already pointed out in Chapter 1, during the latter part of the nineteenth century and the early years of the twentieth, the use of narcotics was fairly widespread, and both morphine and heroin were readily available through legal channels. When the Harrison Act was passed, users had to embrace the black market to obtain their drugs. Since that time, the possession of heroin has remained a crime, and most users seem to have criminal records.

The theory also has a basis in empirical research. As noted in Chapter 5, from the 1920s through the 1970s, the findings almost overwhelmingly indicated that narcotics use preceded criminal activity. Hence, as the enslavement theorists suggested, the inference of causality seemed clear—drug use caused crime. Perhaps it was so, but more likely it was an outgrowth of research biased by the reliance on arrest records as the sole indicators of criminality. For it is clear, at least within highly criminal populations, that only an insignificant proportion of the offenses committed by drug offenders actually result in arrest.[8] There were other biases as well, for as pointed out in Chapter 5, subsequent research demonstrated that while drug use tends to intensify and perpetuate criminal careers, it does not necessarily initiate them.

Within this context, the British system began in 1926 when a Ministry of Health committee headed by Sir Henry Rolleston recommended that addicts should receive narcotic prescriptions in the hope that they would eventually be withdrawn from their drugs.[9] For decades the system was simply a policy that permitted private physicians to prescribe maintenance doses to heroin and morphine users. Addicts were registered in that their names were kept in a file at the Home Office, and at any time it appeared possible to readily calculate the rate of heroin addiction by simply counting the names on file. It did seem to work. In the mid-1950s Britain had but a few hundred known addicts, and crime in the streets by heroin users was unheard of.[10]

Not too long after the American post–World War II heroin epidemic had begun, some argued for bringing the British system to the United States. Almost always, the frame of reference was reducing the crime problem. New York neurologist Hubert S. Howe contended before the American Association for the Advancement of Science in 1957:

> After more than 40 years of diligent enforcement, the Harrison
> Act has failed to accomplish its purpose. Instead, we have a
> black market, with its insidious train of crime.[11]

Dr. Howe went on to suggest implementation of the British approach, adding that "the only way to get rid of the black markets is to undersell them."

There were others who favored what was going on in Britain, but the issue received only minimal publicity. This all changed with the publication of Edwin M. Schur's *Narcotic Addiction in Britain and America* in 1962.[12] Professor Schur presented a thorough and rational argument, contrasting the punitive laws and enforcement procedures in the United States with the solution in Great Britain that appeared to be considerably more sane, humane, and successful.

In retrospect the British approach to narcotic addiction seemed to work for a good many decades primarily because the addiction rate in England was low and most patients were medically addicted. Moreover, there was no street subculture of addicts. As such the system was tailored to fit a favorable addiction situation and for that reason, and probably for that reason alone, it was successful. But when the cultural and drug revolutions emerged in the United States during the 1960s, they arrived in England at the same time. New populations of drug users began to surface, and the heroin addiction rate began to increase as did the abuse of other drugs and the presence of a drug subculture and black market. Because of this, in 1967 the system was adjusted in Great Britain. No longer could addicts obtain opiate prescriptions from private physicians. A government-sponsored program took charge, putting strict controls over opiates and requiring addicts to be registered officially and treated through clinics or specially licensed physicians.[13]

As the British system moved into the 1970s, addiction continued to increase, the drug black market prospered, and the system began shifting its patients from heroin to methadone. Moreover, most heroin users were not registering because the clinic system was not providing them with the amount of heroin and other drugs they desired. By 1980 England's thriving black market in heroin, cocaine, and other illegal drugs had become a major enterprise. One needed only to walk the back streets of London's East End to draw that conclusion.

Then in 1982 Arnold S. Trebach's monograph *The Heroin Solution* was published.[14] Trebach had undertaken a thorough examination of both the American and British drug scenes. He was aware that the treatment system in England was failing, that there was an active drug black market, that rates of addiction and drug abuse were on the rise, and that there was the growing problem of drug-related street crime. Nevertheless, he made the prediction:

. . . Nor do I see the English addiction problem coming even close to the dimensions or character of the American. In comparative ornithological terms, I still see a gentle English addiction sparrow and, across the ocean, a predatory American heroin eagle.[15]

There was more. Trebach went on to argue that the British had given up prematurely on their original system, that the prescribing of heroin and cocaine to drug users by private physicians should have been left intact, and that physicians in the United States should be given a free hand to do the same:

. . . by extending to many doctors the power to prescribe narcotics, including heroin, for addicts, we would be taking addicts off the streets, out of police lockups, out of prisons, and placing them in doctors' offices.[16]

Although Trebach's proposal was unquestionably humanitarian, it was also, at the very best, naive. The British system was adjusted in 1967 to shift away from the private physician for some very good reasons. It had worked for the small cohort of addicts that represented England's drug problem for decades, but when the 1960s witnessed the spread of drug abuse on a worldwide scale, drug taking in Britain began to increase sharply with a new breed of user—one who was part of a growing drug subculture that purchased its drugs on an already developed black market.

There are also more pragmatic issues. So many cultural differences exist between England and the United States that a successful transplant is anything but assured. Moreover, the heroin-using population in the United States is a highly criminal population. In all likelihood most American physicians would prefer that addicts remain out of their communities—not to speak of their offices. The success of the transplant is grounded in a belief in the enslavement theory of addiction—that the high cost of drugs leads to crime. And perhaps most importantly, despite the purported logical and pragmatic nature of the so-called British system, throughout the 1980s the number of addicts continued to expand.[17] By the beginning of the 1990s a report from England's Institute for the Study of Drug Dependence put the number of heroin addicts at 100,000, representing a doubling since 1985.[18] Interestingly, what this means is that from 1985 through 1990, the heroin addiction rate in England went from 88.6 to 174.2 per 100,000 population. In the United States, where the number of heroin addicts has remained relatively stable at 500,000, the addiction rate actually declined over this same period, from 209.3 per 100,000 population in 1985 to 198.8 in 1990.[a]

Shifting back to Alfred R. Lindesmith, even he, whose endorsement of this approach came before drug abuse spread across Western Europe causing the British clinic system to falter, cannot be excused for such an indiscretion. It was apparent well before the drug revolution of the 1960s that the addict population in Great Britain was unique—small and composed primarily of medical addicts. As for Rufus King and the others, the best that can be said is that they were armchair crusaders who had little direct contact with life in the street worlds of heroin, cocaine, and crime. Moreover, even if the British system worked, that would address only the heroin problem. And since most heroin users are involved with other drugs as well, even then the system would be problematic.

If not the British system, what then?

IS THE WAR ON DRUGS BEING WON?
CAN THE WAR ON DRUGS BE WON?
SHOULD THE WAR ON DRUGS BE FOUGHT?

To these three questions, one could answer, respectively, ''Yes, to some extent, at least in the middle class''; ''Perhaps, to some degree at any rate''; and ''Yes, why not?''

The high-tech/military-assistance/asset-forfeiture approach to drug enforcement described in Chapter 8 has had some successes, but it also has had its critics.[19] Some hold that the expenditures involved outweigh the gains achieved. And this may be a justifiable criticism. It has been reported, for example, that since 1986 the U.S. Customs Service spent more than $100 million to test, build, and deploy seven radar balloons along the U.S.-Mexican border, with less than 50 smugglers being apprehended in the effort.[20] The same report noted that in 1989, after sailing for a combined 2,347 ship days costing $33,200,000, the U.S. Navy and U.S. Coast Guard seized only 7 ships and arrested only 40 smugglers.[21] No doubt the Navy and Coast Guard were involved in

---

[a] The population figures used to compute these rates are based on Population Reference Bureau estimates: England—56.4 million in both 1985 and 1990; United States—238.9 million in 1985 and 251.4 million in 1990.

other business as well during these sorties, but these and other data support the contentions of those who argue that since the war cannot be won at all, why squander military and other government resources?

Such criticisms do make some sense. After all, the borders of the United States present a difficult control problem. There are 96,000 miles of land border and coastline in addition to the many internal ports of arrival for international air cargo and travelers. Large numbers of people and conveyances cross these borders each year: 309 million legal travelers, 50,000 vessels, 13 million tons of containerized cargo, and tens of thousands of small vessels and general aviation aircraft.[22] Finally, there are many who continue to argue that drug abuse is either a medical problem or a definitional issue and should not even be a matter dealt with by the government. Given these varying opinions, what then?

In answering this question one is reminded of Sir Winston Churchill's well-known comment about democracy: that it is the worst system devised by the wit of man "except for all the others." For despite the many criticisms and objections, there are indications that contemporary American drug control policies might be backed with at least some of the appropriate weaponry. After all, to a very visible extent the war on drugs has won a few major skirmishes in recent years.

Heroin addiction is far from being solved, and perhaps it never will be. But at least it has been contained to some degree, and rates appear to be declining. In fact it is very probable that of all the nations in the world where a heroin problem exists, the United States is the only country where the rates of heroin use are actually going down. In addition there are other positive indicators: as already noted, the proportion of mainstream youth who report trying illicit drugs has declined, and the percent of high school seniors who are daily users of drugs has also declined. In addition, the perceived harmfulness of using such drugs as marijuana and cocaine has increased substantially during the past decade; smaller percentages of American youths are reporting approval of drug use and larger percentages are reporting their friends don't use drugs; and the social, political, economic, and religious attitudes of young America are increasingly conservative and anti-drug.[23] Finally, in the drug treatment field, higher levels of patient success have become apparent.[24] In other words, although America may not as yet have turned the corner on the drug problem, at least the end of the street is finally seen over the horizon.

Yet despite these gains there are some central weaknesses in the current U.S. approach to drug-abuse control. The war on drugs indeed has the right weapons, but many of them are not pointed in the right directions. The major shortcomings appear to be in the areas of resource allocation and leadership.

It is eminently sensible to maintain effective supply-side programs aimed at keeping heroin, cocaine, marijuana, and other illegal drugs

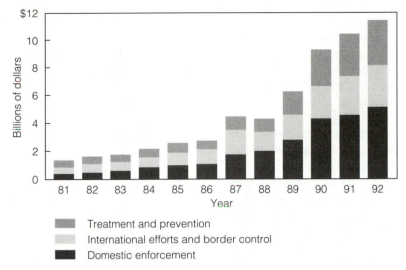

The Drug War's Growing Budget. Obligated budget allocations for fiscal years through 1990, Congressionally enacted spending for 1991, and the Administration's budget request for 1992.

out of the country. However, the emphasis of federal policy has been a bit lopsided. Between 1981 and the passage of the Anti-Drug Abuse Act of 1986, federal funding for drug treatment was cut by 40%. The results included sharp reductions in the available number of treatment slots, overcrowded treatment centers, and the turning away of tens of thousands of drug abusers seeking help. Then, as illustrated in the graph above, of the billions of dollars authorized each year for drug control, most were earmarked for domestic enforcement and interdiction efforts (e.g., international activities and border control). For Fiscal Year 1992, for example, the budget request for federal antidrug efforts was $11.6 billion, a considerable amount of money. However, only 30% of these resources were slated for demand reduction activities (treatment, prevention, education, and research), with the remaining for supply reduction activities.[25]

The difficulty lies in the fact that allocating resources for warring on drugs is always more of a political rather than a commonsense process. Arrests and seizures are easy to count, making for attractive press releases and useful political fodder. And these numbers can indeed be dramatic—each year, tens of thousands of arrests and even greater numbers for the amounts of drugs seized. By contrast, reporting on the number of persons in treatment is far less impressive to a constituency. But the tragedy of it all is that the waiting time for treatment entry in some cities is up to a year. This is an especially critical issue with regard to injecting heroin and cocaine users, for as already noted in Chapter 6, their needle-sharing practices have made them the second highest risk group for HIV and AIDS.

Then there is the matter of leadership. Winning any war requires strong and decisive guidance on all fronts; it demands unified and attentive strategies and the cooperation of the joint chiefs of staff. Saddam Hussein learned that the hard way during the early weeks of 1991. But in terms of leadership and cooperative strategy, there have been times when the war on drugs has looked more like the rag-tag antics of a Saddam Hussein than an effort orchestrated by the most powerful nation on earth. For example, there are no less than 11 cabinet departments, 32 federal agencies (from the FBI and the National Parks Service to the Department of Education), and at least 5 independent agencies with some responsibility for drug control. Not unexpectedly such a situation can undermine drug control endeavors through duplications of effort and agency turf battles, which it has.

To remedy this situation, on more than one occasion during the Reagan administration, Senator Joseph R. Biden (D.-Del) sponsored a bill known as the National Narcotics Leadership Act, which called for a new cabinet-level position to head the federal war on drugs, a post that the media dubbed "drug czar." "Without some central, coordinated mechanism in place," Biden argued, "with the statutory and political authority to do the job, each agency will continue to pursue its own narrow agenda, with little or no concern for the effectiveness of the overall program."[26] Reagan rejected the drug czar idea, and the war on drugs went on—stumbling but forward nevertheless.

With the coming of George Bush to the White House in 1989, with it apparent that the drug czar idea and a new drug initiative appealed to him, Democrats in the House and Senate began hastily drafting their own approaches to the matter. There were a host of antidrug strategies, which were at first modest but gathered rather expensive moss as they were rolled from committee to committee. And knowing that a new drug war was close at hand and that it was politically acceptable, politicians across the nation—Democrats and Republicans alike—began vaulting over one another hoping to reach the frontlines of the antidrug parade, attempting to demonstrate how thoroughly and unconditionally they disapproved of crack, cocaine, heroin, marijuana, and other illegal drugs. It was politics at its best and politics at its worst, and it became clear to many Americans that their representatives all too often appeared more interested in narrow political advantage than the welfare of the country. However, what did result was the passage of Title I of the Anti-Drug Abuse Act of 1988 (21 U.S.C. 1504), which was the National Narcotics Leadership Act. Finally, America would have its first drug czar.

During the early months of 1989 William J. Bennett, Ph.D., J.D., was selected, appointed, and confirmed as the head of the Office of

National Drug Control Policy (ONDCP). A former U.S. Secretary of Education, former college football player, and a life-long rock 'n roll fan, Bennett was an iconoclastic, irreverent neoconservative with an acerbic tongue, a taste for the bully pulpit, and a mission that most people felt was impossible. At best Bennett knew that his job would be difficult, for he was a czar without an empire and a general without troops. The difficulty was that when President Bush appointed Bennett, his position was not cabinet rank, and ONDCP was given only a modest operating budget. As such the new drug warrior had neither the power nor the funds to wage an organized war. But this was not Bennett's only problem.

Bennett's second problem was the Democrats. Although Bennett had no army of his own, it was clear from the outset that a multi-billion dollar antidrug package would be available and that his thoughts would be influential in how these funds would be allocated. In fact Bennett's initial mandate was to prepare a National Drug Control Strategy by September 1, 1989, which was to function as the President's blueprint for the nation's war on drugs. As it began to take shape, partisan politics kicked in, or as Senator Biden put it:

> Quite frankly, the President's plan is not tough enough, bold enough, or imaginative enough to meet the crisis at hand. The President says he wants to wage a war on drugs, but if that's true, what we need is another "D Day," not another Vietnam, not another limited war fought on the cheap and destined for stalemate and human tragedy.[27]

Bennett's third problem was the academics, free market economists, and civil libertarians who wanted to see a movement toward the legalization of all illicit drugs. The legalizers, as pointed out in Chapter 8, saw legalization as a quick and easy solution to the morass of drug-related crime that had engulfed the police, courts, and prisons in states from coast to coast. In the early months of his term, Bennett ignored them, tending to the business of preparing the President's drug strategy. And although the legalizers represented an infinitesimally small minority, by the close of 1989 they had become quite vocal, and among their ranks there were such notables as former Secretary of State George Shultz, arch-conservative ideologue and editor William F. Buckley, the noted liberal columnist Anthony Lewis, Nobel laureate Milton Friedman, the editors of Great Britain's *Economist* magazine, *Harper's* magazine editor Lewis Lapham, federal judge Robert W. Sweet, and Baltimore Mayor Kurt Schmoke—the first prominent elected official to call for a debate on legalization.[28] Although Bennett knew that the nation was solidly against legalization, he found the debate to be bothersome, and complained that the pro-legalization rhetoric was a distraction from the important drug policy issues and initiatives.[29] Further, Bennett challenged the "intellectuals" as he called them to "get with the program, or at the very least, get with the game," and added:

> It is indeed bizarre to see the likes of Anthony Lewis and William F. Buckley lining up on the same side of the issue; but such is the perversity that the so-called legalization debate engenders. To call it a "debate," though, suggests that the arguments in favour of drug legalization are rigorous, substantial, and serious. They are not. They are, at bottom, a series of superficial and even disingenuous ideas that more sober minds recognize as a recipe for public policy disaster.[30]

In the end, reason and logic prevailed. By the early months of 1990 the legalization debate had disappeared not only from sections one and two of the daily and weekly media, but from sections three, four, and five as well. At the same time, the debate retreated to the few small discussion groups from whence it had emerged, capturing the attention of none but the original cheerleaders of an idea that was far too problematic to have been considered as a serious policy alternative in the first place.[b]

Bennett's fourth problem was Washington, D.C. Mayor Marion S. Barry, Jr. Months before the National Drug Control Strategy was unveiled on September 1, 1989,[31] Bennett characterized the nation's capitol as a "high-intensity drug trafficking area" and designated the city as a "shock treatment" test case in the war on drugs. And Bennett was not exaggerating about the District's problems. During the first three months of 1989, Washington, D.C., had had 120 murders—most of them drug-related—and almost double the number during the same period in 1988.[32] Moreover, police seemed virtually powerless to stop the warfare in the streets between rival drug dealers.

The Bennett plan ultimately called for additional DEA and FBI agents for drug enforcement duties in the Washington area, the

---

[b] As a footnote to this discussion, most of those who favored the legalization of drugs never got far enough beyond their own rhetoric to suggest concrete strategies for implementing a legalization policy. Among the few that did, ideas were superficial and ill-conceived as Bennett had maintained. And in this behalf, perhaps the most ludicrous suggestion came from the Washington, D.C.–area journalist Richard B. Karel, who advocated the idea of cocaine chewing gum—available in packages of 20, each piece containing 10 to 20 milligrams of pharmaceutical cocaine, dispensed through vending machines activated by ATM bank cards, with purchases limited to one package every 48 to 72 hours. See Richard B. Karel, "A Model Legalization Proposal," in James A. Inciardi, ed., *The Drug Legalization Debate* (Newbury Park, CA: Sage, 1991), pp. 80–102.

increased use of mandatory prison sentences for certain drug-related crimes, a special narcotics prosecution unit in the court system, 300 slots added to the existing drug treatment system, and an expansion of drug education in the city school system.[33] But the complication in Mr. Bennett's Washington strategy was D.C. Mayor Barry. While struggling to gain control over the city's drug epidemic, Barry was also battling allegations that he himself used drugs. Later in the year Barry was arrested. During his six-week trial, government witnesses testified that Barry had indeed used drugs—cocaine, opium, and marijuana— more than 200 times in homes and hotels, on ships, and even at the 1988 Democratic National Convention. An FBI videotape showed Barry twice inhaling from a crack pipe in a downtown Washington hotel room to which had been invited by a former girlfriend. The jury found Barry guilty of one misdemeanor count of possessing cocaine, acquitted him on a second drug possession charge but deadlocked on twelve other counts, including three felony charges of lying to a grand jury.[34] Unquestionably, Barry's use of cocaine not only disgraced his office and city but undermined the fight against drugs. Or as William Bennett put it: "It's kind of hard to fight a war against drugs when your chief executive officer is a user."[35]

The Barry verdict did not play in Bogota, Medellin, and other cities in Colombia, where judges, prosecutors, and journalists had been casualties of their country's war against the cocaine cartels.[36] The Barry trial was seen as a symbolic test of the American commitment to reduce drug consumption, and with his conviction on only 1 of 14 counts, the United States was accused of having a double standard. Or as *Semana*, Colombia's leading news weekly, wrote in a cover story on the Barry verdict: "In the war against drugs, the United States is ready to fight to the last Colombian."[37]

Bennett's fifth problem was what can only be described as a rather lopsided approach to addressing the drug problem. It had been Bennett's view from the outset that in order to reduce drug use and sales and the related crime and violence, the nation had to "take back the streets" from the dealers and violent predators. No one could argue with him that the violence in the streets had to be addressed, but without going into all the details of the what was unveiled in the *National Drug Control Strategy* on September 1, 1989, the new scheme called for the government to do essentially more of the same things it had been doing for years with only marginal success: make tougher laws, hire and train more cops, expand street level enforcement, make more arrests, build more prisons, intensify efforts to break up drug-trafficking organizations, escalate drug testing in the workplace, elevate the certainty of punishment for drug crimes, increase the penalties for casual users, and cut back foreign aid to drug-producing nations not cooperating with coca and poppy eradicating efforts.

Copyright 1990 by Herblock in The Washington Post.

Although most of these supply reduction activities were indeed essential parts of a coordinated war on drugs, they represented roughly 70% of the Bennett/Bush strategy—a ratio that had remained the same since Richard M. Nixon's war on heroin two decades earlier. Once again, demand reduction—prevention, education, treatment, and research—received limited allocations.

SHIFTING THE FOCUS OF THE WAR ON DRUGS

For a more efficient and cost-effective war on drugs, supply reduction strategies should continue but with considerably less emphasis—at least a 50/50 share of the resources between supply and demand reduction initiatives rather than the historical 80/20 or 70/30. If there were no drug users, then there would be no drug problem, and it is for this reason that a greater emphasis on demand reduction is the most logical course. But this should not suggest that enforcement initiatives be abandoned, for they are crucial to any effective demand reduction strategy. In fact, demand reduction initiatives must take into account a number of important considerations.

1. The argument has been made over the years that drug dependence is a medical problem, not a criminal problem, and hence, drug control should be taken out of the hands of the criminal justice system and put into those of the public health and human service delivery networks. But in counterpoint, drug control must remain within the criminal justice sector for some very good reasons. The Drug Use Forecasting (DUF) data presented in Chapter 5 clearly demonstrates that the majority of arrestees in urban areas throughout the United States are indeed drug involved. At the same time, recent research has demonstrated not only that drug abuse treatment works,[38] coerced treatment works best! Although logic would dictate that voluntary treatment might have more beneficial effects than mandatory treatment, it would appear that the opposite is the case. What the research demonstrates is that the key variable most related to success in treatment is "length of stay in treatment," and that those who are forced into treatment remain longer than those who volunteer.[39] By remaining longer, they benefit more. As such, compulsory treatment efforts should be expanded for those who are dependent on drugs and are involved in drug-related crime.

2. Perhaps the most humane and effective use of criminal justice in drug control activities is its linkage with the treatment system through the Treatment Alternatives to Street Crime (TASC) initiative. TASC represents a humane use of the criminal justice system, for it acts as an objective bridge between two separate institutions: justice and the drug treatment community. The justice system's legal sanctions reflect concerns for public safety and punishment, whereas treatment emphasizes therapeutic intervention as a means for altering drug-taking and drug-seeking behaviors.

Under TASC, community-based supervision is made available to drug-involved individuals who would otherwise burden the justice system with their persistent drug-associated criminality. More specifically, TASC identifies, assesses, and refers drug-involved offenders to community treatment services as an alternative or supplement to existing justice system sanctions and procedures. In the more than 100 jurisdictions where TASC currently operates, it serves as a court diversion mechanism or a supplement to probation supervision. After referral to community-based treatment, the client is monitored by TASC for progress and compliance, including expectations for abstinence, employment, and improved personal and social functioning. TASC then reports treatment results back to the referring justice system agency. Clients who violate the conditions of their justice mandate (diversion, deferred sentencing, pretrial intervention, or probation), their TASC contract, or their treatment agreement are typically returned to the justice system for continued processing or sanctions.[40]

Although there has not been a national evaluation of the entire TASC effort, more than 40 local programs were assessed from 1972 through 1982.[41] In general it was found that the majority effectively linked criminal justice and treatment systems, identified previously untreated drug-involved offenders, and intervened with clients to reduce drug abuse and criminal activity. Two more recent examinations—one in 1986 and the second in 1988—suggested that the TASC initiative continued to meet its intended operational goals.[42] In short, the TASC experience has been a positive one. TASC has been demonstrated to be highly productive in: (a) identifying populations of drug-involved offenders in need of treatment; (b) assessing the nature and extent of their drug-use patterns and specific treatment needs; (c) effectively referring drug-involved offenders to treatment; (d) serving as a linkage between the criminal justice and treatment systems; and (e) providing constructive client identification and monitoring services for the courts, probation, and other segments of the criminal justice system. Perhaps most importantly, evaluation data indicate that TASC-referred clients remain longer in treatment than non-TASC clients, and as a result, have better post-treatment success.

As such, it is important that TASC be expanded because of the role it can play in reducing the growing rates of violent drug-elated street crime, alleviating court backlogs, and easing crowded prison conditions.

3. There needs to be an expansion of therapeutic community treatment in prison settings. The therapeutic community, better known as the "TC" by practitioners in the drug field, is unquestionably the most appropriate form of drug abuse treatment in correctional settings because of the many phenomena in the prison environment that make rehabilitation difficult. Not surprisingly the availability of drugs in jails and prisons is a pervasive problem. In addition there is the violence associated with inmate gangs, often formed along racial lines for the purposes of establishing and maintaining status, turf, and unofficial control over sectors of the penitentiary for distributing contraband and providing protection for other inmates.[43] And finally, there is the prison subculture, a system of norms and values which, among other things,

holds that "people in treatment are faggots," as one Delaware inmate put it in 1988.

In contrast the therapeutic community is a total treatment environment isolated from the rest of the prison population—separated from the drugs, the violence, and the norms and values that militate against treatment and rehabilitation. The primary clinical staff of the TC are typically former substance abusers—recovering addicts—who themselves were rehabilitated in therapeutic communities. The treatment perspective of the TC is that drug abuse is a disorder of the whole person—that the problem is the person and not the drug, that addiction is a symptom and not the essence of the disorder. In the TC's view of recovery, the primary goal is to change the negative patterns of behavior, thinking, and feeling that predispose drug use. As such the overall goal is a responsible drug-free life-style.[44]

Recovery through the TC process depends on positive and negative pressures to change, and this is brought about through a self-help process in which relationships of mutual responsibility to every resident in the program are built. Or as the noted TC researcher Dr. George De Leon once described it:

> The essential dynamic in the TC is mutual self-help. Thus, the day-to-day activities are conducted by the residents themselves. In their jobs, groups, meetings, recreation, personal, and social time, it is residents who continually transmit to each other the main messages and expectations of the community.[45]

In addition to individual and group counseling, the TC process has a system of explicit rewards that reinforce the value of earned achievement. As such, privileges are earned. In addition, TCs have their own specific rules and regulations that guide the behavior of residents and the management of their facilities. Their purposes are to maintain the safety and health of the community and to train and teach residents through the use of discipline. TC rules and regulations are numerous, the most conspicuous of which are total prohibitions against violence, theft, and drug use. Violation of these cardinal rules typically results in immediate expulsion from a TC.

Therapeutic communities have been in existence for decades, and their successes have been well documented.[46] Yet few exist in jail and prison settings. It has been demonstrated, however, that prison-based TCs are effective not only in addressing the problems of drug dependence but also in dealing with issues of prison management. On this latter point prison TCs have been found to be the cleanest and most trouble-free sectors of the institutions in which they are housed.[47]

4. Expansions in drug-abuse treatment services, increases in the number of TASC programs, and development of additional prison-based therapeutic communities should represent only the beginning

of the extended treatment initiative. Funding is also needed for
establishing new and innovative treatment approaches, for researching
treatment effectiveness, and for the recruitment and training of those
who will staff the new programs.

Going further, there should be serious discussion of the treatment
on demand concept, a policy alternative aimed at supplying treatment
space to whomever requests it, whenever they request it. Yet the Office
of National Drug Control Policy has ardently opposed it, on the
grounds that:

> . . . treatment on demand . . . ignores the more immediate
> and fundamental problems that confront the treatment system.
> While it is certainly true that there are addicts who do seek
> treatment voluntarily, many of these volunteers repeatedly
> enter and impulsively drop out of treatment. Their goal, unlike
> the goals of their treatment providers, is to return to "controlled
> use" or to "stay clean" for a few days to reduce their tolerance
> so the same high can be achieved from lower and cheaper
> doses. Others who seek treatment on their own do so only after
> they have "bottomed out;" they have reached a point where
> their addiction has so consumed them and devastated their
> lives that they can no longer function; they cannot care for their
> children, show up for work, or even associate with people who
> don't use drugs.
>
> For addicts like these, simply providing additional treat-
> ment slots does nothing by itself to ensure that treatment
> generally is made more effective and provided in a more
> rational way. A policy designed primarily to provide treatment
> on demand would create a costly, unbalanced system that
> brings no guarantee of higher treatment success rates.
> Moreover, the call for such a system obscures the far more
> pressing and practical needs of drug treatment. Addressing
> those needs requires us to come to grips with the fact that
> while the need for treatment is high, the actual demand for
> it is relatively low.
>
> The overwhelming majority of addicts must be "jolted"
> into drug treatment and induced to stay there by some external
> force: the criminal justice system, employers who have
> discovered drug use, spouses who threaten to leave, or the
> death of a fellow addict.[48]

Without question, there is some truth to the ONDCP remarks. Most
addicts do not volunteer for treatment; many who do are indeed
attempting to reduce the sizes of their habits; and coerced treatment
does seem to have better program retention and success rates. Nevertheless, the ONDCP position opposing treatment on demand is a

bit rigid, particularly since extensive data have demonstrated that reduced drug intake is typically accompanied by reduced criminality.[49] Undoubtedly, there is a need for dialogue and compromise.

5. In the prevention and educational sectors, existing initiatives are in need of evaluation and new ones need implementation and testing. Yet education is the answer only when ignorance is the problem, and prevention efforts don't seem to be working everywhere. While the NIDA National Household Survey and the University of Michigan High School Senior Survey report declines in drug use, these positive indicators relate only to mainstream America. Drugs continue to be abundant in inner-city neighborhoods throughout the country. The antidrug messages from government, schools, parent groups, sports figures, and the entertainment media are either not reaching, not being heard, not being listened to, or have little meaning to inner-city youth. As such, the questions are clear: "Why is this so? What changes are in order?" The answers lie not in the funding of a technological war on drugs, but in a well-funded prevention and educational research program. And at the same time there is the even more important matter of better understanding the frustrations and deprivations of inner-city life and developing the appropriate mechanisms for bringing the residents of inner cities into the mainstream.

6. At both state and federal levels, a focused reexamination of the fairness and logic of the evolving legislative war on drugs would appear to be in order. In this regard, in response to the user accountability provisions of the Anti-Drug Abuse Act of 1988—the idea that "if there were no drug users there would be no drug problem"—many jurisdictions have passed some rather severe penalties for "casual drug use." Granted, casual drug users do contribute to the demand that supports the drug black markets and trafficking cartels. However, arrest, court processing, and incarceration for the possession of a single marijuana cigarette, half a gram of cocaine, or a hit of LSD seem a bit repressive to say the least. When there are no other crimes involved, perhaps civil penalties, rather than criminal sanctions, would be a more appropriate avenue for those found in possession of small amounts of drugs for personal use. Interestingly such a policy is already being tested at the federal level.[50] As such civil penalties applied within the canons of due process of law might prove to be a fair and effective deterrent against recreational drug use.

At the same time, the prosecution of pregnant addicts is even more repressive. In a number of jurisdictions across the United States a women can be convicted of child abuse for using cocaine while pregnant.[51] Without question, unborn children should be protected from drugs. However, prosecution may be in direct violation of the Eighth Amendment ban against cruel and unusual punishment.[52] And even

WE'RE TAKING A WHOLE NEW LOOK AT THE CASUAL DRUG USER.

792363

In Maricopa County, you can no longer do drugs and expect to get away with it. A tough new anti-drug police task force is now on the streets. And if they catch you with drugs, they're taking you to jail. You then face felony charges, a prison sentence and stiff financial penalties. Or pay to enter a year-long rehab program. So before you do drugs, think about how they could make you look.

DO DRUGS. DO TIME.
Maricopa County Demand Reduction Program.
©1989 Maricopa County Demand Reduction Program.

"Do Drugs. Do Time." is a Phoenix, Arizona campaign which guarantees jail even for the casual use of illegal drugs.

more importantly prosecution and incarceration fail to adequately address the problem. There are special consequences of drug use by women that can be remedied not by prison but by comprehensive medical and drug abuse treatment regimens that address issues in both substance abuse and prenatal care.

7. Finally, the fields of economics and finance might explore alternatives to hard currency as a mechanism of drug control. Consider, for example, that without cash there would likely be few transactions involving illegal drugs. Drug dealing and drug trafficking depend completely on a cash economy. Any other system (such as checks, credit cards, or electronic transfers of funds) create paper trails, that is, documentation that a transaction has taken place. The elimination of hard currency would go a long way to eliminate not only illegal drug sales, but also most sales of stolen goods, illegal gambling, and the whole underground economy that evades taxation every year. One might argue that a cashless economy would be difficult and would discriminate against the poor. However, much of the industrialized world is already moving toward cashless systems. Checks and credit cards are well-established aspects of money and banking systems; ATM cards are used throughout the United States in grocery stores in lieu of cash; college students in many parts of the United States use school ID cards for purchasing books, supplies, and food at campus outlets; checks, food stamps, and other vouchers are used with success by federal and local public assistance agencies; tokens and coupons are used at toll booths, theaters, copying machines, and other outlets. And there are likely others. Systems could be developed that would make the need for cash obsolete and eliminate most illegal economies.

POSTSCRIPT

If anything has been learned from the history of drug taking in the United States, it is that drug use is a changing phenomenon. There are fads and fashions in drugs and drug use, suggesting that persistent vigilance is needed. Different drugs come and go. By the close of the 1980s and the beginning of the 1990s new potential drugs of abuse were evident. Basuco, the coca paste of Colombia, had made its way to the streets of Miami by 1986.[53] There will be new designer drugs that simulate the effects of opiates, stimulants, and hallucinogens. A recent entry in this behalf is N,N-dimethylamphetamine, chemically related to methamphetamine and sold on the street as crack and speed.[54] Throughout the United States, cocaine and crack users are adding smokeable heroin to their drug-taking menus.[55] As noted earlier in Chapter 4, heroin not only extends the euphoria associated with crack and cocaine use, but also mediates the edginess and irritability associated with stimulant abuse. This pattern may ultimately create a whole new generation of heroin addicts who may eventually become intravenous users, and hence, a new population at high risk for HIV and AIDS.

There are substances elsewhere in the world that might find popularity in the United States. For example:

- In Southeast Asia there are the drugs known as mambog and kratom. Both are derivatives of *Mitragyna speciosa*, a shrubby member of the coffee family with branches terminating in balls of yellow flowers.[56] Kratom is a leafy material that is smoked like marijuana, whereas mambog is a syrup made from the leaves. Although both substances have been classified as hallucinogens, they engender cocaine-like effects on the central nervous system. Drug officials in Thailand have expressed concern with the potential of these and other *Mitragyna speciosa* derivatives.[57] Although the chewing or smoking of the leaves produces only mild euphoria, a considerably more potent product can be chemically extracted from the plant.
- In Egypt, there is *Maxton Fort*—a combination of ephedrine, red phosphorous, iodine, ethyl alcohol, glycerine, sodium bicarbonate, and acryflavine which yields an injectable amphetamine-like substance with stimulant reactions.[58]
- In India, Hong Kong, many parts of Africa, and the Peoples Republic of China a major drug problem involves *Mandrax*, what Americans refer to as Quaalude and methaqualone.[59] Moreover, unique to South Africa is the so-called "white pipe" method of using this drug, which involves the smoking of a mixture of marijuana or hashish with Mandrax.[60] It is clearly within the realm of the possible that Mandrax supplies could find their way to the United States one of these days, ushering in a third methaqualone epidemic.
- And then there is the matter of qat, mentioned only briefly in a Chapter 8 footnote. On June 27, 1989, at the San Francisco International Airport, approximately 6.5 lbs. of qat leaves were seized. On August 7, 1990, qat leaves were seized at Lambert Field in St. Louis, Missouri. Quantities of qat leaves have also been seized by European customs agents.

  Qat, also known as khat, chat, gat, mirra, tohai, tschat, and kus-es-salahin, is a flowering evergreen shrub which grows both wild and cultivated in Eastern Africa and Southern Arabia. The dried leaves are often referred to as ''Abyssinian Tea'' and ''Arabian Tea.'' The fresh leaves and young shoots contain a psychoactive substance that when chewed and the juices swallowed engenders a stimulant effect similar to that of amphetamines. Unlike high doses of amphetamine, however, the use of qat rarely, if ever, produces toxic psychosis or aggressive behavior. Also, tolerance for increasing amounts of the drug does not develop. It is believed that the means of ingestion (chewing) limits the quantity which can be consumed. Qat is classified as a Schedule IV controlled substance.[61]

And to all of these can be added the more bizarre forms of drug abuse that now and then emerge. Perhaps the most unusual in this regard involved the use of bufotenine, which first appeared in South Florida during the early weeks of 1990.[62] It seems that someone discovered that the toxic slime secreted by *Bufo marinus*—the cane toad—caused hallucinations, and suddenly "toad licking" became a new way to get high. But as the Drug Enforcement Administration warned, "Licking too much can kill you, and so can licking just a little from a particularly potent toad."[c]

Notes

1. Thomas Szasz, *Ceremonial Chemistry: The Ritual Persecution of Drugs, Addicts, and Pushers* (Garden City, NY: Anchor Press, 1974), pp. 11–12.
2. Rufus King, *The Drug Hang-Up: America's Fifty-Year Folly* (New York: W. W. Norton, 1972).
3. David F. Musto, *The American Disease: Origins of Narcotic Control* (New Haven: Yale University Press, 1973).
4. *The Nation*, 21 Apr. 1956, p. 337. See also Alfred R. Lindesmith, *Addiction and Opiates* (Chicago: Aldine, 1968).
5. Szasz, p. 180.
6. King, p. 350; Lindesmith, p. 234.
7. David W. Maurer and Victor H. Vogel, *Narcotics and Narcotic Addiction*, 3rd ed. (Springfield, IL: Chas. C. Thomas, 1978), pp. 286–287 (italics added).

---

[c] Amphibians Anonymous, whose motto is "Never Has It Been So Easy To Just Say No," reported the following telltale signs of toad slime addiction in the *Miami Herald* (2 Feb. 1990, p. 2A):

You know you are in the company of a toad-sucker if you are approached in a singles bar by someone who says:
"Your swamp or mine?"
"You show me your warts and I'll show you mine."
You know you have a toad-sucker in the family if your son or daughter:
Hops right out of bed in the morning.
Has breath that smells like the Everglades.
Develops an appetite for live flies.
Is fascinated by Kermit the Frog.
Has the nickname "Bullfrog" or "Tadpole."

8. See James A. Inciardi, "Heroin Use and Street Crime," *Crime and Delinquency,* July 1979, pp. 335–346.

9. See D. J. West, ed., *Problems of Drug Abuse in Britain* (Cambridge: Institute of Criminology, 1978); Horace Freeland Judson, *Heroin Addiction in Britain* (New York: Harcourt Brace Jovanovich, 1974).

10. Alfred R. Lindesmith, *The Addict and the Law* (New York: Vintage, 1965), p. 166.

11. *Newsweek,* 7 Jan. 1957, p. 66.

12. Edwin M. Schur, *Narcotic Addiction in Britain and America* (Bloomington: Indiana University Press, 1962).

13. See Griffith Edwards and Carol Busch, *Drug Problems in Britain: A Review of Ten Years* (London: Academic Press, 1981).

14. Arnold S. Trebach, *The Heroin Solution* (New Haven: Yale University Press, 1982).

15. Trebach, p. 173.

16. Trebach, p. 269.

17. Jason Ditton and Kevin Speirits, "The New Wave of Heroin Addiction in Britain," *Sociology,* 16 (Nov. 1982), pp. 595–598; *New York Times,* 11 Apr. 1985, p. A15; Geoffrey Pearson, Mark Gilman, and Shirley McIver, *Young People and Heroin: An Examination of Heroin Use in the North of England* (Hants, England: Gower Publishing Company, 1987).

18. *London Times,* 8 Jan. 1991, p. 3.

19. *U.S. News & World Report,* 4 Oct. 1982, pp. 54–55; *Miami Herald,* 31 Mar. 1983, p. 4B; *New York Times,* 13 Sept. 1984, pp. A1, A16; *Wall Street Journal,* 9 Apr. 1985, p. 30.

20. State of Florida, Department of Corrections, DATRC Memo for February 1991.

21. Ibid.

22. The White House, Drug Abuse Policy Office, Office of Policy Development, *National Strategy for Prevention of Drug Abuse and Drug Trafficking* (Washington, DC: U.S. Government Printing Office, 1984), p. 52.

23. University of Michigan News and Information Services Release, 24 Jan. 1991.

24. See Robert L. Hubbard, Mary Ellen Marsden, J. Valley Rachal, Henrick J. Harwood, Elizabeth R. Cavanaugh, and Harold M. Ginzburg, *Drug Abuse Treatment: A National Study of Effectiveness* (Chapel Hill: University of North Carolina Press, 1989).

25. *Drug Enforcement Report,* 8 Feb. 1991, pp. 1–3; *Drug Enforcement Report,* 25 Feb. 1991, pp. 3–4; *Alcoholism and Drug Abuse Week,* 6 Feb. 1991, p. 1.

26. Quoted in James A. Inciardi, "Revitalizing the War on Drugs," *The World & I,* Feb. 1988, pp. 132–139.

27. *Alcoholism and Drug Abuse Week,* 6 Sept. 1989, p. 3.

28. *Alcoholism and Drug Abuse Week,* 20 Dec. 1989, pp. 1–3; Lewis H. Lapham, "A Political Opiate," *Harper's,* Dec. 1989, pp. 43–48; *New York Times,* 13 Dec. 1989, pp. A1, B10; *New York Times,* 27 Nov. 1989, p. A15. Also see *Legalization of Illicit Drugs: Impact and Feasibility,* Hearing Before the Select Committee on Narcotics Abuse and Control, House of Representatives, One Hundredth Congress, September 29, 1988.

29. *Miami Herald,* 14 Dec. 1989, p. 5A; *Newsweek,* 25 Dec. 1989, pp. 46–47.

30. William J. Bennett, "Drug Policy and the Intellectuals," *International Journal on Drug Policy*, 1 (6), 1990, pp. 16–18.
31. The White House, *National Drug Control Strategy* (Washington, DC: Executive Office of the President, Office of National Drug Control Policy, September 1989).
32. *Time*, 3 Apr. 1989, p. 24.
33. *New York Times*, 18 Mar. 1989, p. 7; *Drug Enforcement Report*, 24 Apr. 1989, p. 3.
34. *Time*, 20 Aug. 1990, p. 48; *Washington Post*, 12 Aug. 1990, pp. A1, A14–A17.
35. *USA Today*, 13 Nov. 1990, p. 2A.
36. Bogota *Radio Cadena Nacional*, 1200 GMT, 27 Oct. 1990; Madrid *EFE*, 2246 GMT, 17 Aug. 1990; Bogota *El Tiempo*, 14 Aug. 1990, p. 5A.
37. *New York Times*, 27 Aug. 1990, p. A6.
38. Robert L. Hubbard, Mary Ellen Marsden, J. Valley Rachal, Henrick J. Harwood, Elizabeth R. Cavanaugh, and Harold M. Ginzburg, *Drug Abuse Treatment: A National Study of Effectiveness* (Chapel Hill: University of North Carolina Press, 1989); Jerome J. Platt, Charles D. Kaplan, and Patricia J. Mc Kim, eds., *The Effectiveness of Drug Abuse Treatment* (Malabar, FL: Robert E. Krieger, 1990).
39. For extensive documentation on the effectiveness of coerced treatment, see Carl G. Leukefeld and Frank M. Tims, eds., *Compulsory Treatment of Drug Abuse: Research and Clinical Practice* (Rockville, MD: National Institute on Drug Abuse, 1988). In addition, the entire Fall 1988 (Vol. 16, No.4) issue of the *Journal of Drug Issues*, edited by M. Douglas Anglin and entitled "A Social Policy Analysis of Compulsory Treatment for Opiate Dependence," is devoted to the topic of coerced treatment.
40. Bureau of Justice Assistance, *Treatment Alternatives to Street Crime* (Washington, DC: U.S. Department of Justice, Office of Justice Programs, 1988); Beth A. Weinman, "Treatment Alternatives to Street Crime (TASC)," in James A. Inciardi, ed., *Handbook of Drug Control in the United States* (Westport, CT: Greenwood Press, 1990), pp. 139–150; James A. Inciardi and Duane C. McBride, *Treatment Alternatives to Street Crime (TASC): History, Experiences, and Issues* (Rockville, MD: National Institute on Drug Abuse, 1991).
41. See Mary A. Toborg, D. R. Levin, Robert H. Milkman, and L. J. Center, *Treatment Alternatives to Street Crime (TASC) Projects: National Evaluation Program, Phase I Summary Report* (Washington, DC: National Institute of Law Enforcement and Criminal Justice, 1976); System Sciences, *Evaluation of Treatment Alternatives to Street Crime: National Evaluation Program, Phase II Report* (Washington, DC: National Institute of Law Enforcement and Criminal Justice, 1979); Duane C. McBride and A. L. Bennett, "The Impact of Criminal Justice Diversion on a Community Drug Treatment Structure," *Drug Forum*, 8 (1978); James J. Collins, Robert L. Hubbard, J. Valley Rachal, E. R. Cavanaugh, and S. G. Craddock, *Criminal Justice Clients in Drug Treatment* (Research Triangle Park, NC: Research Triangle Institute, 1982); James J. Collins, Robert L. Hubbard, J. Valley Rachal, E. R. Cavanaugh, and S. G. Craddock, *Client Characteristics, Behaviors and Intreatment Outcomes: 1980 TOPS Admission Cohort* (Research Triangle Park, NC: Research Triangle Institute, 1982).

42. Linda P. Tyon, *Final Report: Baseline Management and Assessment Data Project* (Portland, OR: National Consortium of TASC Programs, 1988); National Association of State Alcohol and Drug Abuse Directors, *Measuring TASC Program Compliance With Established TASC Critical Elements and Performance Standards* (Washington, DC: NASADAD, 1989).

43. See Mark S. Fleisher, *Warehousing Violence* (Newbury Park, CA: Sage, 1989); Robert Johnson, *Hard Time: Understanding and Reforming the Prison* (Monterey CA: Brooks/Cole, 1987); Lee Bowker, *Prison Victimization* (New York: Elsevier, 1980).

44. See George De Leon and James T. Ziegenfuss, *Therapeutic Communities for the Addictions* (Springfield, IL: Charles C. Thomas, 1986); Lewis Yablonsky, *The Therapeutic Community: A Successful Approach for Treating Substance Abusers* (New York: Gardner Press, 1989).

45. George De Leon, "The Therapeutic Community: Status and Evolution," *International Journal of the Addictions*, 20 (1985), pp. 823–844.

46. See George De Leon, "Treatment Strategies," in James A. Inciardi, *Handbook of Drug Control in the United States*, pp. 115–138.

47. Hans Toch, ed., *Therapeutic Communities in Corrections* (New York: Praeger, 1980); Harry K. Wexler and Ronald Williams, "The Stay 'N Out Therapeutic Community: Prison Treatment for Substance Abusers," *Journal of Psychoactive Drugs*, 18 (July–Sept. 1986), pp. 221–230; Douglas S. Lipton and Harry K. Wexler, "Breaking the Drugs-Crime Connection," *Corrections Today*, Aug. 1988, pp. 144, 146, 155; Dan Gursky, "Innovative Drug Treatment in Delaware," *Corrections Today*, July 1988, pp. 49, 79; James A. Inciardi, Steven S. Martin, Dorothy Lockwood, Robert M. Hooper, and Bruce M. Wald, "Obstacles to the Implementation of Drug Treatment Programs in Correctional Settings," National Institute on Drug Abuse Technical Review on Drug Abuse Treatment in Prisons and Jails, Rockville, Maryland, 24–25 May 1990.

48. Office of National Drug Control Policy, *Understanding Drug Treatment* (Washington, DC: The White House, 1990).

49. See David N. Nurco, Timothy W. Kinlock, and Thomas E. Hanlon, "The Drugs-Crime Connection," in James A. Inciardi, ed., *Handbook of Drug Control in the United States* (Westport, CT: Greenwood Press, 1990), pp. 71–90; Jan M. Chaiken and Marcia R. Chaiken, "Drugs and Predatory Crime," in Michael Tonry and James Q. Wilson, eds., *Drugs and Crime* (Chicago: University of Chicago Press, 1990), pp. 203–239.

50. *Drug Enforcement Report*, 23 Jan. 1991, pp. 1–2.

51. *New York Times*, 5 Feb. 1990, p. A14; *Time*, 22 May 1989, pp. 104–105; *Miami Herald*, 5 Jan. 1990, p. 8A; *Insight*, 29 May 1989, p. 61.

52. See Robert Batey and Sandra Anderson Garcia, "Prosecution of the Pregnant Addict: Does the Cruel and Unusual Punishment Clause Apply?" *Criminal Law Bulletin*, 27 (Mar.–Apr. 1991), pp. 99–113.

53. James A. Inciardi, "Beyond Cocaine: Basuco, Crack, and Other Coca Products," *Contemporary Drug Problems*, 14 (Fall 1987), pp. 461–492.

54. See *Substance Abuse Report*, 1 Mar. 1990, p. 8.

55. *New York Times*, 21 July 1990, pp. 1, 26; *Newsweek*, 19 Feb. 1990, pp. 74, 77; *Insight*, 5 Feb. 1990, p. 9; *U.S. News & World Report*, 14 Aug. 1989, pp. 31–32; *Drug Enforcement Report*, 23 Feb. 1989, p. 8; *Drug Enforcement Report*, 23 Feb. 1990, p. 8; *Alcoholism and Drug Abuse Week*, 19 July 1989, p. 7.

56. William Emboden, *Narcotic Plants* (New York: Macmillan, 1979), p. 49.

57. Bangkok *Siam Rat*, 30 Sept. 1986, p. 14.

58. Memo from American Embassy/Cairo, 3 Apr. 1989, 8:05 EST; Cairo *Rose Al-Yusuf*, 22 Jan. 1990, pp. 38–41; Cairo, *Al-Akhbar*, 13 July 1989, p. 7; Cairo, *Al-Wafd*, 1 Nov. 1989, p. 6.

59. For example, see Johannesburg (South Africa) *City Press*, 2 Jan. 1990, p. 5; Johannesburg *Sunday Times*, 11 Nov. 1987, p. 6; Johannesburg *Sowetan*, 7 Jan. 1991, p. 20; Cape Town (South Africa) *Argus*, 12 Oct. 1989, p. 1; Durban (South Africa) *Daily News*, 1 Feb. 1988, p. 3; Lusaka (Zambia) *Times of Zambia*, 12 Jan. 1990, p. 1; Bombay *Times of India*, 3 Feb. 1987, p. 3; Hong Kong, *Sunday Standard*, 5 Apr. 1987, p. 2; Hong Kong, South China *Morning Post*, 6 July 1987, p. 3; Hong Kong, *South China Morning Post*, 10 July 1987, p. 3.

60. Johannesburg *Citizen*, 7 Dec. 1990, p. 15.

61. State of Florida, Department of Corrections, DATRC Memo for March 1991.

62. *Miami Herald*, 31 Jan. 1990, p. 1A; *Washington Post Magazine*, 30 Dec. 1990, p. 22.

GENERAL DRUG TERMS AND CONCEPTS

A common difficulty in many published discussions of drug abuse is the limited attention given to the basic concepts used to describe and analyze the problem. As such, Appendix I provides widely accepted definitions of drug abuse phenomena.

A. Basic Drug Groups

Psychoactive drugs   Drugs that alter perception and consciousness, including analgesics, depressants, stimulants, and hallucinogens.

Analgesics   Drugs used for the relief of varying degrees of pain without rendering the user unconscious. There are both narcotic and non-narcotic varieties of analgesics.

Depressants   Drugs that act on and lessen the activity of the central nervous system (CNS), diminishing or stopping vital functions.

Sedatives   CNS depressant drugs that produce calm and relaxation. Alcohol, barbiturates and related compounds, and minor tranquilizers are sedative drugs.

Hypnotics   CNS depressant drugs that produce sleep. Barbiturates, methaqualone, and chloral hydrate are hypnotic drugs. Like barbiturates, there are a number of drugs that are both sedatives and hypnotics.

Stimulants   Drugs that stimulate the central nervous system and increase the activity of the brain and spinal chord. Amphetamines and cocaine are CNS stimulant drugs.

Hallucinogens   Drugs that act on the central nervous system producing mood and perceptual changes varying from sensory illusions to hallucinations. Sometimes referred to as psychedelics, hallucinogenic drugs include marijuana, hashish, LSD, PCP, and psilocybin.

B. Dependency Terms

Addiction   Drug craving accompanied by physical dependence that motivates continued usage, resulting in a tolerance to a drug's effects and a syndrome of identifiable symptoms when the drug is abruptly withdrawn. Narcotics, barbiturates, and cocaine are all addicting drugs.

Tolerance   A state of acquired resistance to some or all of the effects of a drug. Tolerance develops after the repeated use of certain drugs, resulting in a need to increase the dosage to obtain the original effects.

Cross-tolerance   Among certain pharmacologically related drugs, tolerance to the effects of one will carry over to most or all others. For example, a person who has become tolerant to the euphoric effects of secobarbital is likely tolerant to the euphoric effects of all other short-acting barbiturates.

Cross-addiction   Also referred to as cross-dependence, a situation in which dependence between drugs of the same pharmacological group is mutual and interchangeable. For example, persons addicted to heroin can use methadone or some other narcotic in place of the heroin without experiencing withdrawal.

Withdrawal   The cluster of reactions and behavior that occurs after the abrupt cessation of a drug upon which the user's body is dependent.

Detoxification   The removal of physical dependency.

C. Drug Reactions

Potentiation   The ability of one drug to increase the activity of another drug when the two are taken simultaneously. This can be expressed mathematically as $a + b = A$. For example, aspirin (a) plus caffeine (b) increases the potency of the aspirin (A).

Synergism   Similar to potentiation, a situation in which two or more drugs are taken together and the combined action dramatically increases the normal effects of each drug. A synergistic effect can be expressed mathematically as $1 + 1 = 5$, and typically occurs with mixtures of alcohol and barbiturates.

Antagonism   A situation in which two drugs taken together have opposite effects on the body. An antagonistic reaction can be expressed mathematically as $1 + 1 = 0$, and typically occurs with certain mixtures of depressants and stimulants.

Idiosyncracy   An abnormal or peculiar response to a drug, such as excitation from a depressant or sedation from a stimulant.

Side effect   Any effect other than what the drug was intended for, such as stomach upset from aspirin.

D. Routes of Drug Administration

Intravenous (IV)   Injected into the vein.
Intramuscular (IM)   Injected into the muscle.
Cutaneous   Absorbed through the skin.
Subcutaneous   Inserted under the skin.
Inhalation   Drawn into the lungs through the nose or mouth.
Oral   Swallowed and absorbed through the stomach.
Vaginal   Absorbed through vaginal tissues.
Anal   Absorbed through rectal tissues.
Sub-lingually   Absorbed through the tissues under the tongue.

E. Pharmaceutical Terms

Tablets   Solid dosage forms of medication prepared by molding or compressing into dies. More specifically, they are made by compressing powdered, crystalline, or granular materials in a tablet machine. This may be either a single punch or a rotary punch machine. The former is more likely to be used in clandestine manufacturing since it is cheaper, smaller, and easier to use. The best method of making tablets is to use what is known as the wet-granulation method, which requires a bowl or blender in which to mix the components of the tablet, along with water and/or alcohol, a mesh screen, shallow trays, and a drying cupboard. Tablets may be of many shapes, sizes, and colors.

Capsules   Doses of solids contained in a soluble shell of hard or soft gelatine. They are usually artificially colored. Hard capsules are normally made in two halves, the end of one slipping over the end of the other. Soft capsules are permanently flexible and may be round, oblong, or elliptical.

Pills   Small round dosage forms made by rolling the pharmaceutical material into a cylinder and cutting the cylinder to provide individual doses. Although once a common variety of pharmaceutical preparation, pills have been largely replaced by tablets and capsules.

Tinctures   Alcoholic solutions of extracts of plant material containing a drug.

Extracts   Concentrated forms of plant drugs typically prepared through distillation or percolation.

Syrups   Solutions of medicine in a concentrated form of sugar dissolved in water.

F. Nomenclature of Medicines

Proprietary Names   Designations given by manufacturers to particular drugs or combinations of drugs. More commonly known as trade or brand names, they generally are not related to the chemical composition of the drug. Moreover, with so many companies manufacturing pharmaceutical products, virtually the same drug or medicine may appear in pharmacies under many different names.

Chemical Names Chemical compositions of drugs. Health authorities in many nations, including the United States, have passed legislation requiring the use of chemical names in drug labeling to allow physicians, pharmacists, and patients to identify the contents of medications. However, chemical names tend to be long, complicated, and virtually impossible to remember.

International Non-proprietary Names (INN) Also known as generic names, INNs were developed by the World Health Organization as substitutes for chemical names. INNs may be used by any manufacturer without legal restrictions, thus providing a system for the easy identification of pharmaceuticals, for example:

1. **INN: methadone**
   (Chemical name: 6-dimethylamino-4, 4-diphenyl-3-heptanone
   Proprietary names: Dolophine, Intensol, Physeptone)

2. **INN: phenobarbital**
   (Chemical name: 5-ethyl-5-phenylbarbituric acid
   Proprietary names: Donnatal, Belladenal, Kinesed, Quadrinal)

3. **INN: diazepam**
   (Chemical name: 7-chloro-1, 3-dihydroi-1-methyl-5-phenyl-2H-1-4-benzodiazepin-2-one
   Proprietary names: Valium, T-Quil)

SCHEDULING PROVISIONS OF THE FEDERAL CONTROLLED SUBSTANCES ACT

The regulatory scheme of the federal controlled substances act classifies substances into five categories, or schedules, to facilitate administration and regulation of the manufacturing, distribution, and dispensing of narcotics and other dangerous drugs without interfering in the legitimate and necessary businesses of doctors, pharmacists, and manufacturers.

The categories are based upon such characteristics of drugs as potential for abuse, accepted medical use, and propensity to create a psychological or physiological dependency for users. Classifications of drugs and periodic updating and re-publication of lists of drugs included in each category are the responsibility of the U.S. Drug Enforcement Administration (DEA).

Schedule I drugs are the most strictly controlled, have a high potential for abuse, no currently accepted medical use in the United States, and no acceptable safe level of use under medical supervision. Many narcotics, such as heroin and other opiates and opium derivatives, fall into this category. In addition, many hallucinogenic drugs that have no recognized medicinal value in this country, such as marijuana, mescaline, peyote, psilocybin, and lysergic acid diethylamide (LSD), are listed in schedule I.

Schedule II drugs have a high potential for abuse, and their use may lead to severe psychological or physiological dependencies; however, they have some recognized medicinal value. Drugs in this category include cocaine, morphine, methamphetamine, and phencyclidine (PCP). Dronabinol, the synthetic equivalent of the active ingredient in marijuana, recently was moved from schedule I to schedule II in recognition of its growing medical uses in treating glaucoma and chemotherapy patients. The DEA has under consideration a petition for reclassification of marijuana from schedule I to schedule II for similar reasons.

Schedule III controlled substances have less potential for abuse than schedule I or II drugs and may lead to moderate or low physical dependence or high psychological dependence but have some accepted medical use. Substances listed in schedule III include limited quantities of some narcotic drugs, amphetamines, and derivatives of barbituric acid.

Schedule IV controlled substances have a low potential for abuse compared to substances in schedule III, and although they may lead to limited physical or psychological dependence, they have a currently accepted medical use. Substances in schedule IV include phenobarbital, chlordiazepoxide hydrochloride (librium), diazepam (valium), and propoxyphene hydrochloride (darvon).

Schedule V controlled substances (such as codeine-based cough syrups) have a low potential for abuse compared to substances in schedule IV and a currently accepted medical use; use may lead to limited physical or psychological dependence relative to schedule IV substances. Substances in schedule V are narcotic compounds containing a limited quantity of narcotic drugs together with one or more non-narcotic medicinal ingredients.

NAME INDEX

Abbott, William, 100
Abelson, H., 129
Aboulafia, D., 198
Adams, Edgar H., 101, 131
Adams, James, 231
Adams, Samuel Hopkins, 13
Adler, Freda, 167, 169, 229
Adriaans, Nico F. P., 200, 201
Agar, Michael H., 55
Alam, M., 198
Alesander, S. S., 198
Alford, B. T., 100
Alksne, Harold, 165
Alldritt, L., 201
Allman, T. D., 130, 216
Almeida, M., 129
Alpert, Richard, 35
Altman, Dennis, 197
Amsel, Zili, 100, 166–167
Anderson, Bernard B., 99
Anglin, M. Douglas, 169, 285
Anslinger, Harry J., 22–24, 34, 44,
    47, 53, 54, 144, 147, 151–152,
    159, 166
Aronow, Don, 236
Asbury, Herbert, 164
Aschenbrandt, Theodor, 7
Asghar, Khursheed, 56
Asher, D. M., 198
Ashman, Margarita A., 200
Asnis, S., 169

Auerbach, D. M., 197
Austin, Gregory A., 167
Ausubel, David P., 73, 99
Ayacucho, Lauren, 231

Baden, Michael M., 199
Bagley, Bruce M., 229
Bailey, Walter C., 165
Bakalar, James B., 129
Ball, John C., 26, 80, 100, 158,
    166, 167, 168, 170, 200, 255,
    258
Barbul, A., 102
Barnes, D. M., 56
Barnett, Gene, 102
Barry, Marion S., Jr., 272, 273
Bartholow, Roberts, 25
Batey, Robert, 286
Battaglia, George, 56
Baukney, Debra, 229
Baxter, Sandra, 200
Bayh, Birch, 39, 41
Beck, Jerome, 55
Belenko, Steven, 131
Bellucci, Patricia A., 131
Belmore, Susan, 99
Belushi, John, 94
Bencivengo, Mark, 169
Bennett, A. L., 285
Bennett, J. E., 174
Bennett, William J., 270–274, 285

294

SUBJECT INDEX

Phencyclidine. *See* PCP
Piracy, 218–221
Pitillo, 110
Pneumocystis carinii pneumonia (PCP), 174–175, 177
"Poppers," 176
Posse Comitatus Act, 235
Pregnancy, and cocaine, 93, 279, 281
President's Commission on Law Enforcement and Administration of Justice, 155, 159
Prices
  coca, 90
  cocaine, 90, 112–113
  crack-cocaine, 113, 117, 124–125, 246
  heroin, 69
  morphine, 69
Prohibition, 17, 21, 142
Propoxyphine, 61
Proprietary Medicine Manufacturers and Dealers Association, 5
Prostitution
  AIDS and, 184–185
  crack-cocaine and, 117, 118, 119, 120, 121–122, 124–127
  heroin addiction and, 75–76
  robbery and, 161
Psilocybin, 38
Psychedelic drugs, 35–38
Psychopharmacological violence, 160–161, 248, 249
Public health, and legalization of drug use, 243–248
Pure Food and Drug Act, 15, 16, 18, 21, 81

Qat, 242, 282–283
Quaalude, 40, 41, 82, 226, 282
Quechua Indians, 207, 214
Quinine, 69, 76

Racism, 32, 82, 148. *See also* Blacks; Minority groups
Rape, 120, 122, 162
Realist, The, 35
Reefer addiction (reefer madness), 29–30, 34, 45

Residence houses, 122–123
Resort, 119–121
Retrovirus, 178
Revolutionary War (U.S.), 3, 138
RICO (Racketeer-Influenced and Corrupt Organizations), 234
RNA, 178
Road to H, The, 30–31, 146
Robinson Crusoe, 2
Rock cocaine, 42, 106. *See also* Crack-cocaine
Rock 'n roll, 147–149
Rock Oil, 12
Rorer, William H., Pharmaceuticals, 41
Rumania, AIDS in, 185–186

Safe houses, 191
Sandoz Research Laboratories, 34
Santa Cruz, Bolivia, 84
Santa Marta, Colombia, 219, 220
Santo Domingo de los Colorados, 215
Scarface, 216
Scheduling of drugs, 77, 245–246
Scott's Emulsion, 4
Screwworm project, 156
Sedative drugs, 40–41
Sendero Luminoso, 85, 211–212
Sernyl, 46
Sernylan, 46
Sexual transmission of AIDS, 173, 174–176, 177, 182, 186, 193–194
Shantytowns
  Bolivia, 207
  in Colombia, 212
  in Peru, 210
Shining Path terrorists, 85, 211–212
Shooting galleries, 188, 191–193
"60 Minutes," 47, 48, 138
Skin-popping, 72, 187
Smugglers' Alley, 236
Smuggling, 95, 221
Snow parties, 17–18, 142
Solvents, organic, 146
Spanish-American War, 142

ABOUT THE AUTHOR

James A. Inciardi is Director of the Center for Drug and Alcohol Studies at the University of Delaware; Professor in the Department of Sociology and Criminal Justice at Delaware; Adjunct Professor in the Comprehensive Drug Research Center at the University of Miami School of Medicine; and a member of the South Florida AIDS Research Consortium. Dr. Inciardi received his Ph.D. in sociology at New York University and has extensive research, clinical, field, teaching, and law enforcement experience in substance abuse and criminal justice. He has been Director of the National Center for the Study of Acute Drug Reactions at the University of Miami School of Medicine, Vice-President of the Washington, D.C.–based Resource Planning Corporation, Associate Director of Research for the New York State Narcotic Addiction Control Commission, and Director of the Division of Criminal Justice at the University of Delaware. He has done extensive consulting work nationally and internationally and has published some two dozen books and more than 100 articles and chapters in the areas of substance abuse, criminology, criminal justice, history, folklore, social policy, AIDS, medicine, and law.